4

Ideology, Politics and Diplomacy in East Central Europe

Rochester Studies in Central Europe

(ISSN 1528–4808)

Senior Editor: Ewa Hauser, Director,
Skalny Center for Polish and Central European Studies,
University of Rochester

Post-Communist Transition: The Thorny Road
Grzegorz W. Kolodko

Globalization and Catching-up in Transition Economies
Grzegorz W. Kolodko

Polish Formalist School
Andrzej Karcz

Music in the Culture of Polish Galicia, 1772–1914
Jolanta T. Pekacz

Ideology, Politics and Diplomacy in East Central Europe
M. B. B. Biskupski (Ed.)

The Yale Center for International and Area Studies

Yale Russian and East European
Publications, No. 14
Editor
Harvey Goldblatt
Editorial Board
Vladimir E. Alexandrov
Laura Engelstein
Harvey Goldblatt
John K. MacKay
Timothy D. Snyder

Ideology, Politics and Diplomacy in East Central Europe

Edited by

M. B. B. Biskupski

University of Rochester Press

Copyright © 2003 M. B. B. Biskupski

All Rights Reserved. Except as permitted under current legislation,
no part of this work may be photocopied, stored in a retrieval system,
published, performed in public, adapted, broadcast, transmitted, recorded,
or reproduced in any form or by any means, without the prior permission
of the copyright owner.

First published 2003

Soft cover edition
published 2004

University of Rochester Press
668 Mt. Hope Avenue
Rochester, NY 14620   USA

and at P.O. Box 9
Woodbridge, Suffolk IP12 3DF
United Kingdom
www.urpress.com

With support from The Polish Institute of Arts and Sciences of America,
and the Kosciuszko Foundation, An American Center for Polish Studies,
Promoting Educational and Cultural Exchanges Between the United States
and Poland since 1925.

ISBN 1-58046-137-9 (Hard cover)
ISBN 1-58046-155-7 (Soft cover)
ISSN 1528–4808

Library of Congress Cataloging-in-Publication Data

Ideology, politics, and diplomacy in East Central Europe / edited by
M. B. B. Biskupski.
    p. cm., — (Rochester studies in Central Europe, 1528-4808 ; 5)
    Includes bibliographical references (p.) and index.
    ISBN 1-58046-137-9 (Hardcover : alk. paper)
    1. Europe, Eastern—Politics and government—20th century. 2.
Europe, Eastern—Foreign relations—20th century. I. Biskupski,
Mieczysław B. II. Series.
DJK48.5 .I33 2003
943'.0009'04—dc21
                                                            2003006865

British Library Cataloguing-in-Publication Data
A catalogue record for this book is
available from the British Library

Designed and typeset by Cornerstone Composition Services
Printed in the United States of America
This publication is printed on acid-free paper

Contents

Piotr Wandycz

Preface

All students of the history of Central Europe are in the debt of Piotr Stefan Wandycz, who has recently retired from his position as Bradford Durfee Professor of History at Yale University. Retirement has not slowed Professor Wandycz's activities, but rather has refocused them. His scholarly production has somehow increased with the passage of years and continues at a prodigious rate. He has of late become the president of the Polish Institute of Arts and Sciences in America, and has launched bold initiatives to steer that venerable institution in new directions that reflect the tremendous changes brought about by the restoration of freedom to much of Europe.

As a small gesture of recognition for his long and varied contributions to history, we who had the honor of earning our doctorates under his tutelage have brought together this collection of essays, which is dedicated to a man we admire as a scholar, mentor, and colleague. These studies focus on many of the areas traditionally addressed by Wandycz, reflecting his fascination with politics and international relations. Wandcyz has striven, with unmatched success, to make the history of East Central Europe—here understood principally as the historic lands of the Poles, Hungarians, Czechs, and Slovaks—comprehensible to the English-speaking scholarly world. His method has been to link these nations to the major events and problems of European history in general, thereby expanding and making more coherent the story of the continent and the world.

Piotr's direct contributions to the historiography of East Central Europe are very large indeed. Indirectly, however, his contributions may well prove yet more considerable. His many students, guided by his early counsel and inspired by his continuing accomplishments, have themselves collectively produced a significant body of worthy scholarship that is increasing exponentially as the students of the students of Wandycz are now entering the academic world.

This volume consists of a "Tabula Honoraria," in which many scholars from around the world have joined to pay tribute to one of the most illustrious members of their company. Antony Polonsky has graciously consented to write what follows, an introductory appreciation of Piotr Wandycz's extraordinary career. The main portion of the volume consists of a series of essays by Piotr's students which the editor hopes will please our teacher. Finally, we follow with a bibliography of Piotr's published works—which expands so rapidly that it will obsolesce even as this volume is in press—which most strikingly demonstrates the range and quantity of his writings.

The tribute began as a result of a conversation between William L. Blackwood, one of Wandycz's last doctoral candidates, and the editor. Friends and colleagues along the way have provided encouragement and good counsel. Many most worthy would doubtless be omitted by any enumeration. However, I must mention Harvey Goldblatt of Yale, Tadeusz Gromada of the Polish Institute of Arts and Sciences and Anna M. Cienciala late of the University of Kansas who helped so well and so often. A place apart is reserved for Timothy Madigan of the University of Rochester Press, who dealt with my tardiness and idiosyncrasies with grace and forbearance. The Kościuszko Foundation and the Polish Institute of Arts and Sciences in New York City were generous in their financial contribution to this project, and I am profoundly grateful. Finally, I should like to thank my daughters: Aleksandra (Olesia) who proofread the manuscript, and Jadwiga (Jadzia) who compiled most of the index.

M. B. B. Biskupski

Tabula Honoraria

(Boldfaced names are deceased)

Ivo Banac, Bradford Durfee Professor of History, Yale University, New Haven, CT

Daniel Beauvois, Directeur du Centre de Recherches sur l'histoire des slaves, Université de Paris I

Stanislaus A. Blejwas, Endowed Chair in Polish Studies, Department of History, Central Connecticut State University, New Britain, CT

Henryk Bułhak, Senior Curator, Biblioteka Narodowa, Warsaw

F. Gregory Campbell, President of the College, Carthage College, Kenosha, WI

Andrzej S. Ciechanowiecki, Professor, London

Janusz Cisek, Deputy Mayor, Stalowa Wola

Norman Davies, Professor (emeritus), School of Slavonic and East European Studies, University of London

István Deak, Set Low Professor Emeritus, Columbia University, New York, NY

Kazimierz Dziewanowski, Ambassador of Poland to the United States, 1990–93, Warsaw

M. K. Dziewanowski, Professor of History (emeritus), University of Wisconsin, Milwaukee

Józef Andrzej Gierowski, Professor, Instytut Historii, Uniwersytet Jagielloński, Kraków

Aleksander Gieysztor, Professor, Instytut Historyczny, Uniwersytet Warszawski

Thaddeus V. Gromada, Executive Director, Polish Institute of Arts and Sciences, New York, NY

Milan L. Hauner, Professor of History, Naval War College, Newport, RI

Przemysław Hauser, Professor, Instytut Historii, Uniwersytet Adam Mickicwicza, Poznań

Karlevi Hovi, Professor of History, University of Turku

Sir Michael Howard, Professor of History, Emeritus, Yale University, New Haven, CT

Jerzy Jaruzelski, Professor, Instytut Nauk Politycznych, Uniwersytet Warszawski

Jerzy Jedlicki, Instytut Historii, PAN, Warsaw

Adolf Juzwenko, Director, Ossolineum, Wrocław

Andrzej S. Kamiński, Professor of History, Georgetown University, Washington, DC

Wojciech Karpinski, CNRS, Paris

Paul Kennedy, J. Richardson Dilworth Professor of History, Yale University, New Haven, CT

Jan Kieniewicz, Professor, Uniwersytet Warszawski

Ryszard Kiersnowski, Professor, Instytut Historii PAN, Warsaw

Col. General (ret.) Béla Király, Professor of History, Brooklyn College, CUNY
Jerzy Kłoczowski, Professor, Instytut Europy Środkowo-Wschodniej, Lublin
Macgregor Knox, Stevenson Professor, London School of Economics and
Political Science
Domokos Kosary, Past President, Institute of History, Hungarian Academy
of Sciences, Budapest
Leszek Kosiński, Secretary General, Conseil International des Sciences
Sociales, Paris
Marcin Król, Professor, Instytut Historyczny, Uniwersytet Warszawski
John J. Kulczycki, Professor of History Emeritus, University of Illinois, Chicago
William Larsh, Yale University, New Haven, CT
Zofia Libiszowska, Professor, Uniwersytet Łódzki, Łódź
Piotr Łossowski, Professor, Instytut Historyczny, Uniwersytet Warszawski
Igor Lukes, Professor of History, Boston University
Kay Lundgreen-Nielsen, Professor, University of Southern Denmark
Antoni Mączak, Professor, Instytut Historyczny, Uniwersytet Warszawski
Jan Malicki, Professor, Instytut Orientalistyczny, Uniwesytet Warszawski
Vojtech Mastny, Washington, DC
John Merriman, Charles Seymour Professor of History, Yale University, New
Haven, CT
John S. Micgiel, Director, Institute on East Central Europe, Columbia
University, New York, NY
Bernard Michel, Director, Institut Pierre Renouvin, Université de Paris I
Williamson Murray, Harold K. Johnson Professor of Military History, U.S.
Army War College
Janusz Odrowąż-Pieniążek, Director, Muzeum Historyczne Warszawy
Janusz Pajewski, Professor, Instytut Historii, Uniwersytet Adam
Mickiewicza, Poznań
Martin Peterson, Professor of History, University of Goteborg
Michał Pułaski, Professor, Instytut Historii, Uniwersytet Jagielloński, Kraków
Tomasz Schramm, Professor, Instytut Historii, Uniwersytet Adam Mickiewicza,
Poznań
Zdenek Sladek, Professor, USD, Prague
Georges-Henri Soutou, Professor of Contemporary History, Université de Paris IV
Fr. Józef Tischner, Professor, Papieska Academia Teologiczna, Kraków
Lech Trzeciakowski, Professor, Instytut Historii, Uniwersytet Adama
Mickiewicza, Poznań
Henry A. Turner, Stillé Professor of History, Yale University, New Haven, CT
Maurice Vaïsse, Professeur des Universités à l'Institut d'Études politiques de Paris
Jaroslav Valenta, Historický ustav, AV CR, Prague
Andrzej Walicki, O'Neill Professor of History, University of Notre Dame,
Notre Dame, IN
Zbigniew Wójcik, Professor, Instytut Historii, PAN, Warsaw
Jacek Woźniakowski, Professor, Katolicki Uniwersytet Lubelski, Lublin
Marian Zgórniak, Professor, Instytut Historii, Uniwersytet Jagielloński, Kraków

Piotr Wandycz

(trans. by M. B. B. Biskupski)

In June, 1997, at my suggestion, the University of Paris I, Pantheon-Sorbonne, solemnly granted Piotr Wandycz a doctorate, honoris causa.

This reflected the fact that he is renowned in France among specialists in international relations, especially with regard to Central Europe. Beginning in 1962 with the publication of his book *France and Her Eastern Allies*, the eminent historian Jean-Baptiste Duroselle made Wandycz known to a generation of young historians, including Georges-Henri Soutou and myself. My personal relations with Piotr Wandycz go back a long time, and we have maintained this relationship through many meetings, most often in Paris, but at many other conferences as well, including one at Yale.

It is particularly noteworthy that his earliest works, written when relevant French, Polish, and Czech archives were not yet accessible, have retained all their scholarly value and have been only corroborated by documents which came to light when these archives were later opened.

Wandycz is a remarkable example of cosmopolitan culture in the best sense of the term. He is, of course, a man of Polish culture, but also French, as a result of his studies at the Université de Grenoble. He has had a career at the most outstanding American universities. He moves gracefully in all social circles in Europe and North America. As a result of his vast culture, he was able to write recently a remarkable synthesis of central European history. He deals with various national histories without any trace of bias. One cannot find in Wandycz any disdain for Poland's neighbors, the Czechs or Ukrainians, sentiments rather common among Poles. His scholarly work reflects the fraternity which has united the peoples of central Europe during their common search for liberty, a search often threatened.

Piotr Wandycz is not only a great historian; he is also a great humanist.

BERNARD MICHEL
Professor at the Université Paris I,
Director of the Pierre Renouvin Institute and of the
Center for Research on Contemporary Central Europe

Piotr Wandycz: An Appreciation

Piotr Wandycz, in whose honor the essays in this volume have been prepared, encapsulates in his life many of the aspects of Poland's fate, both tragic and fortunate, in the last most violent of centuries. He was born in Kraków in 1923 and went to school in Lwów, which, according to Norman Davies, is the city which "he feels more than anywhere, to have been his Polish home."[1] His father, Damian Wandycz, was an engineer and a former soldier in the Piłsudski Legions and, together with many others, left Poland with his wife and son during September 1939, moving to Romania and then to France. While in France, Piotr studied at the University of Grenoble. In the late autumn of 1942, the family made its way through Spain to Portugal and from there flew to the United Kingdom. Here the young Wandycz joined the Polish Army in Scotland, where he was later commissioned as a second lieutenant in the First (Armored) Division of General Stanisław Maczak.

After the war, like many other Polish ex-servicemen in the United Kingdom, he was drafted into the Polish Resettlement Corps. His great academic ability was soon recognized and he was accordingly sent to Fitzwilliam College in Cambridge, where in 1948 he took his B.A. in history. He then moved to the London School of Economics and Political Sciences, where he wrote his Ph.D. dissertation under the direction of the redoubtable Professor Charles Manning.

One of Professor Wandycz's most striking characteristics is his ability to combine an internationalist and liberal perspective with an emphatic Polish patriotism. This combination was already evident in his doctoral dissertation. He took as his subject "Liberal Internationalism: The Contribution of British and French Liberal Thought to the Theory of International Relations." It was a thorough and lucid survey of the development of liberal thought on foreign policy from Bentham and Mill to T. H. Green and L. T. Hobhouse and from Thiers, Lamennais and de Tocqueville to Laboulaye, Prevost-Paradol, Leroy-Beaulieu, Molinari and Revouvier. Among the topics it analyzed were the view of these thinkers on the question of national identity, the principle of nonintervention, peace, international morality and international law. All these topics have been central to Professor Wandycz's scholarly interests, and also reflect some of the preoccupations of Manning. What is striking about the dissertation is its obviously deliberate eschewing of any specifically Polish motifs. Indeed, there seem to be no Pol-

---

1. Norman Davies, "Introduction to the Lecture", in Piotr Wandycz, *Polish Diplomacy 1914–1945: Aims and Achievements* (London, 1988), 1.

ish sources in the bibliography (one wonders if any were to be found in the LSE library). Yet the one reference to a Polish topic is also characteristic. In a section entitled "The Balkanisation of Europe," he quoted a letter from Clemenceau to Paderewski, then Polish foreign minister, in which the French leader baldly observed, "I must also recall to your consideration the *fact* that it is to the endeavours and sacrifices of the [Allied] Powers...that the Polish nation owes the recovery of its independence." This elicited the characteristically understated but caustic comment from the young Wandycz that "this tone hardly showed an understanding or sympathetic attitude."[2]

From LSE Wandycz moved to the Collège d'Europe at Bruges and then to the United States where he took a position as a history instructor at Indiana University, eventually attaining the rank of associate professor. Indiana is one of the great centers in the U.S. for the study of the history and culture of East Central Europe and it has a remarkable library and facilities for research and teaching. But the bleakness of the Midwest was very far from Wandycz's earlier experiences. He once described Indiana as "like being on board a great passenger liner—you had everything you wanted within reach but all around you was the ocean, vast and limitless."

In 1968, he moved to the Department of History at Yale, where he has remained ever since and where in 1988 he was granted the distinguished position of the Bradford Durfee Professor of History. He has been a visiting professor at Columbia University and has held the post of Guggenheim Foundation Fellow and Fellow of the Russian Research Center at Harvard. Among his academic honors are the Jurzykowski Foundation Award and the Józef Piłsudski Institute of America Award (1973). He has also been honored by the Rockefeller Foundation and in 1989, was awarded the Wayne Vucinich Prize of the American Association for the Advancement of Slavic Studies. In 1991, he was elected to the Polish Academy of Arts and Sciences and to the Polish Academy of Sciences and in the following year, he received the Hlavka Medal of the Czech Academy of Sciences. In addition he is a member of the editorial boards of *Kosmas, Slavic Review, International History Review, East European Political Studies Niepodległość, POLIN: Studies in Polish Jewry,* and *Przegląd Wschodni.* He is also a member of the editorial board of the book series *Przeszłość i Teraźniejszość.*

Throughout this period, he has been an inspiring teacher of both undergraduates and graduates. Many students at Yale gained their first introduction to the complex world of East Central Europe in his lucid and always stimulating lectures. He has been a dedicated and careful supervisor of graduates and many of those who have established themselves in his field throughout the United States and beyond owe much to his encouragement and criticism. Many of those students are represented among the contributors to this volume.

---

2. Ibid., 2–3.

It is above all by his scholarly works that Wandycz has become known and will be remembered. His writing reflects his three principal preoccupations—the reasons for the collapse of the Versailles system and its consequences for the Polish cause, the similarities and differences between the nations of northeastern Europe and the reasons why they have felt it so hard to combine in the face of external threats from Germany and Russia, and the factors which have determined the evolution of Polish society in the modern period. His first book dealt with a crucial episode that illuminated the first two of these themes. In *Czechoslovak-Polish Confederation and the Great Powers* (Bloomington, 1956), he described the failure of the attempt by the Poles and Czechoslovaks to work together to secure their independent future after the war. Wandycz has always been a strong advocate of Polish-Czechoslovak understanding, but he is well aware of the difficulties in achieving such a reconciliation. In his essay on Polish diplomacy between 1914 and 1945, he wryly quoted the diary of the Kraków conservative, Juliusz Zdanowski, who observed on 11 November 1928 that "everything tells us to love the Czechs and...stand together unflinchingly. But one cannot overcome a certain feeling which makes a *rapprochement* impossible."[3] Wandycz described with great impartiality and detachment how during the Second World War any Polish-Czechoslovak understanding was doomed because of the different perception of the Soviet Union by the two countries' leaders. In Wandycz's words:

> In the sense that Sikorski sought to make the East Central European region less vulnerable and dependent on the two mighty neighbours, his vision was not totally different from the older Polish concepts. It differed from Beneš' concept of a Czechoslovak-Polish regional organization, being really a transition to a wider grouping in which Soviet Russia would either participate or over which it would extend its sponsorship. For all his criticism of anti-Czechoslovak pre-war policies, Sikorski did not envisage Beneš as a mediator between Poland and Russia.[4]

The same careful and meticulous examination of the documents and of the newspapers of the time marks his two linked studies of the breakdown of the French attempt to create a security system to contain Germany after the First World War: *France and her Eastern Allies 1919–1925* (Minneapolis, 1962); and *Twilight of the French Eastern Alliances: French-Czechoslovak-Polish Relations from Locarno to the Remilitarization of the Rhineland* (Princeton, 1988). (Both of these books were awarded the George L. Beer Prize of the American Historical Association for the best book in international history, the first in 1962, the second in 1989.) Together they paint a sympathetic but critical picture of a France deeply weakened by the

---

3. Wandycz, *Polish Diplomacy 1914–1945*, 18–19.
4. Ibid., 38–39.

First World War and unable effectively to contain Germany. Polish foreign policy after Locarno is shown in its vain attempt to fill the security vacuum in which it found itself. The second volume also gives what is probably the best account of the controversy over whether Piłsudski proposed to his French allies a "preventitive war" against Germany in the wake of Hitler's accession to power. As Wandycz shows, it is doubtful whether there was any explicit offer, rather a series of trial balloons that were intended to test the determination of both France and Germany. The outcome, as is well known, was what Wandycz has described as Piłsudski's "most spectacular and controversial coup," the nonaggression declaration with Germany of January 1934. As Wandycz demonstrates, the pact was arrived at without French involvement, but did preserve the Franco-Polish alliance. It had become possible because of what proved to be a temporary breach between Hitler and Stalin and its aim was to strengthen Poland vis-à-vis France and make a Franco-German deal at Poland's expense impossible. In the words of the pro-government journalist Cat-Mackiewicz: "Only since January 26, 1934 does France begin to count us as an ally." As Wandycz commented acidly, "This was largely an illusion."[5]

A similar cautious skepticism and unwillingness to accept patriotic myths marks his *Polish-Soviet Relations, 1917–1921* (Cambridge, MA, 1969). This was based on the archival material that was then available—above all the émigré Polish and Russian archives in the U.S.—it has lost none of its relevance with the recent opening of both the Polish and Soviet archives. Against those who have argued that what Piłsudski was involved in was a preventative war and that a Soviet invasion of Poland was only a matter of time, Wandycz attempted, in my view convincingly, to argue the opposite thesis. In his opinion, although it was an article of faith for the Bolsheviks that the revolution could not maintain itself unless it was followed by revolution in the rest of Europe, above all in Germany, they were prepared to sign treaties, on the pattern of Brest-Litovsk, with the states which emerged to the west of Russian in order to gain a breathing space to end the civil war and consolidate their power. Piłsudski, now the dominant figure in the newly independent Polish state, distrusted these approaches; moreover he saw in Soviet Russia's weakness following the Civil War an opportunity to dislodge Belarus and especially Ukraine from Russia and link them with Poland, believing that in this way he could finally secure the country's independence. As he asked rhetorically, was Poland "to be a state equal to the great world powers or a little state in need of the protection of the mighty? ... [It is vital that Poland] should be the greatest power not only militarily, but also culturally, in the East."[6] Wandycz's assessment of Polish policy in 1920 is characteristically measured and understated:

---

5. Ibid., 23.

6. Józef Piłsudski, *Pisma zbiorowe* (Warsaw, 1937–38), V, 137–38.

...one can perhaps blame Piłsudski for undertaking, largely on his own, a most dangerous operation, which Poland was not strong enough to carry through. Undoubtedly, the Kievan expedition was a gamble, but if Piłsudski had overestimated Polish capabilities and Soviet weaknesses, the temptation to reverse the course of the last 200 hundred years of history was overwhelming. Indeed, only a realization of this great eastern design might have made Poland sufficiently powerful to withstand external pressures. With the Peace of Riga in 1921, Poland became a middle-size state too large to be anyone's satellite, but too small and too weak to be a great power. Many of the subsequent problems of Polish diplomacy stemmed from this half-way house position.[7]

His other works in the field of diplomatic history comprise a study of U.S-Polish relations, *The United States and Poland* (Cambridge, MA, 1980) and four books written in Polish. They include an early study of European integration, *Zjednoczona Europa* (London, 1956); a much-needed biography of August Zaleski, Polish foreign minister from 1926 to 1932, *August Zaleski: Minister spraw zagranicznych RP w świetle wspomnień i dokumentów* (Paris, 1980); and two books on the character of diplomacy intended for a Polish audience: *Polska a zagranica* (Paris, 1986) and *Z dziejów diplomacji* (1988). He summed up his lifelong study of Polish diplomacy in the M. B. Grabowski Memorial Lecture that he delivered in 1987 and which was published under the title *Polish Diplomacy 1914–1945: Aims and Achievements* (London, 1988).

His interest in the specific features of the Polish past is well reflected in the book he wrote for the multivolumed *History of East Central Europe* edited by Peter Sugar and Donald Treadgold and published by the University of Washington Press. Entitled *The Lands of Partitioned Poland 1795–1918* (Seattle, 1974), it is above all a history of the Polish nation, but also deals judiciously and fairly with the multireligious and multiethnic character of the lands which had made up the Polish-Lithuanian Commonwealth. Wandycz summed up his approach in the preface:

As conceived this book is both more and less than a history of the Polish nation in the nineteenth century. Its emphasis on the state territory of the commonwealth explains why such predominantly ethnic Polish lands as parts of Teschen (Cieszyn, Těšín), East Prussia, or Upper Silesia are only barely touched upon. At the same time predominantly Lithuanian, Ukrainian, and Belorussian areas are included, although the histories of these nations could not be treated here in a comprehensive fashion. Lithuanian, Ukrainian, and Belorussian developments are mainly discussed from the point of view of their interaction with Polish trends, as well as in terms of the gradual departure of these nations from the common historic tradition of the commonwealth. While the Germans and the

---

7. Wandycz, *Polish Diplomacy 1914–1945*, 16.

Jews, who constituted sizable groups in the historic *Res Publica,* are discussed, the stress once more is on their relations with the Poles.[8]

He developed this approach still further in his *The Price of Freedom: A History of East-Central Europe from the Middle Ages to the Present Day* (London and New York, 1992, translated into German in 1993). It was dedicated to two great historians of the area, Oskar Halecki and Hugh Seton-Watson, and it sought to explain the specific features of the area by adopting a regional and comparative approach. In Wandycz's words:

> This book is a survey and an attempted synthesis of the modern history of East Central Europe. A regional approach is meant to take the reader beyond national histories that can be, and sometimes are, parochial, isolated, and self-centred. A comparative regional history seeks to overcome this drawback by bringing out similarities and differences and putting national histories on a larger canvas.[9]

Piotr Wandycz's life has been inspired by two ideals—the love of political liberty and the quest for national freedom for his people. In concluding his study of Polish diplomacy between 1914 and 1945, written in 1987, he adjured his countrymen:

> We do not know what the future will bring. But I strongly believe that the Poles, pondering the story of the thirty years of diplomatic efforts, will remember one goal which has been tenaciously pursued and defended: independence.[10]

It must be gratifying to him that this goal has now been achieved and that Poland is now attempting, rather successfully, to accomplish the difficult task of creating a pluralistic and outward-looking democracy. Wandycz has often warned how difficult a goal this is, but has always stressed that freedom is something that the peoples of Central Europe have held dear. He concluded *The Price of Freedom* as follows:

> It would be pretentious to maintain that freedom means more to Poles, Czechs, Hungarians and Slovaks than to other nations of Europe. It is just that history has forced them to defend and to fight for it more frequently than in many other lands. But freedom, as everything else, has a price and its price varies. At present the price seems largely economic, but it has other dimensions. Freedom is not an absolute in itself, but a condition of meaningful existence of individuals and society. It must be self-limiting in order not to become license and lead to op-

---

8. Piotr Wandycz, *The Lands of Partitioned Poland* (Seattle, WA, 1974), xii.

9. Piotr Wandycz, *The Price of Freedom: A History of East-Central Europe from the Middle Ages to the Present Day,* London and New York, 1992.

10. Wandycz, *Polish Diplomacy 1914–1945,* 49.

pression of others. Freedom in East Central Europe has been gained at a high price and must not be lost. As John Paul II expressed in his Encyclical Letter "Solicitudo Rei Socialis" of 1987, "Each [nation] must discover and use to its best advantage its *own area of freedom.* Each must likewise realize its true needs as well as the rights and duties which oblige it to respond to them." Thinking about the past and pondering the present and future, these deceptively simple words need to be remembered.[11]

ANTONY POLONSKY

---

11. Wandycz, *The Price of Freedom*, 273.

Chapter 1

A Comparison of Czech Politics in Bohemia with Czech Politics in Moravia, 1860–1914[1]

Bruce M. Garver

During the late nineteenth and early twentieth centuries, Czech political parties and programs in Moravia developed in many respects differently from those in Bohemia, despite much similarity in the objectives and tactics of like-minded parties in both of these Habsburg crown lands. This essay is based on two premises: first, that these differences partially reflect the somewhat dissimilar histories, economies, religious traditions, and popular cultures of the two largest Czech crown lands, and second, that a critical comparison of the same differences will facilitate historians' efforts to understand the making of the modern Czech nation.

Most histories of the Czech people have understandably concentrated primarily upon developments in more populous and economically advanced Bohemia as opposed to Moravia.[2] Seldom have such histories compared similar situations and events in both crown lands even though late nine-

---

1. The author made a shorter presentation in Czech on this subject at the World Congress of the *Společnost Věd a Umení* (*SVU*) on June 26–29, 1994, in Prague.

2. Among the better general surveys are Karl Bösl (ed.), *Handbuch der Geschichte der böhmischen Länder*, Vol. III: *Die böhmischen Länder im Habsburgerreich 1848–1919* (Stuttgart, 1968); Marcela C. Efmertová, *České země v letech 1848–1918* (Prague, 1999); Zdeněk Karnik, Česke země v éře Pruní republiky, Vol. 1: 1918–1929 (Prague, 2000); Adolf Srb, *Politické dejiny národa českého od roku 1861*, 2 vols. (Prague, 1895–1901); and Zdenek Tobolka, *Politické dejiny československého národa*, 4 Vols. in 5 (Prague, 1932–37). Bohemian developments predominate in tendentious Marxist surveys like František Červinka, *Český nacionalismus v XIX. století* (Prague, 1965). Czech Moravian political and cultural life of the era 1890 to 1918 is most thoroughly examined and documented by Richard Fischer, *Pokroková Morava*, 2 Vols. (Prague, 1937).

teenth century politicians and journalists occasionally made such comparisons in trying to understand the pace and direction of nationwide political, economic and social change. Several of these observers even anticipated the speed and extent to which Moravian Czechs would become an integral, yet in some respects distinct, part of the modern Czech nation. The author's book on *The Young Czech Party, 1874–1901, and the Emergence of the Multi-Party System* addresses specific differences in the rate and nature of social and political change in the two largest Czech lands but does so primarily in order to reveal how such differences help explain the growth of the Young Czech Party in Bohemia from its founding in 1874 to the turn of the century and the rather different development of its affiliate, the Moravian People's Party, established in 1890.[3] This essay further explores this topic by examining the multiparty system of Czech politics in Moravia as well as in Bohemia up to 1914. This system included the two middle class parties of the notables—the Young Czechs (1874–1914) and their, by 1901, already moribund rival, the National, or Old Czech, Party (1848–1914)—as well as four mass parties—Social Democrats, Agrarians, Christian Socials, and National Socialists—and three progressive parties of the intelligentsia: State Rights Radicals, Radical Progressives, and Realists (the People's, later Progressive Party).

I

This essay first examines the main developments in Czech politics from 1860 to 1914 by concentrating upon the objectives, tactics, and constituencies of Czech political parties and related institutions. Second, it reviews succinctly some of the main differences between the social, economic, and cultural development of Bohemia and that of Moravia. Third, it explicitly compares the main trends in Czech political and social development in Bohemia to those in Moravia, including some examination of agrarian and working class as well as middle class interests and endeavors. Finally, this essay indicates how an assessment of the differences noted above can help historians better understand the extent to which political values and institutions, economic development, religious affiliation, and social change have conditioned nineteenth and twentieth century Czech history.

Most Czech and Slovak and many Western scholars have recognized the great extent to which the development of Czech middle class, agrarian, and working class politics has been anything but monolithic. In fact, from the Revolutions of March 1848 to the Communist takeover of Czechoslovakia in February 1948, Czech politics was characterized by a factionalism equal

---

3. Bruce Garver, *The Young Czech Party, 1874–1901, and the Emergence of a Multi-Party System* (New Haven, CT, 1978).

to if not greater than that found in the politics of any other Slavic-speaking people. This was due primarily to the fact that Czechs, earlier and to a greater extent than other Slavs, experienced the social transformation wrought by industrialization, urbanization, and the expansion of communications. Such factionalism also derived partly from the fact that in comparison to other Slavs of the period from 1860 to 1914, Czechs generally maintained more liberal political institutions and a more comprehensive system of free, compulsory, and state-funded elementary schools. Noteworthy too is the fact that the Czechs have been among the least churchgoing and most religiously divided of all Slavic nationalities. Also evident among the Czechs, as among other Europeans, are strong regional loyalties. Even though such loyalties have produced less political partisanship than have the interests of occupational groups, social classes, and religious denominations, they are nonetheless worthy of investigation if only to shed light upon the nature and extent of the aforementioned factionalism.

Most Marxist scholars, especially after 1948, assumed that Czech politics in the later nineteenth century almost exclusively reflected class or material interests and that this was best explained as a response to social changes wrought by industrialization, urbanization, and the expansion of communications. The fairly recent and well-documented works of Otto Urban, Zdeněk Šolle, and Jiří Kořalka among others suggest that Czech politics to some extent developed in this way.[4] The author of this paper has argued elsewhere that Czech politics was also very much conditioned by the civil libertarian values and aspirations of the founders of the first Czech political parties and newspapers and also by the institutions of limited self-government established by Czechs during the 1860s at the advent of constitutional rule in the Habsburg Monarchy. Still, the precise degree to which Czech politics responded to economic and social change is unlikely to be determined until someone writes a very thorough and explicit study of the development of Czech society and the economic growth of Bohemia and Moravia during the nineteenth century.[5] Nonetheless, by comparing what is already known about past Czech politics and society in Bohemia to that in Moravia, we can enlarge our understanding of the main characteristics of Czech political and social development.

---

4. See, for example, Jiří Kořalka, *František Palacky: životopis* (Prague, 1998); *Všenemecký svaz a česká otázka koncem 19. století*, Rozpravy ČSAV [Československá Akademia Ved], Vol. 73, No. 12 (Prague, 1963), and *Vznik socialistického delnického hnutí na Jihlavsku* (Liberec, 1956); Otto Urban, *Česká společnost* (Prague, 1982); and Zdenek Šolle, *Delnické hnutí v českých zemích konocem minulého století* (Prague, 1954), and *Delnické stávky v čechách v druhé polovine XIX století* (Prague, 1960).

5. A clear and concise summary of five decades of scholarship on the subject of "the social structure of the Czech lands" may be found in Efmertová, *Česke země*, 232–315.

The similarities between Czech politics in Bohemia and Moravia become quite evident when compared with developments in Austrian Silesia, the home in 1900 of 147,000 Czechs, a minority of less than one-quarter of the total population of that province. Because more than half of these Czechs were industrial workers or their dependents, not surprisingly the Social Democratic Party consistently captured a large majority of Silesian Czech votes, 65.9 percent in 1907 and 69.3 percent in 1911.[6] Both the occupations and politics of most Czechs in Silesia thus resembled those of many Czechs in other industrializing areas where Czechs constituted a large national minority: northern Moravia, the industrial suburbs of Brno, and northern Bohemia. What made Silesia very different was the fact that its Czech inhabitants included few middle class people and therefore, given restricted "three-class" suffrage, had no political representation comparable to that enjoyed by Czechs in provincial and local self-government in Bohemia and Moravia and in district self-government in Bohemia.[7]

Popular interest in specifically Moravian, as opposed to Bohemian, developments was much stimulated by some Moravians having suggested in the spring of 1968, and again after November 1989, that a tripartite division of Czechoslovakia be made to include an autonomous Moravia-Silesia as well as an autonomous Slovakia. The division of Czechoslovakia into independent Czech and Slovak Republics on January 1, 1993, appears to have dampened Moravian Czech advocacy of increased political autonomy for Moravia, in part because most citizens remain well aware of the manifold differences between Slovak history and nationalism on the one hand and Moravian Czech history and sense of identity on the other. Nonetheless, a small minority of Moravian Czechs continues to express interest in enlarging Moravian autonomy, despite the fact that in free elections in 1990, 1992, 1996, and 1998, Czech voters gave little support to parties advocating such autonomy.[8] That Czechs continue to acknowledge Moravian identity is evident in the January 1, 2000, redrawing of the boundaries for

---

6. Oscar Krejčí, *Kniha o volbách* (Prague, 1994), 72–73.

7. The late Professor Otakar Odložilík first suggested to me in June 1967 that in all instances, one ought to be sure to consider Czech politics in Moravia as well as in Bohemia. In contrast to Czechs in Moravia and in Bohemia, those in Silesia controlled no institutions of self-government at any level and had very little voice in the Diet of Austrian Silesia because most of them were industrial workers or poor to moderately prosperous peasants who had been excluded from politics by suffrage based on wealth and education—voting by curia to the Silesian Diet and by class to district and communal assembly boards. Given the working-class origins of so many Silesian Czechs, no wonder 65 percent of all Czech votes in Silesian *Reichsrat* elections went to Social Democratic candidates.

8. Also, in 1968 both the Czechoslovak Communist Party and state agencies rejected the advice of the Committee for Moravia and Silesia and other groups that

administrative districts (*kraje*) in the Czech Republic to include almost all of historic Moravia within the five new districts whose capitals are Jihlava, Brno, Zlín, Olomouc, and Ostrava.[9]

After Czechs and Slovaks established the Czechoslovak First Republic in 1918, they made three principal modifications to representative governmental institutions. First, universal suffrage for men and women was instituted at all levels of government. Second, proportional representation was introduced by holding elections in accordance with the Hare system.[10] Third, Czechs and, to a lesser degree, Slovaks now dominated the central government, while German and Magyar citizens of the republic became national minorities with considerable cultural and local political autonomy. Furthermore, educational opportunities for Czechs in Moravia were equalized by the founding in 1919 of the comprehensive Czech-language Masaryk University in Brno. Simultaneously, Moravian Czechs created a Greater Brno by annexing the more populous and predominantly Czech industrial and residential suburbs to the historic inner city in order to give Czechs political control of what was now the second largest Czech metropolis. Within a decade, the Czech inhabitants of Brno made it a political, economic, and cultural center comparable in some respects with Prague.[11]

The establishment after 1918 of identically organized and empowered self-governmental and educational institutions in Bohemia and Moravia, along with the democratization of suffrage, helped promote greater cooperation between Czech political leaders in these two regions and also between regional affiliates of national political parties. Such cooperation was further facilitated by the new republic's enlargement of state-supported educational and social welfare services, and by the mutual desire of most Czechs and Slovaks to maintain the independence, territorial integrity, and democratic polity of their new republic.

---

lobbied for a tripartite division of Czechoslovakia. Most Slovaks and Bohemian Czechs appear then to have opposed this tripartite solution. See H. Gordon Skilling, *Czechoslovakia's Interrupted Revolution* (Princeton, NJ, 1976), 470–74.

9. Three new kraje (*Jihlavský, Brnenský,* and *Zlínský*) include all of what formerly was the South Moravian District (*Jihomoravský kraj*) except a small area assigned to the *Olomoucký kraj.* The two others (*Olomoucký* and *Ostravský*) include the entire former North Moravian District (*Severomoravský kraj*) except for the areas in Valašsko and around Vsetín incorporated in the northeasternmost part of the new *Zlínský kraj.* See Miroslav Korecký, "Kraje: bližší vladnutí, vice šredníku," *Lidové noviny* (Prague, March 16, 2000), 7.

10. Krejčí, *Kniha o volbách,* 306, Table 66.

11. On successful Czech efforts before 1914 to improve the government, culture, and public facilities of Brno and its many suburbs, see Jan Sedlák, *Brno v době secese* (Brno, 1995).

II

A comparison of Czech politics in Moravia with that in Bohemia during the years 1860 to 1914 reveals a remarkable similarity of objectives and institutions. These objectives may be broadly defined as the promotion of economic growth and the acquisition of political rights for individuals, communities, occupational and professional groups, and the nation as a whole. Both individual prosperity and communal well-being were to be achieved primarily through accelerated industrialization, expansion of communications, mass education, the emancipation of women, and the application of scientific knowledge to farming and manufacturing.[12]

After the advent of constitutional rule in the Habsburg Monarchy in October 1860, Czechs in Bohemia and Moravia helped advance their interests through voluntary associations of at least six types, each of which originated in Bohemia and was promptly taken up in Moravia. These included political parties, mass circulation newspapers, corporations, cooperatives, fraternal and patriotic organizations, and national foundations to support Czech minorities. Czechs in Bohemia and Moravia developed virtually identical institutions of each type, although their establishment in economically less developed Moravia often occurred somewhat later than in Bohemia.

Czechs of almost every social class founded or joined political parties to advance national as well as regional and local objectives. Middle class and agrarian political parties sought to enlarge Czech national autonomy within the framework of what many voters hoped would be a less authoritarian and more constitutional Habsburg Monarchy. Czechs of almost every occupational group and political persuasion sought to advance civil liberties, including freedom of association and the press as well as universal manhood suffrage. Progressives and Social Democrats also advocated giving women the right to vote. From 1848 onward, anticlericalism and the separation of church and state continued to be advocated by all Czech political parties except the Catholic ones, founded in the 1890s, and the Old Czechs. All Czech parties, especially the Social Democratic and the Christian Social Parties, recognized that the material and intellectual advancement of the Czech nation necessitated considerable improvement in the lot of the workers and peasants who constituted the vast majority of that nation. These parties, of course, disagreed over the extent to which and the pace at which such transformation was to take place and also did not agree on who, precisely, should design and implement specific improvements. The Social

---

12. On women's emancipation, see Jana Buresova, *Proměny společenského postavení českých žen v pruní polovině 20. století* (Olomous, 2001), and chapters by Karen Freeze, Bruce Garver, and Sharon Wolchik in Sharon L. Wolchik and Alfred G. Meyer, *Women, State, and Party in Eastern Europe* (Durham, NC, 1985).

Democrats and all progressive parties believed that addressing the social question was a prerequisite to all efforts to resolving the Czech, or nationality, question. Middle class parties, especially those of the notables, thought otherwise and suggested that their professional leadership would be essential to creating the technological and educational infrastructure for a modern and cultured European Czech nation.

Almost every Czech political party received support from several newspapers and periodicals, some of which it either controlled or had created. A patriotic and liberal Czech-language press rapidly acquired a mass circulation in Bohemia after the founding in January 1861 of the *Národní listy* (*The National Newspaper*), edited by Julius Grégr (1831–96), who soon made it the principal advocate and defender of Young Czech policies.[13] In Moravia, by contrast, the first Czech newspapers emphasized local activities and generally supported the conservative Old Czechs whose Moravian affiliate was then led by Alois Pražák (1820–1901). A strongly liberal Czech-language opposition party press did not appear in Moravia until Adolf Stránský's (1855–1931) founding in Brno in 1889 of the biweekly *Moravské listy* (*The Moravian Newspaper*). Its circulation did not begin to approach that of the *Národní listy* and other Bohemian Czech liberal journals primarily because of the much smaller Czech intelligentsia and upper middle class in Moravia. *Rovnost* (*Equality*), the first Czech Social Democratic weekly in Moravia, likewise originated in Brno and became as influential among Czech workers in Moravia as the Prague biweekly *Právo lidu* was among their counterparts in Bohemia. All newspapers experienced imperial harassment and such onerous restrictions as censorship according to the law of 1862 and the deposit of "caution money" until 1895. Moreover, until December 1899, a tax stamp (*kolek*), which doubled the price of every issue sold, severely restricted the circulation of popular Social Democratic and agrarian newspapers.

Educated and propertied Czechs began to organize corporations in 1852 when imperial law first authorized the formation of these limited liability joint stock companies. After cooperatives of all sorts had been authorized by law in 1873, farmers and, to a lesser degree, industrial workers founded and tried to make maximum use of cooperatives and savings and loan societies. In both provinces, profits obtained from agriculture and food processing, especially from the "national industry" of sugar beet refining, provided much of the investment capital required for Czechs to achieve ascendancy in the manufacture of automobiles, machine tools, and chemicals in Austria-Hungary later in the century. Complementing

---

13. See especially František Roubík, *Bibliografie časopisectva v Čechách z let 1863–1895* (Prague, 1936), introductory essay; and Milada Wurmová, *Soupis moravských novin a časopisů z let 1848–1918* (Brno, 1955), *passim.*

this industrial expansion was the large and growing network of Czech banks, the first of which was the Živnostenská banka chartered in 1868. Fraternal and patriotic organizations included the patriotic gymnastics organization, *Sokol* (Falcon), the most popular institution of its type, and *Orel* (Eagle), its smaller Catholic counterpart and rival. Those organizations dedicated primarily to the advancement of cultural and intellectual life included the committee to build the Czech National Theater, the patriotic singing group *Hlahol*, and local organizations to support the visual and performing arts. National Foundations, or National Unions (*Národní jednoty*), received support from Czechs throughout Bohemia and Moravia to promote the interests of Czech minorities in the predominantly German areas of the two provinces, primarily along their northern periphery. Those in Bohemia included the Sumava National Union, founded in 1884, and the North Bohemian National Union, founded in 1885. In Moravia, they included the National Union for Southwestern Moravia, founded in Brno in 1886, and the Political Association for Northern Moravia in Olomouc, founded in February 1892. A related organization, the *Matice školská* (School Foundation), helped establish and support private Czech schools in predominantly German areas where there resided fewer than the forty Czech-speaking students who had to reside in the district of a Czech-language school in order to obtain governmental tax monies.[14]

Czechs also established a comprehensive and state-financed system of Czech-language public schools at all levels, beginning with free, universal, and compulsory secular elementary education under terms of the imperial school law of 1869. Liberal arts secondary schools, called *gymnasia*, prepared abler students for a higher education, while trade schools gave practical instruction to students who would become skilled workers, factory foremen, or small businessmen. The first Czech institution of higher learning, the Prague Institute of Technology, began to offer a Czech-language curriculum in 1869, and trained most of the technicians and managers for the burgeoning industrial and agricultural economy of Bohemia and Moravia.[15] The second such institution was the Charles University, where

---

14. On National Foundations, see Antonín Boháč, *Boj o české menšiny v zemích českých v posledních dvou letech* (Praha, 1909); Leander Čech, et al., *Pametní list k jubileu 20 letého trvání Nár. Jednoty pro Jihozáp. Moravu* (Brno, 1906); and Emanuel Hrubý, ed., *Náš vývoj v severních Čechách od ochranou Národní Jednoty Severočeské 1910–1935* (Prague, 1936). Fr. Belehradek et al., *Pametní list vydaný na oslavu pulsleleté činnosti ústřední Matice školské v Praze* (Prague, 1931). Claire E. Nolte, *The Sokol in the Czech Lands to 1914* (New York: Palgrave,Macmillan, 2002)

15. These developments are discussed in Bruce Garver, "Representative Czech Masters of Science and Technology as Leaders in Czech National Politics: Jan Evangelista Purkyne, František Tilšer, and Josef Hlávka," *Nationalities Papers* 24, no. 1 (1996): 31–50.

all liberal arts courses were offered in Czech upon the division in 1882 of the Charles-Ferdinand University in Prague into separate Czech and German institutions.

Finally, Czechs in all predominantly Czech-speaking areas of Moravia and Bohemia took control of the self-governmental institutions established during the early 1860s at the communal level and, in Bohemia alone, at the district level. Given curial representation in the diets, Czechs, despite constituting roughly two-thirds of the population in Bohemia and three-quarters in Moravia, were able to control no more than two-fifths of the seats.[16] Besides, the authority of self-governmental institutions at all levels was circumscribed by their subordination to imperial agencies under the "two-tracked" system of government. Nonetheless, Czechs, through self-government, not only promoted public education, economic growth, and internal improvements but also acquired limited control over their own tax monies and public works programs and an invaluable training in the responsibilities of citizenship.[17] Given the election of delegates to self-governmental bodies on the basis of either three-class or curial voting, propertied and educated Czechs predominated and often acted in their own as well as in what they perceived to be the national interest.

Czechs in Bohemia and Moravia advanced their cultural and intellectual life and sought to extend civil liberties and suffrage despite the opposition of the authoritarian Habsburg regime and the opposition of the middle class German parties and the Constitutional Great Landowners. In both Bohemia and Moravia, the Conservative Great Landowners often made common cause, primarily on their terms, with the Old Czech Party and occasionally with the more liberal Young Czech and Agrarian Parties; but they did not support the extension of suffrage and governmentally subsidized social welfare measures advocated by the Progressive and Social Democratic Parties and by the more liberal Agrarian and Young Czech politicians.[18]

---

16. Representation by curias in the diets of Bohemia, Moravia, and Silesia is outlined in Table 16 in Garver, *Young Czech Party*, 346. The results of elections from predominantly Czech districts to the Diet of Bohemia from 1883 to 1908 are presented in Table 17 in *ibid.*, 347.

17. On the Czechs' use of samospráva as a primary means of civic improvement and promoting civic responsibility, see František Schwarz, *Působení Vácalva Dobrovského jako okresního starosty* (Prague, 1890), and *Výklad zákona obecního pro království České ze dne 16. dubna 1864* (Prague, 1877).

18. Antonín Okáč, *Rakouský problém a list Vaterland, 1860–71*, 2 Vols. (Brno, 1970), nicely introduces the politics, organization, and press of the Conservative Great Landowners during their formative years. See also Garver, *Young Czech Party*, 23–25, 50–51, 60–61, 217–18, and 234–35, for a discussion of relationships between the Conservative Great Landowners and the leading Czech middle class parties.

III

Bohemia and Moravia are distinct geographical areas separated by the rugged highlands that form part of the divide between the river systems flowing into the Baltic and North Seas and those flowing into the Black Sea. Bohemia, surrounded by mountains on its other three sides, is drained by the Labe (Elbe) and its tributaries into the North Sea, whereas Moravia, bordered by mountains to the north and east, takes its name from its main river, the Morava, which along with its tributaries flows into the Danube. However formidable, geographical barriers did not hinder the Czechs from establishing close political and economic ties between Bohemia and Moravia beginning as early as the ninth century.[19] The fact that Moravian and Bohemian Czechs speak dialects of the same Slavic language and have usually lived under one government has helped to bind these two peoples together culturally and economically despite the foreign interventions and geographical obstacles that have at times kept them apart. Up to the 1930s, eight Czech dialects were equally divided between Bohemia and Moravia; each of the four Moravian Czech dialects differs a bit more from the central Bohemian dialect than does any dialect in Bohemia.[20]

---

19. Archaeological evidence indicates that Moravia along with most of the present-day Slovak Republic and the northernmost part of lower Austria were, during most of the ninth century, within the borders of Great Moravia (*Velká Morava*). Never subject to this state were the Czech tribes who organized the first principality in Bohemia. After the Magyars overran Great Moravia and incorporated most of its eastern and south central territories into the new Hungarian kingdom, the Czech princes of Bohemia took over Moravia and ruled it through a generally autonomous administration. Thereafter, except for a few years when Moravia fell under Hungarian domination at mid-fifteenth century, Bohemia and Moravia have been linked by political administration as well as by a common language, albeit one with at least eight distinct dialects. The Margravate of Moravia, like the Kingdom of Bohemia and for a time the Duchy of Lusatia and until 1740 the whole of Silesia, were the Lands of the Bohemian Crown, also known as the Czech lands or Czech crown lands.

20. The four dialects of Czech in Bohemia are the Central, the Western, the Southern and the Northeastern. The majority of Moravian Czechs, including all who live in the Haná, the fertile South Moravian plain, speak a dialect called Hanáčká nářečí. Others, living within twenty to thirty miles of the Moravian Slovak border between Moravia and Slovakia speak a Moravian-Slovak dialect that of all Czech dialects most closely resembles Slovak and that is in fact identical in some respects to the westernmost Slovak dialects. In southeastern Moravia, from the hills south of Kyov through Úherské Hradište to Kromeříč, a third dialect, called Dolská nářečí, separates the speakers of the Hanáčká from those speaking Moravian-Slovak. The Lašská nářečí is spoken by the Czech inhabitants of the extreme northeastern corner of Moravia and the eastern part of what was until 1918 Austrian Silesia. Bohuslav Havránek, "Česká nářečí," *Československá Vlastivěda*, Vol. III: *Jazyk* (Prague, 1934), 84–218.

Strong regional identity may still be found in those areas of Moravia or Bohemia where a distinct dialect is complemented by unusually distinctive local customs and folk costumes and by some remarkable historical experience. An outstanding example in Bohemia is the Chodsko area around Domažlice. Cases in point in Moravia include the Haná plain, the Kyov area, and the Valašsko region around Valašské Meziříčí and Vsetín. Proportionally more distinctive local customs and dialects survived in predominately rural Moravia than in heavily industrialized and urbanized Bohemia, where greater, though by no means complete, standardization of dress, language, and customs was evident by the third quarter of the nineteenth century. This phenomenon was reinforced by the fact that in Moravia, every local, or communal, self-governmental body was autonomous, whereas in Bohemia, each such body was subordinate to an elected district governing board situated in an urban area.

Leadership of the Czech national movement by Bohemian Czechs was facilitated by their preponderance in wealth and in population. At the turn of the century in the Czech lands, 29.5 percent of all Czechs lived in Moravia as opposed to 68 percent in Bohemia and 2.5 percent in Silesia. As a percentage of the total population of Bohemia, Czechs grew from 62.4 percent in 1880 to 62.7 percent in 1910, while the German percentage of the total population declined from 37 to 36.5 percent, reflecting an increase in the numbers of Czechs from 3,470,000 to 4,242,000 and of Germans from 2,054,000 to 2,468,000. In Moravia, by contrast, Czechs increased from 1,507,000 to 1,868,000 or from 70 percent of the population in 1880 to 71.8 percent in 1910. During the same period, Germans grew in numbers from 629,000 to 719,000 while decreasing from 29.2 to 27.6 percent of the population. The slightly more rapid proportional increase of the Czech population in Moravia as opposed to Bohemia may be explained by the fact that Czechs in Moravia had a slightly higher birth rate than those in Bohemia and a slightly lower rate of emigration to the United States.[21]

The fact that Czechs comprised a larger share of the total population in Moravia than they did in Bohemia did not translate into their obtaining proportionally greater political representation in the former province; this was not only because suffrage was based on property qualifications but also because urban districts received higher per capita representation than did rural areas. Thus, Germans in some parts of predominantly Czech-speaking Moravia were able to translate their proportionally greater per capita wealth into a disproportionately greater representation than that enjoyed by comparably situated Germans in Bohemia. By sheer weight of

---

21. Data from Richard Charmatz, *Deutsch-österreichische Politik* (Leipzig, 1907), 84–85; *Statistisches Handbuch des Königreiches Böhmen*, 2nd ed. (Prague, 1913), 14–15; and Karel Adámek, *Z naší doby*, 4 Vols. (Velké Meziříčí, 1886–1890), Vol. 4 (1890), 86–87.

numbers, Czechs controlled the fourth or real curia of the Moravian Diet as well as communal self-governmental bodies in Czech-speaking rural areas. But in the third or urban curia of the Diet and in many municipal self-governmental bodies, Germans predominated, giving them a proportionally greater representation in the Moravian than in the Bohemian Diet and control of municipal government until 1919 in the two largest cities of Brno and Moravská Ostrava.

The leadership of Bohemian Czechs in Czech national political, cultural, and commercial life was greater than their 68 percent share of the total Czech population would indicate. Czech society in Moravia was preponderantly rural as late as 1900 as opposed to Bohemia where Czechs by 1870 came to dominate the governments of all cities, including Prague, in predominantly Czech-speaking areas. Of the forty largest cities in the Czech crown lands in 1910, thirty were in Bohemia, eight in Moravia, one in Austrian Silesia (Opava), and one on the Silesian-Moravian border (the conurbation of Frýdek in Silesia and Místek in Moravia).[22] Of these eight Moravian cities, Germans controlled municipal government until November 1918 in four (Brno, Ostrava, Jihlava, and Znojmo) and until 1910 in a fifth: Olomouc. The remaining three Moravian cities—Prostějov, Přerov, and Kroměříž—ranked fourth, sixth, and eighth in size in Moravia in 1910, were predominantly Czech-speaking, and had long been the principal centers of the Czech National Renaissance in that province. Even when slightly outnumbered by Czechs elsewhere, Moravian Germans retained control of self-governmental bodies through the unrepresentative class or curial voting which gave disproportionately large representation to persons well-established in business and the professions. An exception was Olomouc, where, after a twenty-five year struggle, Czechs took over the municipal government in 1910.[23] Even thereafter, Olomouc, a "city of barracks and churches" (město kasaren a cirkvi) and seat of a bishopric and a theological seminary, retained a decidedly imperial and Catholic appearance that differed markedly from that of typically Czech cities of comparable size where a decidedly secular and Czech national outlook prevailed among all social classes.

The Czech lands of Bohemia, Moravia, and Silesia together constituted the leading industrial region of the Dual Monarchy. In Cisleithania, the western half of the Monarchy, Bohemia led in industrial production, followed by Lower Austria and Moravia. Per capita income in these three

---

22. See Table 14 in Garver, Young Czech Party, 341–344, based on official census data presented by Ludmila Kárníková, Vývoj obyvatelstva Českých zemí 1754–1914 (Prague, 1965), 78–101, 112–19, 143–82, 218–69.

23. Julius Ambroš, Z malých kořenu: Vzpomínky a úvahy z národního života v Olomouci (Olomouc and Kroměříž, 1912), gives the most complete and graphic account of this prolonged struggle.

provinces remained higher than that elsewhere in the Monarchy. In Bohemia, Czechs largely controlled several important industries including sugar beet processing, the brewing and bottling of beer, and the manufacture of machine tools, heavy transportation equipment, electrical goods, motorcycles, bicycles, and automobiles. In Moravia, Czechs achieved preeminence only in some of the food processing industries.

Czech banking in Moravia was likewise less well developed than that in Bohemia, where the *Živnostenská banka* and other industrial banks had given Czechs fiscal independence of Bohemian German and Viennese capital. Czechs in Moravia were still dependent upon Viennese capital or upon the larger German banks of Brno and Moravská Ostrava, though penetration of Bohemian Czech capital into Moravia steadily increased. For example, the *Živnostenská banka*, chartered in Prague in 1868, had set up branches in Moravia by the 1880s and expanded abroad, especially into the Balkans, by the turn of the century. As late as 1914, five Czech banks headquartered in Bohemia were larger than the largest in Moravia, the Moravian Agrarian and Industrial Bank (*Moravská agrární a promyslová banka*). Its capital stock was only 13.3 percent of that of the *Živnostenská banka,* Bohemia's largest, and only 6.5 percent of that of the five largest Bohemian Czech banks. The largest Moravian bank had only 12,000,000 crowns in capital stock compared to 80,000,000 in the *Živnostenská banka* and 185,000,000 in the five largest Bohemian Czech banks.[24]

Given the concentration of most Czech-owned industries and banks in Bohemia, one did not find in Moravia a Czech managerial and professional upper middle class at all comparable in absolute or relative size to that in Bohemia. This is also partly explained by Prague's ability to attract ambitious and talented young Moravian Czechs eager to make a national name for themselves in business, politics, and the arts. At the same time, Czechs in Moravia did not dominate retail trade in the predominantly Czech towns and cities to the same extent as did Czech shopkeepers in all comparable towns and cities of Bohemia. In turn, the virtual absence of a strong Czech upper middle class in Moravia helps explain the comparative weakness of Czech liberal and progressive political parties there as opposed to Bohemia, just as the comparative weakness of the Czech lower middle class in Moravia helps explain the fact that the Czech National Socialist Party had virtually no appeal outside Bohemia, the place of its establishment in 1898 and of all of its greatest electoral successes.

The distribution of farmland differed slightly between Bohemia and Moravia, both in the percentage of landholders in any given category and in the percentage of land they held. For example, in 1896, Bohemia had a somewhat higher percentage (20 percent) of land owned by "large farm-

---

24. See comparative figures in Antonín Pimper, *České obchodní banky za války a po válce* (Prague, 1929), 39.

ers" whose farms included 20 to 50 hectares than did Moravia where the figure was 16.1 percent. By contrast, middling Czech farmers who held 5 to 20 hectares were proportionally stronger in Moravia where they owned 29.6 percent of all hectares as opposed to the 26.2 percent they held in Bohemia. The principal difference in landholding between the two provinces was in the greater amount and higher percentage of arable land owned by great landowners whose estates, or latifundia, exceeded 2,000 hectares. In Bohemia, these estates constituted .02 percent of all holdings and controlled 28.3 percent of all hectares. In Moravia, the comparable figures were 0.01 percent and 25.6 percent. This translated into a less powerful position there for both political parties of Great Landowners whose economic prosperity and political influence was facilitated by law, thanks to curial suffrage and laws of entail and primogeniture.[25] Furthermore, the fact that Czech farmers constituted a higher percentage of voters in Moravia than in Bohemia surely facilitated Czech domination of the fourth, or rural, and fifth, or universal, curia in elections to the Moravian Diet.

The economic development of Moravia generally lagged behind that of Bohemia in per capita wealth, value of industrial and agricultural production, and the number and percentage of persons employed in commerce and industry. But, not all parts of Moravia developed less rapidly than all parts of Bohemia. In the Czech lands from 1860 to 1918, demographers have identified four distinct areas of economic development, the first characterized by agricultural depression and backwardness, the second by the introduction of intensive agriculture, the third by the predominance of older industries like textiles, and the fourth by the predominance of the coal and steel industries and new heavy manufacturing industries.[26] Areas of depressed agricultural conditions included most of southern Bohemia as well as some of southern Moravia and were characterized by the presence of large latifundia and by low crop yields, reforestation, subsistence agriculture, and a high rate of emigration to recently industrialized areas and to the United States.[27] Areas of intensive agriculture in Moravia included the Haná in the south and central parts of that province. There one found, as in the Labe Valley of Bohemia, many prosperous small towns and cities, notably Prostějov, Přerov, and Kroměříž, whose growth had been stimulated by railway transportation, food processing, and other light industries.

The areas in which industrialization first occurred were almost exclusively in northern Bohemia where textile manufacturing began and remained the leading industry. Newer industrial areas included most of north central

---

25. Data was obtained from Tables 7, 8A, 8B, and 9 in Garver, *Young Czech Party,* 332–36.

26. These are the divisions clearly delineated by Ludmila Karníková, *Vývoj obyvatelstva v Českých zemí,* 196–201, 348–51.

27. Garver, *Young Czech Party,* 19ff.

and east central Bohemia, northeastern Moravia, and greater Brno in south central Moravia. By the turn of the century, firms in these regions manufactured the larger part of Austro-Hungarian iron and steel, chemicals and electrical goods, machine tools, and heavy transportation equipment. Germans controlled most of these industries in Moravia, whereas Czechs controlled the larger part of all but the coal, iron, steel, and glass industries in Bohemia. Thus, in those few parts of Moravia where industrialization and urbanization had advanced at a pace equal to anywhere in Bohemia, Moravian Czechs had only a small share in owning and managing the technologically most advanced sectors of the economy. This, more than anything else, explains why no party developed in Moravia comparable to the Young Czechs after 1901 under the leadership of Karel Kramář (1860–1937), Bedřich Pacák (1846–1914), and Václav Škarda (1861–1912), who became increasingly beholden to Czech industrial and banking interests.

The far greater strength and influence of the Czech intelligentsia and the industrial and managerial upper middle class in Bohemia as opposed to Moravia were also in part due to the fact that the only Czech-language university before 1919 was located in Prague. It became a magnet for younger Moravian Czech intellectuals who, upon graduation, more often than not returned to their native province to establish newspapers, businesses, or other institutions, very often along lines suggested to them by what they had observed or worked with in Prague. Others like Tomaš G. Masaryk (1850–1937) and Jan Herben (1857–1936) remained in Prague to make their professional reputations.[28] The delay until 1919 in establishing a Czech university in Moravia, in contrast to Bohemia's having obtained one in 1882, had everything to do with politics and cannot be attributed, after the later 1880s, to Moravia's slower economic growth or its relatively small Czech middle class. Moravian German political opposition to the establishment of a Czech-language university in Brno, a policy supported by Germans elsewhere in the monarchy and by the emperor, defeated all annual Moravian Czech attempts beginning in 1891 to create such a university. The absence in Moravia until the turn of the century of a Czech polytechnic institute comparable to that established in Prague in 1869 somewhat restricted the entry of Moravian Czechs into managerial

---

28. A representative selection of recent studies on T. G. Masaryk would include Jaroslav Opat, *TGM: Evropan, světoobčan* (Prague, 1999); Stanislav Polák, *T. G. Masaryk: Za ideálem a pravdou*, Vol. I: *1850–1882* (Prague, 2000); Vratislav Doubek, *T. G. Masaryk a česká slovanská politika, 1882–1910* (Prague, 1999); Roland Hoffmann, *T. G. Masaryk und die tschechische Frage* (München, 1988); Eva Broklová, ed., *Sto let Masarykovy české otázky* (Prague, 1997); and the three volumes published in London in 1989–90 by Macmillan on *T. G. Masaryk (1850–1937)*: Stanley B. Winters, ed., Vol. 1: *Thinker and Politician* (London, 1990); R. B. Pynsent, ed., Vol. 2: *T. G. Masaryk: Thinker and Critic* (London, 1989); and Harry Hanak, ed., Vol. 3: *T. G. Masaryk: Statesman and Cultural Force,* (London, 1989).

jobs and technical fields in industry just as the absence of a Czech university diminished opportunities for Moravian Czechs to pursue a liberal arts or professional curriculum and hence may have retarded their entry into the learned professions. The establishment of a Czech university in Moravia became an important Czech political objective in all elections beginning with the *Reichsrat* elections of 1891 in Bohemia, with Czech parties in Bohemia endorsing it wholeheartedly but never giving it quite the high priority assigned to it by Czech politicians in Moravia. Thus, the fact that the post-turn-of-the-century Young Czech Party was twice persuaded by imperial authorities to bargain away support for a Moravian university may have contributed somewhat to the relative weakness of political liberalism among Moravian Czechs.

Primary and secondary schools did not differ markedly between the two provinces. Czech success in virtually wiping out illiteracy by 1890 was quite impressive, thanks in large part to the fact that Czechs controlled and funded the local and provincial school boards that set most policies for public schools in both crown lands.

The slower growth of large and influential Czech liberal and progressive political parties in Moravia as opposed to Bohemia is also to some extent explained by the fact that after 1864, Bohemia had self-governmental boards at the district level to oversee communal representative bodies whereas Moravia did not. These boards, elected by three-class voting, supervised all self-governmental activities of communal bodies within each district, thereby giving considerable political influence to Czechs of the upper middle class and intelligentsia who controlled these boards from 1864 to 1914. After the turn of the century, liberal and progressive Czech parties relinquished many of their seats in the diets of Bohemia and Moravia and in the *Reichsrat* to representatives of the Agrarians and Social Democrats and, to a lesser extent, the National Socialists but retained their control over the district boards of Czech-speaking Bohemia until 1913 when the Habsburgs suspended all representative government. Thus, the absence of district boards in Moravia along with the presence of a smaller Czech upper middle class and intelligentsia best accounts for the proportionally greater strength in Moravia of the Agrarian and Social Democratic Parties as opposed to liberal parties and helps account for the relatively greater strength of clerical parties in Moravia. There, the large influence of the latter parties is due primarily to the fact that Czechs in both urban and rural areas of that province supported the Catholic Church in proportionally much larger numbers than did Czechs in Bohemia.

IV

The continuing importance of Moravia in Czech politics was also revealed by the fact that some of the most prominent Czech political and intellectual leaders had come from Moravia, including the leading Czech historian and "father of the nation" (*otec národa*), František Palacký (1798–1876), and the president-liberator Masaryk. Other Czech statesmen of national as well as regional importance from Moravia included Alois Pražák (1820–1901), chairman of the Moravian Old Czechs during the seventies and eighties and several times cabinet member in the Taaffe ministry (1879–93), and Msgr. Jan Šrámek (1870–1956), founder of the Czech Christian Social movement and leader of the clerical People's Party in the first Czechoslovak Republic, and Vlastimil Tusar (1880–1924), editor of the Social Democratic *Rovnost* in Brno before 1914 and the second premier of Czechoslovakia.

The typically greater religiosity of Moravian as opposed to Bohemian Czechs generally is evident in Palacký's and Masaryk's preoccupation with ethical or moral questions—an outlook in part attributable to their Protestant faith. Evident, too, in their publications is the Moravian Czech recognition that Czech national interests are much more than the interests of Bohemian Czechs writ large. Pražák's and Tusar's careers illustrate the somewhat greater willingness of Moravian Czechs in the late nineteenth and early twentieth centuries to give some economic issues precedence over nationality questions and to expect tangible gains from cooperation with like-minded parties regardless of their national affiliation. Šrámek's career attests to the fact that the Christian Social movement became popular among a large percentage of Czechs only in Moravia and that Czech clerical politics could on occasion be strongly nationalistic as well as Catholic.

One of the main objectives of later nineteenth century Czech politics, perhaps more keenly perceived in Moravia and in Bohemia, was the full integration of Moravian Czechs into the Czech nation through education, the raising of national consciousness, the encouragement of political activism, and the acquisition of civil liberties and equal opportunities for the use of Czech language in public life. Czechs in all the Czech lands were heartened that by the 1890s, Czech Moravia was assuming a position of full equality with Czech Bohemia in national culture and politics.[29] Bohemian Czechs did so in part because they had long recognized that the Moravian Czechs were their most direct link to the Slovaks and Poles as well as to the eastern and southern Slavs.[30] For example, in southeastern Moravia, Czechs established many cultural as well as political ties with Slovaks just across the border as in the Vesna, an academy dedicated to promoting the fine and decorative arts, in which the Moravian artist, Joža Uprka, was a prin-

---

29. See Antonín Hajn's and Richard Fischer's 1901 and 1902 recollections of František Vahalík. Fischer, *Pokroková Morava*, Vol. I, 125.

30. This point is expressed by T. G. Masaryk among others in his "Moravo, Moravičko milá! Otisk starší práce profesora T.G. Masaryka z II. ročníku *Času* (číslo 2 ze dne 5. ledna 1888)," (Břeclav, 1935), 10.

cipal leader.[31] Not coincidently, the principal advocate of Czech-Slovak solidarity and of Czechoslovak independence, Masaryk, had a Moravian mother and Slovak father and grew up in Hodonín and Čejkovice near the Slovak frontier.[32] Furthermore, as the Moravian Czech progressive František Vahalík contended in 1892, "for all Czechs, bringing Moravia permanently into the Slavic sphere of influence is the greatest addition to the strength of Czech collective endeavor and of greater importance to the Czech national cause than any immediate favor or gift that can be obtained from the powers of the world."[33]

The best indication of party strength in Moravia as opposed to Bohemia are the voting returns from predominately Czech districts in elections to the lower house of the *Reichsrat* held under universal manhood suffrage in 1907 and 1911. These reveal that the principal difference in party strength between the two provinces was the far stronger Czech electoral support for the clerical parties in Moravia—29.8 percent in 1907 and 36.6 percent in 1911—as opposed to Bohemia with 11.9 percent in both cases.[34] The other striking difference in voting behavior is the extraordinarily weak showing of the Czech National Socialists in Moravia, where they obtained 1.1 percent of the Czech vote in 1907 and 2.2 percent in 1911, compared to their obtaining 10.3 percent and 9.7 percent respectively in Bohemia. Equally notable was the absence of any support in Moravia for two progressive parties of the intelligentsia—the Radical Progressives and State Rights Radicals—which combined in 1908 to form the State Rights Progressive Party. Taken together with the poor showing of the National Socialist candidates in Moravia, this indicates that radical nationalism held little appeal for the Moravian lower middle class and intelligentsia. Voters from these classes in Moravia primarily backed the Moravian People's and Progressive parties, individually in 1907 and jointly in 1911. A comparison of the percentage of votes received by the Young Czechs and their non-agrarian progeny in Bohemia with the percentage of votes obtained by the People's party—formerly a Young Czech affiliate—and its offspring, the Progressives, reveals the relative weakness of liberal and progressive Czech middle and lower middle class voters in Moravia: 12.5 percent in 1907 and 10.7 percent in 1911, as opposed to Bohemia, 22.7 percent in 1907 and 21.9 percent in 1911.[35]

---

31. Sedlák, *Brno v době secese*, plates 6 through 9ff.

32. Polák, *T. G. Masaryk*, 15–58.

33. *Pozor*, April 9, 1892, cited by Fischer, *Pokrová Morava*, I:126.

34. See Tables 1 and 2 below. These tables appear in Garver, *Young Czech Party*, 357–58, and are based on information in *Statistisches Handbuch des Königreiches Böhmen*, 2nd ed., 56; Miroslav Buchvaldek et al., *Dějiny Československa v datech* (Prague, 1968), 464–65; Oldřich Říha and Július Mésároš, eds., *Přehled československých dejin* (Prague, 1960), Vol. 2, part 1, 1000, 1012; and R. Fischer, *Pokroková Morava*, 2:318.

35. See Tables 1 and 2 below.

Table 1. Czech Party Representation in the Lower House of the *Reichsrat* under Universal Suffrage in 1907.

Party	No. of votes received	Total seats	Bohemia %	Bohemia No.	Moravia %	Moravia No.	Silesia %	Silesia No.
Social Democrats	389,960	24	39.8	17	30.7	5	65.9	2
Agrarians	206,784	28	22.0	23	15.8	4	14.5	1
Clericals	182,500	17	11.9	7	29.8	10	—	–
Young Czechs & Moravian People's	16,524	19	11.3	14	11.4	5	2.2	–
Old Czechs	32,524	6	1.4	2	6.7	4	—	–
Natl. Socialists	75,101	9	10.3	9	1.1	–	17.4	–
Radical Progressives	9,899	–	0.6	–	—	–	—	–
State Rights Radicals	7,879	–	0.5	–	—	–	--	–
People's Progressives ("Realists")	14,704	2	0.9	1	2.4	1	—	–
w/o party affiliation	—	2	1.3	1	2.1	1	—	–

Table 2. Czech Party Representation in the Lower House of the *Reichsrat* under Universal Suffrage in 1911.

Party	No. of votes received	Total seats	Bohemia %	Bohemia No.	Moravia %	Moravia No.	Silesia %	Silesia No.
Cz.Social Democrats (a)	357,263	25	36.5	14	26.5	11	35.5	–
Centralist Soc. Dems.	19,367	1	0.2	–	2.5	–	33.8	1
Agrarians (a)	257,714	38	26.4	30	18.9	6	24.5	2
National Catholics (b)	127,992	7	11.9	–	36.6	7	—	–
Christian Socials	83,124							
Young Czechs	56,573	14	9.8	14	—	–	2.2	–
Moravian People's Progressives	34,443	4	—	–	8.5	4	—	–
Old Czechs	9,872	1	0.4	1	2.1	–	—	–
Natl. Socialists	95,906	14	9.7	13	2.2	1	—	–
State Rights Progressives	20,916	2	2.4	2	—	–	—	–
Progressives ("Realists") (a)	10,168	1	0.7	–	1.5	1	—	–
w/o party affiliation	10,802	1	2.0	1	1.2	1	6.2	–
Others (c)	14,931	1	1	–				
TOTAL:	1,099,171	108	100.0	75	100.0	30	100.0	3

(a) In Moravia only, these parties formed "the Progressive Bloc."

(b) The two clerical parties ran a joint slate of candidates.

(c) Includes the Tradesmen's Party of Moravia with 3,199 votes, the Czech National Party in Silesia with 1,893 votes, and *Zählkandidaten* in three provinces with 8,839 feet.

How did the growth of liberal middle class politics in Moravia differ from that in Bohemia? The Old Czech Party, which was less overtly civil libertarian, anticlerical, and nationalistic than its Young Czech rivals, retained its preeminence in Moravia until the emergence of mass political parties in the later 1890s, whereas in Bohemia it lost its majority of seats to the Young Czechs in elections to the *Reichsrat* in 1891 and to the Bohemian Diet in 1895.

The founding of the Czech People's Party in Moravia, the first outspokenly liberal middle class party in that province, occurred almost sixteen years after the founding in Prague of its Bohemian counterpart and patron, the Young Czech Party. Adolf Stránský, founder in November 1889 and editor of the biweekly *Moravské listy* (*The Moravian Newspaper*) in Brno, took the lead in organizing the Moravian People's Party on June 22, 1890, in order to support liberal candidates in that year's election of delegates to the Moravian Diet. He was inspired by the success of the Young Czechs in sweeping almost all fourth and some third curial seats in elections to the Bohemian Diet in 1889. In part because a ten-gulden direct tax requirement for voting still applied in Moravia as opposed to a five-gulden requirement in Bohemia, only one candidate of the People's Party as opposed to six Old Czechs won election in the fourth, or rural, curia. In anticipation of the *Reichsrat* elections of March 1891, the People's Party reorganized on February 15, 1891, with the help of Young Czech financial contributions. These subsidies continued after the March 1891 *Reichsrat* elections in which Young Czechs defeated all Old Czech candidates in Bohemia and in which the People's Party for the first time challenged Old Czech preeminence in Moravia.[36] These Young Czech victories came after a majority of Czech voters became persuaded that Czech efforts to advance civil liberties and national autonomy would be jeopardized were the Bohemian Diet to approve the agreement (*punktace*) for Bohemia concluded in 1890 between Minister-President Eduard Taaffe (1833–95) and the Old Czechs, German Liberals, and Conservative Great Landowners. Similarly, Taaffe's forcing the resignation in 1892 of the popular Old Czech Alois Pražák as minister without portfolio for Czech affairs in order to please the ministry's German Liberal partners helped discredit Taaffe's Old Czech supporters and increase the popularity of the People's Party in Moravia. As a result of Pražák's dismissal, and the earlier electoral defeat of the Old Czechs in Bohemia, many disillusioned Moravian Old Czech deputies transferred their allegiance to the Moravian People's Party, thus increasing the size of its delegation in the Moravian Diet and of the joint Young Czech and People's Party club of delegates in the *Reichsrat*. As a result, the Young Czechs ceased subsidizing the People's Party and appointed to their executive committee not only Stránský and his lieutenant, Josef Tuček, but also Josef

---

36. The People's Party won no seats in Moravia at these elections.

Vychodil, head of the Peasant Union for Moravia. The latter organization joined the People's Party and the Political Association for Northern Moravia to try to advance civil liberties, universal suffrage, urban and rural cooperatives, and tax relief for small farmers. The leading figure in this coalition was the lawyer and editor Adolf Stránský, a Czech Jew who had converted to Roman Catholicism but had remained liberal and anticlerical nonetheless. To promote the growing People's Party and increasingly popular civil libertarian policies, Stránský began to publish the first liberal daily in Moravia, the *Lidové noviny* (*The People's News*) in December 1893 as the successor to his biweekly *Moravské listy*. Under his direction, this new daily eventually came to rival the *Národní listy* as an advocate of liberalism and as a Czech paper of record.[37]

At Nymburk, Bohemia, in September 1894, the Young Czech Party's trustees confirmed the autonomous status of the Moravian People's Party, allowing it to continue to place three representatives on the Young Czech executive committee and to maintain its independent organization. Furthermore, every change in policy or tactics on the part of one party that might affect the other still had to be approved by the executive committees of both. The impressive Young Czech landslide in the November 1895 elections to the Bohemian Diet, followed by the People's Party's joint victory in the October 1896 elections to the Moravian Diet, appeared to vindicate the Young Czechs' policy since Nymburk of encouraging alliances with more conservative parties. The Bohemian Old Czechs ceased to be formidable competitors of the Young Czechs, while the Moravian Old Czechs had come to terms with the People's Party.[38] In the elections of March 1897 to the *Reichsrat*, the Young Czechs and the People's Party together captured sixty of the seventy Czech seats from Bohemia and Moravia to become the largest party delegation in the *Reichsrat*.[39] Before these elections, the Moravian People's Party had even concluded an electoral agreement with the Moravian Old Czechs in the spirit of the Nymburk Resolution that authorized cooperation with the Conservative Great Landowners in principle just as the Young Czech agreement to support the Badeni government after 1896 did so in fact. The People's Party continued to support the

---

37. Fischer, *Pokrová Morava*, I:15–19, II:349–67.

38. The October 1896 diet elections in Moravia also brought returns favorable to Young Czech interests. Stránský's People's Party won a plurality of Czech seats for the first time, taking seventeen seats in the third and fourth curias as opposed to thirteen for the National, or Old Czech, Party and five for the clerical parties. An electoral agreement between Stránský and the Old Czechs contributed to the victory. Two of the five clerical mandates went to the leaders of the newly founded Czech Catholic National party (*Katolická strana národní*). See Garver, *Young Czech Party*, 223–24; Fischer, *Pokrová Morava*, I: 49–61, 65–79.

39. Garver, *Young Czech Party*, 245–64.

Young Czechs through the rest of the decade, despite occasional disagreements on policies and tactics.

Leaders of the People's Party were disheartened as were the agrarian, progressive, and state rights radical allies of the Young Czech Party at the Young Czech leadership's inability to realize, in cooperation with the Badeni and Thun ministries, the ambitious program of placing the Czech language on an equal footing with German in the civil bureaucracy and in public life. As a result, the People's Party was not alone in declaring the "bankruptcy" of the Young Czechs' policy of cooperating with imperial ministries in exchange for promised concessions.[40] Thus, the Moravian People's Party went its own way after 1902, much like the similarly disillusioned agrarian, radical, and progressive allies of the Young Czechs had done in 1898 and 1899 in Bohemia, by forming independent National Socialist and Agrarian Parties and three progressive parties of the intelligentsia. To be sure, the breakup of the Young Czech coalition had its roots in the growing social differentiation among Czechs that, beginning in the 1870s, had encouraged political organization according to economic or class interest. But, the failure of the Young Czechs' positive policies in 1898 and 1899 as well as imperial authorization in 1896 of a fifth curia based on universal male suffrage in elections to the lower house of the *Reichsrat* explain why a multiparty system emerged in Czech politics at the end of the 1890s and not sooner. The fifth curia encouraged the formation of mass parties that could now expect for the first time to elect delegates to that relatively powerless forum for public opinion, the *Reichsrat,* instead of having to rely upon a predominantly middle class liberal party of the notables—the Young Czechs— to represent them there as it continued to do in the second and third curias of the Bohemian Diet and on district and local self-governmental bodies elected by highly unrepresentative class voting.[41]

Shortly after the Young Czechs of Bohemia and the Progressives of Moravia began to go their separate ways, the autonomous Czech agrarian movement in Moravia in May 1905 joined forces with the Czech Agrarian Party of Bohemia, which had been independent of the Young Czechs since January 1899. This development prompted the Young Czechs in Bohemia, under the leadership of Kramář, Pacák, and Škarda, to establish closer ties to two parties of the right— the Old Czechs and Conservative Great Landowners. In Moravia, the People's Party, by contrast, moved to the left to establish a closer association with the Moravian Progressives, Agrarians, and Social Democrats. Its first step was to merge in January 1909 with the

---

40. "Jinou cestou," *Selské listy,* December 30, 1902, speech by Adolf Stránský, reprinted in part by Fischer, *Pokroková Morava,* I: 142–43. In this speech, Stránský critically evaluated Young Czech "positive politics" and described the more progressive course about to be taken by the Moravian People's Party.

41. This process is described by Garver, *Young Czech Party,* 277–99.

Progressive Party to form the Moravian People's Progressive Party. In turn, this new party in 1911 took the lead in creating an anticlerical Moravian Progressive Bloc with the Agrarians and Social Democrats to turn the tide against Czech clerical party candidates in the elections of 1911 to the *Reichsrat* and 1913 to the Moravian Diet.[42]

The most striking difference between Czech politics in Bohemia and Czech politics in Moravia was the presence of strong clerical parties in the latter province. Like their counterparts in Bohemia, these parties did not emerge until after the Old Czech Party had sustained defeat at the hands of strongly liberal and anticlerical forces in both rural and urban areas.[43] As soon as the Old Czechs and Conservative Great Landowners appeared incapable of protecting clerical interests or of holding Young Czech and People's Party anticlericalism in check, the church hierarchy, with the support of most Czech priests and many laymen, and in the spirit of Leo XIII's 1891 encyclical *Rerum novarum*, organized the Catholic National Party in 1896 and the Christian Social Party between 1894 and 1899.[44]

In elections to the Bohemian Diet in 1895 and 1901, all Czech Catholic candidates suffered defeat. In Bohemia, the Christian Socialist Party reorganized in 1904 and managed to elect one delegate to the diet in 1908 and again in 1913. Thanks primarily to universal manhood suffrage, Czech clerical candidates first won election to the *Reichsrat* from Bohemia in 1907, receiving 11.9 percent of Czech votes and seven seats. Four years later, all seven delegates were defeated, given an agreement by Czech Social Democrats and Agrarians to support the same anticlerical candidate in

---

42. See Tables 1 and 2 above.

43. A Czech Catholic political movement first formed in Bohemia after the Old Czech defeat of 1891 as Czech Catholics' evaluations of the electoral returns indicated that the replacement of Old Czech cadres by an avowedly Catholic party would increase popular acceptance for clerical and conservative policies and eventually diminish Young Czech support. See Garver, *Young Czech Party,* 285–86.

44. "In the spring of 1896, Mořic Hruban, formerly an Old Czech, and Antonin Cyril Stojan, Th.D., in Moravia established the Catholic National Party (*Katolická strana národní*), which in October acquired five mandates to the Moravian Diet and in the following year sent Stojan to the *Reichsrat*. While the Catholic National Party served wealthier and more conservative Czech Catholics, the Christian Social Party for Moravia and Silesia (*Křest'ansko-sociální strana*), founded in 1894 and reorganized on a popular basis in 1899, appealed to Catholic peasants, tradesmen, and workers, seeking to combat liberalism and Social Democracy and to resolve the social question in accordance with *Rerum novarum*. Under the able leadership of Jan Šrámek, a young parish priest, this party and its local affiliates for political education and economic self-help enjoyed great success throughout rural Moravia. In 1902, Šrámek set up a Catholic trade union (*Všeodborové sdružení křest'ansko-sociálního delnictva*), which grew by 1914 to 410 branches and 32,000 members." See footnote 45 and Fischer, *Pokrová Morava,* I: 79–84.

almost every strongly Catholic district. Thus weakened by repeated electoral defeats, the already divided clerical movement in Bohemia fell apart as its three constituent parties followed separate ways—the Catholic National Party, the Conservative People's Party, and the Christian Socialist Party.[45]

In Moravia, the alliance of 1905 between the Catholic National and Christian Socialist Parties preserved their preeminence among Moravian parties until their close defeat by the Moravian Progressive Bloc of Czech Social Democrats, People's Progressives and Agrarians in elections to the *Reichsrat* in 1911 and to the fourth and fifth curias of the Moravian Diet in 1913. The decline of clerical influence in Moravia after 1908 may be attributed primarily to the mobilization of anticlerical strength by the Progressive Bloc and to a lesser extent to the growing conservatism in both Catholic parties. Pope Pius X's condemnation of modernism in his 1907 encyclical *Pascendi gregis* increased the influence of conservative elements within the allied clerical parties at the expense of priests and laymen who endorsed Czech efforts to advance civil liberties, national autonomy, and social reform. Within the limits prescribed by Catholic doctrine, both parties declared their support for the Habsburgs while seeking to advance the commonweal and obtain equal rights for all Cisleithanian nationalities. Their efforts to suppress criticism of the church, as in the Juda case in Moravia in 1905, and their efforts to establish, in the *Orel*, an attractive Catholic alternative to the *Sokol* (Falcon) met with only limited success.[46]

With the establishment of universal suffrage in a fifth curia to the Moravian Diet in 1905 and to the lower house of the *Reichsrat* in 1907, closely contested electoral battles occurred in urban areas between Czech Social Democratic and Czech clerical candidates and in the countryside between Czech Agrarian and clerical candidates, with the People's Progressives in every instance opposing the latter. Neither the Czech National Socialists nor two of the three Czech progressive parties of the intelligentsia—the Radical Progressives and State Rights Radicals—ever acquired much Moravian support. The third, Masaryk's People's—subsequently Progressive—Party, won one of its two *Reichsrat* mandates in 1907 and its only mandate of 1911 in Moravia in the heavily Protestant Valašské Meziříčí

---

45. See J. Doležal, *Politická cesta českého katolicismu* (Prague, 1928), 7ff.; Jan Heidler, *České strany politické v Čechách, na Moravě a ve Slezsku* (Prague, 1914), 47–50; Ivo Ducháček, ed., *Mandatář národa: Studie a projevy k 75. narozeninám Msgre. Dr. Jana Šrámka* (Prague, 1946); and Ludvík Nemec, *Antonín Cyril Stojan* (New Rochelle, NY, 1983).

46. According to the *Ottův slovník naučný*, Vol. 23 (1905), 625–26, the Sokol in 1903 had 51,505 members and 467 lodges in Bohemia and 154 in Moravia and Silesia. By contrast, Orel had over 12,000 members in 1914 in comparison to nearly 120,000 in the Sokol. Josef Rezníček, "Vývoj čsl. Orla," *Zivot*, Vol. 11(1929), 9.

region, where, in order to defeat the clerical candidate, and impressed by Masaryk's civil libertarian and progressive politics, the Social Democrats, the People's Party, and the Progressives ran no one against him in 1907 or in 1911.[47]

In 1905, Czech Social Democrats, Czech National Socialists, all Czech progressives, and the Moravian People's Party advocated the introduction of universal manhood suffrage, not only for elections to the lower house of the *Reichsrat,* but for the diets in the three Czech crown lands. Only in Moravia in that year did a limited extension of the franchise occur. The Moravian Agreement of November 27, 1905, supported by all German and Great Landowners' parties, the Old Czech Party, and both Czech clerical parties, added a fifth, or universal, curia to the Moravian Diet and otherwise confirmed the long established balance of power in the diet between Czechs, Germans, and Conservative Great Landowners, leaving the latter in control of the first curia, the Germans in control of the second and predominant in the third, and the Czechs predominant in the fourth and fifth.[48]

Czech trade unions developed in Moravia in close association with the "Czechoslavonic Social Democratic Party" established in Prague in 1878 and associated from 1889 to 1911 with the All-Austrian Social Democratic Party established at Hainfeld in December 1888. Because of curial voting, Czech Social Democratic representation in the Moravian Diet under terms of the agreement of 1905 was, in comparison to other parties, proportionally the weakest in relation to total votes received as the party obtained 23.3 percent of all Czech votes in the elections of November and December 1906 but were awarded only 6.9 percent of all Czech delegates. By contrast, the Moravian People's Party, with only three-fifths as many votes, placed more than three times as many delegates—sixteen as opposed to five. This was at least an improvement over conditions in Bohemia, where in the absence of any fifth, or universal, curia in diet elections, working class Czech voters were effectively disenfranchised. Moreover, the Czech Social Democrats improved their representation in the Moravian Diet in the elections of June 1913 by two seats, in large part because their candidates in predominantly industrial districts of the fifth curia ran as the sole candidates of the Progressive Bloc against the clerical opposition.[49] From 1905 to 1913, Czech Social Democrats in Moravia established closer ties

---

47. On Masaryk's two electoral victories in the Valašské Meziříčí area, see Miloslav Trapl, *Vedecké základy Masarykovy politiky* (Brno, 1946), and Miloslav Trapl, *Masarykův program: demokracie—socialismus—česká otázka* (Brno, 1948).

48. See Garver, *Young Czech Party,* 279ff. and 320 for a discussion of the agreement.

49. "Representation in the Moravian Diet before and after 1905" may be seen in Table 24, Garver, *Young Czech Party,* 360.

to their counterparts in Bohemia after rejecting a small minority's desire to draw nearer instead to Austrian Social Democracy in Vienna. This trend is best revealed by the overwhelming support of eleven to one that Moravian working class voters gave to the autonomist, as opposed to the centralist, slate of Czech Social Democratic candidates in the 1911 *Reichsrat* elections.[50]

Czech Social Democrats in Moravia more often made electoral agreements with agrarian and middle class progressive parties than did their comrades in Bohemia. Such cooperation was most effective in the Progressive Bloc primarily because each party in the bloc considered the clerical parties to be more dangerous foes than any bloc partners. The absence of large numbers of Czech entrepreneurs in Moravia, in marked contrast to Bohemia, may also have blunted differences of opinion between Czech Social Democrats and Progressives in Moravia. Most importantly, because no district boards existed in Moravia, the People's Party had no bastion of privilege comparable to that enjoyed by the Young Czechs in Bohemia. This surely encouraged it to come to terms with the Czech Progressives and Social Democrats in Moravia. Besides, the addition of a fifth curia to the Moravian Diet gave Czech Social Democrats in Moravia an opportunity denied to their comrades in Bohemia and Silesia to participate in provincial politics and to do so under circumstances that required some agreement between all anticlerical parties. Quite logically, therefore, in 1919, the Czechoslovak Social Democratic Party chose as its candidate for premier, Vlastimil Tusar, a long-time Moravian Czech Social Democratic advocate of the Progressive Bloc which may be seen as a forerunner of the red-green coalition government of Social Democrats and Agrarians that he helped establish in 1920.

Czech Agrarians, like Czech Social Democrats, were proportionally not quite as popular among Czech voters in Moravia as in Bohemia.[51] Beginning in the early 1880s, the Czech Agrarian movement in Moravia grew up with, but independently of, the Czech Agrarians in Bohemia.[52] The Agrar-

---

50. See Tables 1 and 2 above.

51. This is evident from a comparison of evidence from Tables 1 and 2 above.

52. The Moravian and Silesian party developed out of the Czecho-Moravian Peasant Association for Moravia (*Českomoravský spolek selský pro Moravu*), established in September 1883 in Olomouc by J.J. Tvrdik and Josef Vychodil, and its successor after 1892, the Peasant Union for Moravia. The Bohemian Czech Agrarian Party to the merger had earlier emerged from the Association of Czech Agriculturists and the Peasant Union for the Kingdom of Bohemia. See Garver, *Young Czech Party*, 289–90. During the 1890s, the several Czech peasant associations had dealt primarily with local issues and had depended upon the Young Czech Party in Bohemia and the People's Party in Moravia to advance agrarian interests in the provincial diets and in the *Reichsrat*. Such policies had conformed to the traditionally parochial peasant outlook but, more importantly, had been fostered by curial

ian Party of Bohemia, established in January 1899, joined the Agrarian movement of Moravia in May 1905 to form a single Agrarian Party for all the Czech lands.[53] The Czech Agrarians won a large following more rapidly in Bohemia than in Moravia where they faced far stronger clerical opposition not only in rural districts but also from a minority in their own ranks. In the *Reichsrat* elections of 1907, the Czech Agrarian Party won twenty-four seats in Bohemia to only four in Moravia. The increase in the Czech Agrarians' representation, after the *Reichsrat* elections of 1911 and after elections to the Moravian Diet in 1913, may be attributed primarily to their participation in the Moravian Progressive Bloc, a participation arranged and encouraged by two of the leading Czech Agrarian leaders in Moravia, František Staněk and Kuneš Sonntag. In contrast to their counterparts in Bohemia, both Czech Agrarians and Czech Social Democrats in Moravia more often made agreements with each other and with Czech Progressives, all primarily with a view to taking seats away from the Czech clerical parties who were so much more powerful in Moravia than in Bohemia.

Conclusions

How do the similarities and differences between Czech politics and society in Bohemia and Moravia help one understand the influence of social change, political institutions, and religion upon the making of the modern Czech nation?

Czechs in Bohemia and Moravia expressed virtually identical aims and tried to achieve these aims through the same sorts of political, fraternal, and economic organizations, indicating that Czechs increasingly realized

---

voting, which restricted peasant representation in the diets and the *Reichsrat,* and by the newspaper tax stamp, which was abolished in December 1899 and had retarded the growth of an agrarian press.

53. This unified party reflected an increasing desire among Czech farmers to advance common political and economic interests through an organized political party of their own. Stimulated by the anticipated introduction of election by universal suffrage to the lower house of the *Reichsrat,* the party contended that agrarian interests could no longer be effectively served in Bohemia by peasant affiliation with a Young Czech Party increasingly dominated by a privileged urban upper middle class. A growing consciousness of distinctive occupational and economic interests also encouraged Czech farmers to try to elect fellow agriculturalists to the diets and *Reichsrat* as opposed to the lawyers or professional men who more often than not had been the Young Czech candidates in rural electoral constituencies. On January 6, 1899, the Association of Czech Agriculturalists formed an independent Czech Agrarian Party (*Česká agrární strana*) for Bohemia which included the association as an autonomous affiliate. See Garver, *Young Czech Party,* 290–91.

their need to make common cause regardless of the province in which they lived. All of this attests to the fact that Czech liberal and progressive as well as agrarian and social democratic movements were powerful enough to overcome local or provincial interests among Czechs in both lands. Likewise evident was the fragmentation of Czech political parties in both provinces along class and occupational lines or in accordance with religious affiliation. Fragmentation occurred less rapidly in Moravia because of that province's less rapid industrialization, the absence of a large Czech professional and managerial class, and the greater strength there of Catholicism and clerical parties.

The political primacy of the Czech middle class and of national and liberal political parties in Bohemia derived primarily from the large size and wealth of this class and to a lesser extent from its ability to dominate district and communal self-government through district boards. By contrast, the much weaker political and economic influence of the Czech middle class and of liberalism in Moravia may be explained less by the absence of district boards than by the fact that Germans owned most of Moravia's large banks and heavy industry and until 1919 controlled municipal government in two of its three largest cities.

In Moravia as well as in Bohemia, the emergence after 1898 of a multi-party system increased popular political participation and the representation of popular political aspirations at all levels of self-government. Because the new mass parties advocated the economic advancement and education of the common people as strongly if not more strongly than they did the extension of civil liberties and suffrage, the Habsburgs and the privileged classes were less able to buy off or restrain these parties than they had been able to accommodate the parties of the notables. This was evident in the success of the coalition of popular parties in the Moravian Progressive Bloc in competing with the powerful clerical movement that alone among mass Czech political parties pledged itself to uphold the Habsburg Monarchy come what may.

The much stronger Czech support for clerical parties in Moravia than in Bohemia can be attributed only in small part to the fact that the economic development of Moravia generally proceeded less rapidly than that of Bohemia. It cannot at all be explained by the only two ways in which Moravia's political institutions differed from those of Bohemia—the absence of district boards and the presence of a fifth curia in its diet. In both provinces, anticlericalism prevailed in the agrarian as well as in Social Democratic and middle class political parties; and the most backward rural areas of Bohemia tended to be strongly anticlerical, evident in the success of Alfons Šťastný and his Peasant Union in southern Bohemia. The greater strength of religious belief, whether Catholic or Protestant, among Czechs of Moravia as opposed to Bohemia can be explained only by the study of historical developments preceding industrialization, a task beyond the scope of this chapter. Though industrialization appears to have strengthened Czech national consciousness and to have weakened traditional religious faith, the rebirth of the former was well underway just as challenges to the latter had already emerged well before the advent of steam power and factory production.

The fact that Czech liberal, progressive, and agrarian parties in Moravia retained an electoral alliance after most of those in Bohemia had gone their separate ways may be attributed primarily to the greater strength of Czech clerical politics in Moravia. For the same reason cooperation between Czech Social Democrats and Agrarians occurred more often in Moravia than in Bohemia.

Though relations between Germans and Czechs were never cordial in any of the Czech crown lands, the two nationalities did reach agreement on several issues in Moravia—notably in November 1905—while remaining at loggerheads in Bohemia from 1890 through 1918. Obviously, greater wealth and political influence were at stake in Bohemia. There, the German middle class turned more often to extremism, since it had competitively fallen behind the Czech middle class in wealth and numbers and in control of municipal government, the learned professions, and the new electrical, automotive, machine tool, and mechanized food processing industries. In Moravia, on the other hand, the German middle class could concede some political influence to Czechs in rural areas, secure in the knowledge that German domination of heavy industry and some municipal governments would likely prevail for at least another generation—given the numerically weaker Czech upper middle class and intelligentsia.

The fact that Czech agrarian and workers' organizations developed autonomously in Moravia as well as in Bohemia beginning in the 1870s indicates that political affiliation by social class or occupational group preceded by at least two decades the formation of a multiparty system during the years 1898 to 1901. On the other hand, however much industrialization accelerated class and occupational differentiation and strengthened Czech national as well as class consciousness, these developments cannot adequately explain why a multiparty system emerged in the later 1890s and not somewhat sooner. The timing of this emergence can best be explained by the simultaneous implementation of political reforms like the extension of suffrage to a universal fifth curia and the abolition of newspaper tax stamps and by the inability of the Young Czech Party to realize its ambitious liberal and national agenda in 1897 and 1898 in cooperation with the Badeni and Thun governments. Ultimately, only the destruction of the Habsburg Monarchy made possible the achievement of Czechoslovak independence as well as the full flowering of a system of freely competing political parties based on Czech and Slovak national identities as well as on class and occupational interests.

To understand Czech politics in Austria-Hungary one must therefore consider the authoritarian constitutional political system within which Czech parties and organizations had to operate as well as the transformation of society through industrialization and the expansion of communications that not only stimulated class and national consciousness but placed increasingly heavy pressure upon an authoritarian political system designed primarily to preserve the prerogatives and serve the interests of the Habsburgs and the privileged classes who supported them. The fact that these elements tried to retard or check popular political responses to economic transformation and social change—whether liberal, nationalistic, or social democratic—vastly increased the political instability of the monarchy. In July 1914, the Habsburgs, under German pressure, chose to resort to war instead of accepting international arbitration of its quarrel with Serbia. The result was the defeat of Germany and the Habsburg Monarchy and the latter's disintegration in the ensuing national and social revolutions.

One important development of the period 1860 to 1914 that became especially pronounced during the years 1898 to 1914 was the growing cooperation between Czech political parties in Bohemia and their counterparts in Moravia. This indicates not only that most differences of opinion between Bohemian Czechs and Moravian Czechs were subordinate to their common national and civil libertarian objectives but also that class conflict and differences of religious opinion divided Czechs one from another to a much greater degree than did any sort of provincial or regional loyalties.

One measure of the strength of Czech national identity and interests as well as Czech agrarian, working class, or Catholic solidarity is the fact that liberal, agrarian, social democratic, and clerical parties were able to flourish in the very different social and political circumstances of Bohemia and Moravia. But, the survival through October 1918 of authoritarian constitutional Habsburg rule and of unrepresentative self-governmental institutions along with the enduring influence of religion in politics clearly indicate that Czech politics of the late nineteenth and early twentieth centuries cannot be understood primarily as a pragmatic political response to extensive economic transformation and social change. That era saw not only the Czechs' creation of their first market economy and first modern representative self-governmental institutions but also the advent of practical cooperation between Bohemian Czech and Moravian Czech political parties, labor unions, and fraternal associations. Moreover, the achievements and shortcomings of Czech politics in that era continue to be of more than academic interest today as Czechs enter their fourteenth year of rebuilding political democracy and a market economy and of defining anew the relationships between citizens of different ages, occupations, interests, religious creeds, and regional affiliations.

Chapter 2

Strategy, Politics, and Suffering: The Wartime Relief of Belgium, Serbia, and Poland, 1914–1918

M. B. B. Biskupski

The history of the First World War presents a striking discrepancy between the magnitude, degree, and duration of suffering of European populations and the extent to which this suffering was addressed. Belgium, which sustained relatively few casualties and whose civilian population knew only brief privation, received enormous aid from both its allies and from such neutrals as the United States. By comparison, both Serbia and Poland, which endured years of the most abject misery and lost substantial portions of their population to hunger, exposure, and disease, received scant outside aid during the war. The relief of Belgium was not repeated in the east of Europe. Why this was true is the subject of this essay.

Relief for large, destitute populations was principally a question of food importation. Because European stocks were inadequate, and tended to fall during the War, this meant transatlantic shipment. Food, in effect, became a question of the Allied blockade.[1] This, in turn, meant it was a problem for British rather than French, Italian, or Russian policy. As Paul Vincent has noted, London's allies' "collective effect upon the functioning of the blockade was negligible. In general, one can assume that the blockade, as it existed between 1914 and 1917, was a British apparatus."[2]

---

1. Edward F. Willis expressed this succinctly: "The central feature of the blockade system was a rationing policy by which every country with uncontrolled access to Germany was strictly rationed, and other countries were rationed as the Allies deemed necessary"; vide his *Herbert Hoover and the Russian Prisoners of World War I: A Study in Diplomacy and Relief, 1918–1919* (Stanford, CA, 1951), 3.

2. C. Paul Vincent, *The Politics of Hunger: The Allied Blockade of Germany, 1915–1919* (Athens, OH, 1985), 36.

The importation of transoceanic food into Europe was a strategic question of the greatest moment for the British, who were linked by what Avner Offer has called the "agrarian bond" to food exporting nations.[3] Control of the channels of this food was perhaps London's greatest strategic concern during the war. As a result, relief issues raised fundamental questions about national and imperial security.

Along with the blockade, the United States, although neutral until 1917, was a factor of the greatest importance as regards international relief questions. The United States provided the majority of both the food and the money that relieved Europe during the war.[4] Such organizations as the Rockefeller Foundation, the American Red Cross, and, of course, the Commission for Relief in Belgium were the principal agents either providing, or attempting to provide, wartime relief.[5]

By comparison, the Central Powers, which had great and rising difficulties in feeding their own populations, were relatively passive agents in the question of international relief. Their principal role was to provide a justification—by requisitioning imported foods—for the British to refuse relief efforts.

The whole question of sustained and massive international relief for a substantial population was without precedent before the First World War. As John F. Hutchinson has shown, it was only in the last few years before the war that the international Red Cross movement had become a major institution, enjoying governmental and popular support and large funds.[6] Such institutions as the Rockefeller Foundation, the Quakers, and the American Relief Clearing House [ARCH] in the United States only involved themselves in wartime relief in stages as they gradually expanded what they regarded as their scope of action. The Jewish Joint Distribution Committee came into existence late in 1914 only as a result of amalgamating several smaller organizations. The most famous wartime relief organization of all, Herbert Hoover's Commission for Relief in Belgium, had to engage in almost perpetual struggle to maintain its activities, as both sides

---

3. Avner Offer, *The First World War: An Agrarian Interpretation* (Oxford, 1989), 3 *et passim*.

4. Vide Herbert Hoover, *An American Epic. Volume III* (Chicago, 1961), 1ff; John Maurice Clark, *The Costs of the World War to the American People* (New Haven, CT, 1931), 120.

5. Vide Frank M. Surface and Raymond L. Bland, *American Food and the World War and Reconstruction Period* (Stanford, CA, 1931), 3ff.

6. John F. Hutchinson, *Champions of Charity: War and the Rise of the Red Cross* (Boulder, CO, 1996), 189, 224ff. and passim; Dimitra Giannuli, "American Philanthropy in Action: The American Red Cross in Greece, 1918–1923," *East European Politics and Societies* 10, no. 1 (Winter, 1996): 108–109.

in the conflict resented Hoover. In other words, the very idea of the relief of large civilian populations, in wartime, by neutral agencies was unprecedented before 1914 and intruded itself only with difficulty into the military and diplomatic realities of a major war. Why this development was more successful in some places than in others raises many intriguing questions, which we shall discuss in due course.

I. The Relief of Belgium

By October 10, 1914, virtually all of Belgium, save a small portion of west Flanders, was under German occupation. From this tiny strip of the patrimony, King Albert and the remnants of the Belgian field army endured until the end of the war. For the rest of the country, however, it meant an occupation that was to last four years. The degree of social dislocation quickly outstripped the abilities of the Belgians, and they appealed for international assistance. By mid-October the rudiments of what was to become Herbert Hoover's Commission for Relief in Belgium were established.[7]

During the next four years the Belgian population, which Hoover estimated at seven and one-half million,[8] received just over three million metric tons of supplies, and almost a million additional tons arrived in the period between the Armistice and the end of August 1919. The total value of this assistance, in 1919 dollars, was approximately $700 million.[9] Not surprisingly, therefore, the actual privation in Belgium was short-lived, restricted in its scope, and resulted in few casualties. Material damage done to Belgium was, however, very extensive.[10]

The CRB was able to organize a massive relief effort for Belgium and overcome the diplomatic obstacle to the transportation of foodstuffs across the British blockade, subsequently distributing them with the cooperation

---

7. George I. Gay and H. H. Fisher, *Public Relations of the Commission for Relief in Belgium: Documents*, 2 vols. (Stanford, CA, 1929), I, iff..

8. Hoover to Eustace Percy, October 7, 1916, in Gay and Fisher, *Public Relations*, I, 165.

9. Vide Surface and Bland, *American Food*, 162–163, 278.

10. Sally Marks has calculated that the relatively advanced industrial infrastructure of Belgium was severely crippled by systematic German destruction, requisitioning, and sabotage. By 1919 at least 85 percent of Belgian industry was still "paralyzed." Vide her *Innocent Abroad: Belgium at the Paris Peace Conference of 1919* (Chapel Hill, NC, 1981), 173. A decade after the war per capita income in Belgium was still markedly below 1913 levels, vide Rune Johansson, *Small State in Boundary Conflict: Belgium and the Belgian-German Border, 1914–1919* (Lund, 1988), 101.

of the German occupation authorities. So successful were the commission's actions that famine was averted, the feeding of the entire population assured, and reserve stocks created to preclude the possibility of shortfall or untoward development. Perhaps more important, the CRB had achieved international celebrity, gaining supporters and an organizational support network around the world. In sum, within several months of the occupation of Belgium, the country was no longer in desperate straits, and indeed, was rapidly becoming the object of international concern and affection.[11] Belgian suffering had been both short-lived and not particularly intense. As early as the autumn of 1915 it was concluded that in Belgium there was no "distressing shortage, even of clothing"; the population was "comfortable and free from hunger."[12]

Despite the rapid recovery of Belgium to decent conditions, it retained an enormous hold on the sympathies and charity of the world. In fact, when it became obvious that other peoples were suffering more greatly than the Belgians it was difficult to refocus popular or governmental attention away from Belgium, which tended to monopolize the world's attention and money. This led to both frustration and bitterness among those who tried to resist the enormous power of the informal Belgian relief mentality that had become demonstrably established in the West from the very beginning of the war.

The explanation for this phenomenon begins with chronological priority. Belgium was the first innocent casualty of the war. Its willingness to stand up to German threats was admired as heroic defiance of an infinitely more powerful foe. The subsequent performance of its army, though strategically insignificant, won for the Belgians, and especially its attractive monarch, Albert I, a hero's mantle. The fact that the army was able to hold on to a scrap of the national territory and fight on was still another page in what was a chapter of admirable gallantry. In the words of Sally Marks: "Anglo-Saxon publicists turned the war in part into a crusade for the rights of small nations, the roi-chevalier in Flanders field became the shining symbol of that crusade." Belgium became "the little corner never conquered," the "reluctant and unofficial spokesman of the smaller nations."[13]

---

11. A historian of the American press notes that the CRB had "great power" by the fall of 1914, and was able to begin a "high pressure campaign in the United States." "Most of the New York papers gave publicity and editorial support to the effort." Vide Keven J. O'Keefe, *A Thousand Deadlines: The New York City Press and American Neutrality, 1914–1917* (The Hague, 1972), 64. Gay and Fisher, *Public Relations,* I, 65–66; Proces-Verbal of CRB meeting of July 20, 1915, in ibid., I, 66–69.

12. Walcott to Rockefeller Foundation, December 23, 1915, Walcott Papers, Sterling Memorial Library, Yale University [Hereafter, SMLY], Box 3, folder 25.

13. Marks, *Innocent Abroad,* 5, 17.

In the words of Stuart Wallace, the invasion of Belgium "was a godsend for the [Herbert Henry] Asquith government," rallying liberal opinion, disinclined to military action, behind the war. Intellectuals in Britain were "swept off their feet by Belgium"[14] which became a cause so pure that "secular considerations–treaty commitments and strategic necessities—first put forward . . . later became consecrated as moral imperatives, finally being replaced altogether with religious arguments." Belgium became the theme of mountains of mawkish poetry, the motif of music hall performances, and was endlessly in the press. Dignitaries of the Church of England spoke of "martyred Belgium" first by comparing it to the tribulations of Israel, later it was elevated to a "Christ among nations": "Belgium became a personification of the Allied cause, God's cause, because it was there, in Flanders, that the new Nebuchadnezzar had set up not a golden idol . . . but an idol of iron."[15]

Western, particularly British, statesmen were quick to make bold, even rash, statements of support to Belgium. Prime Minister Asquith promised grandiloquently in November 1914: "We shall never sheath the sword . . . until Belgium recovers in full measure all, and more than all, which she has sacrificed."[16]

In fact, as V. H. Rothwell has noted, "the restoration . . . of Belgium remained for long the one essential and declared British war aim."[17] For the French, similarly, only the restoration of Alsace-Lorraine rivaled Belgium as a basic war aim. By February 1916, the Allies promised, i.a., that Belgium would be "generously indemnified" for all damages. This became the basis for Belgium's claim for "special consideration."[18] Before the war the Foreign Office had concluded that war over Belgium would be popular within the country, whereas involvement in the Balkans would not be.[19] This prediction was borne out by the extraordinary reception given to Belgian refugees by the British who took in more than 250,000 during the war.[20]

14. Stuart Wallace, *War and the Image of Germany: British Academics, 1914–1918* (Edinburgh, 1988), 61, 69, 129, 151.

15. Albert Marrin, *The Last Crusade: The Church of England in the First World War* (Durham, NC, 1974), 126–127, 129.

16. Paul Guinn, *British Strategy*, 122.

17. V. H. Rothwell, *British War Aims and Peace Diplomacy, 1914–1918* (London, 1971), 18.

18. David Stevenson, *French War Aims against Germany, 1914–1919* (Oxford, 1982), 17–18; Walter A. McDougall, *France's Rhineland Diplomacy, 1914–1924* (Princeton, 1978), 20; Baron Pierre van Zuyern, *Les Mains libres: Politique extérieure de la Belgique, 1914–40* (Brussels, 1950); Jane Kathryn Miller *Belgian Foreign Policy between Two Wars, 1919–1940* (New York, 1951), 27.

19. K. M. Wilson, "The Foreign Office and the 'Education' of Public Opinion before the First World War," *The Historical Journal* 26, no.2 (1983): 403ff.

20. Peter Cahalan, *Belgian Refugee Relief in England During the Great War* (New York, 1982), 1ff., 511.

The British defense of Belgian interests was a compound of geopolitical self-interest, and a dedication to moral purpose; the distinction between the two being, in Lawrence Martin's word, essentially "arbitrary." Foreign Secretary Sir Edward Grey, from the beginning of the war, was convinced of the strategic importance of Belgium, linking the fall of that county, domino-like, to the collapse of Holland and France and the concomitant undermining of British security.[21] Self-interest alone, however, would not have galvanized public support sufficiently; hence, Belgium became transmuted into a moral cause:

> It was therefore extremely convenient to use the Belgian cause as a symbol, depicting the war as a struggle against exceptional iniquity, the removal of which would produce the kind of world in which war would really be unnecessary. Initially this process was at least partially conscious.[22]

As H. W. Koch has noted, Britain was not interested in the defense of Belgium until the creation of the High Seas Fleet gave that cause strategic consequence; the link between that self-interest and the celebration of Belgian sacrifice was bridged by "propaganda."[23] Hence, Belgium linked liberal opinion, motivated by an ethical disposition regarding international affairs, and the realpolitik behind British strategic thinking and, as a consequence, enjoyed unique status in London. In Michael Howard's happy phrase, the Belgian cause "harmonized British strategic interests on the Continent with her claim to be the vindicator of international law."[24]

Hence, quite apart from the strategic and political attachment to Belgium, the plight of Belgium fit perfectly into the larger British effort to portray the Germans as barbarians during the war. The plight of suffering Belgium was a constant and eloquent reminder of the "furor Teutonicus" the British did so much to propagate throughout the world as a justification for their war effort:

> The invasion of Belgium consolidated parliamentary and press support of the war and . . . nullified the isolationist case overnight. British officials

---

21. Lawrence W. Martin, *Peace without Victory: Woodrow Wilson and the British Liberals* (Port Washington, NY, 1973 [1958]), 24–25.

22. Martin, *Peace without Victory*, 53.

23. H. W. Koch, introduction to his *The Origins of the First World War: Great Power Rivalry and German War Aims*, 2nd ed. (London, 1984), 22.

24. Michael Howard, "British Grand Strategy in World War I," in Paul Kennedy, ed., *Grand Strategies in War and Peace* (New Haven, 1991), 33. On Belgium in British propaganda, vide Trevor Wilson, "Lord Bryce's Investigation into Alleged German Atrocities in Belgium, 1914–1915," *Journal of Contemporary History* 14 (1979): 369–383.

hoped that this diplomatic trump card would have a similar effect in securing the opinion of the rest of the world, and they dispersed the story of Belgium around the globe.[25]

German actions at the first stage of the war were sufficiently brutal to make verisimilar subsequent atrocity stories. As a result: "The Germans seemed to Allied citizens to have discarded concern for humanity in Belgium."[26] Any distraction from Belgium as an ideal of especial martyrdom would weaken this first, and most convenient, demonstration of German perfidy.

Third, we must note that the British attached enormous significance to the Allied blockade during the war. Nonetheless, they were willing to allow it to be transgressed by Belgian relief shipments, something they would not later do to relieve the far larger and far more destitute populations of Serbia and Poland. The Belgian exception as regards the blockade was due, doubtless, to the status enjoyed by the country, as we have already noted. However, there are other causes as well. The German occupation of Belgium was of a piece with its occupation of a good part of northern France. The CRB's efforts toward the Belgians also included, it should not be forgotten, the population of occupied northern France. It would have been enormously difficult for the British to refuse cooperation in allowing relief supplies that were destined, in part, for the population of its major ally.[27] This was especially true because Paris never attached the same importance to the blockade, as did London.[28]

This had extraordinary consequences for other possible claimants for relief shipments which would have to receive dispensation from the blockade. The exception of Belgium, in effect, made London far less willing to entertain other exceptions. If the blockade were to work, it would have to be stringent. Having violated that once, greater vigilance was required elsewhere lest the entire strategic significance of the blockade be vitiated.

---

25. Nicoletta F. Gullace, "Sexual Violence and Family Honor: British Propaganda and International Law during the First World War," *American Historical Review* 102, no. 3 (June, 1997): 717.

26. James F. Willis, *Prologue to Nuremberg: The Politics and Diplomacy of Punishing War Criminals of the First World War* (Westport, CT., 1982), 9.

27. The CRB counted approximately 9.3 million in its relief operations; of these 7.4 million were Belgians, and 1.4 million in occupied France; vide George I. Gay, *The Commission for Relief in Belgium: Statistical Review of Relief Operations* (Stanford, CA, n.d.), 16.

28. Marjorie Milbank Farrar, *Conflict and Compromise: The Strategy, Politics, and Diplomacy of the French Blockade, 1914–1918* (The Hague, 1974), 190ff.

II. The Decimation of Serbia

At the outbreak of the war, Serbia was "badly handicapped in British popular esteem, for she had a rather sinister political record behind her." The popular image of Serbia in the West was composed of barbarism and incompetence in equal measure. The Sarajevo assassination, featuring at least a degree of Serbian complicity, further damaged Serb standing in liberal opinion. In late July, Prime Minister Asquith met with the Anglican primate and concurred that the defense of Belgrade against Austrian threats was quite impossible for Serbia was "a wild little state . . . for which nobody has a good word, so badly has it behaved."[29]

But the war soon changed all this.[30] Serbia was invaded by the forces of the Dual Monarchy at approximately the same time the Germans crossed the Belgian frontier. The Serbs were able to repulse the Austrian thrust and a series of bloody battles brought the year to end in stalemate.[31] With initial Serbian victories over the Austrians, "English enthusiasm for the Serbs knew no bounds." Paris and London quickly hailed Serbia as a second Belgium, defying great odds, defeated but not destroyed. A Serbian Relief Fund was established in London, and a similar body began functioning in New York City.[32]

Such aid was sorely needed by the Serbs. The country had been at war almost continuously since 1912 in the First and Second Balkan Wars.[33] The new combat of 1914 had killed almost 200,000 from a prewar population of 4.3 million. Widespread damage and social dislocation led to the breakdown of transportation and communication, financial chaos, hunger, even isolated areas of famine. Epidemics began to appear, more fearsome because one-fourth of all physicians in Serbia had died by the end of 1914,

---

29. Hugh Seton-Watson, "British policy towards the South-East European States, 1914–1916," in *Greece and Great Britain during World War I* (Thessaloniki, 1985), 69; Marrin, *Last Crusade*, 72; Gullace, "Sexual Violence," 717.

30. Zara Steiner has noted that both the government and public opinion in England evolved from condemnation of "impossible Serbians" in late June to considerable sympathy by early August; vide her *Britain and the Origins of the First World War* (New York, 1977), 220–239.

31. An important new interpretation of the war, based on, i.a., Serbian documents is James M. B. Lyon, "'A peasant mob': The Serbian Army on the eve of the Great War," The *Journal of Military History*. 61, no. 3 (1997).

32. Harry Hanak, *Great Britain and Austria-Hungary during the First World War: A Study in the Formation of Public Opinion* (London, 1962), 36ff.

33. Lyon, "Peasant mob," 482ff. In these wars the Serbs also lost a very high number to disease.

34. Dragoliub Divlianovich, "Pegavi tifus u Srbii," in *Srbiia 1915 godine* (Belgrade, 1986), 95ff; Yu. A. Pisarev, *Serbiia i Chernogoriia v pervoi mirovoi voine* (Moscow, 1968), 103; Dragoslav Yankovich, *Srbiia i yugoslavensko pitanie 1914–1915* (Belgrade, 1973), 236; G.N. Trubetskoi, *Russkaya diplomatiia 1914–1917gg. i voina na Balkanakh* (Montreal, 1983), 109ff.

and the country's medical system had been primitive to begin with. Cholera, diphtheria, and dysentery spread rapidly, but the worst was typhus. The taxed and hungry population was particularly susceptible and the mortality rate quickly reached 60 percent; more than a half million were ill, and the disease was spreading rapidly throughout the country. Correspondent John Reed termed Serbia "the land of death."[34]

Medical missions from Switzerland and Holland arrived late in the year, and similar assistance from France, England, the United States, and other neutrals quickly followed. Belgrade officially appealed to the United States for major aid, a request whose merits were corroborated by American officials stationed in the Balkans.[35] The State Department, the American Red Cross, the Rockefeller Foundation, and other agencies began intense negotiations involving London and Paris.[36] In March 1915, the Red Cross sent a medical commission of more than forty under Richard Strong. He was able to equip the French and British teams already operating, and with their cooperation establish the "International Sanitary Commission" to combat typhus in Serbia. Under their direction Serbia was "drenched in disinfectants and smoked in sulphur."[37]

---

35. Vladimir Stojanchevich, *Srbiia i srpski narod za vreme rata i okupatsiye* (Letskovats, 1988), 19–20; Clara Sturzenegger, *La Serbie en Guerre, 1914–1916* (Paris, 1916), 134ff.; Nelson Page to Secretary of State, October 22, 1914, United States National Archives, Record Group 59, Records of the State Department Relative to the Internal Affairs of Serbia and to Political Relations between the United States and Serbia, 1910–1929, Microfilm 357 [hereafter USNA, RG 59, M357, followed by roll number], roll 1.

36. Vopicka to Secretary of State, October 20 and 28, 1914; Robert Lansing to Mabel Boardman, October 22 and December 11, 1914; State Department to Consul Thomson at Nis, April 6, 1915; Memorandum by [William] Phillips, State Department, April 21, 1915, Thomson to Secretary of State, April 26, 1915; Karl Robinson, Committee of Mercy, to Frank Polk, State Department, October 14, 1915; in USNA, RG 59, M 357, roll 2. Lansing to Boardman, October 23, 1914, USNA, RG 59, M357, roll 1; Wickliffe Rose to Lindley M. Garrison, March 31, 1915, Rockefeller Archive Center, Rockefeller Foundation Archives, Record Group 1.1, Projects, Series 100N [hereafter RAC, RG 1.1, followed by Box and folder number (if any)], Box 75, folder 712. An outline of the activities of the Rockefeller Foundation relative to Serbia can be found in Ubavka Ostojich-Fejich, "Misiia Rokfelerove Fondatsiie u Srbii 1915–1916 godine, in *Srbiia 1916 godine* (Belgrade, 1987), 237–243.

37. "Preliminary Report of Richard P. Strong, M.D., Director of Sanitary Commission to Serbia of the American Red Cross," October 25, 1915, RAC, RG 1.1, Box 74, folder 705; Walter Hines Page to Secretary of State,, November 16, 1914, USNA, RG 59, M357, roll 1; Pupin to Pasic, March 8 and 15, 1915 and Pasic to Pupin, March 18, 1915, RAC, RG 1.1, Box 74, folder 706; Red Cross to Jerome Greene, March 6, 1915; Rose to Greene, March 13, 1915; Rockefeller Foundation to Greene, March 13, 1915; NN to NN, March 31, 1915, RAC, RG 1.1, Box 75, folder 712; Bicknell to Ryan, March 25, 1916, RAC, RG 1.1, Box 75, folder 712.

Disease nonetheless raged through the spring of 1915, reaching nine thousand new cases daily in April, leading the Red Cross to deem the typhus epidemic in Serbia "the most severe one of this disease which has occurred in modern times." Beyond military deaths, there were already at least 150,000 civilian casualties.[38]

Concerned by the military plight of the Serbs, the British contemplated some major operation in the Balkans, to "show khaki at Belgrade." Lloyd George was a major proponent, and Prime Minister Asquith was "obsessed with helping Serbia." However, they were also desirous of encouraging neutral Bulgaria and Romania as well as Italy to join the Allies. All demanded territory at Serbian expense as partial payment for belligerency. The Serbs were bitter at being "disposed of" by their allies who were "partitioning her like an African colony."[39] None of this rather sordid business aided the Serbs, and military efforts on her behalf foundered on the opposition of the French and powerful Cabinet figures like Lord Kitchener. The alternative to a direct Balkan effort was the ill-fated Gallipoli campaign of which the abandonment of Serbia was merely one result.[40]

While Serbia's strategic fate was being decided elsewhere, the domestic struggle against typhus made headway in 1915. By the summer the Rockefeller Foundation reported the disease contained, moreover, the country was "not in any great distress for food." Serbia was "very much in the

---

38. "War Relief Report No. 3: Servian Relief," March 10, 1915, RAC, RG 1.1, Box 62; "Preliminary Report," RAC, RG 1.1, Box 74, Folder 705; Dragan Zivojinovic, "Serbia and Montenegro: The Home Front, 1914–1918," in Bela K. Kiraly and Nandor F. Dreisziger, eds., *East Central European Society in World War I* (New York, 1985), 242–248.

39. Regarding the efforts to pressure Serbia to make territorial concessions and their results, vide Seton-Watson, "British Policy," 71ff.; *The Memoirs of Raymond Poincaré, 1915* (London, 1930), 180–181, 303; Viscount Grey of Fallodon, *Twenty-Five Years, 1892–1916*, 2 vols. (New York, 1925), II, 202–212; Lord Beaverbrook, *Politicians and the War, 1914–1916* (London, 1960), 156–157; Woodward, *Lloyd George*, 59–69; Hanak, *Great Britain and Austria-Hungary*, 65–99; and Victor S. Mamatey, *The United States and East Central Europe, 1914–1918: A Study in Wilsonian Diplomacy and Propaganda* (Princeton, NJ, 1957), 26–27.

40. Oliver, Viscount Esher, ed., *Journals and Letters of Reginald, Viscount Esher, Vol. 3, 1910–1915* (London, 1938), 208–214. After being very interested in direct aid to Serbia for a few weeks, Asquith noted, on February 17, 1915: "Our Serbian *demarche* is off for the moment . . . so our eyes are now fixed on the Dardanelles," vide The Earl of Oxford and Asquith, *Memoirs and Reflections, 1852–1927*, 2 vols. (Boston, 1928), II, 75. An informed discussion of the temporary infatuation of the British government with military aid to Serbia and the leading role of Lloyd George is David R. Woodward, *Lloyd George and the Generals* (Newark, DE, 1983), 33–40; cf. Martin Gilbert, *Winston Churchill. Volume III, 1914–1916: The Challenge of War* (Boston, 1971), 273ff.

minds of the great nations and was "receiving much assistance," hence, no further aid efforts were contemplated after the summer of 1915. Strong left Serbia in the fall of 1915, after a month without a new case of typhus. He pronounced the medical condition of the military and civilian population alike as "excellent."[41]

It had been a brief and rather inexpensive effort. In all of 1915, the Rockefeller Foundation spent no more than $150,000 for medical aid, and only $40,00 for food for the Serbs.[42] Beyond medical supplies little else was sent to the country: this despite indications that food and clothing were necessary. The reason was that London and Paris would not cooperate regarding the shipment of supplies from the United States across the blockade.[43]

Late 1915 brought disaster for the Serbs. Overwhelmed by a German-Austrian offensive launched in October, the Serbs found their retreat cut off by an attack from Bulgaria. Forced to retreat across the mountains of Montenegro and Albania in winter, the Serbian army lost 50 percent casualties to exposure and disease. The battered remainder of the army and government were evacuated to Corfu by Allied shipping. Serbia and its tiny ally Montenegro were completely occupied until November 1918.

The great retreat was ghastly for the Serbs; more than 150,000 died and the living were exhausted and starving. The abandoned civilian population was left without provisions, for the retreating army removed all the food from the lands it traversed.[44] Serbia became an occupied territory and, as a consequence, relief to its population would require crossing the British blockade.

The result was paradoxical. Stunned by the horrors of the winter retreat, the world was convinced that Serbia was desperately in need of food. However, Serbia, largely an agricultural country, was only in temporary distress from hunger. As soon as the 1916 harvest came in—which was 40

---

41. "Preliminary Report," esp. 3–15; Strong to Bicknell, May 15, 1915, RAC, RG 1.1, Box 75, folder 712; Elliot Wadsworth, "War Relief Report No. 8: Servian and Montenegrin Relief. Report of the War Relief Commission to the Rockefeller Foundation," August 7, 1915, RAC, RG 1.1, Box 74, folder 705.

42. "Serbian War Appropriations," January 6, 1916, RAC, RG 1.1, Box 74, folder 705.

43. Vide "Copies of cablegrams, with replies, received at headquarters re Serbian relief," in RAC, RG 1.1, Box 75, folder 712. According to the Rockefeller Foundation, the French expressed the view that "The question of relief . . . [was] closely connected with the blockade policy which, broadly speaking, is directed from London," vide J. Grant Forbes to Warwick Greene, July 4, 1916, RAC, RG 1.1, Box 74, folder 706.

44. E. Simmonds to Red Cross Headquarters, November 1916, RAC, RG 1.1, Box 75, folder 714.

percent over normal yield—the food problem disappeared.[45] The Rockefeller Foundation concluded with perplexity that "there is so much sympathy for Serbia in the outside world and such a widespread belief her population is starving" that reality did not matter. Despite a public conviction that "The whole race was likely to disappear," in fact "there is no starving Serbia." There had been, but that had been due to the unique conditions occasioned by the retreat to the Adriatic. In fact, by the summer of 1916, the Serbian population was cared for "in an exceedingly generous manner, too generous perhaps." So much food was locally available that imported charitable supplies constituted an overabundance that was being re-exported by the Austria occupation authorities.[46]

The British responded with a series of actions. They were so convinced that the Austrians were plundering Serbia that they prevented food from all other countries from being imported. Their principal focus was nearby Romania.[47] Reports from medical workers in Serbia, as well as the American minister in Bucharest, confirmed that London had joined the French in systematically buying up Romanian stocks. If that proved impossible, the British would pressure the Romanians not to honor deliveries to Serbia.[48] London also insisted that all neutral relief workers leave Serbia.[49] Henceforth, the British announced, the Central Powers would be exclusively re-

---

45. Otto T. Bannard to Ernest Bicknell, September 28, 1916, RAC, RG 1.1, Box 74, folder 705.

46. Vide Warwick Greene's two reports to Jerome Green of the Rockefeller Foundation, dated August 30, and September 12, 1916, and Robinson Smith to Warwick Greene, August 8, 1916, RAC, RG 1.1, Box 74, folder 705; vide "War Relief Report No. 13: Report of the Director of the War Relief Commission, April 1, 1916 to October 1, 1916," RAC, RG 1.1, Box 62, folder 620.

47. Paris and London cooperated to buy up Romanian foodstuffs, specifically to prevent any reaching the Central Powers, but more generally to gain strategic control of food in the Balkans; vide Denys Cochin, *Les organisations de blocus en France pendant la guerre (1914–1918)* (Paris, 1926), 129–132.

48. Vopicka to Secretary of State, July 5, 1916; Stuart to Red Cross Headquarters, July 6, 1916, USNA, RG 59, M357, roll 2; Page to Secretary of State, August 30, 1918, USNA, RG 59, M357, roll 1.

49. Bicknell to Jerome Greene, July 15, 1916; Greene to Bicknell, July 18, 1916 (which encloses Edward Grey to Walter Hines Page, July 20, 1916), Penfield to Secretary of State, October 11, 1916; Alvin Adee [State Department] to Rockefeller Foundation, November 24, 1916, RAC, RG 1.1, Box 74, folder 706; Stuart to Red Cross, November 24, 1916; Red Cross to Stuart and Ryan, November 29, 1916; Red Cross to Stuart, December 5, 1916, RAC, RG 1.1, Box 74, folder 714. For an official Austrian account of the occupation regime vide Hugo Kerchnawe, "Die K.u.K Militärverwaltung in Serbien," in *Militärverwaltung in den von den österreichisch-ungarischen Truppen besetzen Gebieten* (Vienna, 1928), 53–270, esp. 208ff.

sponsible for providing food to the population, a position identical to that which they adopted regarding German-occupied Poland.[50] Paris seconded the British actions and informed American relief agencies that sending aid to Serbia would only "encourage . . . organized pillage" by the occupiers.[51] For their part, the Austrians admitted that international aid for Serbia was unnecessary. However, the Allied charges of wholesale requisitioning were adamantly denied by the Red Cross director for the Balkans who personally vouched for the fact that "not an atom of the food brought in . . . [for relief purposes] has gone to any but Servian mouths."[52]

Having decided to restrict access to Serbia, the British subsequently would not relent. After the summer of 1916, the importation of foodstuffs from Romania became impossible because Bucharest joined the war, and the British would not allow the blockade to be lowered for shipments from abroad. London's insistence that all food to Serbia went, ultimately, to Austria was maintained for the rest of the war, despite efforts by neutrals and appeals from the Serbian government-in-exile. After American belligerency, in April 1917, the State Department used virtually identical words to refuse the urgent appeals from the Serbian government for aid. It became increasingly difficult to repeat the assertions because the Austrians had furnished whatever guarantees against requisitioning the British—and later the Americans—had insisted were crucial.[53] Nonetheless, the policy remained unaffected. In a particularly revealing "confidential" post scriptum to an internal State Department memorandum, it was noted: "Neither the Department nor the British Government are [sic] inclined to consider this matter at all favorably and we are endeavoring to refuse the request politely without antagonizing the Serbian Government.[54]

---

50. Edward Grey to Walter Hines Page, July 20, 1916, RAC, RG 1.1, Box 74, folder 706.

51. Jules Cambon to Sharp, February 3, 1916; Sharp to Secretary of State, February 6 and 7, 1916; Ryan to Red Cross, April 29, 1916, and Bicknell to Secretary of State, April 24, 1916, USNA, RG 59, M. 357, roll 2. J. Grant Forbes to Warwick Greene, July 4, 1916 (wherein it is reported that the Foreign Ministry in Paris informed the Rockefeller Foundation that London would speak for France as regards blockade matters affecting relief), RAC, RG 1.1, Box 74, folder 706.

52. NN to Warwick Greene, June 19, 1916, RAC, RG 1.1, Box 75, folder 714.

53. Maurice de Bunsen to Page, November 9, 1916; Spring Rice to Secretary of State, September 12,1917; "Memorandum" by Spring Rice, December 1, 1917, USNA, RG 59, M357, roll 2. Regarding the American reactions vide Lansing to Hans Sulzer, December 6, 1917; Polk to R. C. Leffingwell, December 21, 1917; Lansing to "LM," January 8, 1918; Lansing to Stovall, May 17, 1918; USNA, RG 59, M357, roll 2.

54. "Memorandum," Division of West European Affairs, February 18, 1918, USNA, RG 59, M357, roll 2.

Remaining efforts to aid the Serbs were restricted to refugees at Salonika and scattered other places. As a result, relief agencies spent very little for Serbia after 1916. The Red Cross, for example, announced in early 1917 that it would suspend all relief operations directed at Serbia and Montenegro, having spent all told perhaps $200,000 since the beginning of the war.[55] This virtual termination of outside aid to Serbia, largely at British insistence, was to be bitterly premature. Deprived of large-scale relief and vexed by Austrian, and especially Bulgarian, exactions, the Serbs were much in need during the last two years of the war.[56] Recent Serbian studies have concluded that by 1917 the number of seriously ill again reached well into six figures and, because of food shortages, the fatality rate soared to one-third of the population.[57] The circumstances of the last year of the war are described movingly in Milovan Djilas' celebrated autobiography, *Land Without Justice*:

> In this very year [1917] there was a drought that can never be forgotten. A frost and then a drought destroyed everything. Even had there not been a war, hunger would have invaded us. People ate wild herbs and sawdust made from beechwood. . . . It was then for the first time that we spoke of death.[58]

This explains why Serbia ended the war in so desperate a fashion in comparison with Belgium.

In sum, Western interest in the plight of the Serbs was considerable, though belated and short-lived. An émigré Serbian historian has lamented that "1915 was the most tragic year in Serbian history . . . and [with] no real help from her allies."[59] This is certainly true in a military and political

---

55. "Information as to the work of the American Rd Cross for Relief in Serbia and of Serb prisoners in the Hands of the Central Powers" [1917], "The Work of the Commission to Serbia" [June, 1918]; USNA, RG 200: Records of the American National Red Cross, 1917–1934 [Hereafter, RG 200: ANRC], Box 904; "Memorandum," Legation of Serbia, March 28, 1917, Serbian Legation to Red Cross, April 4, 1917; "Serbia" [Red Cross memorandum], October, 1917; Box 906; Red Cross to L. R. Brisbee, January 8, 1917, Box 903. The Red Cross later aided the scattered Serb refugees in Greece and elsewhere, spending, by war's end, about 4600,000; vide Henry P. Davison, *The American Red Cross in the Great War* (New York, 1920), 250–255.

56. Danitse Milich, "Stanie u privredi Srbiie pod Austro-ugarskom okupatsiyom 1917 godine," in Slavenko Terzich, ed., *Srbiia 1917 godine* (Belgrade, 1988), 37–44; cf. Kerchnawe, "Militärverwaltung in Serbien," *loc. cit.*

57. Vladimir Stojanchevich, "Polozhai stanovnishtva u Srbii 1917 godine," in Terzich, *Srbiia 1917 godine*, 11–18.

58. Vide Milovan Djilas, *Land Without Justice* (New York, 1958). Djilas spent his childhood in Austrian occupied Montenegro, 73ff.

59. Alex M. Dragnich, *Serbia, Nikola Pasic, and Yugoslavia* (New Brunswick, NJ, 1974), 109.

sense, but only partially so as concerns relief. The Allies were willing to extend considerable medical aid to the Serbs, though they failed to prevent catastrophic casualties. Later they—especially the British—seemed very concerned about oversupplying the Serbs, a phenomenon not in evidence as regards Belgium. Doubtless, the poor synchronization between need and response was due in large part to the suddenness and immensity of the Serbian difficulties: epidemics, and later military disaster, with the concomitant breakdown of the infrastructure of food and medicine. As a result, the magnitude of the Serbian plight was incomparably greater than that suffered by the Belgians.

The decision not to aid Serbia militarily and the subsequent occupation of the country by the Central Powers caused London to lose interest: Serbia offered no more strategic possibilities. The result was continuing, if ill-defined, sympathy for the population, yet these humanitarian concerns never challenged the putative strategic demands of the blockade.[60] This phenomenon was later duplicated in the United States which, while still neutral, had acted to aid Serbia, and after belligerence both government and public opinion adopted attitudes very similar to those demonstrated in Great Britain and France.[61]

We should, however, not exaggerate even the brief interval of Western sympathy for the Serbs. Despite the efforts directed towards it in the early years of the war, Serbia was never a real rival to the Belgian relief cause. By 1916, when the Rockefeller Foundation (which had been the principal financial supporter of medical aid to Serbia) calculated that it had spent perhaps $100,000 in Serbia and Montenegro, it was musing over a new drive to garner forty times that for *additional* aid to Belgium. The foundation concluded that "Belgium had a special claim upon the sympathy and help of the rest of the world."[62] More important, the British and French governments made it clear that Serbia was not to be equated with Belgium. The British ambassador to Washington, Sir Arthur Spring Rice, told the secretary of state in the spring of 1916 that London would object "most strongly" were an analog to the CRB to be contemplated for Serbia. The British insisted, despite assurances from relief personnel on the spot, that the Austrians were "stripping" Serbia and that relief efforts would "merely relieve the Austrian Government of their responsibility." Because the guaranties in effect regarding Belgium were, according to Spring Rice, "unsatisfactory," a second relaxation of the blockade, this time for Serbia, was absolutely out of the question.[63] It is noteworthy that neither Spring Rice

---

60. Hanak, *Great Britain and Austria-Hungary,* 65–99.

61. Vide the recent study by Vojislav Pavlovich, "Shtampa u SAD o Srbii," in Slavenko Terzich, ed., *Srbiia 1917 godine* (Belgrade, 1988), 249–253.

62. Jerome Greene to Walcott, December 17, 1915, RAC, RG 1.1, Box 75, folder 713.

63. Spring Rice to Secretary of State, April 21, 1916, USNA, RG 59, M357, roll 2.

nor his superior, Sir Edward Grey, made the argument that Serbia did not need food, which was at least arguable at some occasions; rather, they insisted that since it was an obligation of the Central Powers to feed the Serbs, importation of foodstuffs would unquestionably be requisitioned.64 In fact, London complained that continuing efforts by American relief agencies were playing into German and Austrian hands by allowing them a propaganda weapon to use against the Allies; in reality, the Central Powers disposed of "enormous stocks" of food, which they were legally required to expend on the Serbs.65 Hence, the needs of the Serbs were not really denied by the British; rather, they were rendered irrelevant by recasting the issue into a debate concerning the legal obligations of occupation regimes. Of course, the same arguments *could* have been adduced regarding Belgium, but there the blockade was relaxed.

The adamant defense of a stringent blockade coincided, notably, with the fact that by the late spring of 1916, it had finally become "water-tight."66 Previously, London assumed considerable leakage resulted in importations of food into Austria or Germany, even if indirectly. Within Britain there took place a major reconceptualization of the blockade after mid-1915. The so-called "ginger group" pressed the government for a far more efficient prosecution of the war, especially through the use of sea power and the blockade. This was matched by a press campaign denouncing the existing blockade efforts as ineffective.67 The ability of the cabinet, and particularly Foreign Secretary Grey, to resist these growing demands for a more stringent enforcement declined in the last half of 1915. The "ginger group" announced by December that they would oppose "any relaxation" of the blockade "on any ground." The result was the creation of a new Ministry of Blockade under an extreme devotee of a tight blockade, Lord Robert Cecil, and his equally ardent subordinate, Eyre Crowe.68 The victory for the extreme pro-blockade faction was complete by 1916, the very time when Serbian—and Polish—relief efforts would be calling for its abridgment. Hence, London was being asked to lower the blockade just when it had become convinced that it was becoming effective.

---

64. Walcott to Rockefeller Foundation, December 20, 1915, RAC, RG 1.1, Box 75, folder 713.

65. Page to Secretary of State, July 16, 1916, USNA, RG 59, M357, roll 2.

66. Esme Howard, *Theater of Life: Life Seen from the Stalls, 1903–1936* (Boston, 1936), 239; Cochin, *Organisation de blocus*, 261.

67. Armin Rappaport, *The British Press and Wilsonian Neutrality* (Stanford, CA, 1951), 60, 77.

68. A useful summary of the consolidation of extreme pro-blockade sentiment in London, written from the perspective of the United States—which, be it noted, was the putative choice of most relief supplies intended for Serbia (or Poland)—is Ernest R. May, *The World War and American Isolation, 1914–1917* (Chicago, 1966[1959]), 305–324.

III. The Failure to Relieve Poland

Poland was by far the largest relief problem of the First World War.[69] A population of almost twenty-five million was rendered destitute by the shifting tide of war and the purposeful efforts by the Russian government to present the Central Powers with only "scorched earth" in the Polish territories over which they advanced.

Within weeks of the outbreak of the war, a team representing the Rockefeller Foundation and the American Red Cross made a preliminary investigation to establish the extent of need of the "suffering non-combatants" throughout Europe. They did not intend to visit the east of the continent at all. Only the urging of the German government caused them to include Poland in this survey. The Germans blamed the hardship of the population in occupied Poland directly on the British blockade and were understandably eager to have neutral relief representatives investigate the situation on the spot. In the first months of 1915—approximately the same time the first teams of physicians were arriving to combat the typhus epidemic in Serbia, and about the same time that the relief needs of Belgium were already being stabilized—the American team toured Poland and were horrified by what they saw, describing it as far worse than anything in Belgium.[70]

The team tried to arrange for the purchase of grain in neighboring countries, but none was available. As a result "the only possible source of any large quantity of supplies seemed to be America." Such shipments, however, would require "concessions from the Allies"; i.e., the abridgment of the blockade. This should have been possible, for as the Rockefeller Foundation accurately concluded, " the principles involved had already been conceded in the case of Belgium."[71]

Hence, in the spring of 1915, Hoover took the lead in attempting to organize an "International Commission for Relief in Poland" and acquired substantial financial support from the Rockefeller Foundation as well as a considerable German contribution.[72] However, neither the Russian nor the British government would cooperate in allowing the importation of food-

---

69. Regarding the Polish relief issue vide M. B. Biskupski, "The Diplomacy of Wartime Relief: The United States and Poland, 1914–1918," *Diplomatic History* 19, no. 3 (1995): 431–451.

70. *Rockefeller Foundation Annual Report, 1915* (New York, n.d), 285–286; "Outline of a Plan for Relief of Poland," Edward M. House Papers, SMLY, Box 61, folder 1924.

71. Jerome Greene to Hugh S. Bird, RAC, RG 1.1, Box 73, folder 700.

72. Rose to Jerome Greene, February 24 and 25, 1915; Rose to Bicknell, April 14, 1915 in RAC, RG 1.1, Box 72, folder 689; "Outline," House Papers, SMLY; James W. Gerard, *My Four Years in Germany* (New York, 1917), 297–298.

stuffs across the blockade, and the whole effort proved abortive. International relations broke down in mutual recrimination. Berlin promised to provide for the Poles from its own stocks, and the British responded that this action justified their intransigence as it demonstrated that the Central Powers had food in sufficiency and must have been guilty of requisitioning. Thus, their obduracy regarding the blockade was, in London's eyes, justified ex post facto.[73]

However, the situation did not end there. The summer of 1915 brought the great eastern offensive by the Central Powers and the occupation of virtually all of formerly Russian Poland. As the Russians retreated, they wreaked havoc over Polish territory: "villages and cities were completely destroyed; foodstuffs burned . . . the livestock killed"; children perished by the tens of thousands from hunger and exposure. The advancing Germans requisitioned wholesale and shipped what they seized back to the *Reich*.[74] An American relief worker described the situation as follows:

> One Million . . . were made homeless in about five or six weeks, and . . . approximately 400,000 of these perished. . . . I motored . . . for over 230 miles with German officers . . . and devastation is almost complete everywhere. . . . the country is a waste, and the people are flat on their backs.[75]

In October, the main Polish relief agency in Warsaw pleaded with Hoover to try again to relieve Poland, now that the situation had both increased in scope and expanded in magnitude. The Rockefeller Foundation informed the State Department that the situation in Poland was "more desperate than it has been at any time in Belgium."[76] The American press was filled with ghastly reports from Poland. A special correspondent of the *Chicago Tribune* reported: "These poor people must starve to death unless America

---

73. Edward Grey to Cecil Spring-Rice, August 31, 1916, in *Correspondence respecting the Relief of Allied Territories: Command 8348* (London, 1916); "Memorandum to Department of State, May 7, 1915 on behalf of the projected commission for relief in Poland," RAC, RG 1.1, Box 71, folder 686; "Germany Relieves Poland," *New York Times*, 27 June 1915

74. Walcott to Vance McCormick, October 6, 1916, RAC, RG 1.1, Box 72, folder 688; Jerzy Tomaszewski, "Bilans gospodarczych skutków pierwszej wojny œwiatowej dla ziem polskiej" in Żanna Kormanowa and Walentyna Najdus, eds., *Historia Polski, Tom III 1850/64–1918. Częœæ 3 1914–1918* (Warsaw, 1974), 441–514; Jan Molenda, "Królestwo Polskie, sierpień 1915" in ibid., 91–92.

75. Frederic C. Walcott to Vance McCormick, October 6, 1916, RAC, RG 1.1, Box 72, folder 72.

76. "Memorandum Presented to the Department of State," May 7, 1915, RAC, RG 1.1, Box 71, folder 686.

feeds them. . . . If something is not done to aid them at once there will be no need to send provisions to them, because they will be dead."[77]

Hoover began intensive negotiations for the importation of food. In general, the Germans were cooperative; the British were not. The major stumbling block was the British insistence on the inviolability of the blockade.[78] As far as London was concerned, the question of Polish relief was, ultimately, a blockade question, which meant it was essentially a "military" decision, and the military necessity of the blockade had already been accepted in London, and hence by the Allies.[79] British public opinion, which became so exercised over Belgium, could countenance a far worse situation in Poland. Stuart Wallace has explained this seeming anomaly:

> Starvation in Poland, as a result of the British blockade of the Central Powers, was a part of the normal means of war'. 'There was no choice'. It was not easy 'to think of actions much more horrible', but the alternative was 'something equivalent to helping the enemy'.[80]

Because of this, British approval of Polish relief was a quest doomed from the start.[81]

Suffering in Poland became a major public issue in the United States, immensely encouraged by the Polish American lobby under the direction of the famous pianist-statesman Ignacy Jan Paderewski.[82] The American government was sympathetic to the Poles and began to press the British for concessions. London, however, was adamant and blamed the whole problem on German requisitioning.[83] The British increasingly viewed efforts to arrange international relief for Poland as either part of, or at least facilitating some gargantuan German plot. Grey and his ambassador in Washing-

---

77. "From Warsaw with the Germans," James O'Donnell Bennett of the *Chicago Tribune, New York Times,* 13 October 1915, 3:3.

78. Walcott to Greene, January 4, 1916, Walcott Papers, SMLY, Box 6; Hoover to Gerard, December 13,1915; Hoover to Walter Hines Page, January 7, 1916; Hoover to CRB Headquarters, January 18,1916; Commission for Relief in Belgium Files, Hoover Institution, Box 5

79. Regarding the "military" nature of the Polish relief question in London vide: Grey to Buchanan, March 12, 1916, PRO, Foreign Office: Grey, 800, 192–193; Walcott to Mrs. Walcott, March 17, 1916, Robinson, *London Times,* to Walcott, March 12, 1916, Walcott to Goode, March 14, 1916 in Frederic C. Walcott Papers, SMLY, Box 4, folder 30.

80. Wallace, *War and the Image of Germany,* 105–106.

81. Eustace Percy, *Some Memories* (London, 1958), 45–46.

82. Vide M. B. Biskupski, "Paderewski as Leader of American Polonia, 1914–1918," *Polish American Studies* XLIII, no. 1 (Spring, 1986): 37–56.

83. Biskupski, "Diplomacy of Wartime Relief" 444ff.

ton, Spring Rice, saw organized Polish American agitation as evidence of German machinations, and the sympathy of the Wilson administration for Polish efforts was explained as crass ethnic politics in an election year.[84] The solution was to appear to negotiate and consider the various proposals, yet insist on impossible conditions and thereby sabotage them.[85]

In the spring of 1916, pressure on London grew and efforts were launched in the American Congress for federal financing of Polish relief. By April the Russians formally endorsed the plan for an international effort to aid the Poles because, as Foreign Minister Sergei Sazonov noted, "Poland's name is constantly put along with the names of Belgium and Serbia," all three enjoying "great popularity . . . among the Western allies."[86] Hence, pressured on many sides, the British seemed to relent, and in May agreed to allow the relief of Poland but only as part of a much larger project that would organize relief for all German and Austrian-occupied territory, including Serbia, Montenegro, and Albania.[87]

This was obviously an effort to sabotage Polish relief, masquerading as assent, because the whole project would require enormous negotiation and involve Berlin, Vienna, and probably Sofia, whereas a practical scheme for Poland had already been worked out between Hoover and the Germans.[88] Despite major efforts by both the State Department, and various relief agencies, notably the Rockefeller Foundation,[89] the whole issue descended into a pointless squabble by the late summer of 1916.[90] The American press

84. A useful discussion of British interest in the minority communities in the United States and their lobbying activities is Kenneth J. Calder, *Britain and the Origins of the New Europe, 1914–1918* (Cambridge, 1976).

85. Grey to Spring-Rice, March 9, 1916; Grey to British Embassy in Petrograd, March 12, 1916; [Spring Rice] to Grey, March 14, 24 and April 17, 1916 in Public Record Office, Foreign Office: General Correspondence: News (115–2124), 191, 192–193, 195, 200ff.; Spring-Rice to Drummond, January 30, 1916, with note by Drummond; Spring-Rice to [Grey], February 12 and March 17, 1916; Spring-Rice to Drummond, March 23, 1916, in PRO, Foreign Office: Private Collections: Sir Edward Grey (800), 40–41, 53–59, 87–92, 99–100.

86. Horst Gunther Linke, *Das zarische Russland und der Erste Weltkrieg: Diplomatie und Kriegsziele 1914–1917* (Munich, 1982), 146ff; Wiktor Sukiennicki, *East Central Europe During World War I* (New York, 1984), 2 vols., I, 174.

87. "Memorandum communicated to the United State Ambassador," in *Correspondence, Command 8348* attached to Grey to Spring-Rice, August 31, 1916.

88. Hoover to Walcott, May 26, 1915; Walcott to Greene, June 10, 1916; Walcott Papers, Box 7; Walter Hines Page, "Journal, 1916," Walter Hines Page Papers, Houghton Library, Harvard University, 126.

89. Imperial and Royal Ministry of Foreign Affairs, Note Verbale, to U.S. Embassy, Vienna, July 24, 1916, Warwick Greene to Ministry of Foreign Affairs, July 24, 1916, in RAC, RG 1.1, Box 74, folder 706.

90. Grey to Page, June 15 and July 4, 1916, *Correspondence, Cd. 8348*; Francis to Lansing, June 15, 1916, *Papers Relating to the Foreign Relations of the United*

reacted bitterly to the failure of the negotiations, and considerable blame was attached to the British. Nonetheless, on the whole, the reaction of both the American government and public opinion was one of disappointment rather than blame. In other words, the British did not suffer any serious loss of public esteem as a result of their refusal to cooperate regarding Polish relief.[91]

Whereas the British conditions—which virtually exploded the negotiations—were obviously insincere, Paris and Petrograd both accepted London's lead in the matter, and the Allied Economic Conference, which coincided with the announcement of the British conditions, specifically endorsed a stringent blockade policy.[92] Hence, Poland, like Serbia, received very little aid despite its enormous wartime suffering.

IV. Conclusions

By the end of the First World War, Belgium had received hundreds of millions of dollars in aid, a major international relief agency had prevented starvation and privation, and the Belgian population was, by all accounts, well fed, well clothed, and in good health. The total casualties suffered by Belgium during the war had not exceeded 75,000.[93] By comparison, Serbia had lost at least one-fourth of its prewar population of four and one-half

---

States, 1916: Supplement (Washington, D.C., 1999), 898; *Transportation of Relief Supplies to Poland, Document No. 494*, U.S. Congress, Senate, 64th Congress, 1st Session (Washington, D.C., 1916), 2ff.; "Le ravitaillement de la Pologne," *La Liberté* (Fribourg), July 30, 1916.

91. A random sampling of the national press showed blame for the deadlock equally attributed to Germany and England; vide: "Berlin Rejects Plan For Relief of Poland," *New York Times*, 1 June 1916; "A Relief Movement Blockaded," Columbus *Dispatch*, 3 June 1916; "Germany's Responsibilities in Poland," New York *World*, 14 July 1916; "Starving Poland," Pittsburgh *Chronicle*; "Meanwhile the Poles Starve," 22 July 1916, St. Louis *Globe Democrat*, 23 July 1916; "Poles are Starving While Aid is Stayed," New York *Evening Post*, 25 July 1916. The Germans also concluded that Germany and Great Britain were equally criticized in the United States for the failure to arrange relief to Poland; vide Bernstorff to Bethmann Hollweg, December 4, 1916, a wireless intercept in PRO, Foreign Office: General Correspondence: News, 115–2302, doc. no. MID 6136/17.

92. Sharp to Lansing, July 28, 1916, *PRFRUS, 1916: Supplement*, 905; Marion C. Siney, *The Allied Blockade of Germany, 1914–1916* (Ann Arbor, MI., 1957), 176–181.

93. Belgian casualties have been variously reported, but all agree as to the low absolute total; vide J. A. Wullus-Rudiger, *La Belgique et la Crise Européenne, 1914–1945*, 2 vols. (Paris, 1941), I, 124–125n.; cf. *La première guerre mondiale*, Vol. II (Paris, 1968), 316.

million.[94] The country was, by war's end, "destitute of supplies," its communications and transportation systems broken down. It had 500,000 orphans, most of them homeless, and a large part of the country was "suffering from semi-starvation," the remainder exhausted and with few medical supplies.[95] Poland presented a similar picture of misery. Wartime deaths were estimated at approximately one million with an equal number wounded or crippled.[96] By the armistice, the country was devastated: starvation threatening at least five million of an estimated twenty-seven million, wreckage everywhere, and the medical system in ruins.[97] Why did the world react with such alacrity and sustained concern for the needs of Belgium and yet prove, relatively, so niggardly with aid to far more grievously beset Serbia and Poland?[98] The answer can be found under several broad headings.

Belgian suffering was chronologically the first and captured world attention, whereas Polish and Serbian problems, however great, became necessarily part of the welter of war news arriving after the public had become gradually inured to reported horrors.[99] Moreover, to Western public opinion, Belgium was a familiar part of Europe, whereas Poland and Serbia were strange and distant places, located, none too precisely, in the exotic east. In practical terms, the Belgians were close to Atlantic-borne importation of food. Serbia and Poland, by comparison, were farther away and far more difficult to access. Second, it cost a tremendous amount to supply Belgium; adding Serbia, and especially large Poland, to relief efforts would have presented the world with gargantuan bills. Third, whereas Belgium was quite industrialized, Serbia and Poland were largely agricultural; they *should* have been able to provide for their populations.[100] If they did not, requisitioning by the Central Powers seemed the inevitable explanation.

---

94. Official post-war figures claimed 1, 330, 925 deaths; vide Stojanchevich, *Srbiia i srpski narod,* 101.

95. Surface and Bland, 207–213.

96. Krzysztof Dunin-Wąsowicz, "Sytuacja demograficzna narodu polskiego w latach 1914–1918," in Kormanowa and Najdus, *Historia Polski,* 504–508.

97. [Vernon] Kellogg,"Preliminary Report on Conditions in Poland," January 6, 1919, and William R. Grove, "A Review of Economic Conditions in Poland," February 16, 1919 in Bane and Lutz, 150–158, 249–253.

98. Shortly after the armistice, Hoover compiled a list of people "wholly or in part in acute famine," the entire population of Poland, Serbia, and Montenegro a total of 38,000,000 people—was on the list; Belgium was not; vide Hoover, *An America Epic, III,* xvi-xvii.

99. I am indebted to Prof. Neal Pease of the University of Wisconsin at Milwaukee for the formulation of this argument.

100. Sally Marks contends that because Belgium was more industrialized than Serbia or Poland this somehow made their plight less compelling; vide *Innocent Abroad,* 171, 176.

But these explanations are not sufficient. They explain why the Western Allies may have been unable to relieve Serbia and Poland, but not why they were unwilling to do so. That requires a consideration of larger factors. Here, two are of equal weight and intimately intertwined. First, we must consider the question of wartime strategy. For France, Belgium was inseparable from the defense of France itself, and London, even before the war, came to regard Belgium as vital to British strategic interests. Neither Serbia nor Poland enjoyed such exalted status in the considerations of the Western Allies. Serbia was significant only so long as it was able to maintain itself against the Central Powers. When it was overrun in 1915, it lost this status. Indeed, because Serbian territorial ambitions complicated British, French, and Russian abilities to bargain at will with Balkan territories in an effort to win the support of Bulgaria, Greece, or Italy, Serbia became a strategic impediment by late 1915. As for Poland, it was until 1917 regarded by Paris and London as exclusively within the penumbra of Russian strategic considerations. Hence, the Western Allies avoided any actions involving Poland as long as Russia was able to assert its preemptive authority over the region.

Of equal importance, both Serbian and Polish relief needs were contradictory to the development of Allied grand strategy during the course of the war. Specifically, the need for major relief to both countries was raised only after the British became convinced that the blockade was vital to defeat the Germans, and that to be effective the blockade must be applied with ever-increasing stringency. The arrangements that allowed the CRB to support Belgium predated this revision of the blockade, whereas Serbian and Polish needs became manifest after. The fact that the British were adamant about the blockade despite very considerable American support for lowering it to relieve Poland demonstrates dramatically how significant the blockade had become in London's eyes.[101]

Indeed, many of those involved in wartime relief feared that the British might eventually impose restrictions even on Belgian relief. Requesting further exceptions for Serbia or Poland, hence, was regarded to some degree as endangering Belgium. Particularly noteworthy in this regard is a May 1915 letter to John D. Rockefeller from his foundation's war relief director, Jerome Greene. The State Department, Greene said, believed that "the continuation of relief to Belgium was most precarious, making it seem very doubtful whether the Allies would be in a state of mind that would lead them to tolerate any further shipments of food" via Germany, regardless of the guarantees as to its use and destination. Greene concluded that Belgian

---

101. As early as February 1915, Grey was being pressured to maintain a strict blockade at any cost, for food was Germany's "Achilles heel" and lowering the blockade in the face of American wishes was "too high a price to pay" for "American friendliness"; vide Stephen Roskill, Hankey: *Man of Secrets, Vol. I, 1877–1918* (New York, 1970), 157–158.

relief had been arranged only over "violent objections" in England and further relief efforts faced enormous difficulties that were essentially "a matter of psychology."[102]

After the United States entry into the war, officials of the Rockefeller Foundation and the Red Cross explained the failure to provide Poland or Serbia with relief as being caused by the war, mutual suspicions, and bad timing. However, documents contemporaneous to the events make it very evident that it was the blockade, and particularly British intransigence— what the Red Cross deemed "a rather petty and cruel policy"[103]—that was the ultimate stumbling block.[104]

One does not need to be an adherent of Avner Offer's thesis[105] concerning the fundamental nature of food importation to British strategy to agree that the British ascribed enormous importance to restricting importations to continental Europe as perhaps the major factor in winning the war.[106] Serbia and Poland ran afoul of so profoundly held a conviction.

We must also consider the importance of propaganda and the management of public opinion as an element in determining relief. Relieving Belgium underscored German rapacity. The singularity of Belgium as victim was useful because it fit the pattern that the Germans had blundered into early in the war that allowed them, so easily, to be portrayed as "Huns." Serbian and Polish relief allowed no such public relations advantages to the Allies. Much of Polish distress was, after all, the result of Russian stripping of the country, and the Germans were insistent about aiding the beset Poles. Indeed, Berlin could well look upon Poland as "their Belgium," or "Belgium in reverse"; i.e., a people suffering as a result of bestial conduct of the war by a far larger power; but in this case, Russia, one of the Allies. Relieving Serbia was the most complex problem of all. Germany might be held to promises of no requisitioning in Belgium, perhaps in Poland, but in the inaccessible reaches of the Balkans guaranteeing the inviolability of imported foodstuffs from seizure by Germans, Austrians, and especially Bulgarians, was virtually impossible.

Finally, we must consider the relative significance of the "cause" of Belgian relief versus Serbian or Polish need. Belgium virtually preempted the

---

102. Greene to Rockefeller, May 8, 1915, RAC, Family Archives, RG 2, Box 38, folder 390.

103. Jerome D. Greene to E. P. Bicknell, July 18, 1916, RAC, RG 1.1, Box 74, folder 706.

104. "No. 8011 Memorandum on the relation of the Rockefeller Foundation to war relief activities," December 4, 1916, RAC, Rockefeller Family Archives, RG 2: Boards, Box 38, folder 390.

105. Offer, *The First World War: An Agrarian Interpretation.*

106. Herbert Henry Asquith, *The Genesis of War* (New York, 1923), 138–139; Vincent, *Politics of Hunger,* 67.

charitable energies of the Western public. Among the British, Belgian relief gained more financial contributions than any other wartime charity if we exclude aid sent to British soldiers. In the United States, which provided by far the greatest financial support for European relief, Belgium was a veritable colossus. By early 1915, the major Polish and Serbian relief funds had each amassed $40,000 in public donations in the United States, but for Belgium the amount was $1,000,000; indeed, Belgian relief had earned almost $50,000 within the first fortnight of the war.[107] This disparity continued throughout the conflict. President Wilson proclaimed January 1, 1916, "National Polish Relief Day" in the United States. The results were pitiful: less than $5,000 was collected throughout the entire country. The appalled administration decided not even to proclaim a similar "Day" for the Serbians— or anybody else—because similarly poor results were anticipated.[108] Secretary of State Lansing advised the president to proclaim no other national relief days. There simply was not enough support from the American public for any country other than Belgium.

It is not that the plight of the east of Europe was not known; the American press regularly noted the problem: An article in the *New York Times* in February 1915 proclaimed "Poles Chief Sufferers,"[109] and in April a *Times* editorial lamented that whereas Belgian relief efforts were "well known," i.e., supported, those for other lands were not. This was particularly unfortunate because: "Worse than the plight of Belgium is that of Poland" and "Serbia . . . in worse case than Poland."[110] A study of Midwestern American opinion concluded that Poland's "suffering was enormous although little recognized by an American public preoccupied with Belgian woes."[111]

Such colossal sums were demanded for Belgium that a "high pressure campaign was maintained on its behalf."[112] This was necessary for the CRB, which raised during the war the staggering sum of nearly $1billion on behalf of Belgium,[113] and was also a convenient focus for public sympathies from the point of view of the Allies.

---

107. "3,000 Tons of Meat to Hungry Belgians" and "Banner Food Week for Belgian Relief," *New York Times,* 4 and 18 April 1915, III, 3:1, and III, 3:4.

108. Memorandum, William Phillips, to Putney, January 7, 1916, USNA, RG 59, M357, Roll 2; Lansing to Tumulty, January 26, 1916, USNA, RG 59, M357, Roll 2.

109. "Poles Chief Sufferers," *New York Times,* 22 February 1915, 3:4.

110. "Poland, Serbia, Armenia," *New York Times,* 25 March 1915, 10:3.

111. Cedric C. Cummins, *Indiana Public Opinion and the World War, 1914–1917* (Indianapolis, 1945), 61.

112. Hoover realized the CRB's absolute requirement to create and sustain a Belgian relief movement; vide Craig Lloyd, *Aggressive Introvert: A Study of Herbert Hoover and Public Relations Management, 1912–1932* (Columbus, 1972), 20ff; Lawrence E. Gelfand, introduction to his *Herbert Hoover: The Great War and Its Aftermath, 1914–1923* (Iowa City, 1979), 6–7; cf. O'Keefe, *Thousand Deadlines,* 64.

Despite the fact that Belgian suffering quickly ceased to be acute, even serious, campaigns for continued, even increased, funds were incessant. In mid-1915 the vice chairman of the CRB demanded that the American public double its donation rate for Belgium (then running twenty-five to forty times higher than the rates for Poland and Serbia).[114] Indeed, the American public never gave substantial amounts to either Poland or Serbia; much of the money collected came from the relatively impoverished ethnic communities in the United States. (This would include the Polish Jews' support for their co-religionists in Europe.) Why the American public was so disposed is an intriguing question, though impossible to answer with certainty. Orthodox Serbia may well have seemed alien to the public, and though Belgium and Poland were both heavily Roman Catholic, the former was part of the unfamiliar east of Europe, which had recently deposited so many not particularly welcome immigrants in the United States. The American public's disdain for southern and eastern Europeans doubtless made their homelands' distress less sympathetic.

Despite the minuscule financial support for relief to these eastern countries, devotees of Belgian relief resented their intrusion into the public conscience and stressed the unique call Belgian had on the sympathies and support of the public. Even the Rockefeller Foundation, which devoted enormous attention, though little actual money, to Serbian and especially Polish relief in 1915–1916, originally was not interested in the relief needs of the east of Europe: "our resources may be preempted in Western Europe," the foundation declared in November 1914.[115] It was in many ways a prophetic declaration.

A pattern of relative neglect for the suffering in Eastern Europe appears when considering the various wartime charitable efforts. The American Quakers, for example, began war relief work in 1917, focusing on France where there was no pressing need. They continued to devote their exclusive attention to that country until the summer of 1919 when "the disclosure of the civil situation of the East" caused them to add "Serbia and Austria," but only after insuring that it could maintain its established level of activity in France.[116] The American Relief Clearing House, another of the major

---

113. Herbert Hoover, *The Memoirs of Herbert Hoover: Years of Adventure, 1874–1920* (New York, 1951), 170.

114. "Belgian Bread Lines Surpass in Misery," *New York Times*, 11 February 1915, 3:2.

115. Jerome Greene to Curtis Guild, [November, 1914]. Guild had informed the Foundation that Poland had relief needs outstripping those of Belgium, and was told that the Foundation was "concentrating" on Belgium; vide Guild to Rockefeller Foundation, November 9, 1914, RAC, RG 1.1, Box 73, folder 697.

116. John Forbes, *The Quaker Star under Seven Flags, 1917–1927* (Philadelphia, 1962), 63, 69.

American charitable institutions, proudly noted its interest in the Serbian typhus epidemic. Nonetheless, the ARCH claimed that Serbia's need "was too big to be accomplished by any individual association," and hence spent less than $100,000 there, while simultaneously spending fifteen times more in France! The organization's official history remarks that the "comparatively small amount" spent on Belgium was due to the existence of the CRB, yet it spent one-third more on the Belgians than it did on the Poles who, of course, had no CRB analog to help them.[117]

The Belgian cause is closely linked to the British propaganda effort in the United States. Count Johann von Bernstorff, the German ambassador in Washington, regarded Belgium as the principal British propaganda weapon during the war.[118] Reports of Belgian woe were vital to British efforts to influence American public opinion. Hoover's CRB was able to profit from this climate of opinion,[119] characterized by James Squires as "an almost nationwide indignation at the German invasion of Belgium . . . which did not grow less but waxed in intensity as the war progressed."[120]

Finally, in a very real sense neither Serbia nor Poland really received relief at all during the war. Only Belgium was the recipient of a steady supply of food, clothing, and medicine that allowed its civilian population to abide. Serbia received teams of physicians, medicines, and technical aid in combating epidemics. This succor was very brief and cost very little. However, when Serbia requested major outside support in food, clothing, and other assistance, it received little or nothing. The Poles, by comparison, did not have the sudden dramatic epidemic that did much of the killing in Serbia. In Poland the population died due to malnutrition, exposure, and exhaustion. No effort to alleviate this distress was consummated. Instead, a steady but pathetic stream of money and supplies flowed in, but it was very little compared to the need. Certainly, this much is true: The only factor that did not play a major role was the distress of the population.

---

117. Percy Mitchell, *The American Relief Clearing House: Its Work in the Great War* (Paris, n.d.), 82, 85–86, 157

118. Count Bernstorff, *My Three Years in America* (New York, 1920), 38–39, 53.

119. Carl Wittke, *German-Americans and the World War* (Columbus, 1936), 14, 18, 46; H. C. Peterson, *Propaganda for War: The Campaign Against American Neutrality, 1914–1917* (Norman, OK, 1939), 64–69.

120. James Duane Squires, *British Propaganda at Home and in the United States 1914 to 1917* (Cambridge, MA, 1935), 65.

Chapter 3

"This Troublesome Question": The United States and the "Polish Pogroms" of 1918–1919

Neal Pease

On April 10 a news dispatch appeared that fifty Jews had been lined up against a wall and executed by command of a Major in the Polish Army. A great outcry broke out in the American press. Paderewski was in Paris and I suggested that he should have an investigation made at once. In the meantime, we sent one of our staff to investigate and found there was really not much truth in the story. But it still raged in the American press and began to threaten our relief work. On June 2nd I wrote President Wilson suggesting that with Paderewski's approval, an official American Mission be sent to look into the matter. General Edgar Jadwin, Mr. Homer Johnson, and Mr. Henry Morgenthau were appointed as the Commission. These gentlemen did a fine service by exposing falsity and creating a generally more wholesome atmosphere.

Herbert Hoover, *The Memoirs of Herbert Hoover: Years of Adventure, 1874–1920* (New York, 1951), 357–58.

In these eight laconic sentences, composed some thirty years after the fact, Herbert Hoover summarized his part in an episode that involved him as director of the American Relief Administration activities in Eastern Europe after the First World War. However, Hoover's memoirs had much ground to cover regarding his busy career, and his account of this incident is considerably condensed, to say the least. In fact, the so-called Pińsk massacre of April 1919 was but one, albeit the most sensational, of numerous outrages reportedly inflicted upon Jews within Poland since the previous November, the month of the restoration of Polish statehood after more than a century of foreign rule. The accumulated charges convinced much of the world that the fledgling Polish government had encouraged or tolerated the slaughter and persecution of not fifty, but thousands of Jews, and the resultant wave of indignation in the United States and abroad persuaded the American authorities that they had no choice but to intervene in the controversy. These efforts culminated, as Hoover stated, in the dispatch of a board of inquiry led by Henry Morgenthau, but not all agreed that the mission had performed a "fine service" or even that it had reached coherent conclusions. Some denounced the Morgenthau report as a whitewash concocted to hide the truth of a ghastly atrocity; many accepted its findings as evidence that allegations of Polish anti-Semitism were wildly exaggerated, while others insisted that it proved precisely the contrary. This was not the sole irony of the U.S. response to the reported "Polish pogroms" of 1918–19, and reexamination of this now obscure *cause célèbre* is useful in several ways. The affair offers insight into American policies concerning Poland and the protection of national minorities at that pivotal time, a fleeting moment when Washington officialdom regarded the restored Polish state as a natural and necessary partner and so took vigorous measures to preserve its good name in the face of unflattering and, they thought, unfair publicity.

For decades, accusations that the Poles "celebrated" the birth of the Second Republic with an orgy of pogroms contributed to a popular and often repeated belief that interwar Poland was viciously anti-Semitic: the violence was, in this view, "a gruesomely fitting inauguration of the kind of treatment that Jews would receive in the independent Poland," where "Jewish life was the cheapest commodity."[1] Like all hardy legends, these extravagant charges rested upon just enough fact to lend plausibility to the elaborations. Over the centuries the Polish lands had become the largest center of Jewish settlement in the world; Jews constituted roughly one-tenth of the population of the Second Republic, and markedly more in the *kresy,* or eastern borderlands of the state. Although scarcely as homogeneous as often portrayed, Polish Jewry at that time was a largely urban group, predominantly Orthodox and culturally distinct from the Poles and other peoples of the region. Despite an increasing diversification by livelihood, the traditional identification of Jews with commerce and retail trade remained strong; in many villages and cities of the *kresy,* the small merchant or shopkeeper was nearly certain to be Jewish. The nineteenth century had injected new strain into the historically intimate but wary relationship between Pole and Jew. In an era of rising Polish nationalism and, with urbanization, the growing attractiveness of occupations once regarded as Jewish preserves, Jews became targets of suspicion and resentment. Roman Dmowski's National Democracy, the most dynamic Polish political

---

1. The quotations are from Harry M. Rabinowicz, *The Legacy of Polish Jewry: A History of Polish Jews in the Inter-War Years, 1919–1939* (New York and London, 1965), 31, 38; and Celia S. Heller, *On the Edge of Destruction: Jews of Poland Between the Two World Wars* (New York, 1977), 47.

movement at the turn of the century, openly called for the reduction of Jewish influence in a free Poland. At the same time, a growing minority of Polish Jewry was abandoning its customary civic passivity and adopting Zionism or other creeds foreseeing a Jewish political destiny separate from the Poles.

The events of the First World War itself had magnified these tensions and led to a palpable increase of anti-Semitic sentiment among the Poles and Ukrainians of the *kresy.* Allegations that Jews had cooperated too readily with the German occupation and that Jewish tradesmen had profiteered from the conflict circulated widely, and the conspicuous if often overstated Jewish presence in radical and Bolshevist ranks aggravated Polish fears that Jews were politically unreliable. In the later stages of the war Dmowski won Allied recognition as the legitimate Polish spokesman, and the expected prominence in reborn Poland of this figure notorious for his slant on the "Jewish Question" aroused unease among Jews worldwide.[2]

These developments partially accounted for the readiness of international opinion to believe that the misfortunes of Polish Jewry in 1918–19 stemmed from deliberate pogroms, encouraged or winked at by the new state authorities, rather than the chaos and warfare still prevalent in the east of Europe. In a sense, the armistice had not ended the world war in the eastern zone of the continent, where the violent and disorderly course of the Russian revolution and civil war and the fixing of new frontiers raged for two more years. In that stormy interlude, Poland battled a variety of Bolshevist, Lithuanian, and Ukrainian forces for control of the *kresy,* which became a no-man's-land of warring factions patrolled by imperfectly disciplined troops and inexperienced officers. Swept up in the maelstrom, the Jews of the region found themselves in harm's way despite their efforts to lie low during the fray. Blatant and brutal attacks against Jews emphatically did occur, but opinions differed then, and continue to differ now, about the applicability of the term "pogrom" to these incidents.[3] Most of

---

2. Charles Reznikoff, ed., *Louis Marshall, Champion of Liberty: Selected Papers and Addresses* (2 vols.; Philadelphia, 1957), v. 2, 585–593.

3. For example, Ezra Mendelsohn, *The Jews of East Central Europe Between the World Wars* (Bloomington, IN, 1983), 40–42, describes these actions as pogroms, while Norman Davies says flatly that they were no such thing, *God's Playground: A History of Poland* (2 vols.; New York, 1982), v. 2, 262–263, and *Europe: A History* (Oxford and New York, 1996), 844. Jerzy Tomaszewski, ed., *Najnowsze dziejów Żydów w Polsce* (Warsaw, 1993) labels the Lwów riots of November 1918 a pogrom, but not the Pińsk affair. The disagreement does not so much concern the facts of what happened, but how to characterize them. For its part, the Morgenthau report consciously strove to limit usage of the word "pogrom" as an elastic and imprecise term applied indiscriminately to a broad range of actions, from individual muggings to concerted mob attacks, instead employing the more general, less emotive "excesses."

the Jewish casualties attributed to pogroms in fact took place within the context of military encounters that afflicted Jewish and gentile civilians alike, and killed more of the latter. Jews plainly suffered a disproportionate share of injuries for many reasons—the concentration of their numbers in the most hotly contested cities, their heightened vulnerability as shop owners to looting and bread riots, bullyragging by licentious soldiers, mob thuggery in anarchic conditions, distrust of Jewish political allegiance—but these were neither sponsored or condoned by the Polish government nor as numerous as reported. In all, approximately three hundred Jews perished by violence in Poland during these months, far fewer indeed than in other troubled areas of East and Central Europe. Even so, the charges that Poles were butchering thousands of Jews, inflated by hearsay and hyperbole, captured the attention of the world.[4]

Accounts of pogroms in Poland first arose in November 1918 in the wake of the Polish capture of Lwów after prolonged combat with adherents of the West Ukrainian Republic. Within days, press dispatches, principally of German and Austrian origin, began to circulate contending that Polish authorities had permitted, or even organized, the slaughter of as many as three thousand Jews in that city. Initiating a pattern that would recur in coming months, a second generation of articles presently disputed the original reports as misrepresentations of a military operation, but the journalistic maxim that accusations outweigh denials held true.[5] The news elicited expressions of shock and indignation, and the protests grew with the appearance of similar tales of anti-Jewish excesses. From the beginning the stories provoked the sharpest response in the English-speaking lands, above all the United States, the country that had waged the war as a crusade for liberal democracy and the liberation of East Central Europe. U.S. public opinion invested much hope in resurrected Poland and reacted reproachfully to these rumored abuses, being untutored in the ethnic and political complexities of the Polish lands and, according to many Poles, conveniently inclined to forget the imperfections in America's own record

---

4. See Norman Davies, "Great Britain and the Polish Jews, 1918–1920," *Journal of Contemporary History* 8, no. 2 (1973): 119–142; Kay Lundgreen-Nielsen, *The Polish Problem at the Paris Peace Conference: A Study of the Policies of the Great Powers and the Poles, 1918–1919* (Odense, 1979), 302–307, 341–348, 371–385. Piotr S. Wandycz devotes several pages to the issue in his *The United States and Poland* (Cambridge, MA, and London, 1980), 157–168. The estimate of three hundred Jews killed in the Polish lands in 1918–1919 represents a consensus of contemporary accounts, following the initial inflated reports, and of subsequent historical research. The Morgenthau report cited a figure of 280, Davies, "Great Britain," guesses four hundred, with most other counts falling within that range.

5. H. H. Fisher, *America and the New Poland* (New York, 1928), 156; *New York Times*, 28 November, 2 December, 3 December, 17 December 1918, 2 January 1919; *Times* (London), 4 December, 23 December 1918.

of treatment of minorities. The United States also was home to a large, influential, and articulate Jewry, whose most visible leadership favored Polish independence but placed little faith in the Poles' intentions toward their Jews. Already by early December Jewish spokesmen had appealed to President Woodrow Wilson to protect Polish Jews, and a groundswell of public censure of Poland had begun to surface.[6]

While not yet the torrent of disapproval it would become, the emerging popular disenchantment with Poland over the Jewish question sparked concern in the U.S. State Department. Not only did the Polish cause occupy a special place in the Wilsonian version of the postwar world, but Washington also counted heavily on the new republic as a bastion of stability and Allied loyalty standing between defeated Germany and revolutionary Russia, and the American authorities took for granted that they should support and strengthen Poland.[7] All the same, they also had long recognized the problems posed by the existence of substantial minorities within a Polish nation-state and now feared that the alleged pogroms might jeopardize the American public enthusiasm for Poland with consequent harm to U.S. policy in East Central Europe.[8] On separate occasions in December 1918 and January 1919, American representatives approached Roman Dmowski, then in Paris preparing to lead the Polish delegation to the coming peace conference, to convey their worries and hear the Polish side of the story. The National Democratic leader responded equably and, to the Americans' ears, plausibly enough. The incriminations against Poland, stated Dmowski, were overstatements spread by enemies of the republic. Jews had sustained isolated injuries, he admitted, but these must be attributed to the anarchy of the *kresy* or to popular resentment of Jewish affronts to the national cause, leading occasionally to disturbances which the army and police were unable to prevent; in any event, he noted ironically, socialists and not his National Democrats controlled the government, so there could be no question of official Polish anti-Semitism. Dmowski frankly restated his thesis regarding the Jewish question: Jews had been an essentially alien and "parasitical" element in the Polish midst, devoted only to their own

---

6. Jacob Schiff to Israel Zangwill, December 13, 1918, in Cyrus Adler, *Jacob H. Schiff: His Life and Letters* (2 vols.; Garden City, 1928), v. 2, 306; *Congressional Record*, December 10, 1918, v. 57, 234; *New York Times*, 15 November, 18 November 1918; Reznikoff, *Louis Marshall*, v. 2, 593–599.

7. A truism of American policy at the time, reflected in such locations as the Edward M. House Papers and "Inquiry" Papers, *passim*, Sterling Library, Yale University; *Congressional Record*, December 21, 1918, v. 57, 725.

8. Charles Seymour, ed., *The Intimate Papers of Colonel House* (4 vols.; Boston and New York, 1928), v. 4, 200; Robert Lansing to House, November 29, 1918, *Foreign Relations of the United States* [FRUS]: *Paris Peace Conference* [PPC], v. 2, 413; Lansing to William Sharp, December 2, 1918, FRUS 1919, v. 2, 746.

welfare, and they would gain acceptance by the majority only upon demonstration of their resolve to become loyal citizens of Poland. These declarations only partially satisfied American misgivings. Colonel Edward House, Wilson's intimate and a decided advocate of Poland, doggedly insisted that the Poles would "try to do the fair thing" but concluded that Polish Jews might require international protection until ethnic hostilities had been "redeemed" by the benefits of democracy and independence.[9]

Subtracting Dmowski's programmatic anti-Semitism, his answers anticipated the defensive tone of Polish official rebuttals to the pogrom reports in coming months. Emphasizing the disordered and warlike condition of the eastern borderlands, the Poles claimed that the atrocity stories were a caricature of the truth, largely propagated with malicious intent both by hostile German sources and Jews seeking to discredit Poland for political purposes.[10] The Polish leadership also resented the suggestion that the country should be subjected to international defamation and scrutiny—groundless, they felt, in the first place—just as it was attempting to consolidate statehood and fix its frontiers. Ignacy Jan Paderewski, the celebrated musician who doubled as premier and foreign minister in the first year of independence, repeatedly assured the world of Warsaw's innocence but grew testy as the pogrom issue dragged on. Chief of State Józef Piłsudski, Dmowski's longtime rival and the Polish luminary most identified with a policy of liberality toward minorities, admitted to a Jewish interviewer that Poles were certainly "not philosemites" but described this as an aberrant condition of the war and its confused aftermath: once the tumult and passions of the moment had passed, Jews would find their existence secure in a Poland that guaranteed them equality of right.[11]

In mid-January 1919, the Paris Peace Conference began, and quickly became the principal forum for discussion of the status of Polish Jewry. The cardinal tasks of the gathering were to conclude treaties and regulate

9. Frank Polk to Sharp, December 4, 1918, Sharp to Polk, December 6, 1918, FRUS 1919, v. 2, 746–747; Stephen Bonsal, *Suitors and Suppliants: The Little Nations at Versailles* (New York, 1946), 123–125.

10. While the Poles overstressed these self-serving arguments, they contained at least a measure of truth. The German press neglected few opportunities to deprecate Poland, a country regarded with enmity and contempt by a solid majority of German opinion. Numerous Zionists and Jewish separatists used the pogrom question as a justification for Jewish autonomy within Poland, despite the lack of any logical connection between the issues: Jewish separatism, as many noted at the time, would provide no protection against anti-Semitic violence. The most noteworthy foreign polemicist for Polish Jewish self-rule was the British Zionist Israel Cohen, whose articles and pamphlets did much to fan the pogrom charges during the first semester of 1919.

11. Israel Cohen, "My Mission to Poland (1918–1919)," *Jewish Social Studies*. 13, no. 2 (1951): 160, 166–168.

the new political order in Europe, but the war also had raised questions of urgency to Jews, chiefly the prospect of a Jewish homeland in Palestine and the wholesale creation of infant East European states that included sizable numbers of Jews. Representatives from virtually all-Jewish colonies flocked to the French capital espousing a variety of contradictory views. One of the many disputes within Jewish ranks centered on the wisdom of advancing a Zionist strategy in East Europe, meaning the demand that Jews in that region be recognized as a distinct nationality endowed with autonomous standing and corporate rights—an aim forcefully pursued by Polish Zionists, but rejected by Warsaw as an unacceptable attempt to create a state within the state. Other Jewish delegations, notably the British and French, opposed the "national-rights" approach and argued that East European Jews should remain content with more modest claims to civil equality.

On the whole, the American Jewish envoys at the conclave adopted the Zionist program for East Europe. Many of the premier figures of U.S. Jewry converged on Paris to uphold the nationalist cause: Supreme Court Justice Louis D. Brandeis; his eventual successor, Felix Frankfurter; the educator Cyrus Adler, and above all, Louis Marshall, the able representative of the American Jewish Congress who quickly established himself as the most tireless and effective Jewish advocate at the conference.[12] By no means did all American Jews support Zionism, however, and in March Henry Morgenthau appeared at the peace parley as spokesman for the anti-nationalist Union of American Hebrew Congregations. While widely disliked within the U.S. Jewish elite both on personal and political grounds, Morgenthau possessed access to the highest ranks of American decision makers. A German-born immigrant who had amassed a fortune in New York real estate, he became an early follower of Woodrow Wilson and managed the finances of the successful presidential campaigns of 1912 and 1916. As a reward he became ambassador to Turkey and enjoyed the confidence of Wilson and his inner circle. Morgenthau sternly opposed Zionism, regarding it as ultimately incompatible with democracy and likely to expose American Jews to the hoary charge of dual loyalty. He also endorsed the Wilsonian view of Poland as a mainstay of U.S. values and interests in the Old World and urged Polish Jews to rally to the state, repudiating autonomist notions.[13]

---

12. Oscar I. Janowsky, *The Jews and Minority Rights (1878–1919)* (New York, 1933), 263–272, 278.

13. Henry Morgenthau, *All in a Life-Time* (Garden City, 1922), 349–351. Felix Frankfurter bore a special animus toward Morgenthau. Speaking of him in 1919, Frankfurter insisted acidly that "the man is without character . . . Take base metal, stamp on it the seal of government, call it an ambassador and you can never drive it out of circulation," quoted in Michael E. Parrish, *Felix Frankfurter and His Times: The Reform Years* (New York, 1982), 142.

If Jewish questions in general became a prominent topic of debate during the early weeks of the peace conference, the matter of the "Polish pogroms" had diminished in visibility through the first trimester of 1919, kept alive by the intermittent press article or protest meeting but not commanding wide attention. The issue revived abruptly, however, with the announcement of the most credible allegation of outrage yet leveled against Warsaw. Previous charges had rested on hearsay, but in this instance none disputed what had happened: that on April 5 Polish soldiers came upon a gathering of Jews in the tense, overwhelmingly Jewish city of Pińsk, only recently secured by the Poles in their war against the Soviet armies. Interpreting the gathering as a subversive political meeting, the officer in command, Major Aleksander Norbut-Łuczyński, ordered the summary execution of at least thirty-five of the participants, who were shot against the wall of the town cathedral. The subsequent revelation that the assembly had been discussing the distribution of food relief in anticipation of Passover lent a macabre touch to the incident, while the Polish imputation of Bolshevist leanings to the victims—not impossible but never proved—seemed callous and unconvincing. The "Pińsk massacre" caused a scandal and catalyzed the topic of pogroms, transforming it into a front-page story that gathered force with each new report of anti-Jewish outbreaks in Wilno and other points in the borderlands, brandishing such headlines as "Jews Massacred, Robbed by Poles."[14] The renewed tales of horrors in eastern Poland exerted a palpable influence on developments in Paris by pricking the conscience of Wilson and fortifying the arguments of the Jewish lobbyists, accelerating the process that would impose a series of minority-protection treaties on Poland and the other newly independent East European states.[15]

---

14. *New York Times,* 26 May 1919. Related articles appeared almost daily in the press in these weeks; see the *Times* of 23 May and 1 June 1919, for notable examples. The pogrom allegations received much attention in organs of American liberals and leftists, already inclined to distaste for Poland as a supposedly militaristic and excessively nationalist beneficiary of the "punitive" Treaty of Versailles. H. N. Brailsford likened the Poles to bloodthirsty oriental despots in *New Republic,* August 20, 1919, 78–81, while the *Nation* noted that "Poland, our energetic young protégé among the new and free nations . . . has already managed to make a notable record in the matter of slaughtering quite a large number of innocent and defenseless Jews," May 31, 1919, 857. See Jerzy Tomaszewski, "Pińsk, Saturday 5 April 1919," *Polin* 1 (1986): 227–251, for a dispassionate summary of the incident. Tomaszewski ascribes the massacre to the Polish troops' jumpiness and sense of impunity in a war zone, abetted by anti-Jewish prejudice and the sheer incompetence of Major Narbut-Łuczyński.

15. Cyrus Adler, *I Have Considered the Days* (Philadelphia, 1941), 312–316; Sir James Headlam-Morley, *A Memoir of the Paris Peace Conference, 1919* (London, 1972), 91; Janowsky, *Jews and Minority Rights,* 351.

The Pińsk affair and its aftershocks also aroused American opinion and touched off a controversy that raged through the spring of 1919. The question not only generated frictions between Polish-Americans and Jews in many localities, but fanned by the press and Jewish organizations, also raised the simmering discontent of the public with Polish minority policies to the boiling point. A bipartisan list of political eminences—William Howard Taft, Charles Evans Hughes, Champ Clark, and Alfred E. Smith— openly condemned Warsaw, and petitions and resolutions in a similar vein poured into Washington. The agitation climaxed on May 21 with a gigantic coordinated day of protest in New York City. Hundreds of thousands of demonstrators marched in the streets, and thousands more jammed into Madison Square Garden to hear Hughes, among other celebrated speakers, denounce the "incredible atrocities" inflicted by Poland upon Jews and call for official U.S. action to end them. These manifestations of public anger impressed Congress. Within days of the New York rallies, the Senate resolved to investigate the reports of pogroms in Poland and Romania, and a bevy of legislators descended upon the State Department to vent indignation and demand explanations.[16]

The sudden furor against Poland alarmed American policymakers in Paris and Washington, whose reflexive action was to seek to quell it by any means. While Wilson saw no contradiction between support for Poland and sympathy for the Jewish plight, many of his subordinates in the peace delegation and the State Department approached the question in the tenor of Colonel House's private admission that "he thought more of the Poles than he did of the Jews." This sentiment embraced matters of policy—the desire to protect the reputation of a country considered an important U.S. interest against injurious and, they believed, overblown accusations—but also a clear measure of pique: the overburdened diplomats at Paris came to consider the Jewish activists as nuisances whose parochial agenda not only conflicted with American aims in East Central Europe but also distracted the peacemakers from weightier matters. In response, the State Department tried to reassure Congress while thrusting the crisis upon the newly ensconced American minister to Warsaw.[17]

---

16. *New York Times,* 21 May, 22 May, 27 May, 30 May, 8 June 1919; *Congressional Record,* v. 58, May 26, 1919, 246, June 5, 1919, 669–670, June 10, 1919, 891, June 19, 1919, 1369.

17. David Hunter Miller, *My Diary at the Conference of Paris* (21 vols.; New York, 1924), v. 1, 286. See as well James T. Shotwell, *At the Paris Peace Conference* (New York, 1937), 322; R. H. Lord to Hugh Gibson, August 22, 1919, Hugh Gibson Papers, Hoover Institution on War, Revolution and Peace, Stanford University; Frank Polk Diary, May 19, May 23, May 26, 1919, Frank Polk Papers, Sterling Library, Yale University; Polk to Gibson, May 21 and May 23, 1919, FRUS 1919, v. 2, 749.

The first chief of the U.S. legation in the Polish capital, Hugh S. Gibson, was a rising star in the diplomatic service. A personable and widely admired protégé of Herbert Hoover, Gibson welcomed his assignment to Warsaw— "the most important legation we have"— and vigorously championed the conception of a strong Poland to stand guard against German revisionism and Soviet Bolshevism.[18] He also stood out for his anti-Semitism even in an era when genteel disdain for things Jewish pervaded the clublike atmosphere of the Foreign Service. Upon their arrival in Warsaw, the Yankee diplomats found their prejudices confirmed by an almost physical repugnance toward the city's exotic Orthodox Jewry and by the growing conviction that the objectives of Polish Zionists and Jewish autonomists endangered the state. To Gibson and his colleagues, the Jews represented antagonists and also a source of sport, and ridicule of Jewish traits, customs, and appearance became the favorite expression of camaraderie within the legation.[19]

This combination of policy and inclination ensured that when the State Department commanded Gibson to accord priority to the investigation of the pogrom charges, superiors as well as envoy would emphasize the search for evidence that would exonerate Poland—as indeed, they genuinely trusted, any dispassionate inquiry would confirm.[20] Pressures from the aroused Congress forced Gibson's probe to proceed at top speed. On June 2 the House Foreign Affairs committee began hearings that, given the mood of the moment, seemed likely to produce a condemnation of Poland. Anxious to avoid this outcome, the State Department sought to stall the legislators, imploring them to postpone action until Gibson had submitted his report while simultaneously hounding him to register his findings before the committee's patience expired—preferably, if improbably, within a week.[21]

---

18. Gibson Diary, April 15, 1919, Gibson Papers. See also Gibson to Lansing, January 22, 1920, State Department Decimal File, R.G. 59 [SDNA] 860.00/3, National Archives, Washington, D.C. Andrzej Kapiszewski, ed., *Hugh Gibson and a Controversy over Polish-Jewish Relations after World War I* (Kraków, 1991) is a useful collection of relevant documents.

19. The culture of jocular anti-Semitism that reigned at the Warsaw legation may be observed *passim* in the Gibson Papers and in the manuscript collections of other mission staff, such as the Arthur Bliss Lane Papers, Sterling Library, Yale University, and the Jay Pierrepont Moffat Papers, Houghton Library, Harvard University. In addition, Robert D. Schulzinger, *The Making of the Diplomatic Mind: The Training, Outlook and Style of United States Foreign Service Officers, 1908– 1931* (Middletown, CT, 1975), 131–132: and Martin Weil, *A Pretty Good Club: The Founding Fathers of the U.S. Foreign Service* (New York, 1978), 34–41.

20. In FRUS 1919, v. 2, William Phillips to Gibson, April 25, 1919, 748; Polk to Gibson, May 28, 1919, 750; Gibson to Polk, May 31, 1919, 752–753; Gibson to Phillips, June 15, 1919, 764.

21. *New York Times*, 3 June, 11 June 1919; in FRUS 1919, v. 2, Phillips to Gibson, June 3, 1919, 760, Polk to Gibson, June 20, 1919, 768.

The harried minister to Warsaw complied dutifully if unwillingly, mounting a hasty inquest in tandem with a Red Cross official and the agent for American Jewish relief in Poland while inwardly seething at the monopolization of his time by the pogrom question. Gibson never completed a comprehensive report but issued a series of dispatches that consistently sounded the themes that the atrocity stories were greatly distorted, that Polish-Jewish hostility was complex and deep-rooted, and that the Jews bore their own share of responsibility for their unpopularity in Poland.[22] Except for the vehemence of their expression, these contentions resembled those of other foreign diplomats and correspondents in Warsaw who were also concluding that the "pogroms" had been a case of much smoke and little fire, but Gibson's views soon became embarrassingly public. To keep the congressional inquisitors at bay, the State Department had fed them copies of the relevant cable traffic between Washington and Warsaw, a ploy that backfired in early June when the House committee chairman leaked to the press an excerpt of a Gibson telegram that largely exculpated Poland while censuring as unwarranted and irresponsible the campaign of "violent agitation" and "propaganda" undertaken by Jews throughout the world. When a Christian Pole suffered harm, said Gibson, it was called a food riot, but if a Jew was the victim in similar circumstances, it was called a pogrom.[23]

Gibson's findings persuaded the congressmen to suspend their hearings, but the publication of his confidential, hence impolitically worded, memorandum infuriated Jewish opinion and prompted accusations that Washington was trying to cover up a series of inconvenient enormities. "Astounding," "whitewash," "inexcusable," and "ignorant" were but some of the epithets Louis Marshall employed to describe the Gibson dispatch,

---

22. Gibson to Phillips, June 17, 1919, Gibson to Polk, June 20, 1919, FRUS 1919, v. 2, 765–769; Gibson to Mrs. Frank Gibson, June 1, 1919, Gibson Papers; Weil, *Pretty Good Club*, 42–43. An account of the Gibson investigations by one of its participants is found in Boris D. Bogen, *Born a Jew* (New York, 1930), 194–201. The degree to which Gibson's prejudice against Jews colored his conclusions is difficult to ascertain. It cannot have helped, but he seems to have been able to separate his private crotchets from his professional judgments to some extent. For instance, he habitually indulged in scathing candid references to Poland and Poles as well, but this did not get in the way of his warm advocacy of political and diplomatic support for the Polish state. For what it is worth, several Jews who observed Gibson during his inquest expressed confidence in his fairness and conscientiousness; see Bogen's relation in *Born a Jew*, as well as Cyrus Adler and Aaron M. Margolith, *With Firmness in the Right: American Diplomatic Action Affecting Jews, 1840–1945* (New York, 1946), 153.

23. Gibson to Phillips, June 2, 1919, FRUS 1919, v. 2, 756–760. Likewise see Phillips to Commission to Negotiate Peace, June 17 and June 28, 1919, FRUS 1919, v. 2, 764–765, 771–772; Lundgreen-Nielsen, *Polish Problem*, 347; *New York Times*, 27 June 1919; *Times* (London), 21 July 1919.

and Cyrus Adler castigated its revival of "old slanders" as an exercise in blaming the victim.[24] When Gibson arrived in Paris later that month to consult with senior U.S. officials, Brandeis and Frankfurter confronted him with threats that the American Jewish lobbies would work to block his confirmation as minister to Warsaw. A man of thin skin and short fuse, Gibson raged at his Jewish critics: if their vendetta provoked anti-Semitic riots in Poland, the "blood guilt" would be theirs.[25] Under fire, the envoy to Warsaw understandably posed no objection when his chiefs decided to transfer custody of the investigation to another, more formal panel.[26]

Even before the Gibson inquest collapsed in fiasco, the plan of constructing an official American commission to examine the alleged Polish pogroms had seemed to many a logical step; indeed, the Polish government and numerous Jewish groups already had accepted the idea in principle when the rumors of atrocities first began to circulate in the last weeks of 1918.[27] The project revived on June 2 when Herbert Hoover of the ARA, following consultations with Prime Minister Paderewski, wrote to President Wilson to warn that the controversy, if left to burn, could do "a great deal of harm"; exaggerated reports of anti-Semitic violence jeopardized the repute of the Polish state, and "it must be a fundamental principle with us that we must support the Polish Republic." To allay the rumors and prescribe any necessary correctives in Warsaw's posture toward the Jewish minority, Wilson should appoint a board of inquiry including American Jews of "broad character"—for example, Henry Morgenthau. The president replied the next day that he favored the proposal both as a means of aiding Poland and as a solution to "this troublesome question of the treatment of the Jewish people." On June 5 Hoover's suggestion won the blessing of the U.S. Commissioners Plenipotentiary, who endorsed the judgment that Morgenthau would make "an excellent Jewish member" of the panel.[28]

---

24. *New York Times*, June 17, 1919; Marshall to Abram Elleus, August 19, 1919, in Reznikoff, *Louis Marshall*, v. 2, 601–611; Adler to Bogen, June 17, 1919, in Zosa Szajkowski, "American Jewish Relief in Poland and Politics, 1918–1923," *Zion*, v. 34, n.3–4, 250–253.

25. Gibson to Phillips, July 6, 1919, Gibson Papers. Also Gibson Diary, June 27, 1919, Gibson Papers; House Diary, June 25, 1919, House Papers.

26. In FRUS 1919, v. 2, Gibson to Polk, June 25, 1919, 769, and Lansing to Phillips, July 2, 1919, 772–773.

27. Pleasant Stovall to Polk, December 10, 1918, FRUS 1919, v. 2, 748; Adler and Margolith, *Firmness in the Right*, 159; *New York Times*, November 29, 1918, June 10, 1919; *Times* (London), June 5, 1919.

28. Hoover to Wilson, June 2, 1919, and Wilson's reply, June 3, 1919, reproduced in Francis William O'Brien, ed., *Two Peacemakers in Paris: The Hoover-Wilson Post-Armistice Letters, 1918–1920* (College Station and London, 1978), 166–168; Minutes of daily meetings of the Commissioners Plenipotentiary, June 5, 1919, FRUS 1919: PPC, v. 11, 224.

Morgenthau attractiveness to the American decision makers in large part derived from the very qualities that rendered him suspect to the U.S. Jewish activists. When Hoover spoke of his "broad character," he meant precisely that Morgenthau differed fundamentally from the other Jewish delegates at Paris: as a Jew who nonetheless opposed Zionism and warmly backed Polish statehood, he could be trusted to lend credibility to the investigation while addressing a delicate issue in an impartial and responsible fashion. However, the American Jews at the conference saw the question in a much different light, and once word of Morgenthau's impending nomination as head of the inquiry started to circulate, to a man they pressed him to step down. Marshall, Adler, and their colleagues argued that no Jew should serve on the commission as a matter of propriety; privately they objected to the selection of Morgenthau himself, doubting his commitment to Jewish interests and worrying that he would merely lend legitimacy to a prefabricated acquittal of Poland. Morgenthau bowed to their advice and asked to be excused, agreeing that the task was best left to a gentile.[29]

All the same, the American officials refused to take Morgenthau's no for an answer. Convinced that he was their man, House and Gibson urged him to reconsider.[30] More importantly, Wilson made clear that he would have Morgenthau or no one. The president met with his choice on June 26 to win him over. Turning aside Morgenthau's objections, Wilson emphasized that he wanted a Jew to serve to guarantee a "sympathetic hearing" for his Polish coreligionists and appealed to his longtime associate's sense of duty and personal loyalty. His arm twisted, and, one senses, pleased to hear of his indispensability, Morgenthau saw little choice but to comply, and on June 30 the United States announced that he would lead the board of inquiry to Poland accompanied by Gen. Edgar Jadwin and the lawyer Homer Johnson.[31]

Considering the notoriety of the controversy the Morgenthau commission was designed to resolve, its formation caused surprisingly little stir, relegated (in the instance of the *New York Times*) to a paragraph on an inside page. The investigation, as it happened, took existence at the exact moment that the issue of the "Polish pogroms" ceased to make headlines after its stint in the spotlight. The abatement of military action in the *kresy* during the summer of 1919 and the consolidation of Polish authority in the

---

29. Morgenthau, *All in a Life-Time,* 352–353; Adler, *I Have Considered,* 319; Harlan B. Phillips, ed., *Felix Frankfurter Reminisces* (New York, 1960), 156; Minutes of daily meetings of the Commissioners Plenipotentiary, June 13, 1919, FRUS 1919: PPC, v. 11, 232–233.

30. House Diary, June 25 and June 26, 1919.

31. Morgenthau, *All in a Life-Time,* 353–354. Likewise Minutes of daily meetings of the Commissioners Plenipotentiary, June 17, 1919, FRUS 1919: PPC, v. 11, 236–237.

region established more orderly conditions in the areas of heavy Jewish settlement. Furthermore, the conclusion of the Polish minority-protection treaty in Paris on June 28, partially in response to the disquieting reports from eastern Poland, considerably reduced the urgency of the pogrom question in the eyes of Jewish leaders. Achievement of this compact had become the centerpiece of the Jewish delegations' East European agenda, and ultimately the peacemakers exacted similar pledges from the other "successor states." While these governments resented the treaties as insults to their sovereignty by great powers unwilling to apply the same standards to themselves, the Jewish spokesmen celebrated them as satisfactory charters of Jewish citizenship in the emancipated countries. With this victory in hand, Marshall and his colleagues called on Polish Jews to set aside the hostilities of the past and offer allegiance to a Poland now obliged to uphold their rights.[32]

If already somewhat anticlimactic, the formation of the Morgenthau mission prompted spirited and varying reactions from the principals. On the Polish side, Paderewski and his advisers thanked the fates that the inquest had been entrusted to a "fair and honest man," and the State Department officers agreed that the Jews disliked the project only because Morgenthau was "too liberal and fair-minded" for their tastes.[33] In fact, the prospect of the investigation appalled the Zionists in Paris, who considered it a patent fraud and dispatched Frankfurter to Poland to keep a conspicuous eye on Morgenthau. In the meantime, Poles, Zionists, and anti-Zionist Jews jostled one another for the ears of the panel and its staff before they departed the French capital, seeking to incline the examiners toward desired directions.[34]

---

32. Adler, *I Have Considered*, 324–325; Marshall, Adler, and Nahum Sokolow to Bogen, July 11, 1919, in Max J. Kohler, "The Origin of the Minority Provisions of the Peace Treaty of 1919," in Luigi Luzzatti, ed., *God in Freedom: Studies in the Relations Between Church and State* (New York, 1930), 793–794. The Polish minority compact is discussed and reproduced in H. W. V. Temperley, ed., *A History of the Peace Conference of Paris* (6 vols.; London, New York, and Toronto, 1924), v. 5, 132–144, 432–436.

33. Jan Ciechanowski to Ministerstwo Spraw Zagranicznych, June 30, 1919, in *Archiwum polityczne Ignacego Paderewskiego* [APIP] (4 vols; Wrocław, 1973–1974), v. 2, 230–232; Sir Ronald Lindsay to Lord George Nathaniel Curzon, July 16, 1919, *Documents on British Foreign Policy* [DBFP], ser. 1, v. 6, 80–81; House Diary, June 26, 1919. In a letter of July 14, 1919, Walter Lippmann told his friend Gibson "I have no confidence whatever in Morgenthau," Walter Lippmann Papers, Sterling Library, Yale University.

34. Morgenthau, *All in a Life-Time*, 357–358; Adler, *I Have Considered*, 319; Zosa Szajkowski, "Western Jewish Aid and Intercession for Polish Jewry, 1919–1939," in Joshua A. Fishman, ed., *Studies on Polish Jewry, 1919–1939: The Interplay of Social, Economic and Political Factors in the Struggle of a Minority for its Existence* (New York, 1974), 152–153; Lippmann to Gibson, July 14, 1919, Lippmann Papers; Phillips, *Frankfurter Reminisces*, 156.

Morgenthau and his entourage arrived in Warsaw on July 13 and wasted no time in assuring all that their goal was less to apportion blame than to foster reconciliation. The board's chairman proclaimed that global stability required "a strong Poland which could keep Russia and Germany apart," but that Poles and Jews must patch up their "family feud" if the country was to thrive and "do its part" for the Allied and democratic cause. General Jadwin also stressed the theme of mutual benefit, intoning that "what is good for the Jews is good for Poland, and what is good for Poland is good for the Jews," although time would show that he accorded far greater weight to the second half of the formula.[35]

Polish reaction to the American mission of inquiry ranged from tumultuous to hostile. Thousands of Jews thronged to greet Morgenthau in Warsaw and other cities of call, but Polish Zionists gave him the cold shoulder for his known opposition to their movement.[36] For their part, the Polish press and officialdom made little effort to disguise their distaste for the examiners as an unwelcome affront to their sovereignty, at best tolerated. Such complaints issued not only from the Dmowski camp, but also from Chief of State Piłsudski. Although Piłsudski had admitted to Gibson that he regarded the attacks on Jews as a disgrace and promised to quell them as best his government could, he was as touchy about nosy outsiders poking into national concerns as he was broadminded toward minorities. In a pair of stiff meetings, the chief of state insisted to Morgenthau that the supposed pogroms had been deplorable but unavoidable "accidents" in no way justifying foreign meddling in Polish affairs.[37] An outbreak of race riots in the United States permitted the critics of the Morgenthau mission to raise questions of hypocrisy and double standards as well. Sarcastic Polish commentators deplored the "negro pogroms" across the Atlantic, and Piłsudski dryly offered Gibson the services of Polish investigators if desired.[38] Despite its resentment of the unwanted guests, however, the government allowed the panel a free hand and made no effort to hinder its researches or restrict its access to Jewish opinion.[39]

---

35. Firsthand accounts of the Morgenthau mission are found in Morgenthau, *All in a Life-Time,* Bogen, *Born a Jew,* and Arthur L. Goodhart, *Poland and the Minority Races* (New York, 1920). The quotations are from Goodhart, 23, 48, and Morgenthau, 358.

36. *New York Times,* 23 July 1919; Bogen, *Born a Jew,* 206–207.

37. Morgenthau, *All in a Life-Time,* 360, 371–376. Also Bogen, *Born a Jew,* 205; Goodhart, *Poland and Minority Races,* 22–23, 165; *New York Times,* February 8, 1920; Gibson to Polk, May 31, 1919, FRUS 1919, v. 2, 754.

38. Goodhart, *Poland and Minority Races,* 108. Likewise Gibson Diary, July 27, 1919; Poland, Sejm, *Sprawozdanie stenograficzne z posiedzenia Sejmu Rzeczypospolitej,* May 23, 1919.

39. Goodhart, *Poland and Minority Races,* 165.

All the same, the commission encountered numerous problems during its sojourn of two months, some inherent in the nature of the task. In the first place, reconstruction of the causes and circumstances of Jewish injuries in the Polish borderlands proved nearly impossible. The panel visited the sites of most reported excesses and took evidence from witnesses of all persuasions, but these efforts clarified the situation little. The accounts conflicted wildly, and the Americans discounted much testimony as unreliable or tendentious.[40] Other complications stemmed from the temperament of the chairman himself. Exploiting the opportunity to continue his running war against Jewish nationalism, Morgenthau hunted for polemical ammunition, going so far, some later claimed, as to offer cash rewards for information that would compromise the Zionists and their cause.[41] Convinced that economic privation fostered enmity between Poles and Jews, he expended much energy in attempts to convince Warsaw and Washington to create an international corporation for Polish investment and development. Whatever the merits of the proposal, all but Morgenthau found it irrelevant to his main purpose, and the suggestion fell on stony ground.[42] Moreover, his ambassadorial service had not taught Morgenthau the virtue of discretion, and he had the habit, as one of his colleagues noted, of doing "his thinking aloud" and in public. This loquacity produced embarrassment in July when newspaper stories claimed that he had dismissed the pogroms as a hoax before the commission had begun its probe. Morgenthau heatedly protested that the journalists had misconstrued him, but the incident highlighted his vulnerability to charges of unshakeable bias in favor of the Poles.[43]

In fact, Morgenthau strove mightily to be evenhanded. Acutely aware of suspicions that he was merely the front for a cover-up, he affirmed that any attempt to hide unpalatable truths would be both unconscionable and futile.[44] This policy led him to chide the Poles somewhat more sharply than expected. While remaining convinced of the basic decency and good intentions of the Polish republic, Morgenthau saw enough evidence of avoidable Jewish hardship to stir unease; in particular, his scrutiny of the Pińsk affair of April shook him profoundly. Gradually he concluded that although

---

40. Davies, "Great Britain," 131; Morgenthau, *All in a Life-Time,* 383–384. In light of this, one is struck by the assertion of the finished Morgenthau report that estimating the number of Jewish casualties was not difficult, and its confidence that the total numbered approximately 280.

41. Morgenthau, *All in a Life-Time,* 383.

42. Morgenthau to Ignacy Jan Paderewski, August 10, 1919, Gibson Papers; Morgenthau, *All in a Life-Time,* 380–382.

43. Bogen, *Born a Jew,* 204–206. Also *New York Times,* 29 July, 8 August 1919; Morgenthau to Howard S. Gans, July 30, 1919, in Szajkowski, "American," 252–253.

44. Morgenthau to Hoover, August 12, 1919, Gibson Papers.

the Polish government had in no way sponsored or condoned outrages, it deserved mild criticism for a complacent and insensitive approach toward Jewish matters that approached culpable negligence. As he neared the end of his probe, he warned his host government that he had no choice but to "rap Poland's knuckles" for these sins of omission.[45]

Morgenthau's partial change of heart produced consternation among the Poles and their staunchest State Department advocates and led him to break ranks with Commissioners Jadwin and Johnson, who were prepared to absolve Poland without reservations. The crucial difference between the chairman and his colleagues regarded definition of the proper scope of the investigation. Morgenthau had served notice that he intended to examine the relevance of the entire complex of Polish-Jewish relations; the others preferred to restrict themselves to the narrower questions of the immediate cause and extent of Jewish injuries by violence, and the responsibility of the Polish government, and on that count Jadwin asserted that "as good order is being maintained in Poland at present as in the United States." The trio consulted in efforts to heal the rift and avoid a public admission of dissension, but in the end the panel had no choice but to resort to separate sets of findings.[46]

Morgenthau issued his report—popularly regarded as the definitive statement of the commission, but in effect a minority opinion—early in October, and its conclusions reflected the author's ambivalence. Concerning the burning question of the inquiry, he denied the authenticity of the alleged pogroms and cleared Warsaw of direct responsibility for the isolated "excesses" that had occurred, attributing them above all to "the chaotic and unnatural state of affairs" of the preceding year. This judgment validated the central contention of Poland and its defenders, but the subsidiary points of the report were more guarded. Morgenthau lamented the existence of "a widespread antisemitic prejudice" in Poland produced by recent social and political conflicts and devoted much of his text to description of substantiated instances of mistreatment of Jews by Polish civil or military authorities, notably the Pińsk incident. He decried both Zionism and Polish chauvinism of the National Democratic stripe as malignant influences on Polish public life but offered the hopeful prediction that "relations between the Jews and non-Jews will undoubtedly improve in a strong democratic Poland."[47] The overall tone of the document was equivocal: the lot of Jews

---

45. Morgenthau, *All in a Life-Time*, 367–370, 376. Speaking to an American audience a few months later, Morgenthau stated that the Pińsk incident had "haunted me ever since" his inspection of the site, *New York Times*, 3 December 1919.

46. *New York Times*, November 23, 1919. In addition, *New York Times*, 30 November 1919; James C. White to Gibson, October 16, 1919, APIP, v. 2, 353–355.

47. Morgenthau's report is reproduced in *All in a Life-Time*, 405–437, and FRUS 1919, v. 2, 774–785.

under Polish rule was in no way as harsh as widely believed but still not satisfactory, and improvement required the cooperation of Poles and Jews of good will against extremists of both camps.

The joint Jadwin-Johnson deposition, released a month later, repeated Morgenthau's determination that no pogroms had taken place but refused to endorse the hedges and qualifications he had attached to the verdict. The discords showed mainly in emphasis and shading rather than assessment of fact. Jadwin and Johnson agreed with Morgenthau that approximately three hundred Polish Jews had died—mostly as civilian victims of war, worsened, they quaintly added, by "the eastern low valuation of human life"—but placed greater stress on the innocence of the Polish government. Indeed, they accepted the relatively low death toll as proof of Warsaw's diligence in shielding the Jewish population from the wrath of a Polish nation provoked by "the attitude of the Jews" at a time of excitement and tension. They highlighted the efforts of German propagandists to frame the Poles as barbarous anti-Semites and expressed confidence in the correctness of Polish minority policies; the world should support the new republic and permit it to develop without undue interference. In short, the Jadwin-Johnson paper replicated, in more measured language, the spirit and substance of the ill-fated Gibson report of June and approximated the stance that many had expected Morgenthau himself to assume.[48]

Couched in nuance, the discrepancies between the two reports were not obvious but showed plainly to those familiar with the subtleties of the controversy. Upon reading the Morgenthau declaration, Louis Marshall termed it, with evident surprise, "quite a good document" and contrasted it favorably to its counterpart. American Jews, he said, should "stand behind Morgenthau" and withhold criticism.[49] On the other hand, Gibson and his fellows at the Warsaw legation objected that Morgenthau had been too hard on the Poles and sought to gain wider publicity for the Jadwin-Johnson statement.[50]

The studied ambiguity of the Morgenthau report, its careful allotment of sympathy and reproach to all parties, permitted diverse interpretations of its message. Lifted from context, isolated passages could offend or please anti-Semites, Jewish activists, and champions or detractors of Poland alike. Outraged Zionists condemned it as "Morgenthau's whitewash," the "de-

---

48. FRUS 1919, v. 2, 786–800. Coincidentally, a British board of inquiry into the status of Jews in Poland conducted investigations in the later months of 1919 with almost identical results: the Jewish chairman of the mission, Sir Stuart Montagu Samuel, found much to criticize in Poland's policies while the rest of the committee rejected these conclusions as too harsh, Davies, "Great Britain," 129–130.

49. Marshall to Julian W. Mack, October 24, 1919, in Reznikoff, *Louis Marshall,* v. 2, 611. In the same volume, Marshall to Phillips, November 26, 1919, 612–621.

50. Weil, *Pretty Good Club,* 42–43.

liberate treachery" of a renegade Jew against his own, but Marshall also could cite it as evidence that Poland needed to raise its standards of conduct toward the Jews.[51] For their part, Polish officials elected to accentuate the positive and focus on the American's dismissal of the pogrom charges and warm regard for Poland as a stronghold of democracy and Allied loyalties, and they greeted his ruling as essentially favorable.[52]

In the United States, the casual reader likewise tended to construe the Morgenthau report as a vindication of Poland, and this opinion prevailed in the press. To the *New York Times,* the "temperate and . . . impartial" Morgenthau inquiry demonstrated that the uproar against Poland had been much ado about little.[53] This reading especially gratified those U.S. officials who had conceived of the commission as a means to exonerate Warsaw and discredit Jewish political leaders as irresponsible calumniators, and their reactions were equal parts of satisfaction and vindictiveness. Hoover claimed that Morgenthau had shown that Polish Jews had "infuriated [the] Christian population" and brought misfortune on themselves. Within the State Department, Undersecretary Frank Polk gloated that the report "will rather jar the Jews," and Assistant Secretary William Phillips forecast, in a telling choice of words, that it would help the department "put the quietus" to the tales of Jewish massacres in Poland.[54]

Phillips's prediction that the pogrom question would fade from notice proved correct, but the Morgenthau report merely confirmed rather than prompted this outcome. Composed as an antidote to the clamor of the American public against the grisly stories of Polish misdeeds, the inquiry completed its work at a time when that public no longer cared. As Poland

---

51. Davies, "Great Britain," 131; Szajkowski, "American," 259; Marshall to Leon Berenson, October 16, 1920, in Reznikoff, *Louis Marshall,* v. 2, 629–630.

52. Franciszek Puławski to Ministerstwo Spraw Zagranicznych, January 20, 1920, Archiwum Adiutantury Generalnej Naczelnego Dowództwa (Archiwum Belwederskie) [AGND], 65a/2361, microfilm edition, Sterling Library, Yale University; Stanisław Patek to Paderewski, September 19, 1919, APIP, v. 2, 329. The degree to which the Morgenthau report could be interpreted variously showed in an exchange in *Current History.* James Jay Kann, "The Jewish Problem in Poland," August 1921, 776–780, contended that Morgenthau had demonstrated the falsehood of all charges of mistreatment of Jews in Poland, implying strongly that Polish Jews were troublesome malcontents. This prompted an indignant response from Maurice Samuel, the mission's interpreter, who rejected Kann's argument as bigoted, simplistic, and indicative of a widespread tendency to misuse the report for partisan purposes, "Poland and the Jews," October 1921, 109–111.

53. *New York Times,* 21 January 1920.

54. Curzon to Sir Eyre Crowe, September 17, 1919, DBFP, ser. 1, v. 6, 241–242; Polk to Lansing, September 22, 1919, Polk Papers; Phillips to Morgenthau, December 1919, Henry Morgenthau, Jr., Papers, Franklin D. Roosevelt Presidential Library, Hyde Park, N.Y.

continued to establish order in the *kresy*, the rumors of atrocities disappeared correspondingly, and the issue lost currency as Americans turned toward other matters. Lacking the prod of popular indignation that had spurred legislative action the previous spring, Congress too allowed the topic to drop. In many ways, these developments reflected the fundamental change in American opinion and diplomacy, already well advanced before the pivotal elections of 1920, that would lead the United States to renounce Wilsonian notions of responsibility for European security and redefine East Central Europe as a region of no compelling U.S. interest. Virtually upon its release, then, Morgenthau's earnest vision of a pluralist, democratic Poland under Allied and American patronage became a relic of a discarded policy of U.S. commitment to the independence and welfare of the Polish republic. In this atmosphere of apathy, the Morgenthau report received perfunctory attention and thereupon sank into oblivion, quickly forgotten by all but a few.

To the extent that the truth of the matter can be determined, and despite the inauspicious political origins of their mission, the American investigators appear to have concluded correctly that the ballyhooed "Polish pogroms" of 1918–19, while not entirely groundless, were exaggerated and not the product of a campaign of terror waged by Warsaw against Jews. The record of the Polish authorities in Jewish questions was not perfect, as they implicitly, though grudgingly, admitted themselves, but primary responsibility for the suffering of Jews in the turbulent first months of independence could not be laid fairly at the door of a newborn government preoccupied with the chores of state building and lacking the power to impose order in all regions of the country. An argument can be made that Poland should have assigned higher priority to the protection of Jews in a volatile situation, or that its tendency to shift blame to German, Zionist, or Bolshevist troublemakers was not the most constructive approach to the issue. Even so, the facts remain that where Polish authority was established, the physical safety of Jews became secure, and that the Poles submitted to foreign examination of a delicate internal matter and offered a free hand to the investigators.

From the outset, official Washington had refused to regard the Poles as the villains of the piece, instead directing its ire toward Jewish advocates, and particularly the American Zionists who lobbied the peace conference, as scandalmongers trading in anti-Polish hysteria. In the eyes of prominent U.S. diplomats, American Jews, pursuing a narrow agenda beyond the bounds of reason or propriety, raised the bogey of pogroms in a cynical and misguided attempt to smear a strategic ally and promising democracy. The Jewish spokesmen did, in fact, overstate Polish wrongdoings, but this was an almost inevitable consequence of their commitment to the cause of Jewish rights. From the perspective of the Western Jews, the common association of Poles with anti-Semitism, the noticeable rise in Polish-Jewish tensions during the war, and the high visibility of Dmowski and the National Democrats added up to a damning consistency. When reports of Polish atrocities against Jews began to proliferate, Louis Marshall and his colleagues concluded that they could not give Poland the benefit of doubt. Lacking other means to be heard, they resorted to publicity that was frequently shrill and politicking that was sometimes heavy-handed, but they could have done little else and remain credible champions of East European Jewry.

As for Henry Morgenthau, for years after 1919 many Jews scorned him as a turncoat who had hidden the ugly truth of the Polish pogroms, a harsh and one-sided characterization of his part in the controversy. In the first place, the objections of Morgenthau's Jewish detractors that he was the wrong man to head an inquiry owing to his Polish sympathies and distaste for Zionism lacked point. Once the decision to mount an investigation under American auspices had been taken, perhaps the only politically possible candidate to head the mission was, as Wilson recognized, none other than Morgenthau, a prominent Jew invulnerable to suspicions of hostility toward Poland, trusted by Washington, and tolerable to Warsaw. The obvious disadvantages to his selection were his lack of credibility with Poland's main accusers and his susceptibility to charges that he was merely accessory to a cover-up. In spite of this handicap—indeed, possibly to compensate for it—the Morgenthau report emerged as an impressively detached and balanced summary of a tangled and supremely sensitive issue. Morgenthau permitted his bias against Zionism to show, and several highly placed American officials plainly would have lost no sleep had he whitewashed any crimes Poland might have committed, but he bent over backwards to be fair according to his lights and surprised partisans at both ends of the polarized debate who assumed they could safely predict the outcome of his researches.

Easily lost in the crossfire of words was the degree to which the entire polemic had become a function of U.S. politics, propelled by the interaction of American public opinion, pressure groups, and official foreign policy objectives. Rarely before or since has a Polish issue gained such importance, even if fleeting, in American civic discourse, or stirred such passion in a country that traditionally has manifested only intermittent interest in Eastern Europe. The furor stirred by the "Polish pogroms" of 1918–19 is rooted in the unusual circumstances of the time: Washington had defined an independent and thriving Poland as an asset of American policy, a principle that appeared to collide with a widespread belief that the Poles were flagrantly violating standards of human rights held sacred by Americans, and therefore undeserving of U.S. support.

In the long run, the Morgenthau commission failed to undo the damage to Poland's reputation wrought by the lurid charges of anti-Semitic outbursts. To the extent that the controversy of 1918–19 made any lasting impression on public memory, the sensational accounts of Jewish massacres in Pińsk and elsewhere outweighed the drier rebuttals of the investigators and reinforced the popular equation of Poland with cruelty toward Jews. John Maynard Keynes spoke for many when, in the course of his celebrated diatribe against the peace treaties, he memorably dismissed Poland as "an economic impossibility with no industry but Jew-baiting."[55] Concerning American opinion, the Polish Foreign Ministry resignedly took for granted that Warsaw would bear the stigma of anti-Semitism indefinitely.[56] The association of Poland with violent animus toward Jews lingered in the U.S., dormant for the time being but easily revived.[57] Moreover, the tales of Jewish bloodbaths in Poland at the end of the World War refused to die, and, with repetition, crystallized into "common knowledge": the "Polish pogroms" had entered the realm of sturdy myth.

55. In his *The Economic Consequences of the Peace* (New York, 1920), 291.

56. Władysław Skrzyński to Polish Legation, Washington, October 3, 1919, Ambasada RP w Waszyngtonie, Archiwum Akt Nowych, Warsaw.

57. In AGND, Prince Kazimierz Lubomirski to Ministerstwo Spraw Zagranicznych, July 24, 1920, 68a/4428, October 13, 1920, 69b/5390, November 9, 1920, 70/5658, Major Kazimierz Mach to Naczelne Dowództwo, January 9, 1921, 72b/6631; *New York Times*, 28 June 1925.

Chapter 4

The Socialist Imprint on International Relations in Interwar Europe

William L. Blackwood

In the middle of October 1925, the world's attention abruptly turned to the town of Locarno, a small resort off the beaten track in southeastern Switzerland. The foreign ministers of the major states of Europe had selected this unlikely spot to finalize an agreement on Germany's borders. The fact that it took place in an obscure venue with limited hotel space and inadequate telephone connections did not prevent the Locarno conference, and the pact it produced, from becoming the media sensation of the year in international affairs. Overnight, a glamorous political counterpart was born to the notably less-hyped Dawes Plan of the previous April.

This American initiative had stabilized the Weimar Republic, Germany's first experiment in full-blown parliamentarianism, by opening the spigot on short-term loans to the ailing German economy. The connection between Dawes and Locarno was an obvious one. Not unlike the Marshall Plan twenty-three years later, Wall Street's decision to take its investments where the Senate had earlier refused to extend political guarantees provided much-needed liquidity. In part, Dawes was a way to dispose of excess capital, but the more profound motive was the American financial community's concern about the link between German reparations, French payments on British loans, and British debts in the United States. Again, similar to the Marshall Plan's requirement that American aid be centrally distributed, the Dawes Plan required an intra-European agreement to regulate and restructure the reparations payments that had been imposed upon Germany at Versailles. With Dawes having thus laid the economic base, Locarno constituted the next, more expansive step in Germany's reintegration into the international system. Whereas Dawes has been posited on the notion that German economic well-being was indispensable, Locarno was rooted in the belief that long-term stability in Western Europe could and should be purchased at the price of recognizing Germany's right to redress the allegedly unjust territorial losses it had suffered in the east and at the end of the war. Driving this one-two combination in what socialists liked to call Europe's "pacification" was a new type of international political economy. Before 1918, it would have been unthinkable that German domestic stability could depend directly on the American bond markets. Right after 1918, it would have been perhaps more plausible, but nonetheless difficult, to envision an attempt to treat defeated Germany as an equal at the expense of the victorious and newly created states of Czechoslovakia and Poland. Developments during the immediate postwar years had changed all of this. One of the critical, though largely ignored, causal factors in this change was European socialism, the same political force that had traditionally devoted the most time and energy to theorizing about the interrelationship between politics and economics.

The immediate background to the Dawes-Locarno package was the unrest that had afflicted Germany ever since the November revolution of 1918. The German crisis had intensified in early 1923, when Belgian and French troops marched across the Rhine into the Ruhr Valley in retaliation for Berlin's unilateral declaration of a reparations moratorium. Four years and a few months after the armistice, militarized foreign control of many of Germany's most important mines and heavy industries exacerbated even further the witch's brew of political violence, social protest, and hyperinflation that inflamed left- and right-wing extremism and threatened to shatter fragile German republicanism. Events such as the massacre of thirteen Krupp workers by French troops played into the hands of radical nationalists and communists alike. The communists' so-called Schlageter line, named after a right-wing German paramilitary executed by the French in the Ruhr, completed the circular connection between right- and left-wing extremism. In the words of Karl Radek, the tireless, multilingual revolutionary journeyman of the Communist International (Comintern), the Weimar Republic's confrontation with France in the Ruhr had transformed "nationalism, used earlier to strengthen the bourgeois governments," into "a means of intensifying the existing capitalist collapse."[1] The communist embrace of nationalism went hand in hand with an appeal for a broad united front "from below" of workers and the lower middle classes. With the specter of an extremist dictatorship in Germany looming large, Europe's socialists moved into the vanguard of the movement to save Europe by rescuing Germany. Discussions among the Belgian socialist leadership at the onset of the Ruhr crisis illustrated how ideology and pragmatic concerns created a rationale for sustaining and collaborating with German democracy. Belgium had a direct stake in reparations, and the still-fresh memory of the German military occupation stroked anti-Germany emotions. The Belgian socialists deemed German payments indispensable, albeit in a reduced amount. At

---

1. Heinrich A. Winkler, *Von der Revolution zur Stabilisierung. Arbeiter und Arbeiterbewegung in der Weimarer Republik 1918 bis 1924* (Berlin, 1985), 581.

the same time, they explicitly framed their discussion of how to go about extracting money from Germany in terms of the need to strengthen German socialism in the internationalist struggle against French "reaction," which, all European socialists argued, threatened to turn the Ruhr into a communist bastion and, for good measure, to wreck definitively the German economy. In Paris, the kind of reasoning gave rise to assertions that socialism's "subordination of national policies to the interests of the proletarian class" sought to undermine the defense of French national interests. Meanwhile, Belgian diplomatic traffic from Berlin made it clear that concern about German stability extended beyond socialist circles. Radek's activities in Germany were tracked closely and portrayed as an attempt to align Germany with Russia by harnessing German nationalism for cummunism.[2] Most socialists in Western Europe had looked askance at Czechoslovakia and Poland's acquisition of formerly Austrian and German territories and the end of World War I. With the fate of the Weimar Republic appearing to hang in the balance in early 1923, the pernicious ideological current flowing from Russia into Germany further strengthened the socialist inclination to deal with Germany at the expense of it immediate eastern neighbors.

By 1925, pro-German sentiments, justified and intensified by the desire to stabilize Europe, made for peculiar bedfellows. Viscount D'Abernon, the British ambassador to Berlin and one of Locarno's key behind the scene architects, explained why Locarno had been chosen over Geneva. As the seat of the League of Nations, the latter, and certainly not an unknown resort, was the most plausible site for grand, headline-capturing acts in the service of peace and mutual understanding. But, in the British aristocrat's opinion, the atmosphere in Geneva contained "too much Polish and Czecho-Slovakian perfume."[3] Distaste for the two successor states to Germany's east formed an important element of the vaunted Locarno spirit, though little evidence to this effect could be gleaned from prominent public statements. These were reflected by one of Locarno's most ardent German partisans and his invocation of "a new conception of the unity and friendship

2. 11, 12 and 30 January 1923 "Seance du Conseil General," in *Archief en Museum van de Socialistische Arbeidersbeweging* (Ghent). 1 June 1923 Berlin-Brussels "L'exécution de Schlageter," 30 June 1923 Berlin-Brussels "Déclarations de MM. Radek et Oustinoff," 22 August 1923 Berlin-Brussels "Le mouvment communiste allemand. Activité du communiste russe Radek," 20 September 1923 Berlin-Brussels "Le mouvment communiste en Allemagne. L'activité du communiste russe Radek," and 9 January 1924 Paris-Brussels "L'internationale at la politique intérieure francaise," *in Archives du Ministère des Affaires Étrangères de Belgique* (Brussels), Correspondance Politique Legations Allemagne, France.

3. Lord D'Abernon, *An Ambassador of Peace*, vol. 3 (London, 1930) 182.

4. Edgar Stern-Rubarth, *Three Men Tried ... Austen Chamberlain, Stresemann, Briand, and their Fight for a New Europe. A Personal Memoir* (London, 1939), 99.

of mankind."[4] The foreign ministers who were the principal signatories of the Locarno treaties—Aristide Briand of France, Austen Chamberlain of Great Britain, and Gustav Stresemann of Germany—jointly received the Noble Peace Prize in 1926, one year after Charles Dawes had gotten the award. As the very first statesmen to be so recognized for a collective effort to promote peace, this Franco-Anglo-German troika thus pioneered a tradition that is now commonplace. Numerous statements echoed the previously cited German paean, and the small Swiss town emerged from out of nowhere as the catchword for a new era in transnational cooperation. Following the disillusionment of the early postwar years, rhetoric reminiscent of Woodrow Wilson's earlier talk of "a war to end all wars" once again began to dominate public discussion about international relations in Europe. When applied retrospectively, this same logic portrayed Locarno as the best chance for avoiding what did indeed come to pass: a second world war.

One war and yet another division of Europe later, Locarno's twenty-fifth anniversary was a time for pondering what might have been. In 1950, Joseph Paul-Boncour, an independent socialist who had represented France at the League of Nations while working closely with Briand to promote Franco-German understanding, christened Locarno "the first tangible manifestation of the spirit of European Union." In an effort to link the past to the present, he conditioned West Germany's transformation into a responsible member of the community of nations on European unification. A further, if somewhat far-fetched contemporary twist on Locarno was to be found in Paul-Boncour's assertion that the principles driving European union also drove the Western commitment to the U.S.-led United Nations' defense of South Korea against invasion from communist North Korea. For his part, a German commemorator of Locarno's silver anniversary postulated that, had Stresemann been alive in 1950, "he and Winston Churchill would have fought side by side for the same lofty cause at the Strasbourg meeting of the Council of Europe." Instead, it fell to Chancellor Konrad Adenauer to make "the choice between East and West, between playing ball with the Soviets or becoming an integral part of a united Europe."[5] West Germany's quest for a usable history aside, Adenauer made for a rather peculiar Stresemann successor. The Catholic politician and lord mayor of Cologne who went on to become the founding father of the Federal Republic had not liked Stresemann, and he had not shared the latter's goals during the crisis year 1923. Nor was it the Christian Democrat Adenauer, but rather the leader of German socialism, Kurt Schumacher, who, after the Second World War, advocated a third path for Germany as part of a united Europe much closer in its underlying goals, if not its ideological

---

5. "Eine Gedenkfeier für den Pakt von Locarno," *Neue Züricher Zeitung,* 17 October 1950. Felix E. Hirsch, "Locarno—25 Years After," in *The Contemporary Review* 175 (Nov. 1950), 279–85.

packaging, to Churchillian conceptions than Adenauer's own nose-to-the-ground policies.

Back in the fall of 1925, the kind of unity for Western Europe supported by the United States twenty years later was nowhere to be had. This made the allusions swirling around the gathering in the remote corner of Switzerland that much more fantastic. The *Times* of London deemed Locarno, not Versailles, the "genuine Treaty of Peace," "a very great and liberating event" destined to be "a landmark in European history." In Paris, *Le Temps* paid homage to "an outstanding act in the development of European politics" that inspired joy "throughout the world, wherever people long for peace and dignified labour." In the bitterly divided journalistic landscape of Berlin, the middle-of-the-road *Vossische Zeitung* predicted that Locarno would enter the history books as the place "where nations ... succeeded in finally attaining real peace" by putting down a "milestone on the path to a closer union of the European states. "Germany's other major liberal daily, the *Frankfurter Zeitung,* hopped on the same bandwagon. It praised "a great historical fact" and "the ascendance of the European spirit." On the other side of the Atlantic, the *Chicago Daily Tribune* headline with the dramatic announcement, "Powers Due to Sign War Death Knell." Not to be outdone by its Midwestern rival, the *New York Times* presented its readers with an even more sensationalistic announcement: "France and Germany Bar War Forever." Manhattan's largest religious venue, the Cathedral of St. John the Divine, staged a "solemn service of thanksgiving for the signing of the treaties of Locarno." Among the assembled luminaries was Nicholas Murray Butler, the president of Columbia University, who spoke passionately in favor of greater American involvement in world affairs.[6]

In Moscow, Locarno sparked very different reactions. *Pravda* speculated about secret anti-Soviet clauses and delivered appropriate caricatures. One featured corpulent bourgeois statesmen leering and encircling a stalwart, lean, and determined German proletarian whose fists were clenched to resist capitalist encirclement. The Russian Communist Party paper embellished its thickly lettered announcement of "Germany's Capitulation at Locarno" with a cartoon featuring the predatory, beak-nosed, and self-satisfied British foreign minister as a schoolmaster. His monocle in place and dressed in a top hat and formal long coat with a whip at the ready behind the back, Austen Chamberlain was shown offering a "treat" to his "obedient boys." Decked out in schoolboy shorts, knee socks and suspenders, the quintessential Bürger-turned-national-leader Gustav Stresemann, with the no less bourgeois chancellor, Hans Luther, at his side, made for a

---

6. The *Times,* 16 October 1925; *Le Temps,* 16 and 17 October 1925; *Vossische Zeitung,* 16 and 17 October 1925; *Frankfurter Zeitung,* 16 October 1925; *Chicago Daily Tribune,* 16 October 1925; *New York Times,* 16 October and 14 December 1925.

belittled adolescent pair. For *Pravda,* they were supplicants to the scion of a British family whose path from provincial screw manufacturing into the upper reaches of social political power provided a ready-made scenario for communist scriptwriters, who no doubt understood that Locarno had dealt a serious blow to Soviet-German cooperation. The aura of peace, stability, and prosperity surrounding the Locarno spirit became that much more luminescent thanks to the belief that Locarno marked the implicit renunciation of the Rapallo Treaty, signed by Weimar Germany and Soviet Russia in 1922. When processed by *The New York Times'* word mill, the anti-Rapallo motif yielded a formulaic verdict: "Germany Turns From East to West, Western Europe Consolidates and Russia Is Excluded."[7] The new international political economy had given the paper of record in the rising center of global capitalism a common analytical language with European socialists.

Unlike the "profound joy," "universal satisfaction," and "feeling of relief" it occasioned in France, Locarno was a particularly troublesome development for the Second Polish Republic, whose appearance on the map had triggered border conflict with every single neighbor, including Germany and Russia. Having shed its status as a defeated outsider, Germany was now beginning to reassert itself with the connivance of the same great powers that had, with varying degrees of enthusiasm, been the patrons of Poland's rebirth. The ubiquitous praise lavished upon Locarno in the West camouflaged, or, as skeptics suspected, purposely obfuscated a cold, hard fact. Germany's western borders may have been stabilized; however, in the bargain, her eastern borders had been conspicuously demoted to a lesser status. This disparity between East and West led one commentator in Warsaw to wonder whether "Europe, having erected a new altar of peace," would, down the road, require "live sacrifices by those who are weakest." Another admitted that, while Locarno did not raise the specter of a new Polish partition right away, it did raise the threat of future German aggression against an isolated Poland. As a consequence, the seven-year-old state was left to contemplate "a dangerous future" made all the more uncertain by the realization that the vital Franco-Polish link had been attenuated.[8]

The other country potentially threatened by Locarno was Czechoslovakia. Like Poland, the First Czechoslovak Republic owed its existence to Germany's defeat and to the new state system sanctioned at the peace negotiations in the Parisian suburbs. The First Republic's borders owed their

---

7. *Pravda,* 15 and 18 October 1925; *New York Times,* 18 October 1925. Thanks to Ted R. Bromund for improving the characterization of Chamberlain.

8. 2 December 1925 Paris-Brussels "Le traité de Locarno et la France," in *AdMdAEdB,* Correspondance Politique Legations France. October 1925 Paris-Prague summary report, in *Archív Ministerva Zahraničních Věcí* (Prague), Politické zprávy, Paříž. 20 and 21 October 1925 *Kurier Warszawski.*

rather haphazard shape to the arbitrary combination of historical, economic, and strategic arguments. The new state they bounded provided the most spectacular example of developments in a region where, to quote a Czech socialist speaking in late 1918, "social demands" and "national questions" had to be addressed parallel to one another.

Although Polish statehood had much deeper historical roots than in the Czechoslovak case, this socialist assertion applied in equal measure to the Second Polish Republic. Both of these states were on the eastern side of the revolutionary fault line that ran through Europe at the onset of the interwar years. The widespread euphoria among all social classes unleashed by the proclamation of independent statehood set them apart from other states, such as France, Germany, Hungary, and Italy, where social radicalism fueled bitter class conflict that made national solidarity a thing of the past, and, in the eyes of many socialists whose heads were throbbing with the hangover left by the *Burgfriede* and the *Union sacrée,* a course of action best left in the past.[9]

Czechoslovakia and Poland both had ample reason to fear German territorial revisionism. In the Czech lands, the western border belt contained a compact German majority that, in 1918 and 1919, had made no bones about its desire to join with Germany. The presence of socialist-controlled cabinets in Berlin and Vienna had intensified this challenge to Czechoslovakia's integrity. Hope had been widespread among Czechoslovakia's German citizens that a Great German Socialist Republic would arise just as socialist support was surging in the territories which would become notorious in the Nazi era as the Sudetenland. In Poland, German irredentism did not pose a threat of the same magnitude. That being said, German designs on the Polish portion of the industrial region of Upper Silesia and the so-called corridor separating East Prussia from the Reich proper were well known. Despite these social, political, and strategic similarities, however, Prague and Warsaw's reactions to Locarno differed markedly.

Some red flags did go up in Czechoslovakia, which were similar in tone, if not effect, to the universally negative reactions in Poland. The main daily paper of the center-right Czechoslovak Agrarian Party, at the time a dominant member of the governing coalition and one of the pillars of "Czechoslovakism," characterized the cooperation between Germany and the West at Locarno as "a great danger" for "the eastern states" which, it

---

9. 19 February 1918 police report on meeting of Czechoslovak socialist leadership in Prague, in *Sborník dokumentů k vnitřnímu vývoji v českých zemích za 1. světové války* 1914–1918, v. 5 (Prague, 1997), 93–97. At the beginning of the First Republic, even centrist and right-of-center parties went out of their way to avoid the *bürgerlich* label. See Antonín Klimek, *Boj o Hrad. Hrad a Pětka /1918–1926/* (Prague, 1996), 26–27.

was predicted, could find themselves at a distinct disadvantage in future disputes with a strengthened and emboldened Germany. Yet the Czechoslovak envoy to the Polish capital had argued against cooperation between Prague and Warsaw when, in early 1925, he reported on the Pole's vehement rejection of the original German security proposals that set the Locarno train in motion. The Czechoslovak diplomat presented the Poles' reaction as a symptom of their endemic insecurity and thus as evidence of their inability to contribute to European understanding. This official interpretive slant proved to be in accord with the main current of opinion in Prague, where Locarno was seen as something that could be reconciled with the basic tenets of the First Republic's foreign policy. French diplomatic reporting from the Czechoslovak capital did take note of some criticism directed against Locarno, but, on the whole, it chronicled public approval that dovetailed neatly with official statements. The French legation in Warsaw, on the other hand, could hardly avoid the impression that the Poles were putting the best possible face on the bad hand dealt to them by others, a hand which, down the road, threatened to unmask the Franco-Polish alliance as a bluff.[10] Even though Czechoslovak diplomacy had strongly supported the Geneva Protocols, a collective security proposal floated in 1924 that would have gone a long way towards permanently stabilizing all of Europe's borders, Locarno was nonetheless deemed palatable in Prague. In Warsaw, Locarno, distasteful as it was, had to be digested regardless of the consequences, because there were no alternative dishes on the plate. Already viewed as obstreperous interlopers with a disturbing habit of bringing unreasonable demands to the international political game, the Poles simply could not afford to abandon the European kitchen on their own.

Taken together, the positive reactions throughout the West, the truculent response in Russia, the visceral rejection in Poland, and the instinctive accommodation in Czechoslovakia were emblematic of Germany's recovery from the defeat it had suffered in 1918. Together with the Dawes Plan, Locarno convinced many that Germany's reincorporation into the interna-

---

10. 14 October 1925 *Venkov*. February 1925 Warsaw-Prague summary report, in *AMZV*, Pz, Varšava. For a discussion of how Locarno fit into the overall contours of Czechoslovak foreign policy in the 1920s, see Frank Hadler, "Locarno im Blickwinkel tschechoslowakischer Aussenpolitik," Ralph Schattkowsky, ed., *Locarno und Osteuropa. Fragen eines europäischen Sicherheitssystems in den 20er Jahren* (Marburg, 1994), 147–53. For a comparison of Czechoslovak and Polish reactions to the genesis of a security arragement confined to the West, see Radko Břach, *Československo a Evropa v polovině dvacátých let* (Prague, 1996), 106–17. 21 October 1925 Prague-Paris "Commentaires de la presse tchécoslovaque au sujet de la Conférence de Locarno," and 23 October 1925 Warsaw-Paris "A/s Retour de M. Skrzynski Les Accords de Locarno et l'opinion polonaise," *In Archives Diplomatiques du Ministère des Affaires Etrangères* (Paris), Sous-série Grande Bretagne, vol. 85, 86.

tional system marked the end of a dangerous interlude in European politics. Locarnites ruled the day with their argument that the moment had come to end, once and for all, the Weimar Republic's internal chaos and to halt its vacillation between half-hearted reconciliation with the West and full-fledged rapprochement with Soviet Russia, the other traditional great power left outside by the Versailles system. Based as it was on Berlin's disavowal of an active eastern policy designed to deepen Russo-German relations, Locarno logic necessitated a quid pro quo that would give Germany something in exchange for concessions in the West on reparations and security. Thanks to the graphical talents of its caricaturists and the angular prose of its editorialists, *Pravda* did make for far livelier reading than its Western counterparts. But the Russian paper's talk of a German defeat in October 1925 missed the mark entirely. Locarno did not subordinate Germany to the West. It did create a new outlet for the projection of German power. With Locarno, a calculus was born that would subsequently define Germany's place in international relations well beyond the 1920s. Namely, how to use ties with the West, which ipso facto imposed certain limitations on German actions, to create opportunities in the East? Whether the issue at hand had to do with borders, as after 1918, or with the division of Germany itself, as after 1945, the problematic interaction between the, at least, superficially desirable "Europeanisation of the German question" and the much less salutary "Germanisation of the European question" became apparent for the first time at Locarno.[11]

Germany's signal diplomatic victory at Locarno leveraged security in the West into a sufficient down payment for the prospect of future territorial changes in the east. In the dry language of diplomacy, this exchange came in the form of a "Treaty of Mutual Guarantee" and "Arbitration Treaties." According to the former, all of the major Western powers—Germany, Belgium, France, Great Britain, and Italy—endorsed "the territorial status quo resulting from the frontiers between Germany and Belgium and between Germany and France and the inviolability of said frontiers as fixed by or in pursuance of the Treaty of peace signed at Versailles." Great Britain's direct participation as a guarantor was crucial. Envisioned by its constructors as the dam that would forever hold back the tides of the war in the West, Locarno left the Rhineland demilitarized, kept Germany disarmed, and forged the Anglo-French security link whose absence after 1918 had so perturbed Paris. But Locarno also protected Germany against another French invasion like the Ruhr occupation of 1923. The Anglo-French link, in other words, hardly came free of charge, since it was anything but a unilateral pledge by His Majesty's government to defend France against

---

11. For a discussion of post-1945 German policy in this light, see Timothy Garton Ash, *In Europe's Name. Germany and the Divided Continent* (New York, 1994), 19–27

future German aggression. The far-reaching implications of this fact all too easily went unnoticed amid the emphatic and florid appeals to peace and understanding. With the British guarantee applying equally to both sides of the Franco-German border, Locarno hamstrung France's ability to support Czechoslovakia and Poland, whether by direct action or through pressure backed by the implied threat of force. Meanwhile, Germany's eastern borders received no such multilateral recognition. At Locarno, Czechoslovakia and Poland had to make do with nonbinding, bilateral arbitration agreements with Germany, which, in theory, established the League of Nations as the default mechanism for the peaceful conclusion of territorial disputes that could not be resolved bilaterally. Locarno, in short, created "second-class borders," to use an oft-cited phrase coined by an Italian participant in the negotiations. Moreover, in no way did the "great and liberating event" announced by the *Times* eliminate the possibility of a future war between Germany and its eastern neighbors. Scenarios were thoroughly imaginable in which the League would or could not involve itself it conflict resolution. In fact, Europe would have come much closer to true socialist pacification had the collective security arrangement foreseen by the Geneva Protocols been enacted. Coming on top of the restriction imposed upon France's ability to project power eastward, and the nod given to German-dominated collective decision-making, the supplementary Franco-Czechoslovak and Franco-Polish treaties initialed at Locarno merely codified the creeping evisceration of the French eastern alliance system. No amount of wordplay could undo the fact that Locarno eclipsed the original French policy put in place after 1918. Hopes of containing Germany by binding France to the two strongest states to Germany's east began to dim in the fall of 1925, and Czechoslovakia and Poland's formal membership in the victors' camp of 1918 lost a great deal of its meaning.[12]

An imposing entourage of leading statesmen gathered in Locarno, where the world's press followed their every move as they strolled, hobnobbed, dined, had coffee, took tea, lingered over aperitifs on sunny verandas, and attended a party thrown on board a boat cruising scenic Lake Maggiore. Lady Chamberlain, whose social graces earned her much praise, organized the cruise to honor her husband, Austen's, birthday, which, it so happened, fell on the day that the accords were unveiled. Locarno was a fitting present

---

12. The Locarno Pact consisted of five separate documents: A "Treaty of Mutual Guarantee Between Germany, Belgium, France, Great Britain, and Italy"; two identical "Arbitration Conventions Between Germany and Belgium and Between Germany and France"; and two identical "Arbitration Treaties Between Germany and Poland and Between Germany and Czechoslovakia." For the text of these documents as well as of the supplementary Franco-Polish and Franco-Czechoslovak treaties, see William J. Newman, *The Balance of Power in the Interwar Years, 1919–1939* (New York, 1968), 205–27.

for the foreign minister of the state whose long-standing wariness of a continental commitment and deep suspicions of French hegemony had now gained the upper hand. Born amid the seamless interweaving of personal and official diplomacy in a sun-drenched setting full of good will, the Locarno spirit was the polar opposite of the grim, conflict-laden bickering and horse-trading in Paris in 1919. Only one socialist participated in this noteworthy enterprise: Emil Vandervelde, the foreign minister of Belgium and the leader of the Parti Ouvrier Belge (POB). In this respect, the caricaturists and editorialists of *Pravda* had gotten it right. Superficially, Locarno was indeed a bourgeois affair. But the socialist contribution to it was decisive. The parliamentary support given to the treaties by the opposition Sozialdemokratische Partei Deutschlands (SPD) guaranteed the Reichstag majority without which the treaties would not have been ratified in Berlin after the main right-wing party chose to bolt from the cabinet rather than to endorse Locarno. True to Radek's "Schlageter line," the entire German right, joined by the communists, condemned Locarno as a sellout, just as, earlier, the Nazis and the communists had castigated Dawes as an act of enslavement to foreign capital. A period of sustained cooperation between the French and German socialists had prepared the way for German socialism's decisive parliamentary intervention on behalf of Locarno. The SPD and the Section Française de l'Internationale ouvrière (SFIO) were the first major forces to break the ice between the two states that had spilled so much blood in the trenches of northern France. In the process, the speculation in Paris about socialism's intent to counter French nationalism with its own class-based foreign policy proved to be prophetic.

The Franco-German socialist collaboration was a sign of just how seriously socialists took developments like the Schlageter line. That being said, another, much weightier and largely ignored historical factor was also at work. In August 1914, the socialist International had collapsed ignominiously, when workers and their leaders all over Europe abandoned the red banner and embraced the national colors in an orgy of patriotism. While the International never became the alternative working-class parliament that many socialists had anticipated when surveying the effects of Europe's first protracted total war, the organization did provide an absolutely vital framework for the formulation and implementation of a specifically socialist approach to international relations. It was through the International that socialists first overcame the enmity induced by the war and then agreed on a common set of economic and political policies that contained all of the key elements subsequently brought to life by Dawes and Locarno. Before 1914, the best the International could hope to do was to act as a pressure group capable of coordinating actions among its member parties. After 1918, by way of contrast, the interparty contacts that the International promoted resonated in cabinets and foreign ministries. Total war had democratized European politics and elevated socialist influenced to a qualitatively new level. To be sure, Karl Kautsky's statement about "a revolutionary party that does not make revolution" and Eduard Bernstein's riposte that the "goal, whatever it may be, is nothing me, the movement is everything" continued to highlight the profound internal contradictions that plagued Marxism in its symbiotic relationship with the capitalist state. The most disastrous consequences of the chasm between theory and practice were to play themselves out in the domestic politics of Weimar Germany in the late 1920s. In international affairs, however, socialists found the going easier at a time when they were no longer merely the passive observers and rhetorical critics of official policies that they had been earlier. In 1919, a Czech socialist marveled at the convocation of an international socialist conference on postwar reconstruction in a Swiss spa, this time Lucerne, where, across a lake, he could gaze at dwellings now occupied by exiled members of the former Habsburg ruling class. In 1923, German communists, hardly satisfied with seeing socialists supplant aristocrats, sought to discredit the socialist International by branding it an "International of ministers" and adorning factory walls with posters that listed the ministerial positions held by leading socialists from most of the major states of Europe. A prominent left-wing French professor and pundit scoffed "at the executive of the Second International, calling it the International Socialist Cabinet," since "all of its members were ministers, ex-ministers, or prospective ministers of State."[13] This is not to suggest that socialism dictated the course of European international relations. It is fair to say, however, that socialism played a decisive role in the selection of options. Without socialist support, there would have been no Locarno. With socialist support, a bona fide collective security arrangement would have stood a better chance of implementation. When what may aptly be deemed "the social democratic moment" dawned in Europe, socialism was ready to play a critical role in the selection of the former over the latter in a way that generated such great expectations and claims that then gave way to bittersweet speculation about lost opportunities.[14]

Franco-German socialist rapprochement within the International became the sine qua non of the change of course in official French policy towards Germany initiated by the Cartel des gauches in 1924. Although this salient

---

13. František Soukup, *Revoluce práce*, vol. 2 (Prague, 1938), 1363. Propaganda flier "to be posted in factories" entitled "Die Internationale der Minister" and listing forty-one prominent socialist politicians and the national offices held by them in Germany, Austria, Czechoslovakia, Belgium, Poland, France, Sweden, and Denmark, in 19 May 1923 *Die Rote Fahne*. Henry De Man, *The Psychology of Marxian Socialism* (New Brunswick, 1985), 312.

14. For a fresh discussion of socialism's place in interwar Europe, see Sheri Berman, *The Social Democratic Moment. Ideas and Politics in the Making of Interwar Europe* (Cambridge, 1998), which focuses on the German and Swedish cases.

fact went missing in the hagiographization of Locarno, and, later, in the historiography, a strong wind blowing from the left powered the sails that propelled the European states towards reconciliation in the West. The shift in course began in late 1923, when British elections paved the way for the first Labour cabinet. The British Labour Party's emphasis on collective security, combined with it's well-known abhorrence of French imperialism and its oftstated belief that Versailles required revision, favored Germany and put the nationalist government then running France on warning. The Czechoslovak ambassador to London believed that the Labour cabinet could count on the SFIO to apply pressure in Paris, and British Labour did put out the word that it intended to use the International to make headway, with a socialist response, to European instability. Joined by its French comrades, British Labour then pushed Dawes forward and seriously broached the collective security question.[15] Labour's brief rule overlapped with the left-wing triumph in French parliamentary elections in May 1924. For Adolf Müller, the SPD member who served as Berlin's ambassador to Switzerland and the League of Nations, the Cartel's triumph was a turning point in "the recovery of European politics," because of the "unmistakable shift to the left" that it denoted. Müller's Belgian counterpart in Paris predicted that the Cartel and the Labour government would create an "entente cordiale" with a dual aim: to resolve the reparations problem and to strike a political deal with Germany. After the Cartel's electoral victory, German diplomatic traffic from Brussels and London also saw a new phase in the offing in Franco-German relations, while the German embassy in the French capital produced a steady stream of reports anticipating the appearance of new methods in French foreign policy. The intersection between socialist postulates and state policies was evident in the Paris embassy's suggestion that Berlin should respond to the Cartel not by ratcheting up the anti-Versailles rhetoric, but rather by underscoring Germany's willingness to meet reformulated reparations demands as a prelude to addressing the real issue: security and borders.[16]

Following the left-wing victories in France and Great Britain, socialism's mantra-like goal of using international political and economic reconciliation to strengthen German democracy received a powerful boost in the

---

15. 10 December 1923 London-Prague report, in AMZV, Pz, Londýn. 19 December 1923 London-Brussels "Politique Anglaise-Elections," in *AdMdAEdB*, Correspondance Politique Legations Grande Bretagne.

16. 12 May 1924 Bern-Berlin telegram, in *Politisches Archiv des Auswärtigen Amtes* (Bonn), Politische Abteilung II, Frankreich, Po 5, vol. 8. 13 May 1924 Paris-Brussels "Les elections du 11 mai," in *AdMdAEdB*, Correspondance Politique Legations France. 13 May 1924 Brussels-Berlin telegram, 14 May 1924 London-Berlin telegram, and 14, 15, and 22 May 1924 Paris-Berlin reports, in *PadAA*. PA II, Frankreich, Po 5, vol. 8.

German parliamentary elections of December 1924. At this juncture, German radicals of all stripes lost votes to the SPD and other parties committed to the "execution of the peace treaty and the Dawes plan." These elections swung the German political spectrum back from the turn it had taken the previous May, when the strong showing of nationalists, "supernationalists," and communists had produced a "debacle" for the SPD and an "incontestable success" for right-wing revanchism. The road to Locarno was marked with significant, interconnected shifts to the left in the politics and societies of the three major state actors. Socialism was now directly linked to official policies in a way that did not jibe well with orthodox Marxists precepts and which also could be exploited in the confrontation between the nationalist right and the internationalist left. Communists throughout Europe regularly accused socialism of having sold out to bourgeois politics. On the other hand, the German ambassador to London cautioned against excessive public support for the Labour government, lest British conservatives accuse the latter of "receiving instructions not only from Moscow, but also from Hamburg," the site of the interwar socialist International's rebirth.[17] Of all the major political actors in Europe, socialists worked the hardest to mold domestic and international politics into a cogent whole between the wars. In the mid-1920s, they could point to abundant evidence of success, as the parallel political developments in France, Germany, and Great Britain appeared to confirm the democratic left's indispensable role in creating a viable, self-reinforcing foundation for reconciliation rooted in the linkage between domestic and international politics.[18] All of the basic tenets underpinning Locarno politics were part of the socialist foreign policy consensus. The intent first put on prominent display at Locarno to bind Germany to European decision-making structures; the related talk of future European unification in conjunction with Locarno; the perceived severing of the Soviet-German link through Locarno;

---

17. 6 May and 11 December 1924 Berlin-Brussels "Elections allemandes," and 6 May 1924 Paris-Brussels "Les élections allemandes," in *AdMdAEdB*, Correspondance Politique Legations Allemagne, France. 20 December 1923 London-Berlin report, in *PadAA*, PA III, England, Po 5, vol. 3. The Labour government was forced to defend itself against accusations from the conservatives that membership in the Labour and Socialist International would infringe upon national sovereignty. See 8 February 1924 position paper from the Labour Party's Joint International Department, in *Public Records Office* (London) 30/69 (MacDonald Papers)/226. Similar concerns generated a much sharper rhetoric in Poland, where the right regularly condemned socialism as a tool of German imperialism. See the very vicious presentation of "facts and documents" by a right-wing politician, Stanisław Lańcucki, PPS *w służbie imperjalizmu Niemiec i Austrii* (Warsaw, 1922).

18. A very cursory indication of socialism's role in this regard can be taken from R. Břach, *Československo v polovině dvacátých* let. 11, and Peter Krüger, *Die Außenpolitik der Republik von Weimar* (Darmstadt, 1985), 239–40.

the implicit rejection of French imperialism at Locarno; the ambivalence towards Czechoslovakia and Poland officially sanctioned by Locarno; and, finally, the attendant differences between the two successor states' reactions to Locarno—all of these key features of Locarno politics were staple elements of the socialist International's approach to European affairs after 1918. It was precisely in the socialist milieu that they were first molded into a coherent policy that found expression at the state level only after socialists had put them into practice among themselves. It is not an exaggeration to say that German socialism's rapid rehabilitation within the International set the stage for Germany's rehabilitation as a great power.

Socialism's pro-German orientation extended back to the immediate postwar period and, indeed, back to the war itself. Already in February 1919, in Bern, Switzerland, the Second International had moved to put a working-class imprint on the pending peace negotiations that were about to ratify the territorial restructuring already under way in the region between Germany and Russia. Already before the West European socialists had buried their war hatchets, the International rejected Czechoslovakia's acquisition of the German-inhabited border areas of Bohemia and Moravia; the prohibition of an Austro-German union; and Poland's acquisition of an outlet to the Baltic. The International also questioned the incorporation of the entire Prussian partition the Polish state as well as the proposed division of the industrially developed region of Upper Silesia between Germany and Poland.[19] In Czechoslovakia and Poland, these territorial changes were widely viewed as a logical consequence of the collapse of multinational rule and as a historical necessity after Germany's blatant bid for imperial domination over Eastern Europe during the war. Doubly disturbing from the Czechoslovak and Polish socialist standpoint was the fact that the International's pro-German territorial postulates of 1919 glibly passed over the wartime record of the majority of Austrian and German socialists, who had embraced Mitteleuropa schemes and their goal of a large, autarchic economic entity that would be forever secure against British-led encirclement.[20] Making matters even worse was the awareness that Germany's

---

19. For the text of the International's territorial resolution adopted at Bern, see "Allgemeine Resolution die territorialen Fragen betreffend, "in Gerhard Ritter, ed., *Die II. Internationale 1918/1919. Protokolle, Berichte und Korrespondenzen* (Berlin, 1980), vol. 1, 343–48. The International did not specify its territorial program in more detail until April 1919, when its Permanent Commission convened in Amsterdam to offer formal socialist counterproposals to the peace treaties. See "Resolution über die Österreichischen Länder" and "Resolution über die deutschpolnischen Grenzfragen," both of which drew heavily on proposals submitted by the Austrian and German socialists, in ibid., vol. 1, 600–601.

20. For a recent study of a well-examined topic which emphasizes that the SPD's war-time thinking about the east began and stopped with its deeply rooted hostility

military control over the "lands in between" had actually peaked just months before the armistice. At this juncture, with German war aims in the east sewed up, the imperial German government had seized on an attempt to rejuvenate the International at Stockholm in 1917 as an opportunity to weaken the Allied war effort. The Czech and Polish socialists had, for their part, sought to use Stockholm as a forum for advancing their own national aims, which received very short shrift among their European comrades, who were fixated on halting the war in the West. Raising certain parallels to Lenin's trip in the opposite direction in a sealed train provided by the German government, after the armistice, European socialism's pro-German proclivities made an effortless journey from Sweden to Switzerland thanks to the deeply ingrained inability to come to terms with the very un-Marxist confluence of national and social revolution among previously stateless nations.

An official British report on the Bern conference recorded that the Labour Party worked hard to build a "golden bridge for the Germans and played into their hands." Moreover, the "majority of delegates listened to speeches of representatives from Poland, etc. with obvious impatience, thereby showing that in their view the question of nationalities is inconvenient as tending to hamper reconstitution of the Internationale."[21] The bridge put up in early 1919 was far from complete. Nor did it lead to an immediately discernible goal. It did, however, point in a direction that, once Franco-German cooperation had created a stable foundation, would have both Dawes and Locarno as way stations. Right after the war, animosities between French and Belgian socialists and their German comrades were too great to permit reconciliation in the West. The right wing of the already seriously divided SFIO was bent on indicting German socialism for its wartime policies and sought to wrest an open admission of war guilt from its German comrades. For its part, the POB did not go to Bern when it became apparent that its members could not stomach the prospect of a reconstructed International that would include the German socialists.[22] The tactlessness and intransigence displayed at Bern by the majority of German socialists proved that

---

towards Russia, see Jürgen Zarusky, *Die deutsche Sozialdwmokratie und das sowjetische Modell* (Munich, 1992), 25. The point to be made here is that the SPD did formulate and pursue a clear conception of foreign affairs in the 1920s.

21. 8 February 1919 Bern-London report, PRO, Foreign Office 371/4309.

22. For reports on the Belgium party's decision to abstain from the Bern conference which emphasize Belgian workers' anti-German attitudes, see 5 February 1919 Brussels-Paris "Conference Internationale de Berne. Abstention Belge," in *AddMdAE*, Europe 1918–1940, Sous-série Internationale, v. 395, and the 4 February 1919 Bern-London report, in *PRO, FO* 371/4309. As these reports make clear, party elites invariably attached more significance to the International than did the rank-and-file. The Belgian leadership supported the attempt to revive the International with the Germans from the beginning.

they were unable at this point to draw the requisite conclusions from their state's weakened position. Despite these conflicts, however, both Belgian and French diplomatic reporting spoke of a prevailing "German atmosphere" at Bern. This recognition of socialism's commitment to reconciliation was qualified by the observation that, on the whole, the International was "ententophile" and "sympathetic to the entente." These official assessments from the two states with the greatest interest in seeing Germany weakened and forced to pay for wartime ravages reflected the Western socialists' unwillingness to make concessions on the war-guilt determination and the reparations' demands that went with it, as well as their unconditional support for French sovereignty over Alsace and Lorraine.[23] The real territorial decisions taken at Bern indicated, however, that the eastern questions belonged to a different category, and it was here that Bern's "German atmosphere" made itself felt in a tangible way. As far as the East was concerned, there could be little question that socialism provided a much more favorable audience for German grievances than any other forum available at the time. In his analysis of Bern, the Austrian ambassador to Switzerland opined that Europe's socialists treated their counterparts "from the defeated countries as domestic political victors" and regarded "the socialists from the Entente states as fallen giants." In the immediate aftermath of the war, German socialism's reputation was tarnished even among those parties that shared the SPD's aversion to communism and saw a strong German socialist movement as a necessary ally in the struggle against the further spread of the radical virus. The SPD's standing was certainly at a nadir among those socialists who cited the German party's recent history as justification for a left-wing brand of socialism, if not communism. However, because of its assumption of state power, the SPD's prestige was intact and even enhanced where it mattered most, among European socialist leaders deeply concerned about the consequences of national and social protest and economic implosion in Germany.[24] German diplomats recognized the

23. 27 January 1919 Bern-Paris "La Conference socialiste internationale de Berne," and 14 February 1919 "Le Congres de Berne (Remarques et impressions)," in *AddMdAE*, Europe 1918–1940, Sous-série: Internationale, v. 395. 21 February 1919 Bern Brussels "Conférence Internationale ouvière et socialiste de Berne, "and February 1919 "Le Congrès International socialiste de Berne (Remarques et impressions)," in *AdMdAEdB*, file 10.813.

24. 20 February 1919 Bern-Vienna "Die politischen Konsequenzen der Intern. Sozialistenkonferenz in Bern," in *Archiv der Republik* (Vienna), Neues Politisches Archiv, box 686. Correspondence between Friedrich Ebert, the trained harnessmaker elected Weimar's first president in 1919, and Scandinavian socialists illustrates the advantages to be had from the advent of republicanism in Germany and the deep fear of German extremism. The SPD was encouraged to act decisively against all forces "whose activity is a crime against the working class and the revolution." The intensity of the SPD's rejection of Versailles gave rise to concerns that

opportunities for pro-German propaganda in the socialist milieu, and during the Paris peace negotiations they expressed displeasure with what they saw as the German socialists' inability to exploit successfully the International's criticism of the peace treaties. As had become apparent at Bern, this criticism had one overpowering focus: Germany's territorial losses in the east.[25]

Notwithstanding such negative assessments of German socialism's international activities, the first major breakthrough for the German cause within the International was not long in coming, and it preceded by several years any comparable breakthrough for German diplomacy. In late July 1920, the International convened a meeting in Geneva. This second significant socialist gathering in Switzerland took place a little more than one year after Versailles and with the acrid smoke from the France-Belgo-German fireworks at Bern still lingering in the air. Blazing a trail that states would later follow, the Geneva conference rehabilitated the SPD. With the Belgians in attendance, but with the SFIO absent because of its drift to the left, the Germans deployed a notable set of interconnected arguments to dispose of the thorny war-guilt matter once and for all. Failure in the struggle against German "militarism" and "imperialism" was openly recognized. This, however, was anything but an unconditional, no-strings-attached admission of guilt on the SPD's part, since it was simultaneously established that the German revolution had taken place "five years too late." By

---

a continued Allied blockade and possible military occupation would further intensify extremism in Germany. Instead of rejecting the peace settlement, the SPD was advised to accept it, with the understanding that "the peace treaty does not need to be viewed as something permanent." In response, Ebert established that "the Versailles conditions with their economic and political impossibilities are the greatest enemy of German democracy and the strongest impetus for communism and nationalism." See 27 December 1918, 23 May 1919 Stauning-Ebert letters, and 16 April 1920 Ebert-Branting letter, in Agnes Blänsdorf, "Friedrich Ebert und die Internationale," in *Archiv für Sozialgeschichte* 9 (1969), 420–26.

25. 2 May 1919 The Hague-Berlin "Schulßbericht" and the attached internal memo, in *PadAA*, Europa Generalia, Arbeiter- und Sozialistenkongresse, vol. 12. Several records in this file document German diplomats' desire to use the International to influence the peace negotiations as well as frustration with the SPD and USPD, both of which were quite busy at the time trying to govern the state and quell internal unrest. See also the 19 April and 23 July 1919 The Hague-Berlin reports, in *Bundesarchiv* (Koblenz), Akten Alte Reichskanzlei, R43I/2677. The latter, especially "Ausführungen Huysmans über die Stellungnahme der Internationale zu Deutschland," show German diplomats serving as intermediaries between the International and the German socialists, whom the International's secretariat implored to become more active in the organization in order to counteract anti-German sentiments by driving home to the Western comrades the magnitude of Germany's "republican" transformation.

implication, therefore, the creation of a "republican Germany" had eliminated the root cause of German aggression. In a reversal from the stance
taken at Bern, the SPD now went out of its way to establish that the "Alsace-
Lorraine question no longer exists for Germany." As further evidence of
the changes in Germany, the SPD offered a denunciation of the imperial
government's violation of Belgian neutrality and the German occupation in
that country. Finally, the German party recognized the validity of reparations designed to "make good the consequences of the attack that Imperial
Germany had undertaken" on Belgium and France. Once German socialism had established the necessary parameters, the International endorsed
the outlines of a territorial and economic understanding confined to the
west and predicated on the belief that republicanism had erected a firewall
against future German revanchism, with the SPD functioning as the necessary brick in the wall. Reconciliation and stabilization thus necessitated
the strongest possible position for socialism within Germany. From here, it
was not far to the supposition that concessions to Germany in the east
could help defang German nationalism and, in the process, strengthen German socialism and, hence, German republicanism. True to this
conceptualization of European reconstruction, the International responded
to the SPD's Geneva pronouncements by passing a resolution against the
"one-sided" aspects of Versailles that posed "a hindrance to the creation of
a lasting, final peace."[26]

Official Belgian and French reporting on the Geneva conference focused
inordinately on the SPD's acceptance of reparations and its renunciation of
Germany's claim to Alsace-Lorraine. The German party's favorable response
to the political and economic questions that directly affected the West over-
shadowed the International's endorsement of a far-reaching political revision of Versailles in Germany's favor. The representatives of the tiny, right-
wing Parti Socialiste Française who attended the Geneva conference were
credited with a "patriotic" stance that "always sought to defend the
country's interests." Almost identical comments were made about the POB's
role at Geneva, as the Belgian socialists' earlier anti-German line passed
into oblivion.[27] Seen through theoretical lenses, the most notable feature of
the Geneva conference was the formal division between right- and left-

---

26. For the text of the resolution on the war guilt question and the text of the
accompanying resolution on the peace treaty and the League of Nations, see *Bericht
vom zehnten Internationalen Sozialistenkongress in Genf 31. Juli bis 5.* August
1920 (Berlin, 1979), 10–11, 19–22.

27. 3 August 1920 Geneva-Paris "A.s. Congrès de la IIe. Internationale," and 7
August 1920 Sûreté (renseignement de Suisse) "A.s. les délégués francais au Congrès
de la IIème Internationale qui tenir à Geneve," in *AddMdAE*, Europe 1918–1940,
Sous-série: Internationale, vol. 379. 3 August 1920 Bern-Brussels "Le Congrès
socialiste de la 2e Internationale à Genève, "*AdMdAEdB*, file 10.813.

wing socialist parties that took place when the latter refused to attend. But the real division at Geneva had to do with national, not theoretical issues. If anything, a meeting dominated by British Labour and the SPD facilitated far-reaching political decisions to Germany's advantage. When the International renewed its condemnation of Versailles' eastern clauses in the summer of 1920, it reiterated the earlier Bern resolutions in a setting free of divisive discussions about bolshevism that made it that much easier to take a practical, international political issues. The Belgians' active participation in the Geneva conference provided further evidence of this shift away from theoretical hairsplitting and towards ideology as a framework for international agreements. Coming so soon after the POB's refusal to meet with the SPD and deemed a positive step in the official sources that stressed the pursuit of state interests, the Belgian presence at Geneva was a harbinger of further developments to come.

The hapless position of the Polish Socialist Party (PPS) at the Geneva conference illustrated the hierarchy of national interests that grew out of the socialist commitment to stabilize Western Europe. While socialists deliberated in Geneva, the newborn Polish state confronted a Russian invasion that brought Tukhachevsky's troops to the gates of Warsaw in a bid to put Trotsky's theory of permanent revolution into practice. All the while, socialists and their affiliated trade unions throughout Europe were active in efforts to block the shipment of arms and ammunition to Poland, which they invariably portrayed as a lackey of France. Class-based opposition to international reaction mixed with sympathy for bolshevism, which many workers in the West viewed as a genuine revolutionary force. Instead of an ideological struggle, the Russo-Polish war was, in the first instance, a national conflict that illustrated how working-class ideology could forge a hierarchy of national, state-based interests. Meeting for the first time since the creation of Czechoslovakia, Czech and Sudeten-German socialists resolved to put aside their nationalist bickering for the sake of the proletarian "struggle against the enemies of Soviet Russia," meaning, first and foremost, France and Poland. The British legation in Warsaw forwarded to London a copy of the PPS's July 1920 appeal for aid, "To All the Socialist and Labour Organizations in the World." The document was annotated with the comment, "I can't imagine it could produce much impression." With his state perilously close to extinction, a Polish socialist stood before the Geneva Conference and made a scathing reference to the International's condemnation of the "one-sided" Versailles system by accusing the organization "of being just as one-sided as the communist Third International." Upon returning to Warsaw, the second Polish delegate to Geneva, Mieczysław Niedziałkowski, the PPS's foreign policy expert who would later perish in a forest outside of Warsaw with a German bullet in his brain, published a critical appraisal of the International entitled "Under Western Eyes—the Polish Question at the Geneva Congress of the International."

The first part of the title came from a Joseph Conrad novel about alienated and isolated members of the Russian revolutionary intelligentsia leading hopeless, abject lives in turn-of-the-century Geneva. Having emerged as the party with the most at stake in the International's differentiation between Western and Eastern Europe, the PPS was giving expression to its own alienation. A Polish socialist dispatched to Rome filed a series of reports in which she emphasized time and again how low Poland's reputation in working-class circles had plummeted because of its armed conflicts with Germany and Russia. PPS envoys sent to London during the same period encountered a torrent of negative assertions from their British comrades, who associated Poland with Western imperialism and anti-Semitism. By succumbing to nationalism, the British Labourites suggested, the PPS had sacrificed its socialist identity. The British audiences had a poor understanding of the nationality of the nationality and political problems in such regions as the vast Russo-Polish borderlands and Upper Silesia. Similarly, a Polish socialist sent to Paris as part of the same outreach effort to the West bemoaned the SFIO's lack of "knowledge about Poland's internal conditions and its international aims."[28]

The clouds casting a shadow over socialist understanding in the West dissipated at Geneva. Shortly thereafter, they broke entirely with the unfolding of a chain of events that culminated in German dominance over European socialism where it mattered most: international relations. In the fall of 1921, the International denounced the division of Upper Silesia's industrial core between Germany and Poland. "Both from the point of view of the political settlement of Europe and of the present industrial distress," the region's partition was deemed "ill-advised." This typically pro-German interpretation of the relationship between economics and politics was given the appropriate ideological spin in the form of a protest against "such problems as this being settled in the interests of capitalist exploitation and in exactly the same frame of mind as the one that animated diplomatists before the war, a frame of mind which regards people as being pawns in imperialist games and produces profit on great financial

---

28. Updated transcript from a summer 1920meeting in the editorial offices of the Czechoslovak party paper, *Právo lido, in Archív Československé Sociální Demokracie* (Prague), fond 70/186. 16 July 1920 Warsaw-London report, in PRO, FO 371/3915. Kazimierz Czapiński's statement in *Bericht vom zehnten Internationalen Sozialistenkongreß*, p. 16. Mieczysław Niedziałkowski, "Woczach zachodu- sprawa polska na kongresie genewskim," in 20 August 1920 *Robotnik*. For reports on the PPS delegation in London, see *Hoover Institution* (Stanford), Poland, Ambasada Great Britain, box 106/3. PPS reports from Italy and several Polish articles submitted to *Avanti* are contained in *Archiwum Akt Nowych* (Warsaw), Archiwum Polskiej Partii Socjalistycznej 305/VI/41, 42. The attitudes in the SFIO are described in Herman Lieberman, *Pamiętniki* (Warsaw, 1996), 160.

interests." After the Ruhr, Upper Silesia was Germany's second-most important coal and steel reservoir. The International's demand that the entire region remain with Germany reflected the SPD's contention that German industrial capacity had to be preserved, if the Weimar Republic was to meet the reparation demands whose legitimacy the German socialists had just recognized at Geneva.[29] Keeping all of Upper Silesia within Germany was tantamount to ignoring the Polish national awakening that had taken place in the region during the latter part of the nineteenth century. This had been a strongly working-class national awakening that demonstrated beyond a shadow of a doubt how the social conflicts produced by capitalist change actually enhanced, not diminished, nationalism. As a political and economic question directly related to postwar reconstruction, Upper Silesia also offered the SPD its first opportunity to advance the amorphous program of a "United States of Europe" as the purported solution to Europe's ills. Acting as reporteur at the launching of a new body, the socialist interparliamentary committee, the SPD leader Otto Wels asserted that "the great European questions like the great socialist questions can to-day solved on an international basis only. To the questions of nationalities, the question of Austria, Upper Silesia . . . to the question of disarmament, of finance, of economic reconstruction there is but one answer. That answer is: the United States of Europe." The SPD's appeal for a united Europe went hand in hand with a proposed redefinition of working-class internationalism. German concerns and German policies dictated that, in lieu of "theoretical combinations," the International's activities should reflect "a calculation of the actual factors of power." Otherwise, Wels ventured, the International would find itself "all too soon ship-wrecked on the rock of fact."[30]

Like the earlier dismissal at Geneva of the war guilt issue in the push to achieve reconciliation in the West, the interparliamentary committee was

---

29. 24 October 1921 declaration by executive of the Second International, in *International Institute for Social History* (Amsterdam), Labour and Socialist International, file 85. For a representative argument about the significance of German control over all of Upper Silesia for "Europe's reconstruction" containing a strong dose of German cultural chauvinism, see the 1921 statement "Die Unteilbarkeit Oberschslesiens," *in Historische Kommission zu Berlin*, Allgemeiner Deutscher Gewerkschaftsbund Rest-Akten, NB 146. For a direct argument about Upper Silesia's vital place in German industrial production and thus its importance for German reparation payments to France, see Carl Legien's 27 November 1921 presentation to the extraordinary trade union congress in London, in ibid., NB 175. This presentation contains numerous statements about the "psychological" impact of the draconian peace on a German working class committed to friendship with France but increasingly desensitized to "bolshevism, imperialism, or other isms" because of the precipitous drop in living standards.

30. 27 June 1921 executive meeting, in IISH, LSI, file 3.

created at German initiative (with British support). It was tasked with ham-
mering out pragmatic positions around which the considerable number of
votes that socialists wielded in Europe's legislatures could be mobilized.
This novel form of socialist cooperation had one overriding purpose: to
influence international relations. Just as the SPD was molding the International into an effective foreign-policy instrument, the Polish Socialist Party
took the unprecedented step of abandoning the organization, thereby em-
barking on a two-year journey through internationalist limbo. The Polish
party's leadership was forced into this dramatic step by a rank and file
incensed over what it saw as the International's uncritical embrace of German socialism. Conditioned by the growing East-West divide within European socialism, the Polish revolt against the International had an entirely
different outcome than the Belgian workers' rejection of cooperation with
the SPD back in early 1919. Projected onto a Marxist mirror, the Poles'
utter isolation within the European socialist community was the invented
and distorted opposite of the Belgians' pragmatically driven return to the
International at Geneva.[31] The Comintern's pithy political intelligence service recorded that "the 'so-called' socialist Party" of Poland had been exiled from a working-class movement that brought together "even the German social patriots with the English, French and Belgian warmongers."
The Polish socialists' predicament was not ideological, let alone theoretical
in nature. Instead, it was the product of national differences. While ideology and theory dictated that these differences be expressed in such stock
phrases as "social imperialism," it was the International's role as a medium
for state conflict that gave them their real meaning.[32]

---

31. Adam Pragier offers a description of the revolt in his memoirs. Like many
Polish socialists who knew Germany much better than most of their Western comrades, Pragier was skeptical of the SPD's commitment to revolutionary transformation in 1918/19. He had sat at the table in the Reichstag that Philipp Scheidemann
had used to stand on when addressing the masses to whom he spontaneously announced the Republic's creation. Shortly after the Reich government's illegal coup
against the SPD-dominated Prussian government in the summer of 1932, a critical
step on the way to the Nazi dictatorship, Pragier traveled to Berlin. Friedrich Stampfer,
the editor of *Vorwärts*, explained away the SPD's passivity towards the coup with
references to the need to preserve the imposing socialist infrastructure. One suspects that the implications of German socialism's "Verbonzung, Verkalkung, and
Verbürgerlichung" for the Polish state, combined with their unusually extensive
experience in Germany, made the International's uncritical embrace of German republicanism that much more difficult for Polish socialists to swallow. See A. Pragier,
Czas prezeszły dokonany (London, 1966), 214–17, 452–73.
    32. 31 December 1921 Berlin-Moscow "Bericht über die Internationale 2 u. 2 1/
2 ," in *Rossiiski Tsentr Khranenia I Izuchenia Dokumentov Noveishei Istorii*
(Moshow), fond 495 (Comintern Archives), op. 1, d. 10.

Not that theory was irrelevant. In the case of Upper Silesia, Marxism's systemic disregard for nationalism and its related subordination of national interests to the greater, "revolutionary" good contributed directly to the International's embrace of German postulates. But, especially as it applied to the German question after 1918, socialist theory was anything but a rigid construct.[33] The malleability of theory had been demonstrated by the SPD's ability to reap the benefits of internationalist inhibitions about dividing Upper Silesia while, at the same time, advancing its own recalibration of internationalism that downplayed abstractions and emphasized practicality. The Germans did play a leading role in the theoretical debates that swept through European socialism as it grappled with the swelling wave of postwar radicalization. The most significant impact of these debates, however, occurred outside the realm of pure theory, because, more than anything else, the brief rise of left-wing socialism facilitated further the International's adoption of a pro-German course in international relations. Between 1921 and 1923, controversies over revolution, state power, class conflict, and socialist wartime policies divided Europe's socialists between the Second International and a rival organization known as the Vienna Union, sarcastically labeled the Second-and-a-Half International by the ever sharp-tongued Karl Radek. On the surface, this intrasocialist split represented a direct continuation of the wartime fracturing and thus functioned as a further symptom of mainstream socialism's inability to staunch the flow of workers to the left. The Vienna Union attempted to tread the ideological middle ground between communism and socialism. As its official English designation indicated, the organization was Austro-Marxist in orientation. During the flux and instability of the immediate postwar years, left-wing socialism was especially attractive to those parties which, like the SFIO and Italians, confronted substantial radicalization in their mass base, or which, like the German socialists in Czechoslovakia, latched onto Austro-Marxism as a vehicle for promoting national autonomy. Yet as a source of practical prescriptions for Europe's postwar problems, the Vienna Union proved to be a complete bust. Stated differently, it had little relevance for a

---

33. One of the best, and only, studies of Marxist theory and its impact on German foreign policy in the Weimar period is Hans Rothfels, "Marxismus und auswärtige Politik," in Paul Wentzcke, ed., *Deutscher Staat und deutsche Parteien. Beiträge zur deutschen Partei- und Ideengeschichte* (Munich, 1922), 308–41. Rothfels emphasizes several things worth noting. He argues that working-class internationalism provide "horizontal" linkages useful to the German state at a time when its power in the "vertically" ordered world of international relations has been reduced. He contends that the revolutionary changes of 1918 transformed foreign policy from a secondary field of socialist activity into one of its main focal points. And, finally, he takes not of "new and multifaceted connections between Marxist and national foreign policy."

policy aimed at securing "a revision of the peace treaties and the realization of the German point of view about reparations."[34] The Vienna Union's two-year existence did, however, overlap exactly with the period when French socialism grappled with two major internal problems: resistance to collaboration with the "social patriotic" SPD and the rise of a Communist Party that, initially, siphoned off the majority of the SFIO's following. In addition to bearing the jackal's mark of German nationalism, the SPD was widely viewed as the standard bearer of right-wing Marxist socialism (the British Labour party did not even pretend to be a Marxist formation). At a time when it was difficult, if not impossible, for the SFIO to openly advocate cooperation with the SPD, the Vienna Union provided a means of maintaining contact between French and German socialism. The latter was represented by the left-wing Unabhängige Sozialdemokratische Partei Deutschlands (USPD), which fulfilled an important, though largely unrecognized, external role. Much more than the SPD, which was stained by its vote for war credits and its sustained support for the German war effort, the independents, which had adopted their name when they had split off from the majority socialists over the war, were seen as legitimate and sincere advocates of reconciliation.[35] While using left-wing ideology to pro-

---

34. 28 February 1921 Vienna-Berlin "Stellungnahme zur Revision der Friedensverträge und zur Wiedergutmachungsfrage," in *PadAA*, PA II, Po 19, vol. 1. Reflecting the concern about radicalization among state-oriented socialists, the long-winded attempts to navigate between bolshevism and "social patriotism" left a broad paper trail in foreign ministries from Warsaw, Vienna, Berlin, Prague, Brussels, Paris, and on to London. The Austro-Marxist connection was not highlighted in the Vienna Union's German designation, Internationale Arbeitsgemeinschaft Sozialistischer Parteien.

35. The SFIO-USPD contacts received favorable coverage at the Quai d'Orsay. See 15 June 1920 Berlin-Paris "Les socialistes allemands et les négociations économiques franco allemandes," and 26 October 1920 Berlin-Paris "Socialistes francaise et socialistes allemands," in *AddMdAE,* Europe 1918–1940, Sous-série: Internationale, vol. 318. French diplomatic reporting portrayed the USPD as the most promising socialist option in Germany, free of excessive nationalism, led by the most intellectually sophisticated politicians, and willing to draw the necessary conclusions from the imperial regime's militaristic excesses and their consequences. Once the SPD and USPD reunited in 1922, French diplomats could only hope that the USPD leadership, which had lost its mass base to the communists, would play a disproportionate role in the new party. See 17 January 1920 Berlin-Paris "Efforts pour la formation d'un nouveau parti socialiste," 25 March 1920 Berlin-Paris "Notice sur les parties de gauche," 27 September 1921 Berlin-Paris "La politique étrangère au Congrés de Goerlitz," and 27 September 1922 Berlin-Paris "Unification socialiste," in AddMdAE, Europe 1918–1940, Sous-série: Internationale, vol. 318, 319. A detailed, official Polish overview of German socialism and communism from the same period is bereft of any suggestion that the Weimar left could, in any way, serve Polish interests. And things only got worse as the interwar period progressed.

mote Franco-German understanding, the Vienna Union also kept the East-West division in the International alive by turning down Polish socialism's request for membership. Employing the same basic theoretical categories that it applied to the SPD and right-wing socialism in general, the Vienna Union condemned the Poles for their "social imperialism." Not surprisingly, this rebuff gave rise to doubts in the Polish Socialist Party about the political legitimacy of any kind of working-class internationalism.[36]

Joined by their trade union counterparts from the International Federation of Trade Unions, socialists from the two competing Internationals began to hammer out the principles that later found their way into the Dawes Plan.[37] Once the Franco-Belgian occupation of the Ruhr kicked socialist diplomacy into high gear, this same pattern repeated itself, although now socialist contacts were driven primarily by political concerns. With the SPD issuing numerous statements and communications tailored to nurture the fear that the imminent collapse of a functioning German society would open the way for an extremist dictatorship, the SFIO made it clear that it wished to see the SPD exit the Ruhr crisis with its internal legitimacy intact. Referring to Berlin's policy of passive resistance to the Ruhr occupation and the economic collapse it accelerated, the same Alsatian socialist who had been one of the SPD's most vehement critics at Bern expressed the

---

In 1929, the Polish socialist leader Ignacy Daszyński was forced to admit vis-à-vis Marshal Piłsudski's chief aid that Léon Blum was spending a conspicuous amount of time in the German embassy in Paris. Then, in 1931, the Polish foreign ministry complied a thick dossier on Emil Vandervelde's public suggestion that the German-Polish borders required revision. 6 April 1921 Berlin-Warsaw "Socjaliści i komuniści niemieccy," in AAN, Ministerstwo Spraw Zagranicznych, Ambasada Londyn, file 70. Kaziminerz Świtalski, *Diariusz* 1919–1935 (Warsaw, 1992), pp. 466–67. "Deklaracje Przedstawicieli II. Międzynarodówki w sprawie Rewizji Granic (Vandervelde)," in AAN, MSZ, file 3581. 21 June 1929 "Visite en Pologne des leaders de la IIe Internationale," and 28 February 1931 Warsaw-Brussels "La Pologne contre la revision des traits," in AdMdAEdB, Correspondance Politique Legations Pologne.

36. W. T-ski., "Jeszcze o odbudowie Międzynarodówki," in September 1921 *Trybuna* (3:37). This journal was the PPS's sole theoretical publication, and it would soon close for financial reasons. The Czechoslovak Social Democratic Labour Party, by way of contrast, maintained as many as three major journals during the First Republic.

37. The first such meeting was held in March 1921 as a gathering of the Second International's executive committee and "parliamentary groups." It brought together the SPD, the British Labour Party, the Belgian Labour Party, and the irrelevant Parti Socialiste Française. In July 1922, however, the second reparations conference brought the SFIO into direct contact with the SPD under the aegis of a meeting between the Second International, the Vienna Union, and the International Federation of Trade Unions. See the transcripts in *IISH, LSI, files 2 and 44.*

French socialists' hope that the German government would "compromise itself to such an extent that at the psychological moment the Socialists would be in a position to give the 'coup de grâce' to the Capitalist Government, and thus be able to assure France that the nationalist danger in Germany had received the death blow." Of course, the SFIO leader also put his finger on the same dynamic that was enabling the SPD to invoke the specter of growing extremism within Germany, and this at a time when "French diplomatic circles in Berlin" were reported to believe that "the hope of French policy is the action of German socialism, which France has already helped often achieve success." Even though the SPD and SFIO remained officially estranged from one another and belonged to two competing ideological formations, this did not prevent the French socialists (joined by the Belgians) from trying to act as an intermediary with the French government in an attempt to broker an end to the Ruhr crisis with the SPD.[38] By the time of the Ruhr crisis, moreover, the SPD's standing in the International had been enhanced even further by the German party's role in establishing a clear dividing line between socialism and communism. As Nikolai Bukharin and Karl Radek made clear in reports back to Moscow, the conference of the three Internationals, held in Berlin in April 1922, left no doubt whatsoever that the SPD attached absolute primacy to reconciliation with its Western comrades.[39] While Rapallo may have been an option available to official German diplomacy in its attempts to gain leverage in the West, the SPD went out of its way to disavow the eastern card in its own internationalist game. The Berlin conference also spelled the end of Austro-Marxist attempts to push the democratic thread through the eye of the Bolshevik needle. In its wake, the merger of the two German parties became the prelude to the reunification of the socialist International. The Austro-Marxist leaders Otto Bauer and Friedrich Adler, authors of some of the most recondite theorizing about how to synthesize socialism and revolution, realized that consolidation in Germany meant consolidation with the International.[40]

---

38. 17 March 1923 "Central European Summary," in *PRO*, FO 371/8723. 9 April 1923 report based on French diplomatic sources, on socialist activities surrounding the Ruhr occupation, in *BA*, Alte Reichskanzlei R 43 I/2662. Voluminous documentation on the socialist response to the Ruhr is contained in *IISH*, LSI, files 57, 107, and 110, and SAI, file 1408, as well as *PRO*, FO 371/8717 and 8725.

39. 5 April 1922 Bukharin Berlin-IKKI telegram, and his 9 May 1922 report to the IKKI, in *RTsKhIDNI*, fond 495, op. 1, d.49 and 51. Lenin closely followed this pursuit of the "Rapallo option" on the left.

40. 17 June 1921 Bauer-Adler letter, 1 July 1921 Adler-Bauer letter, and 9 August 1921 Adler-Bauer letter, in *Verein für Geschichte* der Arbeiterbewegung (Vienna), Altes Partei-Archiv, folder 84/26, 27, 34.

The most significant success in the SPD's campaign to make practical internationalism a reality actually took place prior to the unification of the two socialist Internationals. At the invitation of the SFIO, representatives of the parties from the states that would later be the principals in the Locarno accords convened in Paris in March 1923. Meeting as parliamentarians in order to avoid any impression of division, the major Western parties linked European economic and political stabilization, vetted specific proposals to bring this about, and pledged to support the agreed upon arrangements in their respective legislatures. They proposed that reparations be limited to a finite sum and that a large external loan be made available so that the Weimar Republic could "rapidly restore her finances and stabilize the mark, and at the same time provide for necessities for the reconstruction of the devastated districts" in Belgium and France. While they persisted in defining reparations as "an obligation of a moral nature," socialists wished to see the size of German obligations reduced to a sum that would reflect "considerations of the means to restore the economic life of Europe in order to facilitate and develop exchanges and export trades and avoid a new and formidable economic crisis." These economic policies built directly on the previous socialist reparations' discussions. Most important, they were inserted into a political formula provided by Rudolf Breitscheid, the former USPD leader who was now the SPD's main foreign policy expert and a close collaborator of Stresemann.[41] Breitscheid directly anticipated the terms of Locarno with his proposal that "the powers composing the Rhine Navigation Commission would conclude a pact for the stabilization of the frontiers of the riparian states." Once such an agreement came into force, Germany, which would commit to continuing to respect the Rhineland's demilitarization, was to be "freed from the economic and juridical restrictions of the Treaty of Versailles..." Finally, in a passage that expressed the essence of the socialist consensus on European pacification, Breitscheid established that "the peace of Europe and the security of France are most surely guaranteed by a strengthening of the republic and democ-

---

41. The links between the SPD and official German foreign policy only emerge clearly when studied from the hitherto unexplored perspective of the International and the individual parties. Stresemann's personal secretary did record in his memoirs that, because of his temperament and arrogance, "Breitscheid's activity in the interest of Stresemann's foreign policy was confined to contacts to foreign social democratic parties." See Henry Bernhard, *Finis Germaniae* (Stuttgart, 1947), 82. In addition to his activities on behalf of Stresemann and Locarno in the Reichstag's foreign affairs committee, Breitscheid also published a piece in 1926 in a collection of articles on the various parties' stance towards foreign affairs that publicly aligned the SPD with Stresemann's rendition of "fulfillment policy." See transcript of 1 July 1925 meeting of the foreign affairs committee, in *PAdAA*, Büro des Staatssekretärs, FS, vol. 10, and Rudolf Breitscheid, "Das außenpolitische Programm der Sozialdemokratie," in *Europäche Gespräche,* vol. 4 (April 1926), 169–75.

racy in Germany, the preliminary condition of which is the renunciation by the French government of a policy towards Germany which favors the nationalist and revengeful elements in Germany."[42]

After this signal German success in the French capital, political geography dictated that the International's pacification campaign move to Germany. Switzerland was no longer needed as neutral territory. In May 1923, Europe's socialists met in Hamburg to launch a new organization, the Labour and Socialist International. Unlike Bern and Geneva, Belgian and French diplomatic reporting portrayed Hamburg as an unequivocally pro-German development. The French consul in the Hanseatic city saw the "German national flag and the red flag" combined and hoisted as the banner of "world revolution under German aegis." At Hamburg, he argued, the French socialists revealed themselves to be "dupes of their own persistent illusions and victims of their own irremediable credulity," because they willingly participated in the public lambasting of Versailles as the greatest problem facing Europe, and, in the process, lent credence to the parallel portrayal of France as an equal if not greater threat to European stability than Germany.[43] For the French ambassador in Berlin, the Hamburg congress was the logical "epilogue" to the unification of the SPD and USPD and a breeding ground for the kind of symbolism that later emerged with such pathos at Locarno. Franco-German reconciliation at Hamburg was "embarrassingly" captured for posterity in the photo of a fraternal handshake linking Otto Wels, one of the SPD's most strident defenders of German national

---

42. 28–29 March 1923 "Interparliamentary Conference at Paris," in *IISH*, LSI, file 60. A "confidential source" alerted the French embassy in Berlin to the SPD's intent to use the forthcoming interparliamentary conference in Paris to work out a common socialist response to inter-allied debts, reparations, evacuation of the Ruhr and the other French-occupied areas in Germany, as well as a "perpetual and unlimited pact of guarantee." However, detailed information about Breitscheid's secret security proposal did not circulate. Had it become public knowledge at this point, it would have unleashed a storm of criticism within the International, among communists, and on the right. See the two 27 March 1923 Berlin-Paris telegrams, in *ADdMdAE*, Europe 1918–1940, Sous-série: Internationale, vol. 384. The French embassy was aware that secret discussions between the French and German socialists had taken place in Berlin just before the Paris meeting. See 26 March 1923 Berlin-Paris telegram, in ibid.

43. 21, 22, 24, and 25 May 1923 Hamburg-Paris reports, in *ADdMdAE*, Europe 1918–1940, Sous-série: Internationale, vol. 384.

44. At an April 1933 meeting of the LSI's executive devoted to the new regime in Germany, Henryk Erlich, a Polish Bundist later executed by the NKVD in Lwów in 1941, expressed dismay about Wels' unrepentant German nationalism. Wels, according to Erlich, had hindered the LSI from taking the strongest possible anti-German position, despite Hitler's declaration of a "bestial war of destruction against Germany's 600,000 Jews." See 6 April 1933 Erlich-Adler letter, in *IISH*, SAI, file 2536.

interests, and the SFIO leader Alexandre Bracke.[44] Compared by Bracke to the embrace between a Russian and a Japanese socialist at the 1904 congress of the International, this public act marked the French party's final abandonment of the national and ideological concerns that had previously inhibited overt cooperation with the SPD. For the French diplomats closely observing the new International, socialist rapprochement was made that much worse by the LSI's embrace of pacifism, a step vividly captured in the appearance of the children of Hamburg, "clad in white and crowned with flowers," who sparked "intense emotions among the audience." Materialistic pacifism laced with a strong dose of political relativism would indeed become socialism's leitmotif in international relations after Hamburg. In the words of a Sûreté report posted from Prague, the LSI was "decidedly germanophile and slavophobe," and the "tactic of the majority of socialists" was "to overcome the will of France and Belgium, to undermine the Peace Treaties, and to force their revision." In short, the LSI was "a German International" designed "to utilize the socialists of other countries to pursue national goals" via class-based cooperation couched in European rhetoric.[45]

On the one hand, such sources could hardly avoid a critical tone at a time when the Nationalist bloc then governing in Paris was the bęte noire of socialists throughout Europe. On the other hand, Hamburg was qualitatively different from the preceding socialist gatherings, which, on the whole, had received positive evaluations from representatives of the Belgian and French states. At Hamburg, Alexandre Bracke and Léon Blum, the SFIO leader with the greatest international cachet, delivered addresses redolent with general endorsements of peace and international understanding, and full of specific condemnations of the Ruhr occupation and the economic and territorial clauses of Versailles. The French socialist description of Europe's distress stopped short of a systematic analysis, however. This was left to their German comrades, who sallied forth with an analysis of international affairs that combined theory and specific policy prescriptions into an intelligible whole. Based on the pragmatic acceptance of German reparations to Belgium and France and the doctrine of practical internationalism, the SPD's theoretical prescription for European stabilization could be reduced to the following construct: a "United States of Europe"

---

45. 30 May 19123 Berlin-Paris "Congrès socialiste de Hambourg," and 29 May 1923 Sûreté (renseignement Prague) "A.s. conference internationale socialiste de Hambourg," in *ADdMdAE,* Europe 1918–1940, Sous-série: Internationale, vol. 384. The large amount of official French material on the Hamburg congress includes three lengthy, very detailed reports bearing the imprint of the Berlin embassy's "Social Studies Service," which had at least one emissary present at the congress. Most of the material was addressed to Poincaré personally as prime minister and foreign minister.

that would counteract the economic and political "Balkanization" brought about by the peace treaties. This admittedly amorphous program was preconditioned on Germany's reincorporation into the international system as a full-fledged partner that would, by necessity, play a central, and probably dominant role in collective decision-making. The Hamburg congress also established that the LSI's "resolutions in all international questions" were to be "binding" for all of its member parties. Otherwise, the new International would fail to become "a living reality." Like the German appeal for a united Europe, this vision of the International as a centralized organization capable of dictating foreign policy decisions to its members remained an abstraction. It did, however, prove that the LSI regarded international relations as its most important field of activity. With German practical internationalism pointing the way, the new International was poised to give concrete meaning to its resolutions on "the struggle against the imperialist peace and the tasks of the working class" and on "the international struggle against international reaction." If ideal goals proved to be unattainable, then less ambitious solutions could be countenanced. Right after the SPD had identified the creation of a "United States of Europe" as its premier diplomatic goal in September 1925, Locarno became one of these solutions.[46]

Between the International's Hamburg congress and the Great Powers' Locarno conference, German dominance in the LSI was brought to bear full force. At a time when many observers saw the British Labour Party as the major factor in the International, the SPD used its blossoming relationship with the SFIO to derail socialist support for the Geneva Protocols, the collective security scheme that was the first Labour cabinet's major foreign policy initiative. The protocols expressed a vision of international relations in keeping with socialist theory, above all, through their stated intent to subordinate national interests to a greater, common purpose. Already in 1919, the preface to the proceedings of the Bern conference had identified

---

46. See the opening speeches by Otto Wels and Alexandre Bracke, the addresses by Rudolf Hilferding and Léon Blum, and the congress resolutions, in *Protokoll des Internationalen Sozialistischen Arbeiterkongresses in Hamburg 21. bis 25. Mai 1923* (Glashütten im Taunus, 1974), 13–18, 53–70. The "Statuten der Sozialistischen Arbeiterinternationale" and "Resolutionen" are printed in the accompanying *Beschlüsse des Internationalen Arbeiterkongresses in Hamburg*, 2–13. To his credit, Blum did recognize that "the Versailles peace treaty has also created new states whose creation as such cannot be rejected by socialists, because it reflects the right to self-determination and the nationality principle." This statement, however, merely confirmed the deep contradictions that plagued the SFIO's relationship with Eastern Europe. A new passage in the international political section of the SPD program, which Breitscheid quoted verbatim in the aforementioned 1926 article, endorsed "European economic unity" and "the construction of a United States of Europe." See *Sozialdemokratischer Parteitag 1925 in Heidelberg* (Glashütten im Taunus, 1974), 10.

"the mission of the International to assume the historic role of creator of a new Society in which collective beings will be as free as individuals."[47] At first glance, the LSI drew the necessary lessons from August 1914 and made substantial progress in this direction by constituting itself as an institution whose members would march separately at the national level but act collectively in the international arena (while the Comintern had been created as highly centralized body of "sections" pledged to strict obedience in all matters via the twenty-one conditions). Yet the underlying reality of German-inspired practical internationalism meant that geographically limited marching columns could arise with the International's blessing. This is precisely what happened when Locarno supplanted the Geneva Protocols. The latter condemned all wars of aggression, provided a transparent mechanism for defining a state as an aggressor, established the primacy of collective arbitration via the Assembly of the League of Nations, and contained a strong juridical commitment to disarmament. Most important, the protocols went further than even Versailles towards recognizing the inviolability of the post-1918 borders. Not only did they propose to remove from arbitration earlier decisions of the League, such as the division of Upper Silesia, they also made the revision of treaties and borders contingent on unanimous consent. These provisions made the Protocols anathema to German foreign policy, because, unlike Locarno, the best that could be said about them was that they "would possibly lead to treaty revision by consensus," a very unlikely prospect.[48] Theoretical orthodoxy aside, the Pro-

---

47. G. Ritter, *Die II. Internationale 1918/1919*, 188.

48. P. Krüger, *Die Aussenpolitik*, p. 263. 25 February 1925 "Amendments to the Protocols," in *Archives of the British Labour Party* (Manchester), International Advisory Committee 2/334. The British Labour Party's support for the Geneva Protocols in no way denoted abandonment of the strongly held belief that German territorial revisionism in the East was justified, if not necessary, for long-term stability. Rather, Labour pushed the Protocols because of the new form of international relations that they endorsed. "The outlawry of war, which at length promises to make the League of Nations a beneficent reality," coupled with the promise of obtaining "a reduction in the scale of Allied armaments, on land, in the air, and at sea, comparable to that imposed on Germany by the Treaty of Versailles," received primacy over more immediate German territorial ambitions. Arthur Henderson and Ramsay MacDonald, the two Labour leaders most closely identified with the protocols, went out of their way to insist that the protocols would not block future territorial adjustments. In this respect, Labour Party's support for the protocols mirrored the similar gulf between principle and policy evident in Léon Blum's recognition at Hamburg that the peace settlements had given legitimate expression to "self-determination" and his simultaneous acknowledgment of the need for their revision. Later disagreement caused by the Labour Party's continued support for the Protocols and the SPD's "purely academic" support for them in favor of a limited security pact was further evidence of how far the SPD had succeeded in seizing

tocols' apparent desire "to perpetuate not only peace, but also the status quo" was a practical millstone. The SPD made this confidential admission in early 1928. By this point, the inexorable development of Locarno logic had, in the SPD's own words, allowed the international system to move beyond equating "peace with the maintenance of borders."[49] The Czechoslovak and Polish socialist parties greeted the protocols as the beneficial and logical consequence of the left's rise in Great Britain and France and as evidence of the International's commitment to reshape international relations in accordance with socialist theory.[50] The SFIO, for its part, did go on record as supporting the protocols. Their "defeat," the French party asserted, "would mean a grave peril, and would be a terrible blow to the cause of peace." But it was German socialism that was calling the shots, and the SPD informed the International that the best attainable outcome would be a limited security pact based on an agreement between the French and German socialists. Once again, the need to solidify German democracy received prominent billing, as the SPD took note of the German nationalists' vehement opposition to any agreement with the West and the German communists' simultaneous desire to portray the SPD "and the entire International as allies of the German ultra-reactionaries." A tangible gain in the form of a limited Western security pact thus promised to kill both extremist birds with one stone.[51]

Concessions in this form to German democracy also promised to open new vistas for German territorial revisionism in Eastern Europe. The Brit-

---

(footnote 48 continued) the initiative, once again, by asserting the need to avoid public fissures in the International's ranks, less they play into the hands of domestic extremists. See the Labour Party's "Draft Memorandum on the Geneva Protocol," Arthur Henderson, *Labour and the Geneva Protocol* (London, 1924); Ramsay MacDonald, *Protocol or Pact. The Alternative to War* (London, 1924); "Labour Hostility to the Pact Proposal," "Socialists and the Protocol. A German Misunderstanding. Pressure Not Exerted by the Labour Party," in 4 and 6 April 1925 *Manchester Guardian,* and 8 April 1925 SPD-Vorstand letter to the LSI, in *IISH, SSAI,* file 1175.

49. March 1928 SPD position paper "Stand der Sicherheitsfrage," in *IISH, SAI,* file 849.

50. For the Polish socialists' view of the protocols, see Mieczysław Niedziałkowski, *Położenie międzynarodowe Polski i polityka socjalizmu polskiego* (Warsaw, 1925), 21–24, and "Wielki dzień w Genewie," in 5 October 1924 *Naprzód.* For the Czechoslovak party's virtually identical analysis, see Josef Chmelař, "Politika ženevského Protokolu," in *Zahraniční politika* 3:21 (1924), 1147–51, written by the socialist editor of the Czechoslovak foreign ministry's official analytical periodical, "Ženeva a Marseilles," in *Nová svoboda* 2:35 (1925): 257–58, and "O ženevský protokol," in 5 December 1924 *Právo lidu.*

51. Lengthy December 1924 SFIO-LSI memorandum on collective security, and 30 March, 2 April, and 3 April 1925 SPD-LSI letters, in *IISH, SAI,* file 1175.

ish Labour Party's International Advisory Committee characterized Locarno as a "limited military alliance or guarantee" of a type that "has been in the past and may be again used for purposes other than those specified." As British diplomatic reporting ascertained, however, the Labour Party's ideologically pure rejection of Locarno and support for the protocols had little practical relevance because the British could not override the Franco-German socialist bloc now setting the International's course. With the LSI gravitating towards a formal endorsement of Locarno against British Labour's wishes, a Czechoslovak diplomatic report that drew on inside information supplied by the Belgian socialists spoke of a "worsening internal crisis in the Labour party," while Léon Blum "was very outspoken in his criticism of the British Labour Party" for its "opposition to the [Locarno] pact." In close consultation with Carl von Schubert, state secretary in the German foreign ministry and one of Stresemann's closest assistants, the SPD had mounted a sustained, high-level action to bring the SFIO in line with German thinking about "the security question in the sense agreed upon" in direct deliberations between von Schubert and German socialists. Breitscheid's concerted seduction of French politicians, who, as early as 1922, "had run after him . . . pursuing him all over Paris to discuss the matters," reaped enormous benefits during the buildup to Locarno; moreover, Breitscheid had foreseen that these benefits would, above all, depend on whether French socialism gained significant domestic influence.[52] No longer treading in the wake of its British counterpart, as it had to a certain extent right after the war (and would again briefly after 1945), the SPD was now firmly in control of European socialism's international political policies.

In the inaugural issue of *Die Gesellschaft*, the theoretical journal of the now-united German socialist movement, the leading SPD theoretician, Rudolf Hilferding, best known for his turgid tome *Finance Capital* and his problematic role at the helm of Weimar's ministry of finance during the last republican cabinet, published an article entitled "Problems of the Times." In it, Hilferding asserted that global capitalism was no longer producing

---

52. October 1925 "Memorandum on the Pact of Locarno," in *ABLP*, IAC 2/340. 4 August 1925 Paris-London report on conversation with Blum, and 18 September 1925 Paris-London report, in *PRO*, FO 371/10737 and 10740. 14 August 1925 Brussels-Prague "II. Internacionála a garanční pakt," in *AMZV*, Pz, Brusel. 3, 20 February and 9 March 1925 records of von Schubert conversations with Hilferding and Breitscheid (the latter took place in the company of the SFIO leader Salomon Grumbach, the same French socialist who had abandoned his earlier outspoken condemnations of German "social patriotism" at Bern for the internationalist campaign against German nationalism), in *PAdAA*, Bsts, FS, vol. 1 and 3. 7 November 1922 Berlin-London report, in *PRO*, FO 371/7539. 27 November 1922 Breitscheid statements, in *BA*, Alte Reichskanzlei R43 I/2662.

ever-greater imperialist tensions. Instead, he argued, the economic imperatives of internationalization were paving the way for common policies that
would bind capitalist states to one another in cooperative arrangements.
Simultaneously, Hilferding admitted that the redistribution of power in
Europe after 1918 precluded forceful revision of the peace treaties. In any
event, the realities of internationalization were erecting systemic obstacles
to war among capitalist states, he argued, because of the growing interde-
pendency between their economies. Like the SPD's advocacy of practical
internationalism, this was a heterodox definition of international political
economy that entailed a revision of the orthodox Marxist understanding
of the relationship between capitalism and war. Instead of devoting their
energies to "transcending capitalism," socialists should, Hilferding argued,
look "to create new forms of international political order through a consis-
tent policy which limits the sovereignty of individual nations in the interest
of a transnational organization." As a "practical political task" keyed to
the long-term goal of a "United States of Europe," socialist internationalism could therefore be used to support the foreign policies of capitalist
governments. Writing after the LSI had been launched but before Dawes
and Locarno had brought socialist pacification to life, Hilferding delivered
a theoretical justification for the German party's policies within the International. Even more important, he justified and anticipated the socialists'
post-Dawes embrace of Locarno at the expense of the Geneva Protocols.[53]

One further aspect of the socialist imprint on European international
relations requires elucidation. Why did the Czechoslovak and Polish par-

---

53. Rudolf Hilferding, "Probleme der Zeit," in *Die Gesellschaft* 1:1 (1924), 1–
17. The Russian Mensheviks, diehard adherents of what passed as orthodox Marxism, were not impressed by the new journal. Their delegate to the LSI claimed that
it made "a sad impression" due to the "very many ministers" involved in it and
"the very many unsound statements" it made. This theoretically driven dismissal of
Die Gesellschaft was accompanied by criticism of the LSI's alleged inability to treat
seriously even such "western questions" as the policies of the SFIO and reparations.
In addition, the International's "unified negative position" towards a security pact
limited to the West was noted. Indeed, were one to believe the Menshevik perception, then concern about the "position of the German working class" was "the sole
question" which gave rise to "effectiveness" and "collective initiative." This analysis missed the point entirely. See report on 5–7 June 1924 meeting of the LSI Executive Committee, in *Hoover Institution Archives*, Boris Nikolaevsky Collection 732/
7, as well as "V rabochem Internatsionale," in *Sotsialisticheskii Vestnik* 4:12/13
(20 June 1924), 12–13. For the Mensheviks, the LSI's abandonment of true Marxism had resulted in international political quiescence and British dominance at the
expense of German Marxism. In reality, the exact opposite was true. See 1923
"Obrashenie k sotsialist. partiiam," in *HIA*, BNC 732/7, and "Rabochii
Internatsional i marksistskie partii," in *Sotsialisticheskii Vestnik* 4:4 (25 February
1924), 7–8.

ties fail to create an East European bloc within the International in an effort to steer the organization away from its role as a de facto instrument of German foreign policy? Such cooperation may very well have failed to change any outcomes, but the absence of such an attempt is quite striking. Before and after the creation of the LSI, the Czechoslovak and Polish socialists did discuss such an option. They decried "Anglo-German" hegemony within the International and expressed reservations about its longterm implications for the Versailles system. Although these Czechoslovak-Polish discussions did not go unnoticed, they proved to be irrelevant.[54] Whereas the Poles never shed their status as outsiders within the International, the same hardly obtained for their Czechoslovak comrades. Following its state's accommodation with Locarno, the Czechoslovak Social Democratic Labour Party was able to use the International to promote state interests. Similar to Prague's commitment to good relations with Weimar Germany, the Czechoslovak success in the International was predicated on good relations with the SPD. These started to develop soon after 1918 at the expense of Austrian and Sudeten-German socialism. In 1927, the International secretly agreed, with the SPD's support, to disavow Austro-German union. This hidden development put an end to any realistic hopes of using socialist theory to promote Sudeten-German political autonomy.[55] In the near term, the Labour and Socialist International's commitment to German republicanism as the key to European stability had quite different implications for the First Czechoslovak Republic and Second Polish Republic. But it was a policy that ultimately cut the legs out from under effective, international socialist solidarity when it counted most. In September 1938, Mieczysław Niedziałkowski, having just returned from a crisis meeting of the LSI executive, assured his Czechoslovak counterparts that demo-

---

54. 24 May 1923 report "Jednání sociálních demokratů s Poláky," and 24 October 1924 Protocol "Českoslovenští a polští sociální demokraté—jednání," in *Státní ústřední archív* (Prague), Presidium Ministerské Rady, file 98. The Czechoslovak and French foreign ministries followed these contacts. 27 April 1923 Beneš memorandum, in *AMZV*, II. sekce, box 280. 8 May 1923 Prague-Paris "Parti social-démocrate en Tchécoslovaquie," in ADdMdAE, Europe 1918–1940, Sous-série: Tchécoslovaquie, vol. 60.

55. 4 July 1927 Prague-Vienna "Die Anschlussfrage und die II. Internationale" (Streng geheim!), in *AdR*, NPA, box 64. Marek, the unusually well-connected Austrian envoy to Prague, recorded that "the Hrad, known for its socialist orientation and great international connections in the socialist world, appears to have succeeded in alarming the entire Second (sic) International against the Anschluß and thus to have rendered it subservient to its policies." Eduard Beneš also made good use of contacts to the socialist world in the Anti-Anschluß action. 12 June 1927 Paris "L'Anschluss et le plan de M. Bènés," and 12 July 1927 Prague-Paris "M. Bènés, la 2ème Internationale et l'Anschluss" (Tres Confidentiel), in ADdMdAE, Europe 1918–1940, Sous-série: Autriche, vol. 78 and vol.79.

cratic Europe would support them in an armed struggle with Nazi Germany. Indeed, Czechoslovakia was to resist any pressure from the conservative British government that "would weaken the security of the state and its defensive capabilities."[56] At this point, such gestures, like the socialist International itself, were hollow, thanks in no small part to socialism's own policies. Eighteen years earlier, disillusionment with the International had led Niedziałkowski to use a literary reference tailored for a Polish audience. In the fall of 1938, Polish-style alienation was about to become familiar to socialists in every nook and cranny of Europe, as the Munich accords initiated Europe's descent into another war.

According to the dominant view among its participants and those who have written about it, the interwar LSI took the journey down the same path of powerlessness that had ended with the International's traumatic collapse of August 1914. It was the LSI that failed to translate anti-fascist rhetoric into reality during the 1930s and stood by helplessly as fascism racked up one victory after another. First came the Nazi seizure of power in 1933, followed by the suppression of the Austrian Socialist Party in 1934. Then came two years of ineffectual attempts to aid the Spanish Republic against Franco, who was supported by Italian troops on the ground and German planes in the air. Finally, there was Munich. From the apogee of appeasement it was not far to the nadir of socialism's impotence. Shortly before the Wehrmacht swept across France and the Low Countries, the LSI disbanded. By the end of 1940, the Gestapo had the run of virtually the entire continent, arresting, imprisoning, torturing, and executing socialists irrespective of their nationality. Coming less than three decades after the Second International's collapse, the LSI's demise was yet another marker in European socialism's bleak history as a would-be international actor. Separated from August 1914 by only one generation, the LSI's dissolution at the outbreak of another war made it that much easier to consign the institution to obscurity.

Yet the LSI did exert a very real and very powerful influence on European international relations. While the short-term impact of socialist policies were couched in very positive terms, their long-term consequences set the stage for socialism's renewed failures in the 1930s. The aesthetic, social, and rhetorical flourishes of Locarno's ambiance could not obscure the profound ambiguity of the moment. Both Locarno and socialism's response

---

56. 4 June and 26 August 1938 Warsaw-Prague reports, in *AMZV*, Pz, Varšava. In April 1937, Blum had dispatched an envoy to the Czechoslovak socialists' party congress who, on behalf of the Popular Front leader and then-prime minister, announced that "France will adhere to all of its commitments and will regard a violation of Czechoslovak territory as an attack on France." This statement led the Czechoslovak party to proclaim that the "Socialists of the Entire World are Behind Czechoslovakia." 19 May 1937 *Právo lidu*.

to the German question after 1918 contained the seeds of a much more ominous policy: appeasement. One of the logical, though hardly inevitable, consequences of Europe's division in October 1925 played itself out in late September 1938, at Munich. It was here, just shy of thirteen years to the day after the Locarno accords had been presented with such fanfare to the world, that the West signed off on Hitler's dismemberment of Czechoslovakia. By Munich time, of course, talk of promoting European pacification in conjunction with German economic and political stability made no sense because of the absence of democracy in Germany itself. Instead, as the Czechoslovak socialists realized when confronting their wrenching abandonment by the SFIO, socialism's lofty ideals had given way to opportunistic pacifism. The International "meant nothing," just like the Belgian socialists' condolence telegram to Prague, which expressed "sympathy and gratitude for the sacrifice on behalf of peace" and "admiration for the dignity with which the undeserved" fate imposed by the great powers had been accepted.[57] As a critical causal factor in the international politics that gave rise to appeasement, however, the International was far from meaningless. Of course, appeasement has traditionally been identified with the right, not the left, an ideological label generated by the political profile of the appeasers themselves. Also, the British Labour Party's opposition to Munich and the conflicts within the SFIO over Munich reinforced the plausibility of such a characterization. However, while the Labour Party had begun to reconsider seriously its attitude towards German territorial revisionism in Eastern Europe, Munich found the SFIO caught up in the feeling of "immense relief" that swept over France in a repeat of the Locarno episode. The "remarkable moderation" in the SFIO's public response to Munich demonstrated just how deeply the pacifism that surfaced so prominently at the LSI's birth in 1923 had taken root.[58]

Such continuity makes it more plausible to argue that, had there been no Locarno, Hitler's road to Munich would have been much more arduous, if not altogether impassable. Without the dramatic headlines of fall 1925 and their insidious appeal to peace and understanding, Western resolve to defend the Versailles order would, in all likelihood, have been more stronger. As far as socialism itself was concerned, the movement's role in the formulation and implementation of Locarno politics created a fundamentally defective foundation for the anti-fascist rallying cry that operated as the left's central orientation point after 1933. Theoretical arguments aside,

---

57. 25 October 1938 Výkonný výbor protokol, in AčsSD, fond 71/6. 3 October 1938 "Séance du Conseil General," in AMSAB.

58. 30 May 1938 London-Brussels "Attitude des milieux travaillistes à l'égard de la politique du Gouvernement, en matière de réarmement," and 29 September 1938 Paris-Brussels "La question tchéchoslovaque," in *AdMdAEdB*, Correspondance Politique Legations Grande Bretagne.

anti-fascism in the late 1930s was a very profound cause with one very simple imperative: halting Germany's territorial expansion into the same region that socialism had helped relegate to an inferior status in the Great Power game. After having had the dubious honor of serving as France's prime minister during the summer debacle of 1940, Paul Reynaud came to see the connection between Locarno and Munich. A nationalist, not an internationalist, Reynaud dismissed Locarno as the policy of an ostrich burying its head in the sand, deluding itself that it could thereby remain oblivious to the "spirit of Munich" already lurking in the air.[59] Far from appearing out of nowhere in the brooding Bavarian capital, Locarno's Mr. Hyde had, in fact, been conjured up in the idyllic surroundings of a Swiss resort. Without European socialism, the pacification-appeasement duo would, in all likelihood, never have seen the light of day.

Much has been said and written about the International's "german-ification" prior to 1914. In reality, German influence was much stronger and much more effective during the 1920s than during the Second International's golden age. Henry DeMan, the internationally renowned Belgian socialist theoretician who later became a renegade because of his collaboration with the Nazis, stood largely alone when, in 1927, he fingered organized Marxism's pro-German bias as one of the greatest weakness of the democratic left.[60] This criticism of German influence was central to DeMan's effort to reconceptualize socialism as a movement beholden not to theory, but rather to the promotion of economic planning and social services within the confines of the nation-state. This kind of socialism did not take root until after 1945, when the welfare-state consensus began to weaken ideological politics throughout Western Europe. Later than many of its counterparts, the SPD did not sever its link to orthodox Marxism until 1959, when it adopted the Bad Godesberg program. Under Kurt Schumacher, the German party remained a vocal and often abrasive defender of German nationalism couched in internationalist, European rhetoric well into the 1950s. After the loss of German territories to Poland and the expulsion of Germans from Czech lands and Poland, the SPD's initial reluctance to change was a testament to the enduring legacy of the party's highly successful use of the International in the 1920s to promote German national interests. Seen in this light, the SPD's principled promotion of reconciliation with Germany's eastern neighbors in the 1970s heralded a true sea change for German socialism. By the era of *Ostpolitik*, the socialist International had long ceased to have any relevance for international rela-

---

59. Paul Reynaud, *La France a sauvé L 'Europe* (Paris, 1947), 47–48.

60. DeMan's major work on this front was *The Psychology of Marxian Socialism* (New Brunswick, 1985), originally published in 1927 as *Zur Psychologie des Sozialismus*. The 1927 and 1928 French titles give a better sense of what Deman was trying to achieve—*Au-delà du Marxisme* and *La Crise doctrinale du socialisme*.

tions, and DeMan's vision of a socialist movement freed from Marxist theory had come to fruition. For this reason, it is fitting to speak of a significant socialist imprint on European international relations only during the interwar period, above all, in the 1920s, with a residual and arguably catastrophic after-effect in the 1930s. These were, after all, the years when ideology had a major and often detrimental impact on society and politics in Europe.

Chapter 5

Hungarian Americans during World War II:[1] Their Role in Defending Hungary's Interests

Steven Béla Várdy[2]

The "great economic emigration" from Hungary and East Central Europe lasted from the 1880s until World War I. It transferred nearly two million Hungarian citizens, among them about 650,000 Magyars, to the United States. The large majority of these immigrants were young working-age men who came as temporary "guest workers." They hoped to make enough money during their short stay so that upon their repatriation they would be able to improve their lives and rise to a higher social status in their native country. Many of them did repatriate, a number of them—like birds of passage—several times over and over again. About three-fourths of them, however, opted to stay permanently in America. They remained for a variety of reasons, including economic, social, personal, and even political causes.

The last of these factors became especially significant after 1918, when Austria-Hungary's, and therein Historic Hungary's, dismemberment altered the political realities of East Central Europe. A majority of the Magyar immigrants had come from regions that after 1918 became part of such newly created or significantly enlarged successor states as Czechoslovakia, Yugoslavia, and Romania. Their return to their homelands would have meant that they would have had to accept a minority status in states that henceforth were to be ruled by Hungary's former minorities. Most of the immigrants were unable to face such a new reality. Nor could they return to the small country that remained Hungary after the Treaty of Trianon (June 4, 1920). The economic opportunities in post-Trianon Hungary were

---

1. This study is based partially upon a section of the author's recently published 840–page book entitled *Magyarok az Újvilágban* [Hungarians in the New World] (Budapest, 2000).
2. In Hungarian the author publishes under the name "Béla Várdy."

far short even of the conditions that the immigrants had left behind at the time of their original emigration to the United States.[3]

Given the evaporation of the chances for repatriation, the attitude of Hungarian Americans also changed markedly. Their temporary presence in the United States increasingly assumed the characteristics of a permanent stay. Thus began their integration into American society. This process became particularly evident among the members of the younger generation, who had been born in the United States. While the immigrants were never really able to adjust fully to the peculiarities of American society, their native-born children became increasingly Americanized. They felt less and less kinship with the world of their immigrant parents, including the institutions and organizations the latter had founded during their purported "temporary stay" in the New World. These developments, however, held untold dangers for the immigrant generation. In the absence of a well-tried social welfare system (e.g., pension plans, health and old age insurance), the older members of the immigrant generation were compelled to rely upon the Hungarian fraternal associations that they had helped to found during their younger days. But the survival and well-being of these associations depended on the participation of their native-born offspring, who were being drawn away from these fraternals by Anglo-American society's much more glamorous institutions.[4]

---

3. Concerning Hungarian emigration to the United States during the Age of Dualism, see the following works: Gustav Thirring, "Hungarian Migration in Modern Times," *International Migrations*, vol. II (1931): 411–39; John Kósa, "A Century of Hungarian Emigration, 1850–1950," *The American Slavic and East European Review*, vol. 16, no. 4 (December 1957): 501–14; István Rácz, *A paraszti migráció és politikai megítélése Magyarországon, 1849–1914* [Peasant Migration and its Political Assessment in Hungary, 1849–1914] (Budapest, 1980); Julianna Puskás, *From Hungary to the United States, 1880–1914* (Budapest, 1982); Steven Béla Várdy, "The Great Economic Immigration from Hungary, 1880–1920," in *Society in Change: Studies in Honor of Béla K. Király*, ed. S. B. Várdy and A. H. Várdy (New York, 1983), 189–216; Julianna Puskás, "Kelet-Európából az USA-ba vándorlás folyamata, 1861–1924" [The Process of Migration from Eastern Europe to the USA, 1861–1924], *Történelmi Szemle*, Vol. XXVII, No. 1–2 (Spring, 1984): 145–64; Steven Béla Várdy, *The Hungarian-Americans* (Boston, 1985), 18–29, 86–112; Albert Tezla, *The Hazardous Quest. Hungarian Immigrants in the United States, 1895–1920* (Budapest, 1993). Puskás's and Tezla's volumes also have longer Hungarian versions. The most recent English language synthesis on this topic is by Julianna Puskás, *Ties That Bind, Ties That Divide: 100 Years of Hungarian Experience in the United States*, trans. Zora Ludwig (New York, London, 2000).

4. The largest of these fraternal associations was the Verhovay Aid Society, which also underwent a major internal convulsion at this time. See Steven Béla Várdy, "The Verhovay Association's Efforts to Perpetuate Hungarian National Consciousness among its Native-born Members, 1930s–1950s," *Hungarian Studies*, Vol. 7, Nos. 1–2 (1991–1992): 161–70; and Béla Várdy, "A magyarságtudat megtartásáért: Verhovay Testvérsegítő Egyesület," [For the Preservation of Hungarian National Consciousness: The Verhovay Fraternal Association], *Forrás* [Source] (Kecskemét, Hungary), Vol. XXIII, No. 3, (March 1991): 63–69.

The secure existence and well-being of the retired older members of the immigrant generation depended to a large degree on the health of their fraternal associations. Moreover, the representation of Hungary's interest to the American political establishment also relied to a large degree upon the emotional attachments of the native-born generation to these institutions, and through them to the land and culture of their parents. At least this is the way things seemed at the end of the 1930s, when no one could as yet foretell that, during and after World War II, several waves of much better educated political immigrants would land on American shores. Consequently, the intellectual preparation and political readiness of the native-born generation remained a central question in the lives of Hungarian Americans. These upcoming members of the young generation were asked to fill the difficult role of representing Hungary in the face of unwelcome developments that occurred in the land of their ancestors. In other words, they were called upon to defend Hungary's interests in spite of that country having become an ally of Fascist Italy and Nazi Germany, and in spite of its promulgation of three separate anti-Semitic laws.[5] The latter, of course, have to be viewed in light of the fact that during the same period Hungary had become the haven for many thousands of Polish, Romanian, and Yugoslav Jews,[6] as well as of perhaps more than one hundred thousand non-Jewish Poles, many of whom ended up in France, where they joined the Polish Legion.[7] Moreover, citing the centuries-old Polish-Hungarian friendship, Prime Minister Pál Teleki (1879–1941) of Hungary refused to

---

5. Most history books speak of only two anti-Semitic laws, but the Hungarian Parliament had in fact passed three such laws in the period between 1938 and 1941. These laws include: Act 1938: XV (May 29), Act 1939: IV (May 5), and Act 1941: XV (August 8). The first of these so-called "Jewish Laws" limited the participation of Jews among journalists, attorneys, engineers, physicians, businessmen, and tradesmen to 20 percent at the time when Hungary's Jewish population was about 6 percent, and defined a Jew as one of the Jewish faith or one who had converted to Christianity only after August 1, 1919; the second Jewish Law reduced their participation in the above professions to 6 percent and defined a Jew—irrespective of his or her religious affiliation—as one who has had one Jewish parent or two Jewish grandparents; while the third Jewish Law forbade marriage and even sexual relations between Jews and non-Jews, and defined a Jew as one who had at least two grandparents born into the Jewish faith, or one who is an active member of a Jewish congregation.

6. For the most extensive treatment of the Jewish question in twentieth-century Hungary see Randolph L. Braham, *The Politics of Genocide: The Holocaust in Hungary*, 2 vols. (New York, 1981); and Randolph L. Braham and Attila Pók, eds., *The Holocaust in Hungary: Fifty Years Later* (New York, 1997). For a short summary of the three Jewish Laws, see Steven Béla Várdy, *Historical Dictionary of Hungary* (Lanham MD and London, 1997), 398–99.

7. On the Polish refugees in Hungary during World War II, see Károly Kapronczay, *Refugees in Hungary, Shelter from Storm during World War II* (Toronto-Buffalo,

let Hitler use the Hungarian railways to transport German troops across the country in their attack against Poland.[8] In contrast to Teleki's brave defiance of Hitler, "Tiso's Slovakia not only permitted German troops to cross, but . . . also participated on Germany's side in the conquest of Poland, and then occupied a few Polish socalled *gural* villages."[9]

Territorial Revisions and Division among Hungarian Americans

Germany's invasion of Russia in June 1941, and the Japanese attack against Pearl Harbor in December of that year had turned the hitherto European war into a worldwide conflict and made the lives of Hungarian Americans even more difficult. The price of the territorial revisions in Hungary's favor in 1938–1940 was an obligatory alliance with Hitler's Germany and Fascist Italy.[10] This fact, however, placed Hungarian Americans in a nearly impossible situation. All Hungarians and most American Hungarians viewed

---

1999). See also *Barátok a bajban: Lengyel menekültek Magyarországon, 1939–1945* [Friends in Need: Polish Refugees in Hungary, 1939–1945], documents selected by Jerzy Robert Nowak and Tadeusz Olszański, ed. László Antal, trans. Beatrix Murányi (Budapest, 1985). This is the Hungarian translation of a Polish work, whose original title is unknown to me, but which, in all probability, is similar to the one given above.

8. See Loránt Tilkovszky, *Pál Teleki, 1879–1941: A Biographical Sketch* (Budapest, 1974), 47.

9. Károly Vigh, "Teleki Pál halálának hatvanadik évfordulójára" [On the Occasion of the Sixtieth Anniversary of the Death of Pál Teleki], *Valóság* [Reality], Vol. 44, No. 8 (August 2001), 79.

10. The territorial revisions in question included the following: (1) The First Vienna Award of November 2, 1938, which returned a narrow southern slice of Slovakia to Hungary; (2) the acquisition of Sub-Carpathian Ruthenia on March 15, 1939 as a byproduct of the dismemberment of Czechoslovakia; (3) the Second Vienna Award of August 30, 1940, which returned Northern Transylvania to Hungary; (4) and finally the reacquisition of parts of Bácska and Bánat (northern Voivodina) from Yugoslavia following the German attack against that country on April 6, 1941. It is to be reemphasized here that Hungary's alliance with Italy and Germany was the direct result of the willingness of those two countries to support Hungarian revisionism at a time when no one else was willing to listen even to the country's ethnically and linguistically justifiable claims for territorial revisions. The most detailed account of this situation in English can be found in the classic work by C. A. Macartney, *October Fifteenth: A History of Modern Hungary, 1929–1945*, 2 vols., 2nd ed. (Edinburgh, 1961). See also John Flournoy Montgomery, *Hungary the Unwilling Satellite* (New York, 1947, reprinted Morristown NJ, 1993); Nicholas M. Nagy-Talavera, *The Green Shirts and Others: A History of Fascism in Hungary and Rumania* (Stanford CA, 1970); Mario D. Fenyo, *Hitler, Horthy and Hungary: German-Hungarian Relations, 1941–1944* (New Haven CT, 1972); and Thomas Sakmyster, *Hungary's Admiral on Horseback. Miklós Horthy, 1918–1944* (New York, 1994).

these revisions as fully justifiable on the basis of the highly touted principle of national self-determination that had been used to justify Historic Hungary's dismemberment. Yet, not all of them agreed that these revisions should have been carried out with Hitler's help at the price of a military alliance with the Axis powers. This was all the more true—so they claimed— because these territorial revisions under such conditions had destroyed Hungary's credibility and made the country—in the eyes of the world— into a criminal accomplice of Hitler's Germany.[11]

There are signs of many highly emotionally charged disagreements among Hungarian Americans concerning revisionism with German help. This is evident from the personal correspondences of their leaders, as well as from the latter's repeated efforts to prove their dedication to the United States and to the Western alliance, while at the same time questioning the loyalty of their opponents. These passionate disagreements appear in the secret reports prepared by a special arm of the Office of Strategic Services [OSS], whose task was to watch the activities of American citizens with dual or multiple loyalties.[12]

In the colorful spectrum of Hungarian American political life during World War II, the most widespread split appears to have developed between the so-called "conservative-nationalists" and the "liberal-internationalists" within the immigrant communities. This split was even more visible, however, between the two extremes of the political spectrum, i.e., between those who called each other "chauvinists" and "communists,"

---

11. For a summary of this situation from the point of view of Hungarian Americans see Várdy, *The Hungarian-Americans*, 108–12.

12. This phenomenon of mutual recriminations and reporting to U.S. authorities was especially true for the two rival factions headed respectively by Rusztem Vámbéry (1872–1948), an important spokesman of the left-leaning Hungarian emigration, and Tibor Eckhardt (1888–1972), the secret emissary of the Horthy Regime in the United States. A sizable portion of the relevant documents can be found among their personal papers, located in the Hoover Institution of Stanford University. For a discussion of aspects of this question in Hungarian, see Béla Várdy, "Az amerikai magyarság a második világháború viharaiban" [Hungarian Americans in the Midst of the Storms of the World War], *Valóság* (Budapest), Vol. XLII, No. 1 (January 1999): 63–74; and Béla Várdy, "Az amerikai magyar emigráció és Habsburg Ottó viszonya a második világháború alatt és után" [American Hungarian Emigrés and Their Relations to Otto von Habsburg during and after World War II], *Valóság* [Reality], Vol. 41, No. 7 (July 1998): 37–48. For a revised English-language version of this article see "Archduke Otto von Habsburg and American Hungarian Emigrés during and after World War II," *East European Quarterly*, Vol. 36, No. 4 (December 2002): 441–63. Concerning these secret OSS reports, see Sándor Szilassy, "Az amerikai magyarság a második világháborúban" [American Hungarians in the Secone World War], *Új Látóhatár* [New Horizon] (Munich, Germany), Vol. 30, No. 1–2 (June 1979): 138–43.

respectively. Both groups tried hard to undermine each other's credibility within American society, while simultaneously blackening their rival's name in front of U.S. authorities.

At the same time, each of these groups had its internal disagreements, resulting in emotional conflicts between individuals and subgroups that were the exponents of basically similar political views. Within the "liberal-internationalist" group, for example, there was the "Jászi contra Károlyi debate," which pitted the well-known liberal social philosopher, Oscar Jászi (1875–1957), against an increasingly communist-oriented Michael Károlyi (1875–1955). Within the "conservative-nationalist" camp, on the other hand, there arose the highly emotional clash between the leaders of the American Hungarian Federation and the spokesmen of the "chauvinist-nationalists." The former's policy of political realism and pragmatism clashed with the narrowly nationalistic and provincial views of the latter.

Manifestations of the "Conservative-Nationalist" Group

One of the most vociferous debates within the ranks of the "conservative-nationalist" group of immigrants erupted around the New York-based daily, *Amerikai Magyar Népszava [American Hungarian People's Voice]*, in 1941. The first open sign of this struggle was the publication of a short notice on April 16 by the well-known Pittsburgh-based poet-journalist György Szécskay (1880–1958), who informed the reading public about his resignation from the *Népszava*'s editorial board and announced that he no longer wished to represent the paper in western Pennsylvania.[13] Szécskay's action immediately started a series of rumors and mutual recriminations. One of these rumors claimed that the elderly poet, known for his Kossuthist nationalism and his strong anti-Habsburgism, had been dismissed from his editorial post because of his political stance, which was in open conflict with the official U.S. foreign policy with respect to Hungary and Central Europe. It also asserted that Szécskay had been arrested for anti-American activities and political disloyalty. The latter claim proved to be groundless, but Szécskay's resignation from the *Népszava*'s editorial board was the direct result of the debate that raged within the ranks of the "conservative-nationalist" camp concerning the Hungarian American community's official policy toward the revision of Hungary's frontiers and the resulting military alliance with Hitler's Germany.

---

13. Concerning György Szécskay, see Leslie Konnyu, *A History of American Hungarian Literature* (St. Louis MO, 1962), 29–31; and Béla Várdy and Ágnes Huszár Várdy, "Az amerikai magyar irodalom multja és jelene" [The Past and the Present of Hungarian American Literature], *Magyar Napló* [Hungarian Diary] (Budapest), Vol. 9, Nos. 5–6 (May-June, 1997): 27–31.

In the political spectrum that developed at the start of the war, Szécskay represented the so-called "populist-nationalist" line, which—in contrast to the "pragmatic-nationalist" orientation represented by the *Amerikai Magyar Népszava*—followed developments in Hungary with considerable sympathy. Szécskay and his followers applauded all Hungarian territorial acquisitions, notwithstanding the country's consequent plunge into the Nazi military alliance. They tried to justify and defend Hungary's territorial gains both to Hungarian Americans and to American governmental circles.

The editors of the *Amerikai Magyar Népszava* had a different view. While agreeing that Hungarian revisionism was fully justified, they questioned the country's slide toward the right and its ever-closer alliance with the Axis powers. They likewise criticized some of the Hungarian government's policies that tried to placate Nazi Germany, and condemned the destruction of Czechoslovakia and Yugoslavia, which had been carved partially out of Historic Hungary. True, this condemnation was motivated to a large degree by political pragmatism and by the desire to conform to the generally accepted American views concerning matters in Central Europe, but it still irritated many of the Hungarian populist-nationalists in the United States. This compromising attitude was simply too much for them. This also held true for György Szécskay and his slightly provincial supporters, who still viewed history from the vantage point of late-nineteenth-century Hungarian developments.

Given the realities of the day, which made all former citizens of the countries within the Axis camp objects of suspicion, few Hungarian immigrants dared to voice their political views concerning revisionism. Not so Szécskay, who freely offered his views on this matter, irrespective of their possible political consequences. He was blatant in his support of Hungarian revisionism, and he refused to bemoan the destruction of Czechoslovakia and Yugoslavia, which he believed to have been artificial constructions that were bound to fall apart.[14] Of course, while expressing his opinions on territorial revisionism, Szécskay also proclaimed his loyalty to the United States repeatedly in writing and in considerable detail.

Following his separation from the *Amerikai Magyar Népszava*, Szécskay elaborated his views partially in the Cleveland-based daily *Szabadság [Liberty]*—the major rival of the New York-based *Népszava*—and partially in his own *Alkalmi Magyar Híradó [Periodic Hungarian Herald]*, which he edited and published himself in Pittsburgh. In doing so, he often used obvious sophism to coordinate his support of the policies of the Hungarian government with his loyalty to the United States and American ideals. On one occasion, for example, he wrote as follows:

---

14. Developments in the 1990s appear to have proven him correct in this matter.

The *Amerikai Magyar Népszava* is guided not by the pure and tolerant American spirit that should serve as guide to all Hungarian newspapers published in America, as well as to all citizens who have sworn fidelity to the constitution of the United States. The *Amerikai Magyar Népszava* . . . aspires to direct the politics of another country [i.e., Hungary], exercises an evil influence upon the spirit of understanding and cooperation, and incites hatred with its tendentious articles, many of which are based on distorted facts and motivated by the desire for revenge . . . Many [Hungarian Americans] do not even regard it a Hungarian newspaper. True, compelled by its business and other selfish interests . . . the paper does publish news on religious congregations written by their pastors . . . , and it likewise invites clergymen to submit occasional pieces for special "holiday" issues that are put out for advertisement purposes around Christmas and Easter. . . . Yet, notwithstanding all these manifestations, one can hardly call a newspapers a "Hungarian paper", in which muddled, barely comprehensible, and hate-inspired articles demand that the cruelly mutilated and weakened Hungarian nation should challenge the wrath of the all-overwhelming German war machine that could maim and destroy it completely and permanently. What sort of newspaper . . . is a so-called "Hungarian newspaper", which celebrates the alleged "heroism" of nations that have shared in the spoils of Hungary, and that—like the Serbians and their government—have persecuted our countrymen and have chased these tortured, plundered and guiltless Hungarians across the Trianon frontiers by the thousands . . . ? Does a newspaper have the right to call itself "Hungarian," which, instead of celebrating and reveling in the return of a portion of dismembered Hungary, calls such an event a day of infamy—as it did on the occasion of Hungary's reacquisition of Bácska [Bačka]? . . . To represent such a "Hungarian" newspaper among the ever decreasing Hungarians of America is not only unacceptable, but it is also shamefully embarrassing . . . .[15]

Szécskay's argument reflects well the emotionally charged, but politically naïve, views of the simple working class majority among Hungarian Americans. Given contemporary developments in Central Europe, and the general American attitude toward them, it was rather dangerous to profess openly this political creed even on the local level. It certainly could not be done by a high profile Hungarian daily such as the New York-based *Amerikai Magyar Népszava*. Moreover, what is even more significant, this political creed that favored territorial revisionism at the expense of Czechoslovakia, Romania, and Yugoslavia found no sympathy whatsoever with the American public and government.

---

15. *Alkalmi Magyar Híradó* [Occasional Hungarian Herald] (Pittsburgh), 1941, 1–2. This periodical was published by György Szécskay, partially to justify his break with the *Amerikai Magyar Népszava*, and partially as an outlet for his nationalistic political views. Some of Szécskay's papers, including a sizable portion of his correspondence, are in my possession, which in due time—along with my own personal papers—will end up in one of the Hungarian archives.

The Tribulations of the "Movement for Independent Hungary"

Notwithstanding the German invasion of Russia (June 22, 1941), until Hungary's ill-considered declaration of war against the United States (December 12, 1941),[16] Hungarian Americans were able to express their sympathies for their native country relatively freely. They were able to do so in spite of the fact that indirectly—through the activities of Tibor Eckhardt (1888–1972) and his "Movement for Independent Hungary"—they were also in contact with the same Horthy Regime that by now was generally viewed as a staunch ally of Nazi Germany.[17]

Here one has to remember that following the German invasion of Poland (September 1, 1939) and the outbreak of the European phase of World War II, the acknowledged spokesmen of Hungarian Americans immediately went to work to put up defense ramparts around the Hungarian American community. The most important bastion of these ramparts was the American Hungarian Federation *[Amerikai Magyar Szövetség]*, which was founded in 1906, and then brought out of its slumber in 1939. This reactivation took place at the association's Pittsburgh convention on November 8, 1939, which brought together the leaders of the most important fraternal associations and a number of noted intellectuals, who hitherto had very little to do with the ethnic community. It was at this convention that they decided to relocate its central office to Washington, D.C., so as to be in the vicinity of the White House and the Congress. It was also at this convention that the there assembled community leaders elected Professor Tibor Kerekes (1893–1969), the chairman of the Department of History at Georgetown University, as the AHF's executive secretary. The latter move was particularly significant, as this was the first time that leaders of the Hungarian American community—all of them members or descendants of the humble turn-of-the-century immigrants—were willing to accept a Budapest-educated Hungarian intellectual as one of their spokesmen.

In this connection, it is important to know that the turn-of-the-century peasant immigrants brought with them an intense dislike of Hungary's ruling classes, including the country's intellectual elite. Consequently, they refused to elect any so-called "educated person" to a position of leadership

---

16. The nature of this unfortunate declaration of war is discussed by Ignác Romsics in his "A magyar hadüzenet amerikai fogadtatása" [American Reception of the Hungarian Declaration of War], *História* (Budapest), Vol. 14, No. 2 (February, 1992): 5–16.

17. Tibor Eckhardt was a prominent interwar Hungarian politician, a noted member of the Association of Awakening Hungarians, and later the president of the Independent Smallholders' Party (1932–1941). During the 1920s he was an exponent of extreme nationalism, anti-Habsburgism, and even anti-Semitism, but in the course of the 1930s and 1940s he became a political moderate and a legitimist.

in their fraternal and cultural associations. In point of fact, around the turn of the century, several fraternals incorporated this view into their bylaws.[18] Later they were obliged to remove these provisions, because these were declared unconstitutional. In actuality, however, they still continued this practice at least until World War II.[19]

Following the Pittsburgh convention, events proceeded very rapidly. At the beginning of 1940, the American Hungarian Federation opened its Washington office (839 17th Street, NW), and in the fall of the same year it called together all of the prominent Hungarian American leaders for a "Consultative Assembly" in the capital city. In addition to Kerekes, who ran the association's affairs in Washington, the assembly's most influential leaders included József Daragó (c.1880–1953), president of the Verhovay Aid Association, and Reverend György Borshy-Kerekes (1892–1971), the executive secretary (1936–1956) and later the president (1956–1964) of the Hungarian Reformed Federation of America [*Amerikai Magyar Református Egyesület*].[20] The coming together of these three was itself a major event in Hungarian American social development, for they represented three distinct components of the Hungarian ethnic community in

---

18. The Bridgeport Federation [*Bridgeporti Szövetség*] added this provision to its bylaws in 1897, while the Verhovay Aid Association [*Verhovay Betegsegélyző Egylet*] did so in 1909. The amended bylaws of the latter organization declared "neither a clergyman, nor a journalist, nor a businessman . . . can ever become an officer of the association." See Géza Kende, *Magyarok Amerikában: Az amerikai magyarság története* [Hungarian in America: The History of Hungarian Americans], 2 vols. (Cleveland, 1927), II, 317–18; and Steven Béla Várdy, *The Centennial History of the William Penn Association* (Pittsburgh, 1986), 15–16 [typescript]. It is also indicative of the peasant immigrants' attitude toward the so-called "educated gentlemen" that in 1887 the Verhovay Aid Association removed its secretary, Károly Juhász, because the latter had uniquely beautiful handwriting. This made him subject of suspicion to the association's other leaders and members, who came to the conclusion that Juhász is simply "too educated" to be trusted. See *Verhovayak Lapja—Verhovay Journal. Golden Jubilee, 1886–1936*, ed. József Daragó (Pittsburgh, 1936), 44.

19. Concerning the activities of the American Hungarian Federation, see Elemér Bakó, "Az Amerikai Magyar Szövetség útja" [The Path of the American Hungarian Federation], in *Emlékkönyv az Amerikai Magyar Szövetség 80. évfordulójára* [Memorial Volume on the Occasion of the 80th Anniversary of the American Hungarian Federation], ed. Elemér Bakó (Washington, D.C., 1988), 13–24 [hereafter Bakó, *Memorial Volume*].

20. See the narrative of István Balogh, the association's subsequent executive secretary: "Mi az Amerikai Magyar Szövetség?" [What is the American Hungarian Federation], *Az Amerikai Magyar Népszava Aranyjubileumi Albuma* [Golden Jubilee Album of the American Hungarian Federation] (New York, 1950), 98–100 [hereafter *AMNSZ Golden Jubilee Album*]; reprinted in Bakó, *Memorial Volume*, 37–44.

the United States, whose representatives had seldom met in the past on such intimate terms: The group comprised the educated intellectual, who had found his place in the American academic world and who up to then had only occasional contacts with the Hungarian ethnic community (Kerekes); the always present and always active clergyman, who, because his presence was needed, was grudgingly accepted by the simple peasant immigrants (Borshy-Kerekes); and finally, the simple working class immigrant, who had liberated himself mentally from the bondage of Hungary's class conscious society and was beginning to view himself as a co-equal and respected member of humanity (Daragó). Notwithstanding his peasant background and his subsequent career as a smalltime butcher in Youngstown, Ohio, the latter eventually rose to become the most successful president of the Verhovay Aid Association (1931–1943), and during World War II was also the primary financial supporter of the politically reactivated American Hungarian Federation.[21]

It was at this Consultative Assembly in Washington, D.C., that the leaders of the American Hungarian Federation decided to lay the foundations for the "Movement for Independent Hungary." The intended goal of this movement was to counterbalance the Hungarian government's misdirected policy that had led to its becoming a powerless instrument of Hitler's ambitions. The movement was initiated in January 1941 at another Washington meeting, but by September of that year it merged with a similarly named movement initiated by the recently arrived politician, Tibor Eckhardt, who immediately assumed the leadership of the two merged organizations.

The events of the eight months between the original foundation and the merger were chronicled by Borshy-Kerekes in his reminiscences as follows:

> The directors [of the American Hungarian Federation] requested that I leave my office at the Hungarian Reformed Federation and asked me to assume for the next six months the leadership of the "Movement for Independent Hungary" under the aegis of the American Hungarian Federation. It was toward the end of this period that Dr. Tibor Eckhardt, the President of the Smallholders' Party in

---

21. In connection with this political activism see the article signed by József Daragó of the Verhovay Aid Association, Professor Tibor Kerekes of Georgetown University, and Professor Ferenc Deák of Columbia University Law School, entitled: "A 'Független Magyarországért' mozgalom és az U.S. politikája" [The American Policies of the 'Movement for an Independent Hungary'], *Amerikai Magyar Népszava*, January 3, 1942. Concerning József Daragó, see Kálmán Káldor, ed., *Magyar-Amerika írásban és képben: Amerikai magyar úttörők és vezetőférfiak arcképes életrajza. Magyar egyházak, egyletek, közintézmények története és működése* [Hungarian America in Words and Pictures. Pictorial Biographies of American Hungarian Pioneers and Leading Personalities. History and Functioning of Hungarian Churches, Associations, and Public Institutions], 2 vols. (St. Louis, MO, 1937–1939), II, 244.

Hungary, arrived in America. He immediately established contacts with the Federation's Board of Directors and announced that, as a Hungarian politician who had fled from Nazism, he intends to establish a general movement embracing all Hungarians living in various countries of the world so as to defend the Hungarian people from the charge of Nazism. He asked the Federation to coordinate its continuing effort with his own movement. This did take place at the Federation's and the Independence Movement's joint meeting in September 1941 in Pittsburgh, where Dr. Eckhardt was accompanied by the ambassadorial counselor Antal Balássy and the industrialist Viktor Bátor. They announced that the leadership of their movement counts among its members Ambassador János Pelényi [of Washington] and the noted diplomat Antal Zsilinszky, who resided in London. . . . The Federation had no intention to crossing the undertaking initiated by Eckhardt and his supporters, but rather wished to cooperate with it. Eckhardt's movement, however, soon lost steam. Zsilinszky committed suicide in London, Balássy left the movement, and the remaining three members of the board soon ceased their public activities. They did not wish to have anything to do with [the] ever louder and ever more aggressive Vámbéry and Lugosi groups, with their pink and red political orientation and pro-Soviet stance.[22]

Naturally, the above summary reflects Borshy-Kerekes's own view of things, and it is far from being the whole story. It does point to the brewing conflict between the "patriotic" Eckhardt group and the "socialist" Vámbéry-Lugosi group, which—while anti-Nazi and anti-Horthy—was not necessarily all that red and all that pro-Soviet. This is best demonstrated by the views express by an editorial in the New York based communist daily, *Magyar Jövő [Hungarian Future]*, which, upon learning about Vámbéry's own political movement, called him and his supporters "imperialist agents." At the same time, this editorial referred to the left-liberal journalists Ferenc Göndör (1885–1955) and Márton Himler (1888–1961), who were close to Vámbéry, as fascists.[23]

The Eckhardt mission was dreamt up in the course of 1939 and 1940, when the idea surfaced that Hungary should have a statesman of some prestige to represent it in the West. Initially they thought about sending former Prime Minister Count István Bethlen (1874–1947) abroad, but then

---

22. For Borshy-Kerekes's summary of these developments, see Bakó, *Memorial Volume*, 49–55; quotations from 49–51. On the activities of Vámbéry and Lugosi, see below. Vámbéry's papers can be found in the archives of the Hoover Institution of Stanford University. See also the article by Várdy, "Az amerikai magyarság és Habsburg Ottó."

23. See the following editorial diatribes in the above-mentioned Hungarian communist paper: "Vámbéry-Fényes zászlót bont az imperialista háború mellett" [Vámbéry-Fényes Unfurl Their Flag in Favor of the Imperialist War], *Magyar Jövő* [Hungarian Future] (New York), June 10, 1941; and "'Jöjjön, aminek jönni kell!'"—kiáltja Fényes, Vámbéry és lelkesen háborúba indulnak" ["Come Whatever May Come" Shout Fényes and Vámbéry and then they set off enthusiastically to the war], *Magyar Jövő*, June 13, 1941.

later the choice fell on Eckhardt. The purpose of this mission was that in case of an Axis defeat, hapless Hungary should at least have a presentable spokesman abroad who could perhaps even form a government in exile and defend Hungary's territorial gains. This idea was picked up and supported both by Prime Minister Count Pál Teleki (1879–1941) and by Ambassador János Pelényi (1885–1974). In order to prepare this undertaking, in early 1940 the Hungarian government transferred five million dollars to Ambassador Pelényi in Washington for deposit in a New York bank for the sole purpose of supporting such a mission. In November of that year, Ambassador Pelényi resigned his post and received political asylum in the United States. A few months later, on May 7, 1941, Tibor Eckhardt left Hungary for the United States via Belgrade, Cairo, and Capetown. He arrived here three months later on August 8.[24]

Upon his arrival Eckhardt immediately established contacts with American governmental circles and the leaders of American Hungarian organizations, and presented himself as a political refugee who wished to fight against the destructive ideology of Nazism. Within six weeks after his arrival (September 27) he started his "Movement for Independent Hungary" and assumed leadership over the similarly named movement initiated eight months earlier by the American Hungarian Federation. He popularized his cause through a series of proclamations and articles published in the American press and in various Hungarian American newspapers.[25]

Eckhardt received the active support of a number of well-known public figures, including the internationally known composer Béla Bartók (1881–1945), who had just arrived in the United States as a political refugee himself; and John F. Montgomery, the former U.S. ambassador to Hungary (1933–1941), who had considerable sympathy for the Hungarians and the Hungarian cause, and viewed Hungary basically as Hitler's "unwilling satellite."[26]

Eckhardt's path, however, proved to be much more difficult than originally presumed. American governmental circles had doubts about the genuineness of his refugee status, and also some qualms about his earlier politi-

---

24. In this connection see Paul Nadányi, *The "Free Hungary" Movement* (New York,, 1942), 3–66; Sándor Szilassy, "Az amerikai magyarság a második világháborúban"; and Várdy, *The Hungarian-Americans*, 109–12.

25. A copy of Eckhardt's English language proclamation can be found among his papers in the Hoover Institution of Stanford University. It is also reprinted in Nadányi, *The "Free Hungary" Movement*, 45–47.

26. Ambassador Montgomery expressed his views concerning Hungary's position in his *Hungary, the Unwilling Satellite*. It is to be noted here that Eckhardt's leftist rival, Rusztem Vámbéry, tried to influence Montgomery against Eckhardt, but without any success. Their letters can be found among the Vámbéry papers at the Hoover Institution of Stanford University.

cal career, which in the 1920s included membership in the somewhat anti-Semitic Association of Awakening Hungarians *[Ébredő Magyarok Egyesülete]*. [27] Consequently, a few months after initiating his movement, he also founded the "American Committee of the Movement for Independent Hungary," specifically for the inclusion of native-born Americans and thus broadening his base of support.

Even so, Eckhardt's efforts proved to be short-lived and less than successful. He was able to gain the trust of most Hungarian American organizations, but he failed to break the distrust of American governmental circles and could not counterbalance the propaganda activities of the Little Entente states. Thus, on the positive side, within a few weeks after initiating his movement, he had the support of all major fraternal organizations (Verhovay Aid Society, Reformed Federation, Rákóczi Aid Society, Bridgeport Federation), all religious groups (Catholics, Reformed, Lutherans, and a liberal Jewish group under Rabbi György Lányi's leadership), the large majority of the Hungarian American press (*Szabadság, Amerikai Magyar Népszava*, Márton Himler's newspaper group, many other weeklies, biweeklies and monthlies), as well as the backing of such noted scholars as Kerekes and Professor Ferenc Deák (1899–1972) of Columbia University.[28] Notwithstanding this widespread sponsorship, Eckhardt was still compelled to resign the leadership of his movement after barely ten months (July 9, 1942) and then recede into the background. Thereafter the Movement for Independent Hungary—nominally under Béla Bartók's leadership—gradually petered out and died. While in existence, it had been forced to fight a two-front war, partially against the powerful anti-Hungarian lobby of such Little Entente states as Czechoslovakia, Yugoslavia, and Romania, and partially against the opposition of the equally determined left-leaning Hungarian émigré leaders. Its chances for winning this war were minimal, and Eckhardt simply proved that he was not up to the task.

Rivals of the "Movement for Independent Hungary"

Opposition from the Hungarian left surfaced even before Eckhardt reached the American shores. His leftist opponents represented a wide scale on the political spectrum. They included such outright Marxists as the journalist János Gyetván (1889–1967), the editor of the Hungarian American communist daily *Új Előre [New Forward]*, and such other political leftists as the London-based exiled politician Count Mihály Károlyi (1875–1955), who during the late 1930s and early 1940s had become an outright Stalin

---

27. See Várdy, *Historical Dictionary of Hungary*, 123.

28. The latter is not to be confused with Professor István Deák (b.1926) of Columbia University.

worshiper. But this opposition also included such liberals as the well-known sociologist Oscar Jászi (1875–1957), the noted legal scholar and publicist Rusztem Vámbéry (1872–1948),[29] and the widely known screen actor Béla Lugosi (1883–1956).[30] The last three mentioned were not communists, but they rejected all possible compromise and cooperation with a representative of the Horthy Regime. True, following the outbreak of World War II they separated themselves from the communists who congregated around the *Új Előre [New Forward]* and its successors, the *Magyar Világ [Hungarian World]* and *Magyar Jövő [Hungarian Future]*. But at the same time they also refused to cooperate with Eckhardt and the American Hungarian Federation. In their view the latter stood for a kind of blind traditional nationalism, which they were unable to accept. Nor were they able to stomach the fact that the majority of the Hungarian Americans who congregated under the flag of the federation continued to applaud the successes of Hungarian revisionism at the expense of Czechoslovakia, Romania, and Yugoslavia.[31]

Activities of the American Federation of Democratic Hungarians

While accepting the post-Trianon status quo in the Carpathian Basin, Jászi and his friends were unwilling to cooperate with the communists even for an allegedly common goal. Not so the equally liberal Vámbéry, who—similarly to Károlyi—did not shrink from working with the communists in the interest of Nazi defeat. This became evident upon his arrival in the United States, when he immediately established contacts with communist groups and put himself forth as Károlyi's American spokesman. Perhaps for this very reason, however, the editor of the *Amerikai Magyar Népszava* referred to him as the "court jester" of the Moscow-worshiping "red count."[32] Whether spokesman or court jester, Vámbéry instantly began his

---

29. Rusztem Vámbéry (1872–1948) was the son of the noted Hungarian Orientalist Arminus Vámbéry (1832–1913) and a prominent legal scholar. After World War II he served briefly as the Hungarian ambassador to the United States (1947–1948).

30. Although Béla Lugosi, famous for his portrayal of Dracula, was connected only peripherally with the political activities of the Vámbéry group, during the McCarthy era he was constantly hounded for his involvement. See Andor Sziklay, "Vámpír a külügyben" [Vampire in the State Department], in Andor Sziklay, *Magyar lábnyomok* [Hungarian Footsteps] (Cleveland, 1988), 151–55. This book was republished in Budapest in 1993.

31. On these problems and developments, see Nadányi, *The "Free Hungary" Movement*, 52–63.

32. Ibid., 53. This assertion by Paul Nadányi is fully substantiated by Vámbéry's correspondence found in the archives of the Hoover Institution of Stanford University.

assault against Eckhardt, the American Hungarian Federation, and the Movement for Independent Hungary. He flooded the U.S. State Department with defamatory reports about Eckhardt's allegedly subversive activities, and, in doing so, cooperated with representatives of the Little Entente in their efforts to undermine Hungary's position within the United States. In these reports Vámbéry supported the latter's politically motivated anti-Hungarian goals and assertions, and went so far as to condemn repeatedly Hungary's ethnically justifiable territorial gains, describing them as a manifestation of Hungary's Nazi sympathies.[33]

Vámbéry reached American shores in June 1941, two months before Eckhardt's own arrival. He immediately went to work to establish the "Democratic Federation of American Hungarians" (AFDH) [*Demokratikus Magyarok Amerikai Szövetsége*] with the intention of advancing his own special political agenda. The board of directors of the new federation included such well-known émigré intellectuals as the already mentioned sociologist-historian Jászi, the noted music director Eugene [Jenő] Ormándy (1899–1985), the distinguished publicist-historian Emil Lengyel (1895–1985), and the former Hungarian parliamentarian László Fényes (1871–1944).[34]

When established, Vámbéry's federation joined the ranks of a number of similar politically inspired organizations that had been formed after the start of the war by various émigré groups of liberal or socialist persuasion. These organizations often rivaled each other, cooperated with each other, merged and then separated again. This was also the fate of the Vámbéry-founded organization, which held a followup convention in Cleveland, in September of that year, where it promptly absorbed several similarly inspired organizations and then renamed itself the "American Federation of Democratic Hungarians" [*Demokratikus Magyarok Amerikai Szövetsége*].[35] In addition to the original board members, the leadership of this reconstituted federation included the noted painter and photo artist László Moholy-Nagy (1895–1946), the former Czechoslovak Hungarian parliamentarian Ignác Schultz, the prominent Chicago medical professor Hugó Rónay, the already mentioned film star Béla Lugosi, and János Terebessy, one of the

---

33. This is clear, for example, from Vámbéry's four-page memorandum to the U.S. State Department, written in or around July 1944. Cf. Vámbéry papers, box #5, Hoover Institution, Stanford University.

34. Concerning the formation of Vámbéry's federation, see the following contemporary report: "Új magyar politikai alakulat" [A New Hungarian Political Organization], *Bérmunkás* [Wage Worker] (Cleveland), June 21, 1941.

35. See Oszkár Róbert, "Demokratikus Magyarok Amerikai Szövetsége a szabad Magyarországért" [American Federation of Democratic Hungarians for a Free Hungary], *Az Ember* [The Man] (New York), September 27, 1941.

founding members and leaders of the left-leaning populist Hungarian "Sarló" [Sickle] movement[36] in interwar Czechoslovakia.[37]

Following the Cleveland convention, the AFDH initiated a general offensive against the Eckhardt-led movement. Vámbéry's goal was to discredit both the "Movement for Independent Hungary" and also further undermine the Horthy regime before the U.S. government. He repeatedly accused Eckhardt of racism and anti-Semitism in conjunction with his past role in the Association of Awakening Hungarians, while at the same time attacking the Horthy regime for its "willful and conscious alliance" with Nazi Germany.

Vámbéry and his associates began their attacks against Eckhardt even before the latter's arrival in the United States by publishing accusatory articles in a number of prominent American newspapers. One of these articles, signed by a certain Ludwig Lore of uncertain origin, was published in the July 21, 1941, edition of the *New York Post*. But the real attacks only began in late September, at the very moment when Eckhardt was launching his own "Movement for Independent Hungary."[38] The most damaging of these articles appeared in the liberal weekly, *The Nation*, where the above-mentioned Ignác Schultz, a Hungarian member of the former Czechoslovak Parliament, published an article under the title "Budapest's Fake Mission."[39] In this article he described in considerable detail Eckhardt's alleged racist and anti-Semitic past, as well as the nature of his current mission. Schultz likewise pointed to the widely known truth that Eckhardt had arrived in the United States with the knowledge and the financial support of the regent, Nicholas Horthy (1868–1957; r. 1920–1944), who at that very moment was officially an ally of Hitler's Germany.

Schultz's attack was followed within a week by an editorial in *The Nation,* which also accused the U.S. State Department with complicity in this matter.[40] This in turn started a whole barrage of accusations in the American press—both mainline and ethnic newspapers. These were written mostly

---

36. A movement of young, progressive Hungarian intellectuals in interwar Slovakia (Czechoslovakia) during the late 1920s and early 1930s. The movement split in 1931, when some of its left-leaning members accepted Marxism as their preferred political ideology. Cf. Várdy, *Historical Dictionary of Hungary,* 610–11.

37. See Robert. "Demokratikus Magyarok Amerikai Szövetsége a szabad Magyarországért." A poster announcing the congress of the new federation can be found among the Vámbéry-papers, Box #8, Hoover Institution, Stanford University.

38. Concerning these attacks, see the first five pages of Eckhardt's twenty-six page memorandum to the U.S. State Department, dated February 11, 1942 Cf. Eckhardt's Papers, Box #1, Hoover Institution, Stanford University.

39. Ignác Schultz, "Budapest's Fake Mission," *The Nation,* September 27, 1941. See also pages 5–9 of Eckhardt's above-mentioned twenty-six-page memorandum.

40. *The Nation,* October 3, 1941.

by advocates of the political left and by the representatives of the Little Entente states.[41]

Similar attacks also surfaced in Canada, where the well-known literary scholar and translator of East European literature, Watson Kirkconnell (1895–1976), also became embroiled in this affair. Kirkconnell, who had spent some time in Hungary, had known Eckhardt for many years and had a high opinion of him. Thus, he decided to speak up in the latter's defense. This action on the part of this Canadian scholar triggered a whole series of attacks against him by the leftist émigré press. The charge was led by István Szőke, the editor of the openly communist *Kanadai Magyar Munkás [Canadian Hungarian Worker]*.[42] But such accusatory articles subsequently also found their way into the popular Toronto weekly, the *Saturday Night*.[43]

Otto von Habsburg's Role

One of these accusatory articles came from the pen of Joseph S. Roucek, a well-known Czech émigré professor of sociology, who published a joint attack against Eckhardt and Otto von Habsburg in Princeton University's *The Public Opinion Quarterly*. Roucek tied Eckhardt's "Movement for Independent Hungary" to Otto von Habsburg's "Movement for Independent Austria," and labeled both of them anti-democratic and anti-American. He asserted that the real goal of these movements was to reestablish the oppressive and reactionary Habsburg Empire in the form of a new version of Austria-Hungary.[44] This plan allegedly also included the establishment of a "Habsburg Legion" in the form of a separate Austro-Hungarian military detachment that was meant to fight the Axis powers.[45] While

---

41. Many of these accusatory articles can be found among Vámbéry's and Eckhardt's papers in the archives of the Hoover Institution, Stanford University.

42. Concerning this anti-Kirkconnell campaign, see N. F. Dreisziger, "Watson Kirkconnell: Translator of Hungarian Poetry and Friend of Canadian-Hungarians," *The Canadian-American Review of Hungarian Studies*, Vol. 4, No. 2 (Fall 1977): 117–43; and Kirkconnell's reminiscences, "A Canadian Meets the Magyars," *The Canadian-American Review of Hungarian Studies*, Vol. 1, Nos. 1–2 (Fall 1974): 1–11.

43. See the article, "The Communists of Canada and Tibor Eckhardt," *Saturday Night* (Toronto), January 9, 1943. The Canadian aspect of the Eckhardt mission is discussed by N. F. Dreisziger in his "Mission Impossible: Secret Plans for a Hungarian Government-in-Exile in Canada during World War II," *Canadian Slavonic Papers*, Vol. 30, No. 2 (June 1988): 245–62; and N. F. Dreisziger, "Bridges to the West: The Horthy Regime's 'Reinsurance Policies' in 1941"—the latter being an unpublished paper.

44. Joseph S. Roucek, "The 'Free Movements' of Horthy's Eckhardt and Austria's Otto," *The Public Opinion Quarterly* (Princeton), Vol. 7 (Fall 1943): 466–77.

45. Ibid., 472–77.

making these accusations, Roucek apparently did not realize that this idea actually came from President Roosevelt, who has had intimate and frequent contacts with Otto von Habsburg ever since the early summer of 1940, when the latter fled Hitler's Europe to the safety of the United States.[46] Apparently, Roosevelt would even have liked to see the reestablishment of the former Habsburg Empire, at least in the form of a Danubian Confederation, a view, which he allegedly voiced several time when meeting with Archduke Otto, or with Empress Zita.[47]

The establishment of the Austrian, Norwegian and Greek Battalions— the first of which was to evolve into the "Habsburg Legion"—was announced on November 18, 1942, two days before Otto von Habsburg's thirtieth birthday. Julius Deutsch, Austria's former socialist Minister of Defense and one of the leaders of the anti-Habsburg Austrian emigration, viewed this act as a birthday gift to Archduke Otto. As recorded in his memoirs: "To advance the cause of the Habsburgs, the American Secretary of Defense commissioned the Austrian heir to the throne, on his 30th birthday, to establish a voluntary regiment, which was to serve in the American Armed Forces. This birthday gift meant the recognition of Otto von Habsburg as Austria's legal representative."[48]

While the proposed Habsburg Legion never fully materialized, it did reach the period of gestation, about which we do have some reminiscences by participants. One of these is by the Hungarian poet György Faludy (b.1910), who in those days was a political émigré in the United States, and who had actually been drafted into this legion.[49] He remembers his experiences in the spring of 1943 as follows: "For a few months I resided in

---

46. For details concerning the relationship between Roosevelt and Otto von Habsburg, see Várdy, "Az amerikai magyar emigráció és Habsburg Ottó," and its revised English-language version, "Archduke Otto von Habsburg and American Hungarian Emigrés during and after World War II." See also Emilio Vasari [Emil Csonka], *Dr. Otto Habsburg oder die Leidenschaft für Politik* (Vienna-Munich, 1972), chap. 11. Otto von Habsburg's role in the establishment of the Habsburg Legion is also mentioned in the article about him in the new *Magyar Katolikus Lexikon* [Hungarian Catholic Encyclopedia], vol. 4 (Budapest, 1998), 447–49.

47. As an example, on September 7, 1943, when Empress Zita represented Archduke Otto at a meeting in the White House, President Roosevelt allegedly assured the Empress that he would prefer to see the rise of a new Danubian Confederation that would take the place of the former Habsburg Empire, and thus end the fragmentation of Central Europe. Cf. Archduke Otto's handwritten notes, as quoted by Emil Csonka, *Habsburg Ottó: Egy különös sors története* [Otto von Habsburg. History of a Unique Destiny] (Munich, 1972), 357.

48. Julius Deutsch, *Ein weiter Weg* (Zürich-Leipzig-Wien, 1960), 361; as quoted by Csonka, *Habsburg Ottó*, 329.

49. György Faludy, who currently resides in Hungary, lived in exile between 1938 and 1946, as well as between 1956 and 1989. During his first emigration he

Camp Atterbury, in the middle of Indiana's scraggy and scrofula-infected forests, amidst six foot high snowbanks, in a short-lived unit of the American Army, as a member of the Habsburg Legion, to which I had been assigned. The Legion was the brainchild of FDR and Cordell Hull. Following the war they planned to reestablish the Austro-Hungarian Empire. This plan, however, succumbed to adverse American public opinion and to Stalin's mustache that trembled with anger."[50] Faludy is probably mistaken about Secretary of State Cordell Hull's role in or support of this undertaking. But the idea of a Habsburg Legion was favored by President Roosevelt, Secretary of War Henry L. Stimson, and Undersecretary of State Sumner Welles—the latter of whom was convinced that the destruction of the Dual Monarchy had been a wrong decision, for it produced only impoverishment and political chaos in the Danube region.[51]

In spite of President Roosevelt's original support of this notion, political circumstances compelled him to drop the idea of a Habsburg Legion, as well as his support for the reestablishment of some sort of a Habsburg-led Central European or Danubian Confederation. The nascent Habsburg Legion was dissolved in May 1943,[52] and subsequently the idea of a Habsburg-Danubian Federation also receded into the background.[53]

Throughout this period, Tibor Eckhardt was in close contact with Archduke Otto. Having shed his early anti-Habsburg sentiments, by the 1930s he had become a legitimist, i.e., a supporter of the restoration of the Habsburg dynasty upon the Hungarian throne. Following his arrival in the United States, Eckhardt immediately established contact with Archduke Otto and began to coordinate his political activities with those of the young

---

served in the U.S. Armed Forces, while during his second emigration he edited literary journals in London, Paris, and Toronto, and has taught literature at various American and Canadian universities. Cf. *Új Magyar Irodalmi Lexikon* [New Hungarian Literary Encyclopedia], ed. László Peter, 3 vols. (Budapest, 1994), I, 553.

50. György Faludy and Eric Johnson, *Jegyzetek az esőerődőbl* [Notes from the Rain Forest] (Budapest, 1991), 15.

51. Cf. Sumner Welles, *Seven Decisions That Shaped History* (New York, 1950), 136. One of Otto's biographer, who interviewed Otto repeatedly, claims that it was actually President Roosevelt who brought up the idea of an Austrian or Habsburg Legion with Archduke Otto, who initially received it with some degree of skepticism. Cf. Csonka, *Habsburg Ottó*, 327.

52. See the report in the *New York Times*, May 24, 1943. The article about Otto von Habsburg in the Hungarian Catholic encyclopedia claims that he continued to be involved in the affairs of the Habsburg Legion until March 1944. Cf. *Magyar Katolikus Lexikon*, IV, 448.

53. President Roosevelt's toying with the idea of reestablishing the old Dualist Monarchy in some form or other has also been commented upon by Carlyle A. Macartney in his monumental history of modern Hungary: *October Fifteenth. A History of Modern Hungary*, II, 112.

Habsburg.[54] It is to be remembered that in those days Otto was known, not only for his strong anti-Nazi and anti-Hitler stance, but also for his desire to reestablish the once mighty Habsburg Empire. In his view—which he voiced continuously during his four years' stay in the United States—the reestablished Habsburg Empire would have served as a "democratic counterweight" in the region between Germany and Russia. At the same time he also emphasized repeatedly that the resurrected Habsburg state would undergo a total social and political transformation, and would not start a quarrel with the Soviet Union, which at that moment was fighting on the side of the Western democracies.[55]

Although favored by President Roosevelt, Vámbéry and his supporters repeatedly condemned Otto's political goals and activities, as they did the aspirations of Eckhardt and the American Hungarian Federation. As an example of this anti-Habsburg crusade on the part of the American Federation of Democratic Hungarians, we may cite Vámbéry's manifesto during Otto's lecture tour in November 1943, in which he proclaimed that: "The restoration of Habsburg feudalism would be a danger not only to the peasants and workers of Hungary, but a danger to all nations adjacent. Any hope that the [reestablished] Habsburg Empire would create a buffer state in Europe is ridiculous."[56] This view rhymed well with the position of the Soviet Union and those of the Little Entente states.

The Liquidation of Eckhardt's Mission

In light of the repeated attacks by Vámbéry and the AFDH, Eckhardt's position became shaky within less than a year after launching his Movement for Independent Hungary. He recognized this himself and said so in the twenty-six page memorandum that he submitted to the State Department on February 11, 1942. In this document he summarized his political activities in the United States and enumerated and discussed the relentless propaganda war against him by the Vámbéry group and by the representatives of the Little Entente states. He documented these attacks by listing the scores of articles published against him, from which he quoted liberally.[57]

---

54. In addition to my cited articles on Archduke Otto, see Montgomery, *Hungary, the Unwilling Satellite,* 96; and Ignác Romsics, *Wartime Plans for a New Hungary: Documents from the U.S. Department of State, 1942–1944* (New York, 1992), 6–10.

55. See the article "Confident Otto Maps Royal Foreign Policy. Pretender Says He'll Make Peace with Russia," *New York Times,* December 1, 1943.

56. Quoted in ibid.

57. See Eckhardt's memorandum to the U.S. State Department, dated February 11, 1942.

Apparently the response from the State Department was not very reassuring, for after this exchange Eckhardt survived at the head of his organization for only five more months. He resigned on July 9, 1942, giving his position over to Béla Bartók. But, as it turned out, his resignation also signaled the fading of the "Movement for Independent Hungary," which thereafter merged increasingly into the American Hungarian Federation. Neither Bartók nor the leaders of the AHF were able fill Eckhardt's shoes. The latter remained in the background and from there he tried to influence the AHF's political activities as best as he could. He also kept in touch with Archduke Otto and continued to send political reports to Hungary, in particular to Count István Bethlen, who was in charge of his "American adventure." In his report dated October 1, 1943, for example, Eckhardt summarized the results of Otto's meeting with President Roosevelt:

> Today, October 1st, Otto was once more received by President Roosevelt, who on his own initiative offered a clear picture as to what Hungary can expect from him. He bemoaned the fact that developments in American-Hungarian relations are far from satisfactory, which also holds true for English-Hungarian relations. He regarded this as lamentable, for if Hungary were to normalize its relations with the Allies, they would accept her as a "co-belligerent" country. Naturally, this would mean that at an appropriate moment Hungary would have to turn against the Germans. Upon Archduke Otto's query whether we [Hungarians] could become members of the "United Nations" (which would assure our place among the victors), Roosevelt answered that it is unlikely that this would be approved by Russia (which means that he would be willing to agree to it!). As a second point, he stated that in case of such a switch, Hungary would have to commit itself to certain personal changes (he did not mention names). Thirdly, he also spoke about territorial questions. In order to achieve a final solution in the Russian Question, he would be willing . . . to assign Romania, and even Bulgaria to the Russian orbit. This would mean that in case of a correct policy change Hungary could regain *all* of Transylvania, which otherwise would also fall under Russian control. . . . In my estimation, the purpose of this repeated and well-thought-out statement was that it should be passed on to Hungary. . . . This pronouncement, in my view, presents us with an acceptable basis for negotiations.[58]

Eckhardt ended his letter with the following words: "I am sending this letter to Budapest, not through the usual American line, but with the help of a messenger from the Polish underground."[59]

We don't know how they received Eckhardt's letter in Hungary, we can only guess. But we know that, in spite of Prime Minister Miklós Kállay's efforts to wiggle out of the German alliance, the Horthy Regime was unable to bring itself to break with Germany even in light of these most favorable

---

58. Eckhardt's letter to Count István Bethlen, New York, October 1, 1943. Eckhardt papers, Box #2, Hoover Institution, Stanford University.

conditions. The fear of the German war machine, combined with the dread of Bolshevik Russia, prevented Hungary's contemporary leaders from acting upon this offer. Moreover, when a year later Regent Horthy finally decided to break with Germany, he did it blunderingly and under much worse conditions, which made Hungary's situation even more hopeless than before.

Eckhardt wrote his final report to Budapest—this time in English—on March 8, 1944. This report was addressed to "Dear Friend" [Count István Bethlen], and was signed by "Peti" [Tibor Eckhardt] és "John" [former ambassador János Pelényi]. This thirteen-page letter presented a Washington-based overview of the political and military situation in the early part of 1944. In general, it was much more pessimistic than any of the earlier reports. It was intended to reach Budapest via Portugal, but never arrived there. According to Eckhardt's handwritten note on a copy of this report found among his papers in the Hoover Institution, its fate was sealed by Hungary's German occupation: "The Hungarian courier was on his way from Portugal to Budapest, but upon learning about the German occupation of March 19th, he turned back. The report was destroyed."[60]

The Continued Role of the American Hungarian Federation

Following Eckhardt's resignation, the protection of Hungary's interests in the United States officially devolved upon the American Hungarian Federation, and more specifically upon its executive secretary, Professor Tibor Kerekes of Georgetown University. Given the political realities of the day, however, neither the AHF nor Kerekes could do much. The leaders of the federation did not even have enough influence to secure an audience with President Roosevelt—as was done repeatedly by Otto von Habsburg. Consequently, next to incessantly repeating their loyalty to the United States, supporting the war efforts of their adopted country, and responding to the

---

59. Ibid. Concerning the Polish Underground's operation in Hungary, see the recently published memoirs of József Antall, *Menekültek menedéke: Emlékek és iratok* [Refugee Haven: Memoirs and Documents] (Budapest, 1997), 91–177. József Antall (1896–1974) was the father of Hungary's first post-communist prime minister, József Antall (1931–1993). In the period between 1939 and 1944 the elder Antall served as the Hungarian government's commissioner for refugee affairs, in which capacity he was in close and continuous contact with the more than 100,000 Polish military and civilian personnel who had fled to Hungary after the German invasion of Poland on September 1, 1939.

60. Eckhardt's and Pelényi's joint report to Count István Bethlen, Washington, D.C., March 8, 1944. Eckhardt papers, Box #2, Hoover Institution, Stanford University. The quoted passage is in Eckhardt's handwriting on the upper margin of the first page.

ever more numerous anti-Hungarian articles that appeared in various American newspapers, the AHF's activities consisted of issuing proclamations to the press and writing memoranda to the White House or the State Department. Naturally, these memoranda seldom, if ever, reached the addressees; they were usually answered by some petty bureaucrat hired specifically for such purposes. Most of the responses were banal and meaningless. When reading them, one has the feeling that one is reading generic form letters that have been dispatched many times before to numerous groups and individuals, without any meaningful changes. At times, it appears that the "author" of the letter does not have the vaguest idea about the issue at hand.

A good example of such a response is a letter signed and dispatched by William D. Hassett, secretary to the President, on June 8, 1944, in which he registered the receipt of Kerekes's earlier letter addressed to President Roosevelt in the name of the American Hungarian Federation.[61] It reads as follows: "Dear Professor Kerekes: Please accept the President's thanks for your letter of June fifth, inspired by the second anniversary of war by the United States on Hungary. The President was glad to receive your letter and shares your hope that a better future for Hungary and for the whole world can be established under the principles of the Atlantic Charter."[62]

Eckhardt and the AHF after World War II

Following the war, the paths of the American Hungarian Federation and Tibor Eckhardt parted. The former—at least for a while—remained under the control of native-born and largely Americanized offspring of the turn-of-the-century economic immigrants. Although still engaged in ethnic politics, following the cessation of hostilities the main activities of the AHF centered on the American Hungarian Relief Fund that had been organized in September 1944. The basic goal of the relief fund was to aid war-shattered Hungary as well as the hundreds of thousands of Hungarian political émigrés who—having fled before the Red Army—found themselves in the western territories of the former Third Reich.[63] In the course of 1945, the

---

61. Tibor Kerekes's letter to President Roosevelt, June 5, 1944. Eckhardt papers, Box #6, Hoover Institution, Stanford University.

62. William D. Hassett's letter to Tibor Kerekes, June 8, 1944. Eckhardt papers, Box #6, Hoover Institution, Stanford University.

63. Concerning these so-called displaced persons or DPs, see Wolfgang Jacobmeyer, *Vom Zwangsarbeiter zum Heimatlosen Ausländer: Die Displaced Persons in West Deutschland 1945–1951* (Göttingen, Germany, 1985); and Mark Wyman, *DP: Europe's Displaced Persons, 1945–1951* (Philadelphia, 1989). For the Hungarian DPs specifically, see Kázmér Nagy, *Elveszett alkotmány: Vázlat az 1944 és 1964 közötti magyar politikai emigráció kialakulásáról* [Lost Constitution:

Relief Fund sent tens of thousands of care packages to Hungary, and in 1946, also to the Hungarian refugee camps in Germany and Austria.[64] Naturally, the activities of the American Hungarian Relief Fund altered nothing in U.S. foreign policy concerning Hungary, but it did improve the lives of many thousands of Hungarians, both at home and abroad.

While the AHF and the Hungarian American fraternal associations that supported it financially concentrated their efforts on relief activities, Eckhardt continued to be involved in politics. As soon as conditions permitted it, he joined forces with the leaders of those political immigrants, who—having remained in Hungary after the war—had been active in the postwar coalition governments. In consequence of the cold war and the resulting communist takeover, however, they were pushed out of power, and by 1947 or 1948 they all were forced to flee their homeland.

On July 21, 1948, these refugee politicians jointly established the Hungarian National Council [Magyar Nemzeti Bizottmány] in New York, which for a while functioned as a potential government-in-exile.[65] Among its eight, later ten-member Executive Committee, Eckhardt was the only active representative of the interwar Horthy regime.[66] As a result of this reality, he was in a constant minority on most political issues. In spite of his minority position, however, he would speak up in defense of the Old Regime. But by that time, what he considered the "old regime" was represented almost solely by Otto von Habsburg, or rather by Eckhardt's dedication to the

---

Outline History of the Hungarian Political Emigration between 1944 and 1964] (Munich, 1974); Gyula Borbándi, *A magyar emigráció életrajza, 1945–1985* [Biography of the Hungarian Emigration, 1945–1985] (Bern, 1985); Ágnes Huszár Várdy, "A magyarságtudat megtartása a német és osztrák DP-táborokban a második világháború utáni években" [Retention of Hungarian National Consciousness in German and Austrian DP Camps in the Years following World War II], *Forrás* [Source] (Kecskemét, Hungary), Vol. 23, No. 3 (March 1991): 58–63; Béla Várdy, "A világháború utáni politikai emigránsok: negyvenötösök, negyvenhetesek, ötvenhatosok" [Post-World War II Emigrés: Forty-Fivers, Forty-Seveners, Fifty-Sixers], *Kapu* [Gate] (Budapest), Vol. 8, No. 9 (September 1945): 48–52; and Várdy, *Magyarok az Újvilágban*, 438–91.

64. Concerning the activities of the American Hungarian Relief Fund, see "American Hungarian Relief, Inc.—Az Amerikai Magyar Segélyakció." *AMNSZ Golden Jubilee Album*, 95–97; and Bakó, *Memorial Volume*, 56–58.

65. Concerning the functioning of the Hungarian National Committee see "Hungarian Politicians in Exile," in *Facts about Hungary: The Fight for Freedom,* ed. Imre Kovács (New York, 1966), 301–14.

66. The Executive Committee of the Hungarian National Council also had a few politically less active representatives of the interwar regime. The majority of its membership, however, consisted of politicians who had been active participants in Hungary's post-World War II coalition governments (1945–1947) and thus were viewed as "leftists" by Eckhardt and his followers.

cause of the House of Habsburg. There are many signs of this dedication in the correspondence between Eckhardt and Archduke Otto, found among the former's papers at the Hoover Institution of Stanford University. This correspondence, which also contains a number of political directives by Otto to Eckhardt, continued unabated until the latter's death in 1972.[67]

Conclusions

Looking at it from the vantage point of the end of the twentieth century, we can safely assume that the American Hungarian Federation's and Tibor Eckhardt's efforts during World War II did very little to affect the basic policy of the United States regarding Hungary. That policy was in fact determined by much more important considerations than the activities of a few interest groups and temporary émigré organizations.

The most significant of these factors included: (1) the overriding desire of the Western Allies to defeat Nazi Germany; (2) their need to accommodate the territorial and great power aspirations of the Soviet Union; (3) the necessity of taking into consideration the alignment of the various successor states in the confrontation between Nazi Germany and the Western Allies; (4) and finally, the ability or inability of Hitler's "unwilling satellites" to switch sides at the appropriate time.

As compared to the other "unwilling satellites"—Croatia, Slovakia, Romania, and Bulgaria—Hungary was in the worst possible position in all of these categories. Being a revisionist state with strong claims to Hungarian-inhabited territories immediately adjacent its new post-Trianon frontiers, and not finding any Western support for its revisionist claims, it was virtually pushed into the embraces of Fascist Italy and Nazi Germany. Moreover, after regaining some of its territories in 1938–1941, it was under even greater German pressure to adjust its policies to those of the Third Reich. This was all the more so as Tiso's Slovakia, Antonescu's Romania, and Pavelić's Croatia were significantly more compliant in satisfying Germany's demands.[68]

---

67. On the relationship between Eckhardt and Otto von Habsburg, see my article cited above; and Vasari, *Dr. Otto Habsburg*, chaps. 11–14.

68. Examples of Hungary's relative noncompliance with Germany's demands included the following: The Hungarian government declined to permit German troops to cross the country in their attack against Poland in 1939. Following the German attack, the country received, protected, and supported a large number of Polish refugees, including civilians, military men, as well as Polish Jews. It also aided many of the Polish military units to reach the West via the Balkans. Moreover, notwithstanding repeated German demands, Hungary refused to collect and deliver its Jewish citizens to Germany until after the country's German occupation on March 19, 1944.

None of these realities, however, could alter the fact that Hungary was an ally of Nazi Germany. This fact alone carried much more weight with the U.S. government and with the Western Allies than anything Hungarian Americans could have done or said. Moreover, whatever they did or said, it was immediately contradicted by the well-oiled political émigré organizations of the Little Entente states, as well as by the left-leaning Hungarian émigrés themselves. In light of these realities, the well-meaning efforts of Hungarian Americans to help their motherland appears more like Don Quixote's hopeless duel with the proverbial Spanish windmill. In effect, their struggle turned out to be virtually meaningless. The best proofs for this are the terms of the Treaty of Paris (February 10, 1947), which, in addition to reestablishing Hungary's Trianon frontiers, also obliged the country to transfer three additional Hungarian-inhabited towns to Slovakia in the vicinity of the capital city of Bratislava.[69] This, in spite the fact that Tiso's Slovakia was one of Hitler's most compliant satellites. Slovakia, therefore, was not judged on its own terms, but rather as a component of the highly favored Czechoslovak state under the leadership of the equally highly regarded Edward Beneš. Hungary, on the other hand, was viewed as Hitler's "last satellite" that deserved whatever it got. And this negative perception could not have been altered by anything that was within the power of Hungarian Americans to do.

---

69. For the circumstances around, and terms of the Treaty of Paris of February 10, 1947, see Stephen D. Kertész, *Between Russia and the West: Hungary and the Illusions of Peacemaking, 1945–1947* (Notre Dame, IN, 1984). See also Stephen Borsody, *The Tragedy of Central Europe* (New York, 1962), 220–22; and *Magyarország történeti kronológiája* [Hungary's Historical Chronology], ed. Kálmán Benda, 4 vols. (Budapest, 1982), IV, 1033–34.

Chapter 6

The Nazi-Soviet Pact of August 23, 1939: When Did Stalin Decide to Align with Hitler, and Was Poland the Culprit?

Anna M. Cienciala

The official reason given by the Soviet government for the failure of Anglo-French-Soviet negotiations for a military and political alliance in late August 1939, was the refusal of Poland and Romania to allow the passage of Soviet troops through their territories in the event of a German attack on those countries. Soviet historians upheld that view, especially blaming Poland, but also accusing the Western powers of planning to set Germany against the USSR, and claiming that this situation gave Stalin no choice but to conclude a pact with Hitler.[1] Although microfilm copies of the secret protocol to the Nazi-Soviet Nonaggression Pact of August 23, 1939, were found in western Germany at war's end, and were published in the West, Soviet authorities and historians consistently denied the protocol's existence, as did the commissar for foreign affairs, Vyacheslav M. Molotov, who signed it.[2] It is clear, however, that high Soviet officials knew the German and Russian originals were

---

1. For an early version of some of these charges, see Vyacheslav M. Molotov's speech to the Supreme Soviet of August 31, 1939: *God Krizisa, 1938–1939* (Moscow, 1990), vol. 2, [henceforth: *GK 2*] no. 620; Jane Degras, ed., *Soviet Documents on Foreign Policy*, vol. III [henceforth: Degras *SDFP* III] (Oxford, 1953), 363–371. For the old party line on 1939, see Boris Ponomaryov et al., eds., *History of Soviet Foreign Policy, 1917–1945* (Moscow, 1969), ch. 11: and Vilnis Sipols, *Diplomatic Battles Before World War II* (Moscow, 1982), ch. IV. On standard Soviet treatments of interwar Polish foreign policy, see Anna M. Cienciala, "Marxism and History: Recent Polish and Soviet Interpretations of Polish Foreign Policy in the Era of Appeasement. An Evaluation," *East European Quarterly* 1, no. 1 (1967): 92–117.

2. Molotov, who signed the secret protocol along with Ribbentrop, told a Russian journalist: "There could not have been any such secret agreement. . . . I can assure you that this is unquestionably a fabrication." See Albert Resis, ed., *Molotov Remembers. Inside Kremlin Politics. Conversations with Felix Chuev* (Chicago 1993), 13.

kept in sealed envelopes in the Presidential Archives in the Kremlin where they were officially "discovered" in October 1992. Earlier, copies were found and verified in the archives, as admitted publicly in late December 1989.[3] The lively debate that took place on the pact among Russian historians in 1989, and carried on in Russian works published in the next few years, showed two schools of thought: one close to the former official interpretation, defending Stalin's policy, while the second condemned it along with other aspects of Stalinism. The 1989 debate began before the official acknowledgment of the existence of the copies and subsequently the originals

---

3. The first information on the negotiations for the secret protocol was given at the Nuremberg Trials by the lawyer defending Rudolf Hess, citing a deposition by the German Foreign Ministry legal expert, Friedrich Gauss, who was present at the negotiations, see Alfred Seidl, *Der Fall Rudolf Hess 1941–1987. Dokumentation des Verteidigers*, 3rd, expanded printing (Munich, 1988), 93–95. However, the Allied prosecutors agreed to the Soviet request that this evidence was inadmissible at the Nuremberg Trials.

On the history of the microfilm containing the secret protocol, see: Ingeborg Fleischhauer, *Der Pakt. Hitler, Stalin unter die Initiative der deutschen Diplomatie 1938–1939* (Berlin, Frankfurt-am-Main, 1990), note 139, 533–534. The Secret protocol of August 23, 1939, was first published in the British press by the *Manchester Guardian*, 30 May 1946. It was then published in *Nazi-Soviet Relations 1939–1941. Documents from the Archives of the German Foreign Office*, Washington, 1948, 78, and republished in *Documents on German Foreign Policy* (henceforth: *DGFP*) ser. D, vol. VII (London, Washington, 1956), no. 229; for the Russian texts see *GK 2* (Moscow, 1990) nos. 602, 603 and *Dokumenty Vneshnei Politiki. Vol. XXII, 1939 god*. Kniga I, [henceforth: *DVP 1939 I*] (Moscow, 1992), no, 485.

On finding verified copies of the secret protocol, see Alexander N. Yakovlev's speech to the Second Congress of People's Deputies, December 24, 1989, Russian text, *Izvestiia*, December 25, 1989, reprinted in: O.A. Rzheshevskii, ed., *1939 God. Urokii Istorii* [henceforth: *1939 God*] (Moscow, 1990), appendix, 492–493. For the Congress's condemnation of the secret protocols announced on December 25, see: Mikhail S. Gorbachev, *Pravda*, December 28, 1989, reprint in *1939 God*, 496–497; brief excerpt in *Current Digest of the Soviet Press*, 1990, no. 42, #09, 11.1; for the full text of the reports, see *On the Political and Legal Assessment of the Soviet-German Non-Aggression Treaty of 1939* (Moscow, 1990).

On the first discovery of original German and Russian copies of the secret protocol in the Russian Presidential Archives, when Gorbachev handed over power to Boris N. Yeltsin, see interview given by Yakovlev—who was present—to Michael Dobbs, in his: *Down with Big Brother. The Fall of the Soviet Empire* (New York, 1996), 447–448. On the discovery of the Secret protocol by Russian archivists and historians in October 1992, see Dmitri Volkogonov, *Autopsy for an Empire. The Seven Leaders Who Built the Soviet Regime*, trans. and ed. Harold Shukman (New York and London), 1998, 528, cf. Lev Bezymensky, "The Secret Protocols of 1939 as a Problem of Soviet Historiography," in Gabriel Gorodetsky, ed., *Soviet Foreign Policy 1917–1991. A Retrospective* (London, 1994), 83–84.

of the secret protocol, though a selection of German and Soviet documents published that year clearly impelled this acknowledgment. Nevertheless, many Russian historians still believe that Western appeasement of Germany, and the Soviet need for time, left Stalin no other option than the pact with Hitler to ensure the country's security.[4]

The policy of the Polish government, touted by Soviet historiography as the decisive factor in the failure of Soviet-Western military negotiations in August 1939, was viewed in the same way by some Western participants. Thus, in the memoirs of Sir Robert Strang (then assistant secretary for foreign affairs and head of the Central Department of the Foreign Office, who assisted the British ambassador in Moscow, Sir William Seeds, from mid-June to early August 1939), Warsaw's refusal of the Soviet demand for the passage of the Red Army through Poland was presented as the decisive factor in the breakdown of the negotiations.[5] This was also the view of French captain (later general) André Beaufre, a member of the French contingent in the Anglo-French military mission in Moscow.[6] He was sent to Warsaw to help persuade the Polish government to accept the Soviet demand; years later, he still believed the Polish refusal led to the breakdown of negotiations. However, two key British participants who were in Moscow at the time, thought otherwise. General T. G. Heywood, head of the army section of the British military delegation, thought France and Britain never had a chance because the Russians had been playing both sides to get the highest price, and the British ambassador, Sir William Seeds, was happy

4. For a brief survey of the debate among Russian historians, see: M.I. Mel'miukhov, "Predyistoriia Velikoi Otechestvennoi Voiny v sovremennykh diskusiiakh," in G.A. Bordiagov, ed., *Istoricheskie Issledovaniia v Rossii. Tendentsii poslednikh let* (Moscow, 1996), 278–307; on 1939, ibid., 278–283. For a condemnation of Stalin for signing the pact, see: V.L. Doroshenko, "Stalinskaia provokatsiia vtoroi mirovoi voiny," in: *Drugaia Voina 1939–1945* (Moscow), 1996, 60–72; Lev I. Ginzburg, "Sovetsko-Germanskii pakt: Zamysel i ego realizatsiia," *Otechestvennai Istoriia*, no 3 (1996), 29–40; and M. I. Semiriaga, *Tainy stalinskoi diplomatsii, 1939–1941* (Moscow, 1992), an earlier version of which appeared as "Sovetsko-Germanskiie dogovorennosti v 1939—iunie 1941: Vzgliad istorika," *Sovetskiie Gosudarstvo i Pravo*, no.9 (1989), 92–104.

5. Lord Strang, *At Home and Abroad* (London, 1956), 189–190. Strang had been the British chargé d'affaires in Moscow in the early 1930s. For a brief biographical sketch, see Donald Cameron Watt, *How War Came. The Immediate Origins of the Second World War, 1938–1939* (London, 1989), 361–362.

6. For Beaufre's account of his mission to Warsaw, see General [André] Beaufre, *Mémoires 1920—1940—1945* (Paris, 1965), 144–151.

to accuse Molotov of bad faith to his face.[7] Nevertheless, Western historians generally sided with Strang and Beaufre. A quarter of a century after the Moscow negotiations, the British historian, A. J. P. Taylor, a defender of British appeasement, condemned Polish foreign policy for being unreasonable and for pretending to great power status, while he credited the USSR with the intention of attacking Germany in case of war. He blamed the Western powers and Poland for the failure of negotiations with Moscow, and contended that the Nazi-Soviet pact was neither an alliance nor a partition of Poland.[8] Although Taylor's views were more extreme than most, Western historians generally agreed that the Poles were either partly or largely to blame for the failure of the Anglo-French-Soviet negotiations and, thus, for the conclusion of the Nazi-Soviet Nonaggression Pact.

As mentioned earlier, in 1989, on the fiftieth anniversary of the outbreak of World War II, much was written about the pact in Russia, but positive interpretations of Stalin's policy held a significant edge. There was no such debate in the West; indeed, the vast majority of Western historical periodicals did not even discuss it. British historians and writers who did so, generally agreed that Stalin had no other option but to align with Hitler, and castigated Poland for her refusal to accept Soviet troops into its territory. Thus, two journalist-historians, Anthony Reed and David Fisher, approvingly cited journalist-historian William Shirer to the effect that Polish "self-destructiveness" had been responsible for the partitions of Poland in the late eighteenth century, and that the Poles were guilty of "willful blindness" in refusing to consider Soviet demands for Red Army passage in August 1939. To this, the two authors added their own disparaging comment: "Like the three little pigs, the Poles still frolicked inside their straw house while the big bad wolf was already drawing breath on the outside."[9]

---

7. For general T. G. Heywood's opinion, see point 8 in his letter of August 23 to the Director of Military Operations and Intelligence, *Documents on British Foreign Policy* [henceforth: *DBFP*], 3rd series, vol. VII (London, 1954), app. II, no. 6, 607. For Seeds to Molotov on bad faith, see Seeds to Halifax, August 29, 1939, in D.C. Watt, ed., *British Documents on Foreign Affairs: Reports and Papers from the Foreign Office Confidential Print*, Part II, Series A. *The Soviet Union 1917–1939*, vol. 15 (Lanham, MD., 1986), 144.

8. For examples of Taylor's disparaging opinion of Foreign Minister Józef Beck and Polish foreign policy, see *The Origins of the Second World War* (London, 1961), 80–81, 251; on the Nazi-Soviet Pact, 262. For a penetrating critique of Taylor's views on Poland, see Piotr S.Wandycz, "Poland between East and West," ch. 8 in Gordon Martel, ed., *The Origins of the Second World War Reconsidered. The A.J.P. Taylor Debate After Twenty-Five Years* (Boston, London, Sydney, 1986), 187–209.

9. Anthony Reed and David Fisher, *The Deadly Embrace. Hitler, Stalin, and the Nazi-Soviet Pact, 1939–1941* (New York and London, 1988), 214–215. William L. Shirer (1904–93) was the Universal News Service correspondent in Berlin, 1934–37, also Columbia Broadcasting Service correspondent in Vienna, 1935–37, Prague

On a scholarly level, the leading German historian of Soviet-German relations in 1938–39, Ingeborg Fleischhauer, contended that the Polish refusal to allow the passage of Soviet troops eliminated Moscow's option of an alliance with the Western powers. However, some German historians disagreed. They perceived Stalin's goal as either expanding communism after an exhausting European war in which the USSR would be neutral, or as Soviet territorial expansion, or a combination of both.[10]

After the publication in 1990–1992 of Soviet diplomatic documents for 1939,[11] most Western historians still hewed to their previous views. Thus, British historian Geoffrey Roberts concluded that, while an agreement with Nazi Germany was always an option for Stalin, "not until the final breakdown of the military negotiations with Britain and France were the Germans invited to cross the threshold." He claimed that this was an act of desperation on Stalin's part, and also endorsed Taylor's view of the Nazi-Soviet pact.[12] Another British historian, Jonathan Haslam, had concluded earlier (1984) that:

> Confronted with the evident unwillingness of the Entente to provide immediate, concrete, and water-tight guarantees for Soviet security in Europe, let alone in Asia . . . the Russians were left with little alternative but an agreement with Germany creating a condominium in Eastern Europe. Nonetheless, the Nazi-Soviet pact was unquestionably the second best solution.[13]

Haslam thought that Stalin kept his options open until it was clear that the Anglo-French military delegation was not ready to grant Soviet demands.

---

and Berlin, 1937–40, then war correspondent 1941–45; see his *Berlin Diary, 1934–1941* (New York, 1941), and *The Rise and Fall of the Third Reich* (New York, 1961). He was very critical of Polish foreign policy, particularly with regard to the USSR.

10. Ingeborg Fleischhauer, "Soviet Foreign Policy and the Origins of the Hitler-Stalin Pact," in Bernd Wegner, ed., *From Peace to War. Germany, Soviet Russia and the World, 1939–1941* (Oxford, 1997), 31, 43. For the view that Stalin aimed to expand communism after a European war, see Gottfried Schramm, "Basic Features of German Ostpolitik, 1918–1939," Wegner, ibid., 24; for a similar view, see Rolf Ahmann, "Der Hitler-Stalin Pakt: Nichtangriffs- und Angriffsvertrag?" in: Erwin Oberländer, ed., *Hitler-Stalin Pakt 1939: Das Ende Mitteleuropas?* (Frankfurt-am-Main, 1989), 26–42; and Jorg K. Hoensch, ibid., 50.

11. See note 3 above. *DVP 1939* I contains more new Russian documents than *God Krizisa*, published in 1990.

12. Geoffrey Roberts, *The Soviet Union and the Origins of the Second World War. Russo-German Relations and the Road to War, 1933–1941* (New York, 1995), 86, 92. For an earlier work by this author, with similar conclusions, see *The Unholy Alliance. Stalin's Pact with Hitler* (Bloomington, IN., 1989).

13. Jonathan Haslam, *The Soviet Union and the Struggle for Collective Security in Europe, 1933–1939* (New York, 1984), 231.

However, in 1994, he concluded that Stalin had opted for Hitler as early as the dismissal of Maxim M. Litvinov from the post of commissar of foreign affairs in early May 1939. This view is shared by some Russian historians, for example, Lev I. Ginzberg.[14] Fleischhauer contends, however, that Stalin finally made up his mind on August 21, when it was clear that the British and French delegations had no answer to give on the passage of Soviet troops through Poland and Romania. An American historian, Teddy Uldricks, rejects all existing theories in favor of the simple explanation that Stalin was a realist and sought security wherever he could find it, a view shared by Gabriel Gorodetsky.[15] According to Canadian historian Michael Jabara Carlay, [Foreign Minister Józef] "Beck was the *bete noire* of just about everyone in Europe" and " . . . Litvinov regarded him as a Nazi pimp." [sic]. Finally, Carlay writes: "Polish opposition to collective security and Polish collusion with Nazi Germany immensely irritated Soviet and French diplomats and led ultimately to Poland's disappearance."[16] As for the Poles, most have always believed—as did the Polish government in August 1939—that Stalin wanted to stay out of the war, preferred a deal with Hitler, and deliberately double-crossed France and Britain. This was also the view of exiled Polish historians, shared later by their colleagues in Poland when they could write freely on the subject after the collapse of communism in 1989.[17] However, with the exception of some German scholars, Gerhard L. Weinberg, the leading American historian of Nazi foreign policy, and Donald Cameron Watt, the premier British diplomatic historian of this period, most Western historians still see the Nazi-Soviet pact as

---

14. Haslam: "Litvinov, Stalin and the Road not Taken," in Gorodetsky, ed., *Soviet Foreign Policy,* 58; also Ginzburg, "Sovetsko-germanskii pakt," 30. However, the majority view is expressed by Vladimir Sokolov: "The question of Litvinov's resignation was ripe for decision if the Soviet government did not intend to pursue a policy oriented to Britain and France, but an independent policy meeting the country's national rather than ideological needs." Sokolov, "People's Commissar Maxim Litvinov," *International Affairs,* no. 5, (Moscow, 1991): 93–107.

15. Fleischhauer, *Der Pakt,* 339; Teddy J. Uldricks, "Soviet Security in the 1930s," in Gorodetsky, *Soviet Foreign Policy,* 73; see also Gabriel Gorodetsky, *Grand Illusion. Stalin and the German Invasion of Russia* (New Haven and London, 1999), 8–9.

16. Michael Jabara Carlay, *1939: The Alliance That Never Was And The Coming Of World War II* (Chicago, 1999), p. 68.

17. Władysław Pobóg-Malinowski, *Najnowsza historia polityczna Polski, 1864–1945,* vol. II, 1864–1939 (London, 1956, reprint Warsaw, 1981), ch. 22; Stanisław Gregorowicz, Michał J. Zacharias, *Polska—Związek Sowiecki. Stosunki polityczne 1925–1939* (Warsaw, 1995), ch. XV; Wojciech Materski, *Tarcza Europy. Stosunki polsko-sowieckie 1918–1939* (Warsaw, 1994), ch. VI, section 5.

either the only, or at least the logical, choice for Stalin.[18] Most historians also view the demand for Red Army passage though Poland as natural, and see the Polish refusal as either key to the breakdown of Franco-British military negotiations with the USSR, or at least a significant contributing factor. In contrast to the above, the goal of this paper is to demonstrate that most of the available evidence indicates Stalin always preferred a pact with Germany, and that he used negotiations with the Western powers to pressure Hitler into an agreement with the USSR. Finally, it will also show that Poland did not play any significant role in Stalin's decision to sign the nonaggression pact with Nazi Germany.

It is, of course, true that the Poles distrusted the Soviet Union. This was not surprising, given Russia's role in the partitions of Poland, and then her oppressive rule over her share of Polish lands.[19] After World War I, Lenin's attempt to destroy the reborn Polish state was foiled by Marshal Józef Piłsudski in the Battle of the Vistula in mid-August 1920. This defeat rankled deep with the Russians, together with great resentment at the loss of western Ukraine and western Belorussia to Poland in the Treaty of Riga (March 18, 1921).[20] As for the Poles, they distrusted both of their great neighbors

---

18. On these German historians, see note 10 above. According to Gerhard L. Weinberg, "A war between Germany and the Western Powers looked to the Soviet leader like the best prospect for both the safety and the future expansion of Soviet power," Germany, *Hitler and World War II. Essays in Modern German History* (Cambridge, England, 1995), 176. D. C. Watt distributes blame for the failure of the Moscow negotiations equally between the British and the French on the one side and the Soviets on the other. However, he adds the proviso that having a paid Soviet spy in the foreign office communications center (Francis Herbert King), and a master spy in Japan (Richard Sorge), the director of Soviet negotiations with Britain and Germany was "like a poker player with marked cards." Watt suspects the conviction that Hitler's main targets were Britain and France was central to Soviet policy, *How War Came*, 231, 369.

19. For Poland under Russian rule and national uprisings, see Piotr S. Wandycz, *The Lands of Partitioned Poland, 1795–1918* (Seattle, WA, and London, 1974); and Norman Davies, *God's Playground. A History of Poland. Vol. II. 1795 to the Present* (New York, 1982), ch. 2.

20. For the diplomatic history of the Soviet-Polish War, see Wandycz, *Soviet-Polish Relations 1917–1921* (Cambridge, MA., 1969); on the military side, see Norman Davies, *White Eagle, Red Star. The Polish-Soviet War, 1919–20* (London, 1972). For Lenin's statements at a closed session of the Ninth Party Conference on September 22, 1920 (first published in Russia in 1992), on the reasons for the Soviet rejection of the Curzon Line and the decision to advance into Poland, see Richard Pipes, *Russia under the Bolshevik Regime* (New York, 1993), 181–183. For the Treaty of Riga, see *Documents on Polish-Soviet Relations 1939–1945*, vol. 1. *1939–1943* [henceforth: *DPSR*] (London, 1961), no. 3.

and conducted their foreign policy accordingly. In view of German claims to Polish western territories and the well known, if muted, Soviet claims to eastern Poland, the cardinal principle of interwar Polish foreign policy was "equilibrium" or nonalignment with either neighboring power, but maintaining equilibrium between them. This policy was bolstered by an alliance with France to secure the latter's aid in case of war with Germany, and a defensive alliance with Romania in case of war with the USSR. The equilibrium policy was characterized by the Polish-Soviet Nonaggression Treaty (1932) and the Declaration of Nonaggression with Germany (1934, for ten years), after which the Polish-Soviet treaty was extended for ten years.[21] However, due to Hitler's policy of courting Warsaw, Polish relations were more amicable with Berlin than with Moscow from 1934 until March 1939. The agreement with Berlin recognized Poland's existing alliances, that is, with France and Romania. Thus, equilibrium was a well known Polish policy, which was reiterated to Moscow several times in the course of the fateful spring and summer of 1939.[22]

Poland's distrust of the USSR was shared by the European peoples who had been subject to Russia in the past; that is: Finland, Estonia, Latvia, Lithuania, and also by Romania whose possession of Bessarabia was never recognized by the USSR. The Soviet Union was also distrusted by most West European statesmen, who saw their views confirmed by Soviet declarations and official statements, especially Stalin's speech to the Eighteenth Party Congress on March 10. He then declared Soviet readiness to help victims of aggression—but also accused France and Britain of setting Germany against the USSR and said the Soviet Union would not pull chestnuts out of the fire for other powers.[23]

Two days after Hitler's destruction of the Czechoslovak state (March 15, 1939), and with rumors flying of a German threat to Romania, the British inquired whether Moscow would declare its readiness to aid Romania in case of aggression. The Soviet government, in turn, proposed a conference in Bucharest for joint consultation.[24] This was turned down by the

---

21. For the texts of the Polish-Soviet nonaggression pact of July 25, 1932 and its ten-year extension on May 5, 1934, see *DPSR*, nos. 6, 10; for the Polish-German Declaration of Nonaggression of January 26, 1934, see *DGFP*, C, vol. II (London and Washington, 1959), no.291.

22. For a brief study of interwar Polish foreign policy, see Anna M. Cienciala, "Polish Foreign Policy, 1926–1939; 'Equilibrium,' Stereotype and Reality," *Polish Review*, vol. XX, no. 1 (1975): 42–58.

23. For extracts from Stalin's speech of March 10, 1939 to the Eighteenth Congress of the Soviet Communist Party, see Degras, *SDFP* III, 315–322.

24. For the British inquiry, see Foreign Secretary Viscount Halifax to Ambassador Seeds, March 17, *DBFP*, 3rd ser., vol. IV (London, 1951). no. 389; for Seeds' conversation with Litvinov on March 18, and his report on Litvinov's proposals of

British government, which proposed, on March 21, a declaration on consultation in case of a threat of further aggression to France, the USSR, Poland, and Romania. The Polish government refused to sign because, as the Polish foreign minister claimed, Poland's signature alongside the USSR would provoke a German attack on her. The real motives, however, were both distrust of Moscow and the goal of keeping the door open to a compromise settlement of the Danzig-Corridor question with Germany, which would be compatible with Poland's security and independence. Instead of signing the declaration, Beck proposed a secret Anglo-Polish agreement on consultation, which the British accepted. This led to the conclusion of a provisional agreement on mutual assistance, signed on April 6, during Beck's visit to Britain. Beck explained the Polish position to Prime Minister Neville Chamberlain saying that the Poles had no confidence in Soviet Russia. On the basis of their experience, they saw no difference between Soviet and Tsarist imperialism, but in the face of the German threat they thought it advisable that, at a minimum, Russia's neutrality should be secured. They did not believe that Russia would honestly join Poland's allies, but they would not oppose British and French efforts to reach an understanding with Moscow. Beck added that, as in the case of the negotiations for the Franco-Soviet alliance (1935), the Polish government would insist that no treaty concluded by its Western allies without their participation could impose any obligations on Poland. But he also declared the Poles would welcome any Allied agreement with the Soviets, which would allow the transit of military supplies and the delivery of Soviet raw materials to Poland.[25]

The Polish attitude toward the USSR was based, not only on memories of the past and hopes of a peaceful resolution of disputes with Germany,

---

March 19, ibid., nos. 403, 421; for the Russian text of the Soviet proposal of March 18, see Litvinov to Stalin, *DVP 1939* I, no. 150, also Litvinov to Soviet ambassadors in London and Paris, March 18, 1939, *Soviet Peace Efforts on the Eve of World War II* [henceforth: *SPE*] (Moscow, 2nd printing, 1976), no. 109. For British documents on the Declaration on Consultation, see *DBFP*, ibid., chapter V.

25. See annotated edition of Józef Beck's memoirs: *Polska polityka zagraniczna w latach 192–1939. Na podstawie tekstów min. Józefa Becka opracowała Anna M. Cienciala* Paris, (1990), 245–246; cf. the French edition of Beck's memoirs, Colonel Józef Beck, *Dernier Rapport. Politique polonaise 1926–1939* (Neuchâtel and Paris, 1951), 93–194; English edition, *Final Report* (New York, 1957). For British records of Beck's London talks, see *DBFP*, 3rd Ser., vol. V (London, 1952), nos. 1,2,10, 16, also Cienciala, *Poland and the Western Powers 1938–1939. A Study in the Interdependence of Eastern and Western Europe* (London, Toronto, 1968), 216–217. This work was based on Polish archival documents in the *Polish Institute and Sikorski Museum*, London (henceforth *PISM*), also on published British, French, German, and Italian documents available at that time. For a later study of the topic in 1939, based on Polish and other archival documents, see Cienciala article cited in note 41 below.

but also on certain key assumptions, some of which were shared by non-Polish observers. Thus, from Warsaw's point of view, a German-Soviet alliance was seen as most unlikely for ideological reasons, which was, incidentally, also the view prevalent in the West. Furthermore, from the military point of view, the Poles did not expect the USSR to participate in any offensive action against Germany because the Soviet officer corps had been decapitated by the purge of 1937—a view shared by both the French and British General Staffs. Finally, the Poles thought a German-Soviet partition of Poland would be unacceptable to the Soviets because it would bring the formidable German army and air force that much nearer to Moscow, thus posing a mortal threat to Soviet security—a view shared by many Western observers, though some entertained such a possibility. Therefore, the Poles expected a German attack on their country to bring them automatic Soviet aid.[26] They were confirmed in their views by Soviet statements that the USSR would supply Poland with raw materials—at least, within the framework of the trade agreement signed in February 1939, ratified on May 16—and probably with military supplies and air support in case of a German-Polish war.[27]

However, friendly public declarations aside, the Soviet attitude toward Poland was characterized by profound hostility and suspicion. Moscow's attempts to pin down the Polish government on the declaration of consultation seem to have been designed less to elicit Polish agreement than to document an expected Polish refusal. Thus, Litvinov told Seeds on March 21 that he was sure Poland would not accept the commitments under the declaration on consultation in case of further German aggression, as proposed by London. He also confided to French Chargé d'Affaires Jean Payart, on March 29, that he felt Beck's "line" was unlikely to change until Poland received a direct blow. Despite these views, the Soviet government made

---

26. The opinion of the Polish ambassador to the USSR, Wacław Grzybowski, was typical. He told Undersecretary of State, Jan Szembek, on June 26, 1939, that he did not believe the rumors of German-Soviet talks because Moscow could not permit a German victory over Poland, and thus have Germany as a neighbor, see Jan Zarański, ed., *Diariusz i Teki Jana Szembeka, 1935–1939*, vol. IV (London, 1972), 641. This was also the policy evaluation given by the Polish General Staff to Col. Stefan Brzeszczyński, Polish military attaché in Moscow, when he visited Warsaw in early June, see Brzeszczyński report to the War Minister, Paris, December 31, 1939, Kol. 79, *PISM*. On June 29, the U.S. chargé d'affaires in Moscow reported a similar statement by a member of the Polish embassy; see *Foreign Relations of the United States. Diplomatic Papers. 1939. Vol. I. General,* [henceforth *FRUS 1939* I] (Washington, D.C., 1956), 196.

27. For the Polish-Soviet trade agreement of February 19, ratified on May 16, 1939, see *Dokumenty i materiały do historii stosunków polsko-radzieckich,* vol. VII, January 1939—December 1943, [henceforth: *DiM* VII] (Warsaw, 1973), nos. 12–17, 63–64.

Poland's signature—along with that of France—the condition for its own adherence to the declaration.[28] One may well ask why Moscow insisted that Poland sign the declaration on consultation, if she was expected not to do so? Perhaps Stalin saw this as a test of whether Britain and France would force Poland to sign? Whatever the case may be, Soviet Deputy Commissar for Foreign Affairs Vladimir P. Potemkin did not, as is sometimes claimed, offer a mutual assistance pact to the Polish foreign minister when they met in Warsaw on May 10, 1939. This was five days after Beck's speech to the Polish Parliament, in which he answered Hitler's statements of April 28. Beck declared Poland's determination to not be cut off from the Baltic Sea, but at the same time, Polish desire for peace—though not at any price, and especially not at the price of honor. Molotov instructed Potemkin to stop in the Polish capital on his way home from a tour of the Balkans and Turkey because Beck had expressed a desire to see him. Potemkin's main task was to learn what was going on between Poland and Germany, but Molotov also authorized him to "hint" at possible Soviet aid to Poland. According to Potemkin's brief, published telegram, that is all he did, saying the USSR would not refuse assistance to Poland if she desired it.[29]

---

28. See Seeds to Halifax, March 21, 1939, *DBFP*, 3rd ser. vol. IV (London, 1951), no. 461; Litvinov's report does not include his remark on Poland, *GK*, 1, no. 209. In his telegram of March 21 to Soviet ambassadors in Britain and France, Litvinov stated the Soviet government would sign the declaration as soon as France and Poland promised their signatures, *SPE* no. 122, *GK* 1, no. 215 and *SVP 1939* I, no.162. For Litvinov's remark to Payart, see extract in: *SPE*, no. 132, 226, not included in published Russian and French documents. For Litvinov's and Potemkin's conversations with Polish Ambassador Grzybowski regarding Poland's signature of the declaration, see *DiM* VII, nos. 32, 37, 42, 43, 46; also *GK*. 1, nos. 226, 251, and *DVP 1939*, I, nos. 183, 189.

29. For Beck's speech of May 5, 1939, see *The Polish White Book. Official Documents concerning Polish-German and Polish-Soviet Relations 1933–1939* [henceforth *PWB]* (London and New York, 1940), no.77. By saying Poland wanted peace but "not at the price of honor," Beck meant giving up Polish independence without a fight. His speech, prepared in consultation with the British government, answered Hitler's speech of April 28, in which the latter denounced the Anglo-German Naval Treaty of 1935, and the Polish-German Declaration of Nonaggression, and listed the proposals Poland had rejected, i.e., the return of Danzig and part of the Polish Corridor to the Reich in exchange for German recognition of the Polish-German frontier, saying he would never offer them again. For Molotov's instruction to Potemkin, May 10, 1939, see *DVP, 1939*, I, no.293; for Potemkin's brief telegram on his conversation with Beck that day, see *SPE*, no. 210; for the same text in Russian, see *DiM*, VII, no. 60, *GK* 1, no. 330. Fleischhauer interprets Potemkin's remarks as a proposal for a Polish-Soviet assistance pact, which was rejected, see her article in Wegner, ed., *From Peace to War*, 34. Elsewhere she writes that Beck's declarations to Potemkin were "a bitter pill" for the Russians, who had hoped for an assistance pact with Poland, *Der Pakt*, 188. There is no documented evidence of a Moscow proposal for a Soviet-Polish assistance pact, or of Russian hopes for same.

Whatever else Potemkin may have said, he managed to give Beck the impression that Moscow understood Poland's nonalignment policy, and that the Poles would never attack the USSR in tandem with Germany. Beck also noted Potemkin's statement that Moscow would adopt a policy of benevolent neutrality in case of a Polish-German war.[30] By this time, of course, Litvinov had been replaced as commissar for foreign affairs by Molotov (May 3), and Anglo-French-Soviet negotiations were proceeding toward a treaty guaranteeing the USSR's western neighbors against German aggression. In order to avoid any misunderstandings of Beck's statements to Potemkin, Ambassador Grzybowski clarified the Polish position to Molotov the following day. He read to him the instruction just received from Warsaw: (1) Poland did not agree with, nor authorize, the French initiative regarding guarantees to Poland; (2) she could not accept a one-sided Soviet guarantee, nor a mutual guarantee because, if she were totally engaged in a conflict with Germany, she could not aid the Soviet Union; (3) the Polish attitude toward collective negotiations would depend on the results of the Anglo-French-Soviet negotiations, but Poland rejected all discussion of matters affecting her other than by bilateral methods; (4) the Polish-Romanian alliance was purely defensive, so it could not be regarded as in any way directed against the USSR.[31]

It is not known what Potemkin actually reported to Molotov when he returned to Moscow because this document is not accessible as yet. It is known, however, that when the new Soviet ambassador to Warsaw, Nikolai I. Sharonov, took up his post in late May, he also professed Soviet friend-

---

30. On May 13, Beck wrote Juliusz Łukasiewicz, the Polish ambassador in Paris, that conversations with Potemkin on May 10 made it clear the Soviet government understood the Polish point of view on relations with the USSR, and realized the Polish government did not intend to reach agreement with either great neighbor against the other. Beck wrote: "Mr. Potemkin also stated that in the event of an armed conflict between Poland and Germany, the Soviets will adopt 'une attitude bienveillante' towards us.," *PWB* no. 163, *DPSR* no.19. Beck confirmed this statement in his memoirs. He also noted that the new Soviet ambassador [Nikolai Sharonov] told him a few days later that Molotov had studied Potemkin's report several times and judged the conversation to be very positive, saying: "I quite understand Colonel Beck"—to which the latter answered he still understood Molotov quite well, see: Beck (Cienciala, ed.), *Polska polityka zagraniczna*, 253.

31. For Grzybowski's statement to Molotov, May 11, see *SPE*, no.212, Russian text: *DiM*, VII, no. 62, *GK* 1, no. 336, *DVP, 1939*, I, no. 298; see also Grzybowski's "Final Report," Paris, November 6, 1939, *PWB*, no.184, reprinted with some abbreviations in *DPSR*, no. 69. "French initiatives" meant French efforts aimed at the conclusion of a triple alliance between France, Britain, and the USSR involving Poland, but not necessarily with the latter's agreement.

ship for Poland and hinted at Moscow's readiness to help Poland.[32] This and similar declarations may have been designed to support Polish determination to resist German demands by force, but it is clear Sharonov did not believe the Poles would really do so. His report to Molotov of August 23 probably reflected not only his opinion but also the views of the Soviet leadership throughout the spring and summer of 1939. Sharonov wrote that Poland was preparing to bow to England's peace policy, if she had not already done so; therefore a German-Polish war over Danzig was unlikely.[33]

It should be borne in mind that Stalin's decision to sign the nonaggression pact with Nazi Germany, however astounding to most contemporaries, had solid historical precedents. Russia and Prussia, later Germany, had enjoyed friendly relations for most of the period 1772–1914, and this relationship—in which the Austrian Empire was the third partner—was founded on the partitions of Poland. After the Bolshevik seizure of power in November 1917, came the peace of Brest-Litovsk with the Central Powers in March 1918, in which Lenin gave up the western provinces of the former Russian Empire rather than continue the war and thus risk losing power. The peace allowed Germany to launch powerful offensives on the western front, but her ultimate defeat nullified the peace of Brest-Litovsk. In April 1922, the Rapallo Treaty normalized German-Soviet relations and canceled mutual claims, while the Treaty of Berlin, signed four years later, was in essence a nonaggression agreement between the two countries. Until the advent of Hitler, relations were very good and military cooperation flourished. Even after Hitler terminated the latter in fall 1933, trade relations continued. Indeed, Stalin, in his report to the Seventeenth Congress of the CPSU on January 26, 1934 (the day the Polish-German Declaration of Nonaggression was signed), said that fascism was not the issue, for it did not prevent good Soviet relations with Italy. This policy line led to the

---

32. Ambassador Sharonov reported on May 25, that he told Beck the Soviet Union would be willing to help Poland if the latter was attacked by Germany, but that earlier talks were necessary to make such help possible, *DiM* VII, no. 66, *GK* I, no. 373, *DVP 1939*, I, no.334. On presenting his credentials to Polish President Ignacy Mościcki on June 2, Sharonov said his mission was to support and develop friendly Polish-Soviet relations based on a series of mutual political and economic agreements. Close and fruitful cooperation between the two countries was, he said, a factor in the consolidation of universal peace and it was in keeping with Soviet policy to have peaceful and friendly relations with all countries, especially with its neighbors, see *PWB*, no. 165, *DiM VII*, no.70. This was two days after Molotov's speech to the Supreme Soviet, in which he used the same phrases on Soviet relations with Poland, see: Degras, *SDFP*, III, 337.

33. Sharonov's report of August 23, 1939, *DVP 1939*, I, no. 489; on Poland and Germany, ibid., p. 640.

conclusion of a German-Soviet trade-credit agreement in early April 1935, whereby Germany gave the Soviet Union a credit of two hundred million RM to purchase German manufactured goods in return for Soviet raw materials.[34] While trade continued, German-Soviet relations deteriorated but Litvinov (perceived then as now as the champion of collective security) declared publicly in December 1937 that collective security was dead and that a rapprochement between the Soviet Union and Germany was perfectly possible.[35]

Whether or not the Nazi-Soviet pact of 1939 was mainly the result of efforts by those German Foreign Ministry officials who wanted a return to Rapallo, as Fleischhauer contends,[36] it is clear that such a return was desired by some members of the German diplomatic and military establishment. All available evidence points to the fact that this was also the Soviet goal. However, the question of when Stalin decided to pursue it is still a matter of debate because authoritative Russian documentation is lacking. The most important source for his policy decisions might well be the records of discussions in Stalin's "Kremlin Cabinet." This body consisted, in order of importance, of Stalin; Molotov, Politburo member, head of the Sovnarkom (Council of National Commissars), and from early May, commissar for foreign affairs; Andrei A. Zhdanov, head of the Leningrad party organization and Politburo member in charge of ideology; Anastas I. Mikoyan, Politburo member and deputy premier in charge of foreign and domestic trade; Lazar M. Kaganovich, Politburo member in charge of agriculture;

---

34. For documents on German-Soviet military cooperation, see Yuri Dyakov & Tatyana Bushuyeva, *The Red Army and the Wehrmacht. How the Soviets Militarized Germany, 1922–1933, and Paved the Way for Fascism* (New York, 1995). For Stalin on Germany, January 26, 1934, Degras, *SDFP*, III, 70. For the German-Soviet trade agreement signed April 9, 1935, see: *DGFP* C IV (London and Washington, 1962), nos. 20, 21.

35. For Litvinov on collective security as dead, see his interview with the Moscow correspondent of *Le Monde*, late December 1937, cit. Hugh D. Phillips, *Between the Revolution and the West. A Political Biography of Maxim M. Litvinov* (Boulder, CO., 1992), 163; French text, Ambassador Robert Coulondre to Premier Yvon Delbos, December 27, 1937, Documents *Diplomatiques Français* [henceforth: *DDF*], 2nd ser. vol. VII (Paris, 1972), no. 30, enclosure, "Note de M. Luciani."

36. Fleischhauer claims that Stalin's remark on not pulling chestnuts out of the fire for others in his speech of March 10, 1939, was taken up by the "old" Wilhelmstrasse officials, who built on this phrase to pursue the German national interest as they saw it, and worked to get Ribbentrop's support for a deal with Soviet Russia—see Fleischhauer in Wegner, ed., *From Peace to War*, 33. This is also the theme of her major work, *Der Pakt*.

Lavrenty P. Beria, candidate member of the Politburo, commissar of the NKVD (National Commissariat of Internal Security); Marshal Kliment Y. Voroshilov, member of the Politburo and commissar for military and naval affairs, also others as needed. Selected officials, including Molotov, who was nearly always present, met almost every night with the "Vozhd" (leader) in his Kremlin office to discuss current problems and policy. However, only the dates and lists of visitors for each day are available. Aside from the lack of these records, Politburo, Central Committee, Foreign Affairs Commissariat documents, also NKVD and GRU (Military Intelligence) documents illustrating Soviet foreign policy decision-making are missing from the Russian sources published thus far, and are still inaccessible in Russian archives.[37]

In the absence of authoritative documents on Soviet foreign policy decision-making, it is worth mentioning that a handful of Soviet defectors reported Stalin had wanted a deal with Hitler for some time before August 1939. Among them was the Soviet chargé d'affaires in Rome, Leon B. Helphand, who defected to the West in summer 1940. However, the first published claim that Stalin preferred a deal with Hitler to one with the Western powers was made by Walter Krivitsky, the head of Soviet military intelligence in Western Europe, then Spain, until his defection in 1937, when he feared the Stalinist purges would engulf him as well. Krivitsky published a series of articles in the *Saturday Evening Post* in April 1939 asserting that Stalin had sought an agreement with Nazi Germany since 1934. Later, he publicized the theory—shared by Polish statesmen and some Western observers—that Soviet negotiations for an alliance with France and Britain were a fraud. In support of this claim, Krivitsky adduced Stalin's refusal to believe in a German threat to the USSR. According to Krivitsky, when the German-Soviet trade-credit agreement was concluded in April 1935, Stalin said that Hitler could not make war on the USSR—because German business circles were too powerful to allow it. Krivitsky also claimed that the head of the Soviet trade delegation in Berlin, David Kandelaki, brought with him the draft of a German-Soviet agreement when he re-

---

37. For names of visitors in Stalin's appointment book for 1938–1939, see "Posetiteli kremlevskogo kabineta I.V. Stalina. Zhurnaly (Tetradi) Zapisy lits priniiatykh pervym gensekom, 1924–1953;" *Istoricheskii Arkhiv,* no. 5–6 (Moscow, 1995): 5–63, [henceforth: *IA* 1995, no. 5–6]. On declassified documents and general comments on Russian archives, Raymond L. Garthoff, "Some Observations on Using the Soviet Archives," *Diplomatic History,* no. 5 (1997): 243–258; also Michael David Fox and David Hoffmann, "The Politburo Protocols, 1919–49," *The Russian Review,* vol. 55 (1996): 99–103.

turned to Moscow in April 1937.[38] If there was such a draft, it did not survive in German archives, though German documents record Soviet soundings of Germany in 1935–36. Thus, on May 8, 1935, Litvinov told the German ambassador in Moscow, Count Friedrich Werner von der Schulenburg, that since the Soviet Union had signed an alliance with France, he hoped it would soon be followed by a general nonaggression agreement, "of the kind suggested by Germany." This would, said Molotov, lessen the significance of the Franco-Soviet pact and lead to the improvement of German-Soviet relations, "which the Soviet Government desired above all things and which they now considered possible."[39] This proposal was made just six days after the signature of the Franco-Soviet alliance in Paris and eight days before the signature of the Czechoslovak-Soviet alliance in Prague. German documents also show that in late 1936, Kandelaki told Hjalmar Schacht, head of the Reichsbank, that the Soviet government had never refused political negotiations with Germany and had even made concrete proposals to improve them at the time of the negotiations for the Franco-Soviet pact—a passage that German Foreign Minister Baron Konstantin von Neurath underlined, adding a question mark. Kandelaki declared that

---

38. Uldricks dismisses this testimony because it was given by lower-level Soviet functionaries, whose information was speculative and because, as defectors, they had rejected the Stalinist system, see Uldricks in Gorodetsky, *Soviet Foreign Policy,* 69, and 74, note 14. For Krivitsky's account, see Walter Krivitsky, *I Was Stalin's Agent* (New York, 1940). For Stalin's reaction to the German-Soviet trade agreement, and Kandelaki bringing a draft agreement, ibid., 31, 38. The book was first published in London, in 1939, titled, *In Stalin's Secret Service* (reprint, New York, 2000). The Russian translation of this edition has an extensive supplement with materials on and by Krivitsky, also documents selected and annotated by Aleksandr Kolpakidi, with photographs and short biographies of people figuring in the book, see Val'ter Krivitsky, *Ia byl agentom Stalina. Zapiski sovetskogo razvednika* (Moscow, 1996). Walter Krivitsky (Samuel Ginsberg, 1889–1941), gave testimony to a congressional committee. He was found dead in room 532, Bellevue Hotel, Washington, D.C. on February 10, 1941, see Flora Lewis, "Who Killed Krivitsky?" *Washington Post,* 13 February 1966), reprint, Krivitsky, *In Stalin's Secret Service* (New York, 2000). Despite an alleged suicide note to Krivitsky's lawyer, it is very likely that the KGB murdered him.

39. Ambassador Schulenburg's report on his conversation with Litvinov, May 8, 1935, *DGFP,* ser. C, vol. IV, no. 78. Litvinov's mention of a German suggestion of a nonaggression pact referred to a vague German proposal made to the British government as a counter to their proposal that Germany join the proposed Eastern Security Pact, see "Communique of the Official German News Agency," 18 April 1935, ibid., no. 29.

his government was ready to enter into open or secret German-Soviet negotiations to improve mutual relations, and on "general peace." However, Hitler rejected the idea, whose time, he said, had not yet come. But he also said that once Stalin showed himself the absolute master of Russia, and especially of the military, Germany would not pass up the opportunity.[40] German-Soviet negotiations for a new trade-credit agreement began in December 1938, with the signature of an agreement on methods of payment. At the turn of 1938–39, the German press toned down its attacks on the USSR and the Soviet press reciprocated. Trade negotiations proceeded in January 1939, but were suspended by the Germans later that month. They were to resume once more in July 1939, and this time they would pave the way to the nonaggression pact.

How can a convincing answer be found to the question of just when Stalin decided on an agreement with Hitler? Krivitsky dated Stalin's decision as far back as the summer of 1934. However that may be, it is clear there were Soviet soundings in 1935–36, but the purpose of this paper is to examine developments during the spring and summer of 1939. The best way to proceed is to survey the available evidence, though this does not require a detailed examination of all known documents. The course of Soviet-British-French negotiations on the one hand, and of Soviet-German talks on the other, has been well known for several decades from published German and British diplomatic documents, and later from French documents. These are now supplemented by selected Russian diplomatic documents. However, a brief outline will help follow what is, after all, a very complex story.

After the Soviet proposal of a conference of interested parties in Bucharest to discuss measures of preventing further German aggression, which was rejected by Britain, and after the failed British proposal of a declaration on consultation, Britain gave Poland a guarantee of the latter's independence

---

40. See Schacht letter to Von Neurath, February 6, 1936, reporting his late December 1936 conversation with Kandelaki, also Neurath to Schacht, February 11, 1937, reporting Hitler's answer, *DGFP*, C, VI (London, Washington, 1983), nos. 183, 185. Whether or not these Soviet overtures were aimed at Hitler, or at German officials interested in renewing the former Rapallo/Berlin Treaty relationship, it is now clear that Czechoslovak President Edvard Beneš had nothing to do with provoking Stalin's purges of the Soviet officer corps, including Marshal Mikhail N. Tukhachevsky, by passing on a Gestapo-provided message on the marshal's alleged secret dealings with the Wehrmacht, see Igor Lukes, *Czechoslovakia Between Stalin and Hitler. The Diplomacy of Edvard Beneš in the 1930s* (Oxford, 1996), 99–107. It is likely that Stalin himself ordered his intelligence service in Germany to "leak" this message to the Gestapo, so he could use it to eliminate the popular Tukhachevsky, whom he may have seen as a rival for power.

on March 31, 1939, which was endorsed by Poland's ally France.[41] The unintended result was increased Soviet suspicion of both the Western powers and Poland. In the communist ideological framework, "bourgeois" states were always assumed as hostile to the world's only "socialist" state. Therefore, even before Hitler's seizure of the Czech lands in mid-March 1939, Stalin suspected the French and British of encouraging the Führer to attack the USSR. Indeed, Litvinov wrote the Soviet ambassador in London, Ivan M. Maisky, that Poland would give in to Hitler's demands, perhaps in return for Lithuania, and that Chamberlain wanted a German-Soviet war to break out over the Baltic States. Litvinov also wrote Iakov E. Suritz, the Soviet ambassador in Paris: "England has in fact concluded a treaty with Poland against us."[42] It is clear that since Stalin controlled Soviet foreign policy, Litvinov's communications to the ambassadors reflected the Soviet leader's views. Thus, the British guarantee and then the provisional Anglo-Polish mutual assistance agreement of April 6 fueled Stalin's suspicions of a Western plot to provoke a German attack on the USSR.

Soviet negotiations with the British and French governments began in earnest in mid-April, but after the Western powers finally agreed to guarantee Latvia, Estonia, and Finland, (though not Lithuania, which did not border on the USSR and for which the latter did not demand a guarantee), negotiations bogged down over the issue of "indirect aggression." This meant the Soviet right to military intervention in these states if Moscow perceived a threat to Soviet security, and this even if the above states were not overtly threatened but changed their policy of their own volition. Stalin's fears were strengthened when Germany signed nonaggression pacts with Estonia and Latvia in June 1939. The French and British governments, for their part, opposed the Soviet definition of indirect aggression because they wished to keep the door open to a peaceful solution of the German demands on

---

41. The guarantee was not Chamberlain's "spontaneous" reaction to his personal humiliation by Hitler, when the latter seized the Czech lands in mid-March 1939, nor did the prime minister fail to consult his advisers and the Foreign Office, as one historian contends, e.g. Gorodetsky, *Grand Illusion*, p. 4 and note 7. On the British road to the guarantee and its meaning, see Anna M. Cienciala, "Poland in British and French Policy in 1939: Determination to Fight or Avoid War?" *Polish Review*, vol. 34, no.3 (1989): 199–226; slightly abbreviated reprint in Patrick Finney, ed., *The Origins of the Second World War* (London, New York, Sidney and Auckland, 1997), 413–432.

42. Litvinov's letter of April 4, 1939 to Maisky on suspicions of Chamberlain's motives, and his letter of April 11 to Suritz on an Anglo-Polish treaty directed against the USSR, *SPE*, nos. 145, and 157. See also Litvinov to Stalin, 9 April 1939, in which the former denigrated French Foreign Minister Georges Bonnet's proposal for Franco-Soviet talks to clarify measures to be taken in case of a German attack on Poland, *DVP 1939 I*, no. 206.

Poland. Furthermore, Chamberlain did not want to lose the support of neutral countries, especially the United States, by sacrificing the Baltic States to the USSR. French Foreign Minister G. Bonnet, though strongly in favor of a triple alliance between London, Paris, and Moscow as a deterrent to Hitler, also opposed the Soviet demand. Nevertheless, in late July, the British and French proposed a secret protocol specifying Soviet intervention if any of these states were threatened, as Czechoslovakia had been in March 1939, but with consultation in other cases. Later, they agreed to the inclusion of this provision in the alliance treaty, and lastly to the Soviet demand for a military alliance. They decided to send a joint French-British military mission to Moscow to negotiate the alliance, assuming the political agreement would be negotiated at the same time. These negotiations began on August 12 but were suspended on August 17, allegedly over the Polish refusal to allow the passage of Soviet troops in case of war with Germany. They were finally broken off by the Soviet side on August 25, two days after the signature of the Nazi-Soviet pact. It is worth noting that France, an ally of the USSR since 1935, always showed more interest than Britain in a concrete military agreement with Moscow, as well as willingness to override Polish objections to the passage of Soviet troops through Poland. Indeed, the French premier and war minister, Edouard Daladier, gave the French government's consent to this Soviet demand on August 21, without Polish agreement. However, French offers were routinely ignored by Stalin.[43] Meanwhile, German-Soviet talks began on April 17 and, as early as May 20, Molotov indicated interest in a political agreement with Germany. The Germans, while showing much interest, were put off by Molotov's rough insistence that Berlin first fulfill all Soviet economic demands as stipulated by the commissar for foreign trade, Mikoyan. Above all, they feared that Stalin might trick them, so they suspended political talks in late June. However, they proposed conditions for a trade-credit agreement in early July, which were favorably received in Moscow. Preliminary talks began in Berlin in late July, at the same time outlining the basis for a political treaty, after which matters progressed rapidly. A trade-credit agreement was signed

---

43. For a succinct presentation of French efforts to secure a separate agreement on military cooperation with the USSR, and French pressure for the conclusion of the triple alliance, see Jean-Baptiste Duroselle, *La Décadence 1932–1939* (Paris, 1979), ch. XIII, 405–440. For French-Polish relations in the period March–end August 1939, see Wacław Jędrzejewicz, ed., *Diplomat in Paris 1936–1939. Papers and Memoirs of Juliusz Łukasiewicz Ambassador of Poland* (New York and London, 1970), 173–271; Polish text in revised and expanded edition, Wacław Jędrzejewicz and Henryk Bułhak, eds., *Dyplomata w Paryżu 1936–1939. Wspomnienia i dokumenty Juliusza Łukasiewicza Ambasadora Rzeczypospolitej Polskiej* (London, 1989), pt. II, 213–322. On Daladier and Poland in late August 1939, see discussion of Anglo-French-Soviet negotiations, Moscow, later in this paper.

in Berlin on August 19, followed four days later by the signature of the nonaggression pact and secret protocol in Moscow.

While the parallel course of Anglo-French-Soviet negotiations and German-Soviet talks is fairly well known, this is not true of a sideline that most historians have virtually ignored. This was a series of "leaks" of Anglo-French proposals to the Soviet government, which regularly reached Berlin through the German embassy in London. They are to be found in published German documents which, in any case, are more helpful in tracing the Soviet path to the nonaggression pact than the British, French, and to some extent, the Russian documents. British historian D. C. Watt has argued persuasively that the leaks stemmed from Francis Herbert King, a paid Soviet agent in the foreign office communications department (code room). King was, indeed, in a prime position to pass summaries, or even copies, of secret British documents to the Soviet embassy in London. Whether or not he was the only person directly involved, it is clear the documents were suitably edited—most likely by an NKVD officer in the Soviet embassy—and then passed on to the German embassy, which in turn telegraphed them post haste to Berlin.[44] Alongside these leaks, there were also Soviet "hints" of Moscow's interest in a deal with Germany; these were made by Soviet diplomats to their foreign colleagues, and sometimes to foreign journalists.

But most important of all were the talks between the Soviet representatives and German Foreign Ministry officials in Berlin, which took place from mid-April to mid-August 1939. However, there are striking discrepancies between some of the German and Russian accounts of these conversations, and their interpretation is part of the debate on Stalin's policy in 1939. Thus, some Russian and German historians, such as Lev Bezymensky

---

44. D.C. Watt, "Francis Herbert King: A Soviet Source in the Foreign Office," *Intelligence and National Security,* vol. III, no. 4 (1988), 62–82. Watt later wrote of John Herbert King, as do some other authors, but this is clearly the same person. According to another British writer: ". . . this monumental breach of British security actually began ten years earlier when King's fellow code clerk Andrew Oldham walked into the Soviet embassy in Paris.," John Costello, *Mask of Treachery* (New York, 1988), 347. King, a retired army captain, was an Irishman, who hated the British and needed money to support his lifestyle, see Nigel West & Oleg Tsarev, *The Crown Jewels. The British Secrets at the Heart of the KGB Archives* (New Haven and London, 1999), 286. On Ernest Holloway [not Andrew] Oldham, see ibid., 286–287.

and Fleischhauer, claim that German officials who favored a return to the Rapallo/Berlin Treaty policy put statements in the mouths of Russian diplomats in Berlin so as to nudge Hitler and Ribbentrop in this direction. Indeed, Fleischhauer, who has written the most detailed account of these conversations—based mostly on German but also a few Russian archival documents—claims that the initiative for the rapprochement between Berlin and Moscow stemmed from those German Foreign Ministry officials, who wished to rein in Hitler by persuading him to sign a German-Soviet nonaggression pact, while also obtaining a Western commitment to maintain the East European status quo.[45] However, Russian historian S. A. Gorlov argues that a coordinated pro-Rapallo orientation among German Foreign Ministry officials—some of whom were Nazis—was unlikely, though some clearly supported a return to good German-Soviet relations. He also points out that Hitler and Stalin must be taken into account. Gorlov admits that the ground for the nonaggression pact was laid in the period between mid-April and mid-August 1939 in the talks conducted between German officials in Berlin and the Russian chargé d'affaires, Georgii A. Astakhov. What is most important, however, is Gorlov's claim that the absence of Molotov's instructions and directives to Astakhov during this crucial period proves the latter was acting on his own initiative. In support of this claim, Gorlov cites the recollection of Hans Herwarth [von Bittenfeld]. Herwarth was then first secretary in the German embassy, Moscow, and thus personal assistant to the German ambassador in Moscow, von der Schulenburg. He wrote that Astakhov was viewed both in the embassy and in the German Foreign Ministry as a bright, untypical, Soviet diplomat who had his own views and worked to restore good German-Soviet relations. Gorlov adds that Astakhov was arrested at the end of 1939 and shot in February 1940,

---

45. Fleischhauer, *Der Pakt*, 404–405. Evidently she meant the new status quo as of late fall 1938, plus some further territorial cessions to Germany. The latter, while proposed by members of the German "opposition," were also envisaged by most German officials who wanted a rapprochement with the USSR. The proposals of the German "opposition," as put to the British government in December 1938 by its leader Dr. Karl Goerdeler, specified that in return for their overthrowing Hitler, Germany was to regain Danzig and the Corridor, also a block of colonial territory and obtain an interest-free loan from Britain. The Under-Secretary of State for foreign affairs, Sir Alexander Cadogan, found these terms unacceptable because they were too much like Hitler's *Mein Kampf*, and Britain would receive only I.O.Us, see his diary entry for December 10, 1938, David Dilks, ed., *The Diaries of Sir Alexander Cadogan, O.M. 1938–1945* (London, 1971),128–129.

but does not give the reasons.[46] Of course, if Astakhov really conducted his own independent diplomacy in Berlin between mid-April and mid-August, this would clear the Soviet government of the charge of double dealing by conducting secret talks in Berlin on the one hand, while officially negotiating with France and Britain on the other. However, aside from the well-known fact that Soviet diplomats worked under tight control from Moscow, a directive from Molotov to Astakhov in late July has been published. Also, an examination of the recorded conversations indicates that Astakhov must have been instructed to behave as if he were acting on his own in order to allow Moscow to sound out German intentions, also perhaps to provide it with an alibi should the secret conversations be discovered, or fail. Indeed, the practice of diplomats allegedly expressing their own opinions to sound out the other side is well known. Thus, in the early stages of these talks, German State Secretary Ernst von Weizsäcker also pretended to be expressing his "personal" views, although he was speaking according to instructions. Furthermore, the fact that no instructions or directives from Molotov before late July are included in the Russian documents published in 1990–1992, and are not accessible in Russian archives, does not prove that none was sent before late July 1939. Finally, the German officials with whom Astakhov conducted these conversations, including Foreign Minister Joachim von Ribbentrop, clearly regarded him as a reliable conduit for transmitting their statements to Molotov or they would not have talked to him as they did. Of course, there were also other indicators of Soviet interest in an agreement with Germany, which could not have been made without Stalin's knowledge and consent. These were the above mentioned "leaks" to the Germans of Franco-British proposals to Moscow, as well as "hints" given the Germans by Soviet diplomats. No such hints of a possible German-Soviet agreement were made to Britain by the Soviet side in order to propel London toward an agreement with the USSR. However, some leaks were made by the Germans to the French, presumably because, since France was an ally of Poland, French armies were expected to fight the Wehrmacht

---

46. See S. A. Gorlov, "Sovetsko-germanskii dialog na kanune pakta Molotova-Ribbentropa 1939," *Novaia i Noveishaia Istoriia*, no. 4 (1993), 13–34. For an English rendering of Herwarth's comment on Astakhov in Berlin, 1939, see Hans von Herwarth with S. Frederck Starr, *Against Two Evils* (New York, 1981),. 144. According to the Soviet diplomatic dictionary, Astakhov died in 1942; see "Georgii Timofeevich Astakhov," in Andrei A. Gromyko et al., eds., *Diplomaticheskii Slovar,* vol. I., Moscow, 1984, 100. Hearsay has it that he was shot. Whatever the date and way of his death, it is clear he knew too much about German-Soviet talks in Berlin in summer 1939.

in the West, and also because Paris always showed more interest in a military treaty with Moscow than the British.[47]

As far as Anglo-Soviet negotiations are concerned, it should be noted that on April 11, Ambassador Maisky asked Foreign Secretary Viscount Halifax why, if the British and French intended to help Poland and Romania, they could not make their aid conditional on these countries' adopting a "reasonable attitude" toward accepting Russian help? Halifax replied that while such a possibility could not be excluded, this could force Poland and Romania to issue formal protests and disassociate themselves from the Western powers, with damaging effects to the common cause. He thought it was up to the Soviet government to remove Polish and Romanian suspicions. Maisky insisted that "collective security" was superior to bilateral agreements—but was reprimanded for this remark by Litvinov. Perhaps to sound out or even encourage London, on April 14, when the new British note to Moscow was ready, Maisky suddenly told Halifax that the USSR wished to play a part in aiding Romania, but first wanted to know how Britain envisaged helping that country. As for the French, they were unhappy with the British stance and took action on their own. On April 14, Foreign Minister Bonnet proposed to Soviet Ambassador Iakov Suritz a Franco-Soviet military agreement covering aid to Poland and Romania. At the same time, however, the French government supported a very different British proposal. This was communicated by Ambassador Seeds to Litvinov on April 15 in the form of an inquiry. Seeds asked whether the Soviet government could declare that it would aid any neighboring state if it was the victim of aggression, providing such a state resisted and that such aid was desired. This question came *after* the signing of the provisional Anglo-Polish mutual assistance agreement on April 6, Mussolini's invasion of Albania the next day, and Anglo-French guarantees of Romanian and Greek independence on April 13. Nevertheless, Litvinov reacted to the inquiry by telling Seeds that the British proposal would bind the Soviet government

---

47. The French ambassador in Berlin, Robert Coulondre (formerly ambassador in Moscow), commented as early as May 7, 1939—four days after Litvinov's resignation—on the basis of information from General Karl Bodenschatz, who was close to Goering, that a fourth partition of Poland was to be expected. On May 24, the Quai d'Orsay noted reports that Berlin-Moscow contacts could change everything. These reports reinforced the French government in its belief that negotiations with Moscow must be concluded as soon as possible, Duroselle, *La Décadence*, 430–431. On May 30, the French ambassador in London communicated to the British a long dispatch from Coulondre reporting that Ribbentrop was pressing for an understanding with Russia, *DBFP*, 3rd ser., vol. VI (London, 1953), no.11, cf. *DDF*, 2nd ser., vol. XVI (Paris, 1983), no. 251. Coulondre continued to pass on warnings of this kind to Paris through the summer.

without committing anyone else.[48] As will be seen from the foreign commissar's dismissal in early May, his statement to Seeds in mid-April reflected Stalin's view rather than his own. Stalin also ignored a French proposal for a bilateral Franco-Soviet military agreement.

On April 17 Litvinov gave Seeds a detailed counterproposal which, as published Russian documents show, had been worked out with Stalin. It stipulated a military assistance agreement between France, Britain and the USSR, as well as their commitment to aid the latter's western neighbors between the Baltic and Black Seas in the event of aggression against them. Furthermore, the British government was to state that the assistance it had recently promised to Poland concerned exclusively aggression by Germany, and that the Polish-Romanian alliance was to be made operative either regarding aggression by any country—or revoked as being directed against the USSR. Furthermore, a political agreement was to be signed by the interested parties at the same time as the military agreement, and a special agreement was to be signed with Turkey. Finally, both sides would commit themselves not to sign a separate peace. The Soviet proposal seemed reasonable and comprehensive, but showed great distrust of both Britain and Poland. Indeed, the Poles were worried. British Ambassador Sir Howard Kennard reported from Warsaw that the Soviet proposals could jeopardize the possibility of Polish-Soviet cooperation, and showed Moscow's inclination to treat Poland as a pawn. He thought that since she would be in the forefront of the battle, her susceptibilities had to be borne in mind.[49] As for Stalin,

---

48. For Maisky conversation with Halifax, April 11, see *DBFP*, 3rd ser., vol. V, no.42, cf. *GK 1*, no.264; for Litvinov's reprimand to Maisky for speaking without instructions about collective security, thus giving the impression that bilateral agreements were not envisaged, *DVP I*, no.217. For Maisky-Halifax conversation, April 14, SPE, nos. 162, 163, *DVP*, ibid., nos. 217, 221, also Halifax to Seeds, April 14, 1939, *DBFP*, ibid., no. 166. For Bonnet's proposal of a Franco-Soviet military agreement to Suritz, April 14, *DDF*, 2nd ser. XV (Paris, 1981), no. 387; this was presented to the British as an "annex" to the Franco-Soviet Pact of 1935, see *DBFP*, ibid., no.183, see also Payart conversation with Potemkin on same, April 17, Potemkin to Suritz,. *DVP*, ibid., no. 231, and Payart to Bonnet, April 16, *DDF* ibid., no. 419. For the British proposals of April 15, see *DBFP*, ibid., no. 170; for Litvinov reaction, ibid., no. 182, and cf. *GK 1*, no. 271.

49. On the working out of the Soviet proposal, see Litvinov to Stalin, April 15, 17, 1939, *DVP 1939 I*, nos. 223, 224, 228, and proposals handed to ambassador Seeds, April 17, ibid., no.229, also *SPE* no.171, *DiM* VII no.50, *GK* I, nos. 275, 276, *DBFP* 3rd ser. V, no.193. See also Litvinov to Suritz April 17, that the British guarantee to Poland could be interpreted formally as aid to the latter against the USSR, *DVP* ibid., no. 230. For Kennard's comments from Warsaw, April 18, 19, see *DBFP* ibid., nos. 204, 222. The Polish-Romanian alliance and secret military convention of March 3 1921, were purely defensive agreements in case of attack on their eastern frontiers, that is, by the USSR; for Polish texts see Tadeusz Jędruszczak

Russian documents do not indicate whether he expected the British government to accept his terms, or regarded them merely as a way of sounding out British intentions. It is also possible they were designed with an eye to frightening the Germans, who were to learn of the Soviet proposal when it was reported by Seeds to the Foreign Office, where John Herbert King was working in the code room.

On April 17, the same day that Litvinov handed Soviet counter-proposals to Seeds in Moscow, von Weizsäcker recorded an interesting conversation with the Soviet envoy in Berlin, Alexei F. Merekalov. The latter requested the unblocking of former Soviet orders to the Czech Škoda Works, now under German control. He also asked for the state secretary's view of Soviet-German relations. After Weizsäcker's rather general answer, in which he mentioned the improved tone of the German press toward the USSR, the Soviet envoy declared that ideological differences did not hamper Soviet-Italian relations, so he did not see any obstacles to normal Soviet-German relations. This was not the first such Soviet hint. Stalin, in his report to the Eighteenth Congress of the Communist Party of the Soviet Union on 10 March 1939, had condemned Western appeasement of Germany and claimed the Western powers wanted to provoke a German-Soviet war, and said the USSR would not pull other people's chestnuts out of the fire. Furthermore, according to a secret German report of April 1, the Soviet Commissar for Defense, Voroshilov, told the German ambassador's wife at a Moscow reception that, in view of Western policy, he thought German-Soviet relations might be based on a different foundation. The Voroshilov and Merekalov statements look very much like a Soviet attempt to interest the Germans in a political agreement. It is worth noting that according to Astakhov's record of the Merekalov-Weizsäcker conversation, Merekalov merely asked Weizsäcker for his opinion on German-Soviet relations, to

---

and Maria Nowak-Kiełbikowa, eds., *Dokumenty z dziejòw polskiej polityki zagranicznej 1918–1939. Tom I, 1918–1932* (Warsaw, 1989), nos. 32, 33. These treaties were revised on March 26, 1925, and later supplemented by new guarantees and technical agreements on January 15 and June 30 1931, respectively; for the texts of the first two, see nos. 75, 102, ibid; on the third, see second Bułhak article cited below. The revised military convention signed at this time had a clause committing both sides to mutual aid through supplies and transit in case of attack by a third country, not the USSR. However, both governments rejected British and Soviet proposals to make the treaty overtly anti-German in 1939, for fear of provoking a German attack against Poland and a Hungarian attack, supported by Germany, against Romania. (The latter declared her neutrality on September 6, 1939). On Polish-Romanian relations in the interwar period, see Henryk Bułhak, "Polska a Rumunia 1918–1939,"in Janusz Żarnowski, ed., *Przyjaźnie i antagonizmy. Stosunki Polski z państwami sąsiednimi w latach 1918–1939* (Wrocław, Warsaw, 1977), 305–344; for documents, see: Bułhak, "Materiały do dziejów sojuszu polsko-rumuńskiego w latach 1921–1931," *Studia Historyczne*, no. 3 (1973), 421 ff.

which the latter jokingly replied he thought there were ideological differences, but that Germany wanted to develop economic ties with the USSR.[50] What is one to make of the divergence between these two reports? Did Weizsäcker, who wished for a return to the good German-Soviet relations of the Rapallo era, put words in Merekalov's mouth to nudge Hitler and Ribbentrop toward a German-Soviet agreement? Or did Astakhov omit Merekalov's statement in order to conceal a Soviet initiative? The answer to this question may lie in some document still inaccessible in the Russian archives.

Whatever the case may be, two days later, on April 19, the German embassy in London reported "from a reliable source" the contents of the Anglo-French proposals to the Soviet government as presented by Seeds to Litvinov on April 15. The "reliable source" stated that the Baltic States were also envisaged in these proposals, and reported the Soviet question whether the proposed Anglo-French guarantee was to cover only Poland and Romania, or the Baltic States as well. The "reliable source" also mentioned that the Soviet ambassador in Paris, Suritz, had said the Soviet Union was ready to guarantee Romanian possession of Bessarabia, while Deputy Foreign Commissar Vladimir P. Potemkin told the French ambassador in Moscow [Émile Naggiar] that the Soviet government had not yet made up its mind on the matter.[51] The alleged Soviet statement on Bessarabia may have been inserted due to some French rumors, for it is not confirmed by any known French or Soviet document. On the contrary, Potemkin told Payart on April 16 that the Soviet government had not promised any aid to Romania if the latter was the object of aggression, and that such a view could only be a misunderstanding. He added that the Romanian attitude toward the USSR was evasive.[52] It is also possible that the misinformation on Bessarabia was meant to frighten the Germans with the possibility of an imminent Soviet-Western agreement, while the alleged express Soviet question on the Baltic States looks like a Soviet hint to Berlin of Moscow's

---

50. See Weizsäcker report on conversation with Merekalov, April 17, 1939, *DGFP* D VI, no. 215; for Astakhov's version of the Merekalov-Weizsäcker conversation, see *DVP 1939*, I, no. 236. For excerpts from Stalin's report of 10 March 1939, see Degras, *DSFP, III*, 315–322. For Voroshilov's remarks to Mrs. von der Schulenburg, see Secret Report, Berlin, April 1, 1939, Politisches Archiv des Auswärtigen Amtes, Berlin, Dienstelle Ribbentrop, Vertrauliche Berichte, Bd. 2, 1939, 293. The document was found in the German archives by Dr. Stanisław Żerko of the Instytut Zachodni, Poznań. The author wishes to thank Dr. Richard Raack, professor emeritus of the University of California at Davis, for making the document available to her.

51. Chargé d'Affaires [Theo Kordt] London, to Foreign Ministry, Berlin, April 19, 1939, *DGFP*, D, VI, no. 233.

52. See Potemkin to Suritz, April 17, 1939, *DVP 1939*, no.231, and Payart on same, *DDF* 2nd ser. vol. XVI, no. 418.

interest in the region. In any case, the German embassy in London used the "reliable source" to inform the German Foreign Ministry about Western proposals at every stage of the negotiations, except for three weeks after July 22. It is likely that the good progress in direct German-Soviet talks in Berlin at that time made such reports unnecessary.

In early May came the astonishing news of the resignation of Litvinov as commissar for foreign affairs—an event closely connected with the dating of Stalin's decision to throw in his hand with Hitler. If the "Vozhd" had not done this much earlier in 1934–36—as per Krivitsky—he could, as mentioned earlier, have made up his mind when he sacked Litvinov. The latter was forced to resign on May 3, allegedly because of his "disloyalty" to Molotov, then head of the Sovnarkom. There is no documented explanation of what this "disloyalty" meant, but it is known that Litvinov never got on with Molotov, and that the latter shouted at him in Stalin's Kremlin office on the day of his dismissal. It is likely that Litvinov's persistence in advocating a compromise between Soviet and British proposals, and especially his suggestion that Moscow give up its demand for British agreement to Soviet guarantees of aid to Poland and Romania—i.e., that France and Britain would force them to accept such aid—was held against him. Indeed, many years later, in 1987, former Soviet Foreign Minister Andrei A. Gromyko claimed that Litvinov had been relieved of his post because he had gone against the party line. As Gromyko then said : " . . . *he was against shifting our focus from England and France to Germany, and so he was fired.*" Furthermore, on May 5, 1939, Astakhov told a French journalist in Berlin that Litvinov's dismissal did not mean a change of Soviet policy, but signaled the Soviet government's reaction to the ambivalent policy of the Western powers, which downplayed the political and military value of the aid that the USSR was ready to give them. It is also known that the Commissariat of Foreign Affairs was thoroughly purged, though Litvinov was spared to await a better day. (He was the Soviet ambassador to the United States in 1941–43). As mentioned earlier, some historians believe Litvinov's dismissal marks the moment that Stalin decided to work for an agreement with Hitler—a view also expressed by some contemporary observers of international affairs and by some diplomats, including the French ambassador in Rome, François Poncet.[53] Gromyko's 1987 statement con-

---

53. In one of Litvinov's last notes to Stalin, dated May 3, 1939, he criticized British delays in answering the Soviet proposals of April 17; suggested insisting on the inclusion of the eastern Baltic States [Finland, Latvia, Estonia], but said that Poland and Romania were already sufficiently protected by British and French commitments. Thus, it seems Litvinov thought the USSR should not insist on giving its own guarantee to these states. He also proposed agreement to the British demand for the inclusion of Holland, Belgium, and Switzerland in the guarantees; see *DVP*

firms the view that Litvinov's dismissal in early May 1939, if not earlier, indicates Stalin had made up his mind at this time to strike a deal with Hitler rather than with France and Britain.

Indeed, German-Soviet relations began to warm up immediately. On May 5, Julius Schnurre, head of Department W IV (Economic Department, Eastern Europe) in the German Foreign Ministry, recorded a conversation with Astakhov. On learning that Soviet orders to the Škoda Works in German-occupied Bohemia would be filled, Astakhov asked Schnurre whether German-Soviet economic negotiations could be renewed, to which Schnurre said he would soon give him an answer. Astakhov then asked whether the Germans thought that Litvinov's replacement by Molotov meant a shift in Soviet policy toward Germany. He went on to say that though Molotov had no experience in foreign policy, he would have a significant impact on it.[54] It is curious that the only Russian record of this conversation is a telegram from Merekalov to Molotov of May 5, reporting that Schnurre had invited him to call, told him that the Soviet order to the Škoda Works would be filled, and that no obstacles were expected. It is also worth noting in connection with Astakhov's question on the renewal of economic negotiations, that in early January 1939, Merekalov had insisted to Schnurre

---

(note 53 continued) *1939*, I, no. 267. For Gromyko's statement, made at a Politburo meeting in 1987, see Anatoly Chernaev, *My Six Years with Gorbachev*, translated and edited by Robert English and Elizabeth Tucker (University Park, PA, 2000), 126, emphasis added A.M.C.). Maisky wrote that Litvinov's resignation was preceded by "a war of words" between Molotov and Litvinov in Stalin's Kremlin office. Furthermore, a former Soviet diplomat, Evgeny Gnedin, claimed that long before this time, the NKVD had been preparing a "case" against Litvinov. See Sokolov, "People's Commissar Maxim Litvinov,"103 (For Sokolov, see note 14 above). See also Jonathan Haslam, *The Soviet Union and the Threat from the East, 1933–1941* (Pittsburgh, PA, 1992), 129, and Haslam, note 14 above. An enlarged "Stalin Cabinet" met on May 3; the record shows that Molotov was there from 3 to 7.50 p.m., while Litvinov came in at 5.15 and left at 5.50 p.m.; see *IA* 1995 no. 5–6, 36. Stalin's terse telegram to Soviet envoys on Litvinov's resignation and his replacement by Molotov mentioned a serious conflict between Molotov and Litvinov stemming from the latter's "disloyal attitude" toward the Sovnarkom, see *DVP*, ibid., no. 269. On Astakhov's remarks to a French journalist in Berlin, see Coulondre to Bonnet, May 5, 1939, *DDF*, 2nd ser., vol. XVI, no. 71. Astakhov must have been acting on instructions, since Merekalov had asked on May 4 for directives on what to say about Litvinov's dismissal, see *DVP* ibid., no. 276. The French ambassador in Rome, François Poncet, told his British colleague, Sir Percy Lorraine, that he believed Stalin sacked Litvinov "to make an arrangement with Germany, which would enable the latter to attack Poland and retake the Corridor with relative impunity." Lorraine to Halifax, Rome, May 5, 1939, *DBFP* 3rd ser. V, no.372.

54. For Schnurre's record of the conversation with Astakhov, May 5, 1939, see *DGFP*, D, VI, no. 332.

on their renewal. In December 1938, the Germans had offered Moscow a credit line of two hundred million reichsmarks (RM) in return for Russian raw materials, and Schnurre was to go to Moscow as the German negotiator. However, the Germans canceled the negotiations, allegedly because of French press reports.[55] As will be seen later, Stalin and Molotov resented this cancellation.

The international background to the next Astakhov-Schnurre meeting (May 17) was a new version of the previous British proposal (April 17). Presented by Ambassador Seeds to Molotov on May 8, it requested a public Soviet declaration that the USSR would aid certain East European countries in case of aggression—but only after Britain and France had become involved. This was reminiscent of the Czechoslovak-Soviet alliance of May 1935, which stipulated Soviet aid only after France acted to aid Czechoslovakia. (The stipulation was inserted by President Edward Beneš). The revised Anglo-French proposal—consulted on with the Poles—was more forthcoming than the first version, but Stalin and Molotov saw it as a request for one-sided Soviet aid to be given Poland and Romania for free, that is, without any compensation to the USSR. Still, Molotov asked Ambassadors Suritz and Maisky for their views on what answer should be given, and both advised that negotiations be continued. Whether or not Molotov was influenced by this advice, on May 14 he handed Seeds the Soviet reply listing three basic Soviet conditions for constructing a barrier against further aggression in Europe: (1) an effective mutual assistance pact between England, France, and the USSR; (2) their guarantee of Central and East European states threatened by aggression, including Latvia, Estonia, and Finland; (3) agreement by the three powers on the extent of material assistance to be rendered to each other and to the guaranteed states.[56] This

---

55. Merekalov to Commissariat of Foreign Affairs, May 5, 1939, *DVP 1939* I, no. 280. On the German offer of December 1938 and postponement of Schnurre trip, see *DGFP* D IV (London and Washington, 1951), nos. 484, 487. The German credit offer of December 1938 was for the same sum as in the German-Soviet trade agreement of April 1935; see note 34 above.

56. For the Anglo-French proposal of May 8, see *DBFP* 3rd ser. V, p.487; *SPE*, no.205, *GK* 1, no.327. On Anglo-Polish consultations on same, see Ambassador Edward Raczyński's cipher telegrams to Polish Foreign Ministry of April 20, May 3, 1939, Polish Embassy London, A.12 , Ciphers, *PISM*, also Raczyński report to Beck, April 26, *DiM* VII, no. 55; for Halifax to Kennard, April 28, and Kennard to Halifax, *DBFP*, ibid., nos. 304, 319. For Molotov's telegram to Suritz, May 8, see *DVP 1939* I, no. 284; extract, *SPE* no. 206; see also TASS communiqué of May 10, 1939, criticizing the English proposal as allegedly reported by Reuters, ibid., no. 208. Maisky thought the English proposal was unacceptable, but that London had not said its last word, *DVP 1939* I, no. 290. Suritz wrote Molotov on May 10 advising acceptance of the English proposal, because this would show the Soviet Union was not playing a double game with Germany, would gain the support of

project did not include Lithuania, which did not border on the USSR, and which Moscow perhaps expected to be defended by Poland. Whatever the case may be, in mid-April 1939, Major Korotkikh, the Soviet military attaché in Kaunas, told his Polish counterpart that the Soviet government considered the Baltic to lie in the sphere of Polish interests and that if Lithuania or any other Baltic state declared for Germany, the neighboring states would have to enter their territory in order to prevent German domination there. This seems to have been a low-level sounding of the Polish position on Lithuania, and, of course, Polish reaction to a possible Soviet entry into the other Baltic States. The Polish minister to Lithuania, Franciszek Charwat, did not mention Korotkikh's démarche when speaking to the Polish Undersecretary for Foreign Affairs, Jan Szembek, on 25 April 1939. But he did emphasize German economic pressure on Lithuania, and said he thought Poland should conduct an anti-German policy there.[57]

Three days later, on May 17, Astakhov saw Schnurre again. According to the German record, Astakhov requested that the Soviet Trade Office in Prague remain there as a branch of the Soviet Trade Delegation in Berlin. He then remarked on the improvement of the German press tone toward the USSR, and went on to say that since there were no outstanding differences between German and Soviet policies, there was no basis for hostility between the two countries. It was true, he said, that the USSR felt threatened by Germany, but this fear could be removed—and in this context he mentioned the Rapallo Treaty. To a question by Schnurre on Anglo-Soviet negotiations, Astakhov said he did not think Britain would attain her goal. He then expatiated on the good Soviet-Italian relations, noting the Duce's statement that, despite the [forthcoming] establishment of the [German-Italian] Axis, nothing stood in the way of further developing political and economic relations with the USSR. All this is, however, missing from Astakhov's short telegram reporting the same conversation.[58]

(*note 56 continued*) majority French opinion, and prevent Chamberlain from "wriggling" out again in Parliament; ibid., no.296. For the Soviet counterproposal of May 15, see *DBFP*, 3rd ser. V, no. 520; *SPE*, no.213; *GK* I, no. 342.

57. On Major Korotkikh's statement to Col. Leon Mitkiewicz, see Polish Envoy to Lithuania, Franciszek Charwat, to Ministry of Foreign Affairs, April 18, 1939, *DiM* VII, no. 51; for his talk with Jan Szembek, 25 April 1939, Szembek, *Diariusz*, IV, 573.

58. Schnurre's report on the conversation with Astakhov, May 17, 1939, DGFP D, VI, no. 406; Astakhov's telegram to National Commissariat of Foreign Affairs, May 17, on conversation with Schnurre, *GK* I, no. 349, *DVP 1939*, I, no. 318. The German-Italian Axis agreement was signed on May 22. What Astakhov was to say to Schnurre, May 17, may have been discussed at a meeting of the Stalin Cabinet two days earlier. On May 15, Molotov, Andrei Zhdanov, head of the Leningrad Party Organization, Andrei A. Andreev, chairman of the Central Committee Control Commission, and Georgii M. Malenkov, head of the central committee depart-

It is worth noting Schnurre's record of Astakhov's reference to the Rapallo Treaty of 1922, which normalized German-Soviet relations and led to secret military cooperation. Furthermore, Schnurre's record of Astakhov's statement on good Soviet-Italian relations was in line with those made by Merekalov in early January to Ambassador Schulenburg, when the latter was in Berlin, and to Weizsäcker on April 17. After Merekalov's departure for Moscow sometime in May, Astakhov carried on conversations with Schnurre. In fact, it is clear that the Astakhov-Schnurre conversation of May 17 prepared the ground for Molotov's declaration to Schulenburg in Moscow three days later. In this instance, both German and Russian records report the commissar's declaration that Soviet-German trade-credit negotiations could continue, *but that a "political basis" had to be established first,* though Molotov refused to say what this would be.[59] Hitler and Ribbentrop at first wanted to take up the Molotov proposal but then decided to wait, fearing the Russians might trick them. Instead, they decided on a cautious exploration of the possibility of better relations, a task they entrusted to Weizsäcker, who was to speak to Astakhov as if expressing his own opinions.[60]

In the meanwhile, Anglo-French-Soviet negotiations showed no progress. Neither Molotov nor Potemkin attended the May session of the League of Nations, though Halifax had expressed the hope of discussing the subject with one or the other. Instead, Maisky traveled to Geneva to be on hand, but does not seem to have been consulted. The British Cabinet Foreign Policy Committee met to discuss the matter on May 19, before Halifax's departure. They agreed that a close alliance with Russia, as proposed by the French, was not desirable, though the Secretary for Home Affairs, Sir Samuel Hoare, said failure to get an arrangement with Russia would mean the failure of the "peace front." Chamberlain, however, noted that both

---

ment dealing with senior cadres, were with Stalin for about two hours each, while Molotov stayed from 8:30 p.m. to 12:30 a.m. See *IA 1995*, no. 5–6, 36. On May 17, after the Astakhov-Schnurre conversation, Molotov met with Stalin from 7–10 p.m., while Marshal Kliment Y. Voroshilov, defense commissar, and Deputy Foreign Commissar Potemkin were there between 7:30 and 9:45 p.m.; they were followed by Lavrenty P. Beria, commissar for national security (NKVD), Malenkov, Potemkin—again—and third Deputy Foreign Commissar Vladimir I. Dekanozov; ibid., 38.

59. Emphasis added, A.M.C. For Schulenburg's report on the conversation with Molotov of May 20, 1939, see *DGFP* D, VI, no. 424; Russian record, *GK* I, no. 352 and *DVP* 1939 I, no. 326. On May 19, Molotov met with Stalin from 6:35–11:50 p.m., while Zhdanov, Andreev, and Malenkov were there 6:40–8:05 p.m., followed by Mikoyan, 7:10–8:05 p.m.. Nikolai I. Sharonov—the newly appointed ambassador to Poland—was there from 8:45–11:50 p.m; others were also present; see *IA* 1995, no. 5–6, 38.

60. *DGFP* D, VI, nos. 414, 437, 441.

the Polish and Romanian ambassadors had said in private conversations with Halifax and himself that any close association between Britain and Russia would also mean their countries' association with Moscow, which would in itself precipitate a European war. He also reminded the committee that there were still important "moderate elements" in Germany, whom a Western alliance with Russia would drive into Hitler's camp.[61] Chamberlain may have had the German "opposition" in mind, but he was clearly unaware of the Rapallo supporters in Berlin. Still, he was right about the Romanians and the Poles. Indeed, the Polish foreign minister gave British Ambassador Kennard his comments and suggestions on May 22. Having already made his position clear to Moscow on May 10–11, Beck emphasized three points to the British: (1) It seemed people in Paris and London did not realize that Russia and Germany had no common frontier; (2) Polish-Russian relations must be reciprocal, so Poland cannot be the object of any agreement made between other states; (3) The projected [Franco-British] agreement [with the USSR] envisioned war and was perhaps good and useful in such a case. However, if there was no war and France and Britain wished to organize Europe on peaceful principles, the Soviet alliance would make conversations with Berlin difficult, while at the same time British policy would be unpopular in some of the states of Central, Northern, and Eastern Europe. Beck concluded by saying that his comments were not motivated by the desire to hamper British and French freedom of action in matters not engaging Poland, for every state had the right to conclude defensive alliances.[62]

The British government kept Polish views in mind, but only as long as they did not interfere with its policy goals—or run counter to public opinion at home. In fact, by late May, public opinion in both Britain and France was calling for an alliance with Moscow and the two governments had to take this into account. Thus, French and British statesmen worked out a joint proposal, presented by Seeds and Payart to Potemkin on May 25. It envisaged a tripartite pact, though without a guarantee of the Baltic States. Furthermore, it proposed the discredited article 16 of the League Covenant as the basis for mutual aid, an idea that appealed greatly to Chamberlain. Molotov criticized the Western proposals to French and British diplomats

---

61. On Cabinet discussion before Halifax's departure for Geneva, see Cabinet Foreign Policy Committee (36) 48th meeting, Friday, May 19, 1939, CAB 27/625, 62–68, Public Record Office, London, [henceforth: PRO]. For the Franco-British talks in Geneva on the new proposal to the USSR, see *DBFP* 3rd ser. V, nos. 576, 578; Foreign Office memo on the pros and cons of an alliance, ibid., no.589.

62. For Polish views and objections, see Kennard's report on conversation with Beck to Under-Secretary of State Alexander Cadogan, May 22, 1939, *DBFP*. ibid., nos. 586, 649; for Polish record of same, see GMM 396/WB/9, Polish embassy London, A.12, *PISM*.

in Moscow on May 27, and did so publicly in a speech to the Supreme
Soviet on May 31. On the same day, Molotov presented the Soviet counter-
proposals, with critical remarks on the Anglo-French proposal. He named
eight states to be defended, including the Baltic States, and demanded that
military and political agreements be signed at the same time. On June 6,
Halifax wrote the British ambassador in Paris, Sir Eric Phipps: "The Russian business is quite infuriating, it blocks everything and frays everybody's
nerves." Still, he hoped it would bring results soon.[63]

It is against this background that one should view an important conversation which took place in Berlin on May 30 between Weizsäcker and
Astakhov. German historian Fleischhauer sees Weizsäcker's account of it
as marking "the first German initiative." This is true, but it was also a
reaction to Molotov's proposal of a political agreement made to Schulenburg
on May 20. Weizsäcker—acting on instructions but pretending to express
only his own views—reported that he asked Astakhov whether the request
to make the Soviet Trade Office in Prague a branch of the Soviet Trade
Delegation in Berlin was meant to lead to a provisional or a longer arrangement. Astakhov answered it was the latter. *He then stated that he was
informed of the Molotov-Schulenburg conversation.* He said the Soviet side

---

63. For the Franco-British proposal presented to Molotov on May 25, see *SPE,*
nos. 229, 230 and *DBFP,* no.649, 679–80, Russian: *GK* 1, nos. 379,380, *DVP
1939,* no.339. Article 16 mandated League members' severance of relations with an
aggressor and foresaw financial and economic sanctions against him; also the League
Council was to recommend what military action should be contributed by member
countries. The article was not invoked against Japan after the latter's aggression
against China, nor against Germany after the annexation of Austria and the Czech
lands. Economic sanctions failed to stop Mussolini's aggression in Ethiopia, and
were not invoked against him when he invaded Albania in April 1939. For French
support of an alliance with the USSR, see *DDF,* 2nd ser. XVI, no.289, also Suritz
report of May 24 that the French General Staff, especially Generals Maurice Gamelin
and Maxime Weygand, pressed for an alliance and military agreement with the
USSR, see *DVP* ibid., no. 331. For Potemkin-Seeds conversation, May 25, see *DVP*
ibid., no.333; for Molotov-Seeds-Payart conversation May 27, see *DBFP* ibid., no.
648, 657, *GK* 1, no.379, and *DVP* ibid., no.339. For Molotov's speech to the Supreme Soviet, May 31, 1939, see *SPE,* no. 232, Degras, *SDFP* III, 332–340; for the
Soviet draft proposal of June 2, see ibid., 340–41, also *DBFP* 3rd ser.V, p.753, *SPE*
no. 233. On Russian business "infuriating," see Halifax to Phipps, June 6, 1939,
DBFP 3rd ser. VI, no.272. There was a meeting of the "Stalin Cabinet" on the night
of June 1–2, at which both political and military matters seem to have been discussed. Molotov stayed from 6:10 p.m.–2:50 a.m. and Voroshilov 7:40–2:50 a.m.;
the chief of the general staff, Army Commander [later General] Boris Shaposhnikov,
attended 11:45–2:50 a.m.; Andreev and Zhdanov stayed from a few minutes after
10 p.m. to 2:50 a.m., and Mikoyan attended, 10 p.m.–1:30 a.m., *IA* 1995, no. 5–6,
38.

did not see economic negotiations as a "game," and cited Molotov as saying that economics and politics could not be separated in German-Soviet relations. He added that Potemkin had "apparently" told the German economic attaché in Moscow [Gustav Hilger] that the planned economic negotiations should not be a game. Weizsäcker, for his part, hinted that Germany had much to offer the USSR, to which Astakhov responded that *the German government had rejected a Soviet offer of alliance before concluding a treaty with Poland,* also that Germany had showed little understanding for the Soviet view that domestic and foreign policy need not conflict with each other. Weizsäcker then noted Astakhov's statement that he would ask Moscow again for its views about the branch Soviet Trade Office in Prague, also for information on what exactly Molotov had wished to tell Ambassador Schulenburg. Astakhov added that, despite mistrust of Germany, Molotov did not wish to shut the door to further German-Soviet discussions.[64]

Astakhov's record generally agrees with Weizsäcker's, but gives a somewhat different presentation. In mentioning Molotov's declaration to Schulenburg, Weizsäcker allegedly said this was different from what Merekalov had told the Foreign Ministry; that is, that economic relations could develop separately from political ones. To this Astakhov answered that he was familiar only with part of Molotov's conversation with Schulenburg and could not give a definite interpretation of the commissar's declaration. However, he had no grounds to believe that Molotov was definitely opposed to Schnurre's trip to Moscow and to economic negotiations. He would ask the "Center" about this and then give a clarification. At the same time, he recalled that Merekalov had often stated in conversations with Weizsäcker that "economics is condensed politics." He also recalled that at a breakfast given by Merekalov for Schulenburg, the latter had agreed that an improvement in political relations could follow improved economic relations. Astakhov then went on to recount Weizsäcker's "personal" statements, noting he could not render them precisely due to

---

64. Memorandum by Weizsäcker, May 30, 1939, *DGFP* D VI, no. 451, emphasis added, A.M.C. There is no published record of the Potemkin-Hilger conversation. On May 29, Ribbentrop told Italian Ambassador Bernardo Attolico that Weizsäcker was to speak to the Russian chargé in Berlin, rather than Schulenburg to Molotov in Moscow. He asked Attolico not to inform Italian foreign minister just yet, because he had not yet fully clarified his own thoughts, but Attolico immediately informed Ciano, see *Documenti Diplomatici Italiani* [henceforth: *DDI*], 8th ser. vol. XII (Rome, 1952), no. 53. Likewise, a member of the Italian embassy in Berlin told one of French Ambassador Coulondre's informants that advances, or at least soundings, were made recently by the Axis powers directly or indirectly to the Kremlin. The Italian diplomat said Ribbentrop would march with the Soviets, but they were turning a deaf ear, see Coulondre telegram to Bonnet, June 1, 1939, *DDF* 2nd ser. XVI no. 329.

the camouflaged and contorted manner in which they were made. The main points were—and here Astakhov's account agrees with Weizsäcker's—that Hitler had given up any designs on Ukraine, giving as an example the fate of Carpathian Ukraine. Also, Weizsäcker pointed out that Hitler had not made any negative comments on the USSR in his speech of April 28, when he denounced both the German-Polish nonaggression agreement of 1934 and the Anglo-German naval agreement of 1935. Weizsäcker said it was now up to the USSR to choose between England and Germany. Astakhov reported that he replied, also informally, by pointing out past German anti-Soviet policy, good Soviet-Italian relations, also the fact that the Soviet Union had always desired good relations with Germany. Here *he recalled that just before the conclusion of the Franco-Soviet and Czechoslovak-Soviet pacts, the Soviet government had proposed mutual assistance pacts to Germany and Poland.* To this Weizsäcker said: "I did not know this," as if catching himself unawares. Astakhov then asked about the significance of the rumors flying around Berlin about a German-Soviet agreement, but did not record an answer. Finally, he told Weizsäcker he would forward his questions to Moscow, while his account of the rest of the conversation would be presented as unofficial statements.[65]

Two aspects of this conversation, present in both records, are significant. First of all, Astakhov indicated that he had been informed of at least part of the Molotov-Schulenburg conversation of May 20, and mentioned a conversation between Potemkin and Hilger, saying he would contact Moscow to clarify certain points. Thus, it is clear that he could hardly have been acting on his own initiative. Secondly, he mentioned Soviet offers of mutual assistance pacts to Germany and Poland, made according to Weizsäcker's account, before the German-Polish treaty [January 1934], but according to Astakhov, just before the conclusion of Soviet alliances with France and Czechoslovakia in [May] 1935. There is no record of such a Soviet proposal to Poland, but proposals to Germany at this time were also mentioned by Kandelaki in his Berlin conversations at the turn of 1936–37.[66] Perhaps both Kandelaki and Astakhov referred to the suggestion Litvinov made to Schulenburg on May 8, 1935, to start negotiations for a nonaggression pact, or there may have been some other "concrete" proposal,

---

65. See Astakhov record of conversation with Weizsäcker, May 30, 1939, *GK* I, no. 384 (emphasis added, A.M.C), and his telegram to Foreign Affairs Commissariat, May 30, *DVP 1939* I, no. 342. The Carpathian Ukraine was part of Austria-Hungary before 1918 and then of Czechoslovakia. It had been viewed as a potential German bridge to Soviet Ukraine, but part of it was awarded to Hungary by the Vienna Accord of 1 November 1938, and the rest in late March 1939, see Paul Robert Magocsi. *Historical Atlas of East Central Europe* (Seattle and London, 1993, reprint 1994), map 39c, 132–133.

66. On Kandelaki, see note 40 above.

the trace of which has been lost. Whatever the case may be, Astakhov's reference to a previous Soviet proposal of a mutual assistance pact to Germany in 1935 looks very much like a calculated hint directed at Hitler and Ribbentrop through Weizsäcker, who certainly favored a return to Rapallo but did not make German policy.

While the Germans were cautious, the Soviets were not shy about dropping hints. Thus, on June 3, Weizsäcker noted a conversation with the Estonian minister in Berlin. The latter, known as a good judge of Russian affairs, said he thought the Russians viewed the democratic states with greater mistrust than totalitarian ones. Also, he had the impression from speaking to the Russian chargé d'affaires that the Russians were only waiting for "a friendly gesture" to say so.[67] Twelve days later, on June 15, Ernst Woermann, the Nazi head of the Political Department in the German Foreign Ministry, recorded some very striking statements by Astakhov, as reported by the Bulgarian minister in Berlin [Parvan Draganov]. According to the latter, the Soviet diplomat stated the Soviet Union had three choices: a pact with Britain and France, further delaying those negotiations, or a nonaggression pact with Germany. Astakhov said the third option was the most desirable for the USSR, and that different "world views" did not have to play any role. He also said the USSR did not recognize Romanian possession of Bessarabia and feared a German occupation of the Baltic States. *If, however, Germany made it clear that she would not attack the Soviet Union, the latter would abstain from concluding a pact with the Western powers—but the Soviets did not know what Germany wanted.*[68] Gorlov admits that Draganov, in a report to the Bulgarian foreign office, confirmed these statements were made by Astakhov, but the Russian historian gives credence to the Soviet diplomat, who in his "Dairy" [sic] presented the statements attributed to him by Draganov—as made to him by the latter. Gorlov also notes there is a detailed, four-page unpublished report by Astakhov on this conversation in the Russian archives, but does not say when it was received by Molotov.[69] Geoffrey Roberts also points out the discrepancy between the Draganov and Astakhov accounts, but speculates

---

67. Weizsäcker note, June 3, 1939, *DGFP* D VI, no. 469; Karl Tofer was the Estonian minister in Berlin.

68. Ernst Woermann's record of a conversation with the Bulgarian minister, June 15, 1939, *DGFP* D VI, no. 529; emphasis added, A.M.C.

69. Gorlov, "Sovetsko-germanskii dialog," 21–23 (see note 46 above), and Astakhov's diary entry for June 14, 1939, *GK* 2, no. 403. Astakhov's detailed report on the conversation, cited by Gorlov as f. 011, op. 4, p.27, d. 59, 123–127, Foreign Policy Archives, Moscow, was not published in *DVP 1939* I. Instead, there is a political report by Astakhov to Molotov, dated June 14, beginning with the words: "The last few days here passed without any special events," see ibid., no. 370.

that Astakhov made the statements on his own initiative, so they could be seen as "an instance of personal kite flying." Roberts admits that Astakhov had asked Molotov for instructions on how to answer persistent questions put to him on Soviet policy, but concludes that Astakhov might have sounded out Draganov on his own initiative.[70] Neither Gorlov nor Roberts is willing to entertain the possibility that Astakhov had been instructed to "fish" for German proposals, though given the Stalin-Molotov control of Soviet diplomacy, this must have been the case.

Furthermore, the Germans did not treat Astakhov as a free lance agent but as a bona fide Soviet representative, whom they expected to transmit their statements to Molotov. Weizsäcker had done this on May 30. The next to do so was Schulenburg, who was instructed to follow up on the Draganov report. During a brief stay in Berlin, the ambassador visited Astakhov on June 17, and told him there were no serious problems between Germany and the Soviet Union. Schulenburg reported Astakhov's claim that Weizsäcker's statements were rather general and vague, noting the Soviet diplomat had said the same to the Bulgarian minister, probably a reference to Astakhov's statement to Draganov that the Soviet Union did not know what Germany wanted. The ambassador denied this, and *repeated the statement, made to him personally by Ribbentrop, that Germany did not fear England and France, because she had a strong line of fortifications, but "an agreement with Russia makes sense."* Schulenburg also reported Astakhov as saying that things had gone well for Germany and Russia when they were friends, and badly when they were not. The ambassador, for his part, said that Germany had experienced difficulties in fulfilling Mikoyan's "A and B programs" [Soviet demands in the projected trade agreement] because of her own needs, but that the situation had improved after the "union" with Czechoslovakia. This was clearly a hint that Germany would welcome the renewal of German-Soviet trade-credit negotiations. Astakhov's account of this conversation is generally in keeping with Schulenburg's, except for his statement on German-Russian relations as reported by the German ambassador.[71]

---

70. Roberts, *The Soviet Union and the Origins of the Second World War*, 78.

71. Schulenburg account, June 17, *DGFP* D, VI, no. 540, emphasis added, A.M.C; Astakhov account, *DVP 1939* I, no. 378. Mikoyan's A and B programs referred to 1938 Soviet demands for German manufactured goods, especially armaments; for these programs and German deliveries to the USSR as agreed on 19 August 1939, see *GK* 2, no. 575, 284–285; for the C program (list) of Soviet deliveries to Germany, not published in *GK* 2, see Zorya and Lebedeva, "Around the Non-Aggression Pact," *International Affairs*, no. 10 (1989), 101. Timber led the way, followed by agricultural goods and phosphates, but raw cotton, manganese ore, gas oil, and other goods were also included. See also note 126 below.

In the meanwhile, Anglo-Soviet negotiations were stalemated because, as Seeds was informed from London on June 12, the British government could not agree that guarantees be imposed on states unwilling to receive them. Indeed, like Poland and Romania, the Baltic States did not want to be guaranteed by the USSR, while the latter insisted that their security must be guaranteed. On June 13, a *Pravda* editorial written by Zhdanov expatiated on the need to defend the Baltic States [Latvia, Estonia, and Finland, but not Lithuania] against aggression. Seeds was to have traveled to London for consultations but came down with flu, so Robert Strang, a high official in the Foreign Office, left London for Moscow on June 14 with a new set of proposals.[72] Seeds handed them to Molotov on June 15. They provided for consultation in case of a threat to one of the states envisaged, but still included article 16 of the League Covenant as the basis for aid. Molotov rejected the proposal the next day, insisting on the inclusion of the three Baltic States and full reciprocity. By this time, Chamberlain and the cabinet, as well as most British officials and diplomats, saw an alliance with the USSR as necessary, if only to prevent a German-Soviet pact. At a meeting of the Cabinet Foreign Policy Committee on June 20, Lord Chatfield, the minister for Coordination of Defense, said a treaty of mutual defense with Russia would at least prevent the Soviets from making a pact with Germany. *Halifax agreed, but said that if Germany invaded Poland, nothing could prevent a Soviet-German arrangement to partition that country.*[73] There were, of course, some British officials and diplomats who still opposed an agreement with Moscow. Sir Nevile Henderson, the pro-German British ambassador in Berlin, wrote Halifax on June 17 that he was uneasy about the negotiations with the Russians because: "History contains nothing but examples of the unwisdom of putting one's faith in the Slavs; they have always and invariably proved a bitter disappointment to their allies from the days of Maria Theresa to 1917." This diatribe earned an ironic marginal comment from one Foreign Office reader: "What about 1812–1815?"[74]

---

72. Foreign Office Memorandum: "Instructions for Sir William Seeds, June 12, 1939," *DBFP* 3rd ser. v. VI, no. 35. Robert Strang was head of the Central Department, Foreign Office, 1937–39, and assistant under-secretary of state, 1939–43.

73. For the British proposal and Molotov reply, June 15, 16, see *SPE*, nos. 245–246; *DBFP,* 3rd ser. VI, nos. 73, 103, 122,123; Zhdanov article of June 13, Franco-British proposals and Molotov rejection, *GK* 2, no. 401, 404, 406, 407; *DVP 1939* I no.373. The visitor record for the "Stalin Cabinet" on June 15, shows Molotov; Voroshilov; Andreev; Nikolai M. Shvernik, president of the Trade Union Federation; Kaganovich, Mikoyan, and Beria. Molotov stayed the longest, 11:10 p.m.– 3:10 a.m., see *I A* 1995, no. 5–6, 40. For the British cabinet meeting of June 20, see CAB. 27/626, 39, *PRO*, emphasis added, A.M.C.

74. For N. Henderson to Halifax, June 17, and marginal comment, F.0. 800.315, 217, *PRO*.

On the Berlin-Moscow sector, the Germans were still cautious, while the Russians insisted on their economic demands. Schulenburg told Molotov on June 28, that he was instructed by Ribbentrop to say Germany desired not only a normalization but also an improvement of mutual relations, and that this was approved by Hitler. Molotov, however, replied that it would be better for the German embassy to answer Mikoyan's questions [regarding a trade-credit agreement], and only then would a decision be made as to whether Schnurre should come to Moscow.[75] Molotov's arrogant stance, confirmed by Potemkin in a conversation with Schulenburg on July 1,[76] led to the suspension of German probing and thus the interruption of German-Soviet diplomatic conversations in both Moscow and Berlin. However, presumably to encourage the Germans, the Russian air attaché in London, Ivan Cherny, told the assistant German air attaché that the Soviet government had no interest in concluding a pact with Britain and France. In a telegram of June 29 reporting this item, the German ambassador in London, Herbert von Dirksen, also transmitted the correct version of the proposal sent that day to the British ambassador in Moscow. He did so without citing the "reliable source," which was perhaps so well established by this time that it needed no mention. In this proposal, presented to Molotov on July 1, Latvia, Estonia, and Finland were to be listed as guaranteed states in a separate, secret annex to the alliance treaty—which was a French suggestion. The British and French also insisted that besides Poland, the guarantees include Romania, Turkey, Greece, Belgium, Luxemburg, the Netherlands, and Switzerland.[77] On June 29, *Pravda* published another article by Zhdanov, titled: "The British and French Governments do not want agreement with the USSR."[78]

On July 3, Molotov handed the British and French ambassadors a counterdraft excluding Luxembourg, the Netherlands, and Switzerland from the projected guarantee. He told the ambassadors orally that the Soviet government would only agree to the inclusion of the last two if Poland and Turkey concluded mutual assistance pacts with the USSR. The Soviet draft also stipulated assistance in case of direct or indirect aggression, defining

---

75. Schulenburg telegram, June 29, 1939, *DGFP* D VI, no. 579; Soviet record *GK* 2, no. 442, also Schulenburg July 3, *DGFP* ibid., no. 607.

76. Potemkin-Schulenburg conversation, July 1, 1939; Russian record, *DVP 1939* I, no. 402; no German record published.

77. German Ambassador, London, Telegram to Ministry of Foreign Affairs, June 29, 1939, *DGFP* D VI, no.581. Anglo-French draft handed to Molotov, July 1, 1939, *DBFP* 3rd ser., VI, no. 209; *SPE* no. 271; *GK* 2, no. 453. Thirty-eight visitors to Stalin were listed on the evening of July 1; of these, Molotov, Voroshilov and Kaganovich stayed about five hours, *I A* 1995, no. 5–6, 42.

78. Zhdanov article, June 29, *SPE* no.269, Degras, *SDFP,* III, pp. 352–353.

the latter as *"an internal coup d'état or a reversal of policy in favor of the aggressor."* Furthermore, Molotov insisted orally on the simultaneous entry into force of the military and political agreements. Of course, he knew very well that Poland and Turkey did not wish to ally with the USSR, so his proposal may have been intended to drag out the negotiations. In any event, on July 6, the British ambassador was instructed to agree to the omission of Switzerland and the Netherlands, but to reject the simultaneous entry into force of the military and political agreements, also the Soviet definition of indirect aggression. However, the instruction to Seeds reiterated the July 1 inclusion of the list of guaranteed states in an *unpublished protocol.* This suggests that Britain and France were willing to bypass Polish, Romanian, and Baltic objections. Indeed, on July 7, the Polish chargé d'affaires in London, Antoni Jażdżewski, was informed "briefly" about the state of Anglo-Soviet negotiations. In particular, he was told that "the Soviet Union must obtain some compensation for coming to our assistance in the event of our having to implement our guarantee to Poland." This implied Anglo-French readiness to conclude a military and political treaty with the USSR and making some concessions to the latter's demands. On July 8, the ambassadors handed a new draft agreement to Molotov, to which the commissar added a draft supplementary letter stipulating the conditional inclusion of the Netherlands and Switzerland. This letter also defined indirect aggression as the action of any of the guaranteed states under the threat of force by another power, *or without any such threat,* involving the use of its territory and forces by that power for the purposes of aggression, and consequently the loss of the state's independence. On July 11, Halifax suggested to the French that, in return for Russian acceptance of the Anglo-French formula on indirect aggression (which was limited to change of policy under direct threat, as in the Czechoslovak case in 1938), both governments should agree to the Russian demand for the simultaneous signing of the military and political agreements. The French at first opposed this, but then advised the British to accept the Soviet demand rather than risk the breakdown of negotiations.[79]

---

79. Soviet counterdraft, July 3, 1939, *SPE* no. 273; *GK* 2, no.458, emphasis added, A.M.C. On the stipulation of conditionally including the Netherlands and Switzerland, see Molotov to Soviet Ambassadors Maisky and Suritz, July 3, 1979, *SPE* no. 274, *GK* 2, no. 459. Halifax instructions to Seeds, July 6, 7, 1939, *DBFP* 3rd ser. VI, nos. 251–253; on conversations with Molotov, see Seeds to Halifax, *DBFP* ibid., nos. 279, 281–282. Correspondence on linking the Anglo-French definition of indirect aggression with signing a military-political agreement, see *DBFP,* ibid., nos. 290, 295, 307. For the Anglo-French proposal of July 8, and Molotov's supplemental letter July 9, see *SPE* nos. 278. 279, *GK* 2 nos. 465, 467, *DVP 1939* I, no. 417. For information to Poles, see Halifax to Clifford Norton, British chargé d'affaires, Warsaw, July 12, 1939, *DBFP,* ibid., no. 306, cf. Jażdżewski telegraphic report on July 7 conversation with Ivone Kirkpatrick of the Foreign Office, Warszawa,

Meanwhile, on July 7, Berlin made a move that proved crucial for rapprochement with Moscow. On that day, the German embassy in Moscow was instructed to offer Mikoyan a credit of 200 million reichsmarks—the same amount as in the 1935 agreement and as offered in December 1938—and also to propose a list of issues to be discussed in negotiations for a trade-credit agreement. Three days later, the embassy reported that Mikoyan had received these proposals with great interest, saying he would inform his government and give an answer soon.[80] On July 19, Astakhov reported to Molotov, with whom he was obviously in close touch, that the Germans let no opportunity slip "to let us understand their readiness to change their policy toward us, and that all depended only on us."[81] Clearly, the German side was anxious to proceed with talks. Moscow was forthcoming as well, for Stalin decided that E. I. Babarin should return to Berlin as deputy head of the Soviet Trade Delegation to negotiate the trade-credit agreement. On July 13, Babarin attended a meeting of the "Stalin Cabinet," so it is likely that he received his new instructions that evening. Schulenburg reported the decision on sending Babarin on July 16, and the Soviet press announced his departure to conduct negotiations in Berlin on July 22. Ribbentrop assumed that Astakhov and Babarin would immediately report every German statement to Moscow, so the German experts were instructed to infiltrate certain statements by Hitler into the negotiations and to keep in close telephone touch with the German foreign minister.[82]

---

teleg. szyfr. no. 120, 121, Polish embassy, London, archives, A.12, ciphers, *PISM*. For French views and advice to the British, see: *DDF*, 2nd ser., XVII (Paris, 1984), pt. II (documents from June 29 through July 11).

80. For Weizsäcker's instruction to the Moscow embassy, July 7, 1939, see *DGFP* D VI, no. 628, also Schulenburg report of July10, ibid., no. 642. No Russian record of this conversation has been published, but Schulenburg reported earlier, June 29, that Molotov told him that day (telegram sent June 29, 2 a.m. so referred to June 28) he approved Mikoyan's attitude in his conversation with Hilger, and that after this matter was settled it might be useful for Schnurre to come to Moscow; ibid., no.579; Russian record, *GK* 2, no. 442. On the evening of July 10, Stalin saw Molotov, Voroshilov, Beria, Kaganovich and Mikoyan; Molotov came at 8.45 p.m., the rest at 9 or 10 p.m., see: *I A* 1995, 5–6, no. 44.

81. Astakhov letter to Molotov, July 19, 1939, *GK* 2, no. 485..

82. For an earlier Mikoyan-Hilger conversation mentioning Babarin on June 2, see ibid., no. 388. Schulenburg's report on this conversation does not mention Babarin, *DGFP* D VI, no.465. Babarin had gone to Berlin earlier but returned, presumably to receive new instructions. The July 13 session of the "Stalin Cabinet" was attended by a total of seventeen visitors, of whom Molotov, as usual stayed longest, from 1:45 to 7:15 p.m; Babarin came at 6:45 and left at 7:05 p.m, see *IA* 1995, no.5–6, 44. For Schulenburg's report on Babarin trip, July 16, see *DGFP* ibid.,no.677. For Weizsäcker's July 22 instruction to Schulenburg on the end of the waiting period mandated to him at the end of June, and instructing him to start political conversations, ibid., no. 700. For Schnurre's daily telephone contact with Ribbentrop during the talks with Babarin, see his letter to Schulenburg, August 2, ibid., no. 756.

Babarin paid a visit to Schnurre on July 18, and stated he had been empowered to negotiate a trade treaty in the German capital, while the German ambassador was to pick up the threads in Moscow.[83] It seems Stalin had decided that trade negotiations could, after all, go forward before establishing a "political base" or, as is more likely, that he expected the trade negotiations to lead to a political agreement. Perhaps sending Babarin to Berlin marked another date at which Stalin decided to throw in his hand with Hitler?

Japan was also an element in Soviet policy in 1939. Some historians see the fighting between Japanese and Soviet forces in summer 1939 in the Far East, on the frontier between Manchukuo and Mongolia, as very important or even central to Stalin's policy at this time. However, it does not seem to have been significant, given the small size of the forces involved.[84] Furthermore, the brilliant Soviet intelligence agent in Tokyo, Richard Sorge—who had excellent contacts in high Japanese government circles—reported in June that the Japanese army would not be ready for a major offensive for another two years or so, and the Japanese government did not plan a war against the USSR.[85] This information, together with Soviet military reconnaissance reports, should have convinced Stalin that there was no threat of a major war with Japan. However, it is impossible to evaluate the role of this protracted, distant conflict in Stalin's European policy, because the records of high-level Politburo and Stalin Cabinet foreign policy

---

83. See Schnurre's report on conversation with Babarin, July 18, 1939, *GDFP* D VI, no. 685.

84. On May 11, Japanese-sponsored Manchukuo (Manchurian) cavalry units had driven Soviet-controlled Outer Mongolian troops across the Holha River on the disputed Nomonhan/Ghalkin Gol section of the frontier between Manchukuo and Mongolia. Three days later, a Japanese reconnaissance unit advanced into this area, but was destroyed by Soviet troops on May 28. The Japanese Kwantung Army then decided to send its 23rd division, later supplemented by additional forces, all of which were combined later into the 6th Army. The Japanese attack began with the bombing of Soviet positions on June 28, and developed into a land offensive in the first days of July, but ran into Georgii K. Zhukov's armored and motorized troops, with good artillery support, so it stalled two days later. The Japanese launched another attack on July 23 and pushed the Soviet forces back in two days, but suffered heavy casualties. What followed was a war of attrition until Zhukov launched a victorious offensive on August 20, totally defeating the Japanese forces by August 31. The Japanese 6th Army numbered about 75,000 men while Zhukov's lst Army Corps numbered 57,000, but the Japanese were spread out over a large area. An armistice was agreed by Molotov and Japanese Ambassador Shigenori Togo in Moscow on September 15, and signed locally the next day, see *DVP 1939*, pt. II., docs. 586, 591. For a discussion of the political and military aspects, see Jonathan Haslam, *The Soviet Union and the Threat from the East*, ch. 5.

85. For Richard Sorge telegram, see Haslam, ibid., 131; this telegram was not published in *DVP 1939* 1.

discussions are unavailable. Another event in the Far East that may have caused some concern in Moscow involved British policy in that region. After the Japanese blockade of the British concession at Tientsin in June, the British government signed an agreement with Japan on July 22, recognizing Japanese gains in China. This was resented in Moscow, which was supporting Chiang Kai-Shek.

However, it is likely that another development concerning Britain was more worrisome to Stalin, because it was closer to home. The British government now showed a renewed interest in reaching an agreement with Hitler, and this became public knowledge through leaks to the British press. Helmuth Wohlthat, a high official in Hermann Goering's Four-Year Plan Office, conducted talks in July with some prominent British officials in London. They included Chamberlain's close adviser Sir Horace Wilson, who allegedly expressed great interest in a peaceful settlement with Germany by way of a nonaggression pact, which would make it possible for Britain to discard her East European guarantees. There was also talk of a large loan to Germany. Some details of Wohlthat's conversations were leaked to the press by Robert S. Hudson, secretary of the Board of Overseas Trade, who had earlier led a British trade delegation to Moscow. These leaks appeared in the British press on July 22, with the charge that at least one member of the government was involved in a new attempt at appeasement.[86]

Meanwhile, however, the British and French governments had agreed on July 12 to include in the treaty a formula on indirect aggression closer to the Soviet version. On July 17, the two ambassadors presented a draft to Molotov including their agreed definition of indirect aggression. This assumed armed Soviet action in case a state changed its policy under a clear threat of force by another power, and this change involved the abandonment of its independence or neutrality, but in other cases there were to be consultations. Assistance was to be given according to League of Nations principles, but without the need to follow League procedure or await its action. They also proposed *a secret protocol listing the countries to be guaranteed—which included Poland, Romania, Estonia, Latvia, and Finland.* Molotov rejected the Anglo-French formula on indirect aggression, saying it did not cover all contingencies. He offered Czech President Emil Hacha's acceptance of Hitler's terms in mid-March 1939 as an example of a state bowing to a threat without it being acknowledged as such. He then

---

86. For Wohlthat's July 24 report on his London talks, see *DGFP* D VI, no.716; for confirmation by German Ambassador Herbert von Dirksen, see ibid., nos.710, 746, 752. British historians deny that Wilson made the proposals reported by Wohlthat, since there is no British documentary confirmation, Watt, *How War Came*, 399–400. For press reports and Chamberlain reactions, ibid., 400–401. Wilson made the same proposal to Dirksen on August 3, 1939, *DBFP* 3rd ser. VI, no. 533.

said that if the British and French did not accept the Soviet formula on indirect aggression, there was no point in continuing the conversations. After this ultimatum, however, he went on to insist that the political and military agreements should be signed at the same time and declared this was the "fundamental principle." Once this was settled, he said: "The question as to how agreement on the text of the political articles was to be recorded was a technical matter of secondary importance." Finally, he asked whether or not the British and French governments "were really willing to open military conversations." The two ambassadors assured him they were and French Ambassador Émile Naggiar even said his government would be willing to begin military conversations immediately, without waiting to sign the political agreement. Seeds, however, stated the British government was ready to start technical conversations only if agreement was reached on the article under discussion. Naggiar then asked whether the Soviet government would agree to open military talks at once before the conclusion of political discussions, but proceeding parallel with them. Molotov said he thought the Soviet government might agree. Stalin won this point, which was presumably the goal of Molotov's diatribe, for the ambassadors were authorized on July 21 to agree to the Soviet demand for the simultaneous entry into force of the military and political agreements. They informed Molotov of this on July 22—the day that the leaks appeared in the London press—whereupon he insisted that military conversations start at once without resolving outstanding issues in a political agreement. The Anglo-French agreement to this demand was transmitted on July 21 by "the reliable source" to the German embassy in London, which reported it to Berlin. On July 25, the appropriate instructions were sent from London to Ambassador Seeds.[87]

The Polish government was skeptical of positive results in these negotiations. It viewed bargaining with the Soviets as shopping in an "oriental bazaar," that is, dealing with a devious merchant who constantly upped the price. In any case, as mentioned earlier, the Poles were certain the Soviets would help them in the event of German aggression, for "the Soviet government would be anxious to see Hitler as far from its frontiers as possible." Meanwhile, Beck warned that any Anglo-French commitments involving Poland or the Baltic countries would have "an unfortunate effect." This was a veiled warning against pushing them into Germany's arms,

---

87. For the Anglo-French proposal of July 17, see *SPE* no.286, *DBFP* 3rd ser. VI, no.338, emphasis added, A.M.C; French urging acceptance of Soviet demands, ibid., no.337; Halifax insisting on the British formula on indirect aggression, ibid., no.338; British agreement to military conversations, ibid., no.435. For secret information on French views and "reliable source" report on Halifax instruction to Seeds of July 21, see Dirksen telegram, July 21, *DGFP* D, VI, no.695.

which the British always feared and thus wished to avoid. It is worth noting, however, that the British envisaged the passage of Soviet troops in the event of a German attack on Poland. Thus, "the instructions to the British Military Mission to Moscow August 1939" for staff conversations with Russia did not preclude Russian entry into Poland, though they indicated some naiveté about the beliefs of the Polish and Soviet governments. The real reason for Polish opposition was fear that the Russians would stay—which was true—but also the alleged fear that the Soviet sojourn there would lead to "communizing the peasantry," which was not a Polish phobia. At the same time, the authors of the memorandum believed the Russians were not enthusiastic about having their troops in Poland for fear they would come under "bourgeois influences," which was not a fear entertained in Moscow. Finally, the "Instructions" perceived the real problem to be that while the Poles might accept Russian "air forces" and raw materials, they did not want Russian soldiers on their soil. The conclusion to this section read: "The position is one that will have to be handled with considerable tact."[88]

Meanwhile, as instructions were being drawn up for the British delegation in preparation for its depature, Anglo-Soviet relations were at a low ebb. On July 31, R. A. Butler, the parliamentary undersecretary of state for foreign affairs, stated in the House of Commons that the chief difference between the Western powers and Moscow was "the question whether we should infringe the independence of the Baltic States or not." This infuriated the Kremlin. *Izvestiia* commented on August 2 that the chief difference was in the British formula leaving a loophole for an aggressor to do just that. That same day, the Anglo-French formula on indirect aggression, defined as a clear threat to the independence of a Baltic State and consultation in other cases, was offered again to Molotov, who did not welcome it. At this point, the Western-Soviet negotiations lapsed, though the British, at least, expected them to continue parallel to the military talks. On August 4, just as Strang was ordered to leave Moscow for London, the French and British delegations set out for Russia on a small, slow merchant ship, "The City of Exeter." They arrived in Leningrad on August 10, and reached Moscow the next morning. Travel on a merchant ship was chosen because the RAF could not spare its two Sunderland flying boats to accommodate the joint mission, while a railway trip through Germany was clearly unadvisable and Halifax thought that sending the mission on a destroyer through the Baltic would be provocative. In any case, the British delegation members were told they were only negotiators, for the final agreement to any military convention rested with the French and British governments.

---

88. For Polish views as reported from Warsaw on July 21 and 31, see *DBFP* 3rd ser. VI, nos. 394, 489. Instructions to British military mission, on Polish-Russian relations, ibid., Appendix V, 772.

Moreover, "the main issue is to define the circumstances in which France and Great Britain would assist the Soviet Government should the latter feel obligated to defend the independence or neutrality of one of the Baltic States. Agreement on this point has not been reached." Thus, they were instructed: "Until such time as the political agreement is concluded, the Delegation should therefore go very slowly with the conversations, watching the progress of the political negotiations and keeping in very close touch with His Majesty's Ambassador." By contrast, the French delegation was given full powers to negotiate and told to return with a signed agreement. On August 12, the day the Anglo-French-Soviet military talks began in Moscow, Chamberlain is said to have approved a new definition of indirect aggression very close to the Soviet one, but as it turned out, there was no opportunity to discuss it.[89] By that time, the Soviet leadership had other, increasingly tempting German proposals to consider, which allowed them to take an ever stiffer attitude toward France and Britain in the Moscow negotiations.

As mentioned earlier, the "reliable source" had informed the German embassy in London on July 21 of the forthcoming Anglo-French-Soviet negotiations. This impelled the Germans to speed up their efforts to reach an agreement with the USSR, which were evident in the talks that now took place in Berlin. The German-Soviet trade-credit negotiations provided an excellent opportunity for both sides to sound each other on a possible political deal. Indeed, at this time the future German-Soviet agreement on spheres of influence was outlined in talks between Schnurre on the one hand and the two Soviet representatives, Astakhov and Babarin, on the other. In a preliminary conversation between Schnurre and Astakhov on July 24, the former gave the German view of three stages in improving relations: a trade-credit agreement, press and cultural relations, and political rapprochement. He said there was no conflict between Soviet and German interests, and Germany did not envisage doing anything in the Baltic or in Bessarabia that would harm Soviet interests.[90] The most significant

---

89. On Butler statement, July 31 and *Izvestiia*, August 2, see *DBFP*, ibid., no. 512, also *SPE* no. 300 and Degras *SDFP* III, 356. For the Anglo-French draft on indirect aggression, August 2, see *SPE* no.301, *GK* 2, no. 519; on Molotov reaction, *DBFP*, ibid., nos. 525, 527. Instructions to British delegation to go slow, DBFP, ibid., pp. 762–763. For instruction to French delegates, *DDF*, 2nd ser., vol. XVII (Paris, 1984), doc. 364. On a definition of indirect aggression allegedly approved by Chamberlain, August 12, see Sidney Aster, *1939. The Making of the Second World War* (New York, 1973), 300; the text of the definition is not given.

90. No German record of this conversation was printed, but see Fleischhauer, *Der Pakt*, 268; for Astakhov record, see *GK* 2, no.294 and *DVP 1939* I, no. 434; see also his diary notes of conversations with Peter Kleist, a member of Ribbentrop's office, and Schnurre, July 24, ibid., no.431.

conversation took place on July 26. According to Schnurre's report, he talked with Astakhov and Babarin during dinner in the Ewest Restaurant, and the conversation lasted until about 12.30 a.m. The German official again listed the three stages for improving relations, then stated there was no conflict of interest between Germany and the USSR in the region stretching from the Baltic to the Black Sea—which was to be the slogan used in German declarations to Moscow from now on. According to Schnurre, Astakhov said it was clear the Danzig and Corridor questions would be resolved one way or another to Germany's advantage. He then asked whether the former Austrian lands would also return to Germany, especially the Galician and Ukrainian regions. Schnurre replied that in all these matters there was no conflict of interest between Germany and Russia. He also said it would be even easier to reach an understanding on Poland, and emphasized that his statements were sanctioned by Ribbentrop. Astakhov said he would report all this to Moscow. At this point, the trade-credit issue came up, but Schnurre gave no details in his report. He concluded by stating his opinion that the Soviet government had not yet made up its mind and was drawing out negotiations with England in order to keep both the British and the Germans guessing.[91]

In his record of the conversation, Astakhov did not report making the statements attributed to him by Schnurre. Instead, he wrote that the German official had gone all out in expressing the German wish for better German-Soviet relations, assuring the Soviet diplomats that Germany had no intention of acting against Soviet interests in the Baltic States, and that she had given up any interest in Ukraine. Astakhov commented that it was not clear whether this included the Ukrainian lands of the former Austro-Hungarian Empire.[92] Molotov congratulated Astakhov in a telegram sent on July 28, for merely listening to Schnurre's declarations and saying he would transmit them to Moscow.[93] Although Gorlov acknowledges this contact between Astakhov and Molotov, he does not admit it implies previous reports and instructions. Nor does he see any indication of this in Molotov's telegram to Astakhov of July 29, replying to the latter's report. The commissar wrote that if the Germans were sincere in their wish to

---

91. By Galician and Ukrainian regions, Astakhov meant former East Galicia—later western Ukraine—then in Poland, and Carpathian Ukraine, then in Hungary; both had belonged to the Austro-Hungarian Empire. Revised Polish estimates of the 1931 census figures show the Ukrainians and Poles of eastern Poland at just under 5 million each; in this part of Poland, there were also about 2 million Belorussians and one and a quarter million Jews, see Tadeusz Piotrowski, *Poland's Holocaust* (Jefferson, N.C., 1998), 297, note 14. For Schnurre's record of the July 26 conversation, see *DGFP*, D, VI, no.729.

92. For Astakhov record, see *GK* 2, no.503, and diary notes, *DVP 1939* I, no.421. The "Stalin Cabinet" met on July 26 and 27, see: *IA 1995*, no. 5–6, 45.

93. For Molotov to Astakhov, July 28, see *GK* 2, no. 503.

improve relations with the USSR, then they must say just how they thought this should be done. He noted Schulenburg had also said recently that Germany wished to improve relations with the USSR, but had made no concrete proposals. Molotov concluded: "The matter depends entirely on the Germans. Of course, we would welcome any improvement of political relations between the two sides."[94] Clearly, Stalin and Molotov wanted the Germans to say exactly what they were willing to pay for a political agreement with Moscow.

Indeed, the Germans were now more than interested; they were anxious. The Franco-British decision to send a combined military delegation to Moscow to negotiate a military alliance with the USSR had a galvanizing effect on Hitler and Ribbentrop. They ordered Weizsäcker to instruct Schulenburg on July 29 to sound out Molotov on his impressions of the Berlin talks between Babarin, Astakhov, and Schnurre. Ribbentrop showed his impatience by making the German position official on August 2; he then repeated personally, to Astakhov, Schnurre's statement on the absence of conflict between German and Soviet interests in the area between the Baltic and Black Seas, and said that an agreement could be reached without difficulty. As for Poland, he thought Germany could destroy it in a military campaign of a week to ten days, though he hoped this would not be necessary. Astakhov repeated Molotov's message that Moscow awaited concrete proposals, to which Ribbentrop answered that he wanted to know first if the Soviet government was interested in conducting talks either in Berlin or in Moscow.[95] Ribbentrop instructed Schulenburg to repeat his statements to Molotov, and the ambassador did so on August 3. However, Molotov was unforthcoming despite Schulenburg's repetition of Ribbentrop's statement on there being no conflict of German and Soviet interests between the Baltic and Black Seas. The commissar reminded the ambassador of German support for Japanese aggression against the USSR, and insisted on the economic agreement being signed first. He also used a phrase similar to the one in his July 29 telegram to Astakhov: "Now everything depends on the German side's line of conduct." Schulenburg had the impression that the Soviet government still mistrusted Germany and would conduct long negotiations with the French and British, whom it also dis-

---

94. For Molotov to Astakhov, July 29, after receipt of Astakhov's full report, see *GK 2*, no. 511; Gorlov, "Sovetsko-germanskii dialog," 28. (See note 46 above).

95. On sounding out Molotov's reaction to the talks with Babarin and Astakhov, see Weizsäcker to Schulenburg, July 29, 1939, *DGFP* D VI, no. 736; on Ribbentrop's statement to Astakhov, August 2, 1939, see his telegrams to Schulenburg, August 3, 4, ibid., nos. 758, 770, and Schnurre report of August 3, ibid., no. 761. For Astakhov report, see *GK 2*, no. 523, longer version in *DVP 1939* I, no. 445. Schnurre wrote of the Astakhov-Ribbentrop meeting as taking place on August 3, but both Astakhov and Ribbentrop give August 2 as the date.

trusted. He wrote that the Germans would have to make strenuous efforts to bring the Soviet government around.[96]

While the Germans pressed for negotiations, Molotov kept insisting that they make concrete proposals and that the trade-credit agreement be signed first. On August 8, Astakhov sent Molotov a list of what the Germans were ready to concede, and it was a great deal: disinterest in the fate of the Baltic States—except for Lithuania—and also Bessarabia, as well as "Russian Poland" [central Poland, including Warsaw, part of the Russian Empire in 1914]. They also distanced themselves from any aspirations to Ukraine. In exchange, they wished to receive confirmation of Russian disinterest in Danzig and in former German Poland [western or Prussian Poland in 1914], with adjustments in Germany's favor up to the Warta, or even the Vistula line, and also in Galicia. Of course, discussions on the above could only take place if there was no Anglo-French-Soviet military and political agreement.[97] Two days later, on August 10, Astakhov cabled that according to Schnurre, who had just returned from seeing Ribbentrop at Obersalzburg on August 8–9, the Germans wanted to know the Soviet attitude toward either a peaceful or military solution of the Polish-German dispute over Danzig and the Corridor. If there was war, Germany would not impinge on Soviet interests, but wanted to know what these were. There was no conflict between German and Soviet interests in the region between the Baltic and Black Seas, but the conclusion of a Soviet pact with Britain and France would be a bad introduction to Soviet negotiations with Germany. Thus, it is clear that on August 8–9 Hitler decided to press Stalin for an agreement.[98] On August 11, Molotov telegraphed Astakhov that the list of German objectives cited in his letter of August 8, "interests us," but their discussion required preparation. Intervening steps should take the form of a

---

96. For Schulenburg's report on his conversation with Molotov, August 3, 1939, see *DGFP* D VI, no.766; Molotov's record, *GK* 2, no. 525, *DVP 1939* I, no.446. Stalin had eleven visitors on the evening of August 4. Molotov and Voroshilov were there twice at the same time: 5 .00–9.15, and again 10.30–11.50 p.m., *IA 1995*, 5–6, 47.

97. By Galicia, Schnurre meant East Galicia, now western Ukraine, see Astakhov letter to Molotov, August 8, 1939, *GK* 2, no. 534, *DVP 1939* I, no. 455. On the evening of August 8, Stalin had 21 visitors; Molotov was there twice: 5.35–6.45, and 9.55 p.m. to12.00 midnight, *IA* ibid.

98. See Astakhov telegram to Molotov, August 10, 1939, *GK* 2, no. 538, *DVP 1939* I, no. 460; there are minor stylistic differences between the two texts. For Hitler's final decision on August 8–9 to seek an agreement with the USSR, see Fleischhauer, *Der Pakt*, 292–295. On the evening of August 10, Stalin had 23 visitors. Commissar for Defense Voroshilov and the Chief of the General Staff, Shaposhnikov, visited twice; Zhdanov came as usual; Molotov was absent but probably saw Stalin earlier. The first visitor, Malenkov, arrived at 3.30 and the last visitors left at 1 a.m.; see: *IA 1995*, 5–6, 47–48.

trade-credit agreement, and agreement on other questions. He expected the negotiations to take place in Moscow.[99]

Astakhov's account of what the Germans were ready to offer, and then his report of what Schnurre had told him on August 10, may have convinced Stalin and Molotov that the time had come to begin "concrete" negotiations, or this may have been due to some military information, or a combination of both. Fifty years later, in late December 1989, Alexander N. Yakovlev, Central Committee member and chairman of the commission to examine Stalinist crimes and rehabilitate the victims, told the Second Congress of People's Deputies about the decision to begin negotiations with the Germans. He stated that Stalin was informed on August 7 of German readiness to start military action [against Poland] any day after August 25. He said the situation was discussed on August 11 at a Politburo meeting, which also took into account Hitler's attempts to establish direct contact with Chamberlain and the pessimistic prognosis of the [forthcoming] military negotiations [with the Anglo-French delegation] in Moscow. In view of all the above, it was decided to begin an official discussion of the questions raised by the Germans and to inform Berlin accordingly. This decision, said Yakovlev, led to the beginning of German-Soviet negotiations at Molotov's meeting with Schulenburg on August 15.[100]

The news allegedly received by Stalin on August 7 may have come from German diplomat Rudolf von Scheliha, a paid Soviet agent in the German embassy, Warsaw, with extensive contacts in high German political and military circles. According to a Russian document, Scheliha reported on August 7 that according to the German military attaché at the German embassy in Warsaw, Colonel Gerstenberg, who had just returned from Berlin, Hitler had decided on war and the start of military action against Poland was expected any day after August 25.[101] This is the same wording as that used in the Yakovlev report. However, there is no record of Hitler

---

99. See Molotov's telegram to Astakhov, August 11, 1939, *GK* 2, no. 540.

100. For Yakovlev's report on the secret protocol, December 24, 25, 1989, see note 3 above. On the commission, the rifts within it, and Yakovlev report of December 23, 1989—but not the key report of Dec. 24—see Bezymensky, "The Secret protocols of 1939" in Gorodetsky, *Soviet Foreign Policy 1917–1991*, 80–83.

101. Some of Rudolf von Scheliha's reports were published in *SPE*, where his name is consistently misspelled as "von Scheliah"; for his report of August 7, see ibid., no. 308. Gerstenberg was presumably Alfred Gerstenberg, the German military attaché in Bucharest in September 1940. Von Scheliha, a counselor in the German embassy, Warsaw, was recruited in 1937 by Soviet intelligence for money he needed to keep up his lavish lifestyle. In August, presumably after he sent this report, he was transferred to the Information Section of the German Foreign Ministry, Berlin, where he continued to gather valuable information for Moscow until his arrest in October 1942; he was executed. See Christopher Andrew and Oleg Gordievsky, *KGB. The Inside Story* (New York, 1990), 240–241, 255–256, 276.

making such a decision around August 5–7, though it is known that he was furious at the Poles over a crisis in Polish-Danzig relations and reports about the mistreatment of Germans in Poland. (The French and British ambassadors cabled their government that these reports were false). It is also known that Hitler fumed at the Poles to Hungarian Foreign Minister István Csáky, whom he received at Berchtesgaden on August 8, but said he still hoped the Poles would be reasonable. Also, the German ambassador to Poland, Hans Adolf von Moltke, was instructed not to return to Poland.[102] Thus, if Gerstenberg had said what Scheliha reported on August 7, this was based probably on rumors in high German military circles and not on any decision by Hitler. Finally, according to German records, Hitler did not tell his military and political leaders of the date of the attack on Poland—August 26—until August 22. Indeed, it is clear he set this date on August 21, when he had the agreement with Stalin in the bag. (On August 25, the attack date was changed to September 1). It is possible, though not mentioned by Yakovlev, that Stalin knew of the meeting on August 7 of a group of British businessmen with Hermann Goering on the island of Sylt to sound out peace possibilities.[103] Whatever the case might be, on August 12—the very day on which the Anglo-French and Soviet military conversations began in Moscow—Astakhov told Schnurre that he had instructions from Molotov to say the Soviet government was interested in discussing the groups of questions that had been raised earlier, but this could only be undertaken gradually and in Moscow, leaving the choice of negotiator to the Germans.[104] Hitler rejoiced and shared the good news with Italian Foreign Minister Galeazzo Ciano, who was visiting with him at the time.[105] Perhaps August 11 marked the moment of Stalin's final decision to align with Hitler—or was it a significant step forward in this direction?

---

102. For Hitler-Csaky conversation, see *DGFP* D, VI, no. 784; instruction to Moltke not to return to Warsaw, *DGFP* D, VII (London, Washington, 1956), no. 99.

103. It was actually Chamberlain who was sounding out Hitler, as witness Sir Horace Wilson's conversation with German ambassador Dirksen on August 3 (see note 86 above). Goering told the British businessmen at Sylt on August 7, that no Anglo-German conversations were possible unless Britain and Poland settled the Danzig question with Germany. Later, Wilson proposed a nonaggression pact, again in secret conversations with Fritz Hesse, press attaché at the German embassy, but Hitler's answer on August 20 was that Germany must have her demands on Poland settled first, see Watt, *How War Came*, 404 ff. On August 11, Stalin saw Molotov at 7.45–10.30 p.m. and Voroshilov, at 7:40–10:30 p.m. See *IA* 1995, no. 5–6, 48. For Hitler's statement of August 22, that the attack on Poland would begin August 26, see *DGFP* D VII,, no. 192.

104. See Astakhov's letter to Molotov, August 12, 1939, *GK* 2, no. 541, *DVP 1939* I, no. 462, and Schnurre telegram to Schulenburg, August 14, *DGFP* D VII, no. 50.

The Germans did not waste time after hearing Astakhov's message of August 12. After two days of frenetic consultations, Ribbentrop instructed Schulenburg to transmit, through Molotov, Hitler's personal message for Stalin, and the ambassador did so on the evening of August 15. Hitler proposed that Ribbentrop come to Moscow as soon as possible to lay the Führer's views before Stalin. The key part of the message read:

> The Reich Government are of the opinion that there is no question between the Baltic Sea and the Black Sea which cannot be settled to the complete satisfaction of both countries. Among these are such questions as: the Baltic Sea, the Baltic States, Poland, South-Eastern questions, etc.

Molotov said he would give an answer after communicating the message to his government, but he made a significant statement. He referred to what had been reported to him in June by the Soviet minister in Rome as the "Schulenburg Plan" to improve German-Soviet relations. He said this "plan" stipulated: (1) German-Soviet cooperation in regulating Soviet-Japanese relations and the liquidation of their frontier conflicts; (2) the conclusion of a nonaggression pact and a mutual guarantee of the Baltic States; (3) a broad economic agreement between the two powers. *Molotov now asked whether the German government was interested in "refreshing" or supplementing existing German-Soviet agreements, or in a nonaggression pact? If so, there could be concrete negotiations.* Schulenburg said he would telegraph Molotov's questions to Berlin.[106] This was certainly a direct Soviet proposal.

---

105. Schmidt record of Hitler-Ciano conversations at Obersalzburg, August 12, ibid., no. 43, p. 49; Italian record, *DDI,* 8th ser., vol. XIII (Rome, 1953), no.4, p. 6.

106. Emphasis added, A.M.C. The German-Soviet agreements Molotov had in mind were the Rapallo Treaty, 1922 and the Treaty of Berlin, 1926. For Ribbentrop's instruction to Schulenburg and the latter's record of conversation with Molotov, August 15, *DGFP* D VII, nos.51, 56, 79; Russian record, *GK* 2, no. 556, *DVP 1939,* I, no.468. This record was first published in Russia, along with records of German-Soviet conversations on August 17, 19, the German-Soviet Credit Agreement of August 19, also a translation of the German text of the nonaggression pact and secret protocol of August 23 1939, and other documents in: *International Affairs,* no. 10 (1989), 81–116, 143. For Soviet Chargé d'Affaires Leon B. Helfand's report from Rome, June 26, 1939, on the so-called Schulenburg Plan, see *GK* 2, no. 437, longer version in *DVP 1939* I no. 399. This may have been an Italian effort, perhaps inspired by Berlin, to speed up the German-Soviet agreement, for the counselor of the German embassy, Moscow, Werner von Tippelskirch, reported on June 26, that the Italian ambassador, Augusto Rosso, told him the previous day he had received a telegram from his government saying the moment had come to bring about the breakdown of the Anglo-French-Soviet negotiations, see *DGFP,* D VI, no.569. Helfand is not listed in vol. I. of the Russian diplomatic dictionary (Moscow, 1984), presumably because he defected to the West in summer 1940.

Though Molotov and Stalin did not seem to be in a hurry to conclude an agreement with Germany, they gave Hitler—who *was* in a hurry—some indirect encouragement. On August 16, an official in the News and Press Department of the German Foreign Ministry reported that a M. Legrenier (not identified) and a Mr. Barnes, described as a former correspondent of the *New York Herald Tribune* in Moscow, both of whom were known to enjoy excellent relations with the Soviet embassy in Berlin, had each given independent but similar accounts of their conversations with Astakhov and the Soviet press attaché, Smirnov. The Soviet diplomats were reported as saying that Moscow intended to draw out negotiations with the Western powers until Germany settled the Danzig question with Poland, a settlement in which Moscow did not expect the Western powers to be involved. After this, Russia would enter into political discussions with Germany. This statement was also noted by an official of Ribbentrop's office.[107] It must have made Hitler even more eager to secure an agreement with Stalin.

It has been known for some time that the German proposals which Schulenburg put to Molotov on August 15 were reported that day to Washington by the American ambassador in Moscow, Laurence A. Steinhardt. They had been communicated to Charles Bohlen of the U.S. embassy by his tennis partner, Hans Heinrich ("Johnny") von Herwarth, first secretary at the German embassy, Moscow, and personal assistant to Ambassador von Schulenburg. Both were covert opponents of the Nazi regime, but wished for the peaceful return of Danzig and part of the Polish Corridor to Germany. Indeed, Schulenburg hoped a German-Soviet agreement would accomplish this aim and thus prevent war. It is worth noting that information on earlier German-Soviet talks had also reached Washington and had provoked a reaction from President Franklin D. Roosevelt. Herwarth had passed on to Bohlen the contents of the Schulenburg-Molotov conversation of August 3, which the U.S. embassy transmitted to Washington. There is no evidence that it was passed on to the British, French, or Polish governments, but Roosevelt warned the Soviet ambassador to the United States, Konstantin A. Oumansky, that if war broke out in Europe and the Far East, and if the Axis powers were victorious, then both the United States and the USSR would be affected, but the latter would be affected immediately. Therefore, the president believed that an agreement against aggression on the part of other European powers would have a stabilizing effect. This message was repeated by Steinhardt to Molotov on August 16, but it

---

107. Report on Soviet diplomats' statements by Legrenier and Barnes, *DGFP* D VII, no.84. Ralph Barnes had been the *New York Herald Tribune* correspondent in Berlin, then Moscow, and in 1939 he was again in Berlin.

did not seem to have any effect.[108] After this, Washington did pass on Steinhardt's second report to the British. On August 17, the U.S. Under-Secretary of State, Sumner Welles, told the British ambassador in Washington, Sir Ronald Lindsay, that the German ambassador in Moscow had seen Molotov two days earlier and transmitted an oral statement from Hitler to Stalin to the effect that Germany had no aggressive intentions towards the Soviet Union, and that there was no conflict of interest between the two powers "from the Baltic to the Black Sea." Thus, Germany was ready to discuss any territorial questions in Eastern Europe and conversations should start very soon because she was ready to send a negotiator to Moscow immediately.[109] However, this message was intercepted and delayed, most likely by Francis Herbert King. Six years later, at the Potsdam Conference, Anthony Eden told Bohlen that due to a communist spy in the Foreign Office code room, it was not received until after Berlin had announced Ribbentrop's forthcoming visit to Moscow. The Lindsay telegram was, indeed, officially registered in the foreign office on August 18 at 9.30 a.m., but was not received in the Central Department until August 22.[110] Halifax told the U.S. ambassador, Joseph F. Kennedy, on August 23, that [Sir Robert G.] Vansittart [the chief diplomatic adviser to the Foreign Office] "believes there is a provision in the agreement providing for the fourth partition of Poland."[111] Perhaps, Vansittart had read the Lindsay telegram, or perhaps also the report sent that day to Paris by the French ambassador in Berlin, Robert Coulondre. Whatever Vansittart's source, he informed Halifax, who passed it on to Kennedy.

---

108. For Steinhardt report, August 15, 1939, see *FRUS 1939, I,* 334–35; see also Charles Bohlen, *Witness to History 1929–1939* (New York, 1973), 80–82, and Hans von Herwarth, with S. Frederick Starr, *Against Two Evils* (New York, 1981), 159–160. For report on German proposals of August 3, see U.S. Chargé in the Soviet Union (Grummon) to secretary of state, Moscow, August 3, 1939, *FRUS 1939,* I, 292–293. For President Roosevelt's warning to Ambassador Oumansky, with request that Steinhardt repeat it to Molotov, see under secretary of state to Steinhardt, August 4, 1939, ibid., 293–294; for Steinhardt's report on conversation with Molotov, August 16, ibid., 296–298; Russian record: *SPE* no.329, *GK* 2, no. 564.

109. For Welles' report on German proposals of August 15 to the British ambassador, see Sir Ronald Lindsay to Halifax, Washington, August 17, 1939, *DBFP* 3rd ser. VII (London, 1954), no.41.

110. See Watt, "Francis Herbert King," *Intelligence and National Security,* vol. 3, no. 4 (1988): 79, and his "An Intelligence Surprise: The Failure of the Foreign Office to Anticipate the Nazi-Soviet Pact," *Intelligence and National Security,* vol. 4, no. 3 (1989): 524; here Watt names the Soviet agent as John Herbert King. For Eden to Bohlen at Potsdam, see Bohlen, *Witness to History,* 80–82. Herwarth writes that the message was not deciphered until after the spy was replaced, *Against Two Evils,* 161, but this is incorrect because King was arrested after September 4, see note 116 below.

111. Kennedy to secretary of state, August 23, 1939, *FRUS, 1939,* I, 339–340.

There is no documentary evidence that the British government communicated the contents of Lindsay's telegram—once it had reached the Foreign Office Central Department on August 22—either to the French or the Polish governments. The same is true of the information regarding the German-Soviet Nonaggression Pact signed on August 23. This news was transmitted again by Herwarth to Bohlen, reported by Steinhardt to Washington on August 24, and communicated by the latter that same day to the British ambassador in Moscow.[112] It must be assumed that the latter informed his government, but there is no published document showing the State Department transmitted this news to the British or French ambassador in Washington. It is also clear that the Polish ambassador in Washington was not informed, even though some high U.S. officials were fully cognizant of what it meant for Poland. Instead, President Roosevelt decided to launch another appeal for peace to European heads of state, including Hitler and President Ignacy Mościcki of Poland.[113] It is also strange that though Ambassador Coulondre had warned Paris on August 22 of an imminent German-Soviet agreement, and two days later communicated reports from high Berlin circles that a German-Soviet understanding had been reached "regulating" the situation in Eastern Europe—including a partition of Poland along the Vistula River—there is no evidence of this being communicated to the Polish ambassador in Paris. Vansittart probably heard of it through his own channels in Berlin or Paris. Perhaps French Premier Daladier hoped that, despite the German-Soviet Nonaggression Pact, French agreement to the passage of Soviet troops through Poland—sent to General Joseph Doumenc in Moscow on the night of August 21—might still allow the conclusion of a Franco-British-Soviet alliance to deter Hitler from war, even if it meant the Soviet annexation of eastern Poland, as reported by Coulondre three days later on August 24. (In fact, Bonnet may have envisaged this in

---

112. See Herwarth, *Against Two Evils*, 166–167, and Bohlen, *Witness to History*, 82–83; Steinhardt to secretary to state, August 24, 1939 noon (received Washington, August 24 11:15 a.m.), FRUS, *1939*, I 342–343; on informing the British ambassador and his incredulity, see Steinhardt to secretary of state, August 24, 5 p.m (received 5:.40 p.m), ibid., 343–344. For Polish text and comments, see Piotr S. Wandycz, "Telegram Steinhardta," *Zeszyty Historyczne*, no. 84 (Paris, 1988): 204–207.

113. Under Secretary of State Adolf A. Berle noted in his diary on August 24 that in view of what was known in Washington about the German-Soviet agreement to partition Poland, "a strong message" to the latter, as urged from London by Ambassador Joseph P. Kennedy, would have to start with some such words as: "In view of the fact that your suicide is required, kindly oblige" etc., see Adolf A. Berle, *Navigating the Rapids, 1918–1971* (New York, 1973), 243. For Roosevelt's peace appeal of August 24 to Mościcki and the latter's reply see *FRUS 1939, I*, 361–62, 368.

May).[114] If so, it would not be in Daladier's interest to inform the Polish government of the Coulondre report.

The grounds for the decision of the British and French governments not to communicate to the Poles the terms of the forthcoming Nazi-Soviet agreement, and then the agreement itself, are not known. It is most likely they still hoped to secure Soviet alliance or neutrality, if need be, at Poland's expense. Furthermore, in the second half of August, Hitler was intensifying his pressure on Poland, so British and French statesmen were primarily focusing on this crisis, which threatened to erupt into war. But it is also a fact that, though Halifax had mentioned the possibility of a German-Soviet agreement at a Cabinet meeting in June, the Foreign Office—like the Poles—refused to take it seriously, and this despite a number of reports received between May and July 1939.[115] In particular, Krivitsky's warnings about the imminence of a Nazi-Soviet pact had been dismissed by the foreign office as "twaddle," "rigmarole," and "directly contrary to all our other information." It was only after the conclusion of the pact that he was listened to with more respect. After this, he was instrumental in unmasking Soviet spies in the Foreign Office. According to an unpublished entry in Under-Secretary of State Alexander Cadogan's diary on September 4, a telegram was received that day from Washington with some information on "leaks over the last four years, from someone in communications." King was arrested soon thereafter and on September 26, Cadogan noted that investigators were "on the track of others" who remain unknown. In any case, the whole staff of the communications department was dismissed and a new order established, though Soviet moles elsewhere would continue espionage on Moscow's behalf for many years to come.[116]

---

114. See Coulondre to Bonnet, August 22, 1939, *DDF,* 2nd ser. XVIII (Paris, 1985), no. 253, 301–302 (the document heading erroneously lists François-Poncet as the ambassador, whereas he was then French ambassador in Rome, A.M.C); for Coulondre report, August 24, on German information about the partition of Poland, see ibid., no.377, 451 (here Moscow is erroneously listed instead of Berlin, as the origin of the telegram A.M.C). For Bonnet's note of a conversation with Suritz, May 26, with the former's comment on abandoning the Baltic States and part of Poland as the price of the Soviet alliance, see *DDF 2nd ser.* XVI, no. 289. However, the editorial note states this may have been written by Bonnet later to justify his policy (presumably, his appeasement of Germany, A.M.C) see ibid., p. 571. For Daladier telegram to Doumenc of August 21, received the next day, see discussion of Moscow negotiations later in this paper.

115. See Watt, "An Intelligence Surprise," especially the appendix listing twenty-two "Warnings or intimations of Nazi-Soviet Negotiations which are recorded as having reached British representatives, April-August 1939," 532–534.

116. On the arrest of King and others, see Watt, "Francis Herbert King," 7.

As mentioned earlier, Poland was frequently blamed by Soviet and Western sources, both at the time and since, for the breakdown of the Anglo-Franco-Soviet military negotiations in Moscow. However, German documents available since the late 1950s, as well as recently published Russian documents, do not support this conclusion. Indeed, one Russian document throws new light on Stalin's thinking just before the Anglo-French mission arrived in Moscow. On August 7, Stalin dictated instructions to Voroshilov on how to conduct the negotiations with the British and French military delegations. By this time, of course, the "Vozhd" knew that Hitler was ready to offer him what he wanted regarding Poland, the Baltic States, and southeastern Europe. What is striking in these instructions is Stalin's deep distrust of France and Britain and the listing of Russian demands that he expected their representatives to refuse. The instructions are worth quoting in full:

1. agreement by both sides on secrecy;
2. first, present our full powers to conduct negotiations, and then ask the leaders of the Anglo-French delegation whether they also have full powers from their governments to sign a military convention with the USSR.
3. If they do not have such full powers, show surprise, throw up your hands, and "respectfully" ask what was the purpose of their governments in sending them to the USSR.
4. If they answer that they were sent to negotiate and prepare the ground for signing the military convention, ask them if they have any plan to defend the future allies, i.e. France, England, USSR etc., against aggression by the aggressors' bloc in Europe.
5. If it appears that they don't have any concrete plan of defense against aggression in one variant or another, which is unlikely, then ask them on the basis of what questions, what defense plan, the French and English think they will conduct negotiations with the military delegation of the USSR.
6. If the French and English still insist on negotiations, then direct these to the discussion of separate, principal questions, mainly on allowing the passage of our armies through the Vilna corridor and Galicia, also through Romania.
7. If it appears that the free passage of our armies through the territory of Poland and Romania is ruled out, then declare that without [the fulfillment of] this condition agreement is impossible, because without the free passage of Soviet armies through the indicated territories any variant of defense against aggression is doomed to failure, [and] that we do not consider it possible to participate in an undertaking that is doomed to fail.
8. To requests that we show the French and English delegations our defense factories, institutes, military units and military instruction centers,

say that after the visit of the pilot Lindbergh to the USSR in 1938, the Soviet government forbade showing defense enterprises and military units to foreigners, except to our allies—when these appear on the scene.[117]

It is true that in his earlier memorandum on Soviet ideas for the negotiations, the chief of the Soviet General Staff, Boris M. Shaposhnikov, had specified the passage of Soviet troops through Poland (against Germany) and through Romania (to aid Turkey).[118] These would, indeed, be the logical directions of Soviet military action against Germany—if it was intended. However, no Russian documents have surfaced to prove that it was. Moreover, Stalin's instructions to Voroshilov indicate that a Franco-British agreement to Soviet demands was not expected. Indeed, Voroshilov told a member of the French delegation almost at the outset that he did not believe the Polish and Romanian governments were asking for Soviet help, and according to a French report, the Soviet demands for troop passage through those countries did not seem to be sincere.[119]

In fact, the Soviet government had not raised the issue until Voroshilov did so at the first official meeting of the delegations on August 12, and made it the key Russian condition two days later. It is worth noting that on that day, August 14, Voroshilov asked for a fifteen-minute interval when the head of the British delegation, Admiral Ernle Drax, asked how Soviet armed forces would be used if permission were given for passage through the Poland and Romania. After the interval—when Voroshilov clearly consulted Stalin—he read a statement that talks could not go on since, without

---

117. See *DVP 1939*, I, no. 453, p.584 (trans. A.M.C). Voroshilov was with Stalin on August 7 between 6.35 and 10 p.m; other visitors included Molotov, Zhdanov, Malenkov, and Kaganovich, see: *IA* 1995, no. 5–6, 47. The Lindberghs had paid flying visits to the USSR in 1931 and 1933, and flew in for a short visit in August 1938. They received royal treatment, so the Russians were greatly angered by a report on Lindbergh's negative remarks on the Russian air force and bad Soviet conditions, also his expectation that the Soviet system would collapse. The report was printed in the London news sheet, *The Week*, see Wayne S. Cole, *Charles A. Lindbergh and the Battle Against American Intervention in World War II* (New York and London, 1974), 29.

118. For Shaposhnikov's memorandum of August 4, 1939, see *GK 2*, no. 527; *DVP 1939*, I, no. 447; on passage through Poland and Romania, p.575.

119. In his end report on the negotiations, Jacques Antoine Williaume, French corvette captain and professor at the École de Guerre Navale, noted that at the August 14 session, there was an atmosphere of great doubt about the sincerity of Soviet demands for troop passage through Poland and Romania. He also recorded Voroshilov as saying: "Je ne crois pas que la Pologne et la Roumanie demandent notre aide," see Williaume report, Monday, August 14, section 29, *DDF* 2nd ser. XVIII, Addenda, V, p. 598.

a positive solution to this question, the attempt to conclude a military convention was "doomed to failure." However, once a positive answer was received, the Soviet military mission would be willing "to set out its plan for joint action against aggression in Europe." Three days later, in the early afternoon of August 17, he announced that the negotiations were suspended until August 20 or 21, justifying this by the lack of a Franco-British reply on the passage of Soviet troops through Poland and Romania. However, he agreed with the British suggestion that the negotiations resume on the later date.[120]

The suspension of the Moscow talks led to strenuous Anglo-French efforts—more French than British—to secure the Polish government's agreement to the passage of Soviet troops. However, the Poles said the Russians were not to be trusted. There was no assurance, they said, that once they were on Polish soil, they would fight the Germans. The USSR was expected to be neutral in a Polish-German war, so once the Russians came in they would not fight but just stay, i.e., annex eastern Poland. There was also mention of the Piłsudski dogma that no foreign troops could be allowed on Polish soil, and of the Polish belief that while the Germans threatened the Poles with physical destruction, the Soviets threatened to destroy their souls. Ultimately, all that could be obtained on August 19 was Polish agreement for the Anglo-French military mission either to convey the Poles' negative answer, or to say the question had not been raised in Warsaw. Captain Beaufre, sent to the Polish capital from Moscow, left with this message on August 20, arriving in Moscow the next day. The French military attaché in Warsaw, General Félix Musse, telegraphed the news to Paris that afternoon and, according to Beaufre, also to General Doumenc in Moscow.[121]

---

120. For the Russian record of the military talks through August 17, see: *SPE* nos. 314–317, 319, 327–328, 33; *GK* 2, nos. 546–548, 559–560, 566, and summary in *DVP 1939*, I, no.506; British record, *DBFP* D 3rd ser., VI, appendix V; French record, *DDF* 2nd ser., XVII , part II, and Addenda; XVIII, part I.

121. For Beaufre's account of his Warsaw mission, see note 6 above; for French documents on the efforts to obtain Polish assent to Soviet troop passage, August 17–20, see *DDF* 2nd ser. XVIII, note 108. See also account by Léon Noël, *Polonia Restituta. La Pologne entre deux mondes* (Paris, 1984), ch. XXI. In writing this negative account of prewar Poland, the aged ambassador did not bother to read the *DDF* documents, but relied on his memory and older sources. For the Polish side, see Łukasiewicz papers, "Franco-British-Soviet Negotiations in Moscow," *Diplomat in Paris*, 233–252 and *Dyplomata w Paryżu*, 283–304. For Polish diplomatic documents on Anglo-French-Soviet negotiations, see "Polskie akty dyplomatyczne odnoszące się do rokowań brytyjsko-francusko-sowieckich w okresie przed wybuchem drugiej wojny oświatowej," *Bellona*, styczeń-marzec (1955): 60–77. See also the notes on the allied negotiations with Russia and pressure exerted on Poland, written later from memory by the Polish Chief of Staff, General Wacław Stachiewicz, *Wierności dochować żołnierskiej*, edited by Marek Tarczyński (Warsaw, 1998), 126–140.

It should be noted that just before and during the Moscow negotiations, Soviet hints to the Germans seemed designed to increase Berlin's desire for an agreement with the USSR. Thus, on August 10, Schulenburg reported from Moscow that according to "a reliable source," the British were conceding the Soviet right, in the event of a direct attack on a Baltic State, to move in troops under the guarantee, even if the state in question did not request assistance. This may have referred to a new formula discussed in the Foreign Office. If so, it could have been obtained by King and passed on to Moscow. On August 14, the German embassy in London passed on another report from the "reliable source" that Strang, who had just returned from Moscow, was optimistic about an alliance between Britain, France, and the USSR Furthermore, as mentioned earlier, on August 16, the German Foreign Ministry learned that, according to Astakhov and Smirnov , the Soviet side was deliberately drawing out the negotiations until the Danzig-Corridor question was settled to Germany's advantage Finally, on August 17, the German embassy in London reported that according to the "reliable source," the Moscow negotiations were going well and the Poles were ready to begin staff talks with the Soviets.[122] This news is unlikely to have come from the Anglo-French mission or the British Foreign or War Offices, so it may have been a Soviet fabrication meant to worry the Germans.

As it turned out, the Soviet leaders did not wait for the results of Anglo-French efforts in Warsaw, but decided to suspend the military negotiations before these efforts began. In fact, there was a direct connection between Hitler's instruction of August 16 to Schulenburg to see Molotov, and the suspension of the military negotiations by Voroshilov the next day. Hitler's directive to Schulenburg to seek an immediate appointment with Molotov led the ambassador to instruct Counselor Hilger at 10 a.m. on August 17 to request an audience for the ambassador with the commissar. On hearing this, Stalin ordered Voroshilov to confront the French and British military delegates with the demand that they provide an answer on Soviet troop passage through Poland, and as mentioned earlier, the negotiations were suspended that afternoon until August 21. Stalin also instructed Molotov on August 17 to see the German ambassador by 8 p.m. at the latest, to hear what he had to say.[123] When Molotov met with Schulenburg that evening,

---

122. Schulenburg report, August 10, see *DGFP* D VII, no. 14. On Strang being optimistic (which he was not), see report of August 14, ibid., no.55. For Legrenier and Barnes on Astakhov and Smirnov statements, see note 107 above; report on alleged on Polish-Russian staff talks, August 17, *DGFP*, ibid., no. 99.

123. For the linkage between Schulenburg's message to Hilger and the suspension of the military negotiations on August 17 by Voroshilov, see Fleischhauer, *Der Pakt*, 320–321 . For the Russian record of the discussions by military delegations on August 17 and the suspension of talks, see *GK* 2, no. 566.

the German ambassador declared his government was ready to conclude a nonaggression pact with the USSR and to give a joint German-Soviet guarantee to the Baltic States. It was also ready to use its offices to improve Soviet-Japanese relations. Furthermore, Hitler believed that given the dangerous situation—imminent war with Poland—Ribbentrop was ready to come to Moscow as the German plenipotentiary any time after August 18, to negotiate and sign the nonaggression agreement. Schulenburg also gave the commissar an aide-mémoire to this effect. Molotov, for his part, *gave the ambassador an aide-mémoire stating that the first step should be the conclusion of the trade-credit agreement, and then the signature of a nonaggression pact or confirmation of the neutrality treaty of 1926; this should be signed simultaneously with a secret protocol on the interest of the two parties in these and other questions of foreign policy. The protocol would be an organic part of the pact.* Schulenburg asked about the secret protocol, but Molotov said that first there must be a draft of the nonaggression pact, or the confirmation of a neutrality agreement. Ribbentrop could come to Moscow that week, or the next.[124]

Two days later, on August 19 at 9.30 p.m. Paris time—11.30 p.m. Moscow time—Daladier received a telephone message from General Musse in Warsaw on the failure of French efforts to get the Poles to agree to the passage of Soviet troops. Even if this news reached Stalin immediately, either from Warsaw or from Paris, it is unlikely it could have been deciphered until late that night, and in any case, Molotov had proposed a nonaggression agreement and secret protocol to the German ambassador two days earlier. What is more, on the afternoon of August 19—that is, before the Polish reply was reported by Musse to Daladier in Paris and/or to Doumenc in Moscow—Molotov twice called in Schulenburg to see him. On the second occasion, he handed the ambassador the proposed Soviet text of the nonaggression treaty, though he did not supply a draft of the secret protocol, saying this would be negotiated later. It is significant that, *unlike previous Soviet nonaggression pacts, this one did not stipulate abrogation if one of the parties was involved in aggression against a third country.* Thus, Hitler knew that Moscow had no objection to his attack on Poland. As in the Soviet aide-mémoire of August 17, the postscript to the Soviet draft of August 19 stated the pact would come into force only with the simultaneous signature of a separate protocol based on points of interest to the foreign policy of both sides, and that this protocol was to form an

---

124. Emphasis added, A.M.C. For the Russian record of the Molotov-Schulenburg conversation, August 17, with Russian and German aide-mémoires, see *GK* 2, no.570, *DVP 1939* I, no. 470; German record and same, *DGFP* D VII, no. 105.

integral part of the pact.[125] Thus, it is clear that the Soviet side stipulated this condition. As for the German-Soviet trade-credit agreement, it was signed in Berlin on August 19. However, as Schnurre told Fleischhauer many years later, the directive for Babarin to sign did not arrive from Moscow until very late that night.[126]

It is not known exactly what impelled Stalin to have Molotov give Schulenburg a draft of the nonaggression pact on August 19, though it can be assumed that Hitler's pressure for Ribbentrop's visit to Moscow within the next few days may have been the key factor. However, Fleischhauer and most Russian historians offer another explanation, which is in general agreement with part of Yakovlev's report of December 23, 1989, on the nonaggression pact. Yakovlev stated that on August 19–20, Stalin received documented indications that England, France, and Poland would not change their attitude. Yakovlev went on to say that Stalin apparently hoped to influence England and France by concluding the pact but miscalculated, for after it was signed the Western powers lost all constructive interest in the USSR.[127] However, it should be noted with regard to the first statement that Molotov had told Schulenburg two days earlier, on August 17, that the Soviet government was ready to sign a nonaggression pact with Germany, and that a secret protocol must be an integral part of it. As for Yakovlev's second statement, it is not true that France and Britain lost interest in a treaty with the USSR, as witness Daladier's agreement on August 21 to the passage of Soviet troops through Poland. The British declared their agreement on August 24, that is, after the signing of the nonaggression pact (see below). Still, it is possible that Stalin intended to use the pact as a lever to force the western powers to grant his demand regarding Poland and Romania, for he could only have welcomed British and French approval of Soviet military entry into those countries. Or he might have calculated that if he had agreements with both sides and Germany seized western, northern, and central Poland, he could annex eastern Poland and

---

125. Emphasis added, A.M.C. For the German record of the Molotov-Schulenburg conversations August 19, see: *DGFP* D VII, no.132; Russian record: *GK* 2, no. *572, DVP 1939* I no.474. Fleischhauer believes the fighting in the Far East was at the heart of Stalin's nonaggression draft proposal, *Der Pakt,* p.332, but see note 84 above.

126. For Schnurre's account of the delays, see Fleischhauer, *Der Pakt,* 522, note 471 to part III; for the text of the agreement, except part C, listing what the USSR was to supply to Germany, see: *GK,* 2, no.575; on part C, see note 71 above. For the text of the Credit Agreement, see also Edward F. Ericson, *Feeding the German Eagle: Soviet Economic Aid to Nazi Germany, 1933–1941* (London, 1999), Appendix B; for lists of goods exchanged by Germany and the USSR, 1939–41, ibid., Tables 2.7–3.1.

justify this by Soviet security reasons without jeopardizing an alliance with the Western powers. Whatever Stalin's calculations may have been, on August 21, he agreed to Hitler's personal request that Ribbentrop come to Moscow and the date was set for August 23.[128] He could hardly refuse the Führer's request without risking the loss of the nonaggression pact.

As mentioned earlier, the German and Soviet governments announced the signature of the economic agreement and Ribbentrop's forthcoming visit to Moscow on August 21 and 22 respectively. The Anglo-French-Soviet talks, suspended on August 17, resumed at 11.03 a.m. on August 21, but were adjourned at 5.25 p.m. for an indefinite time. They were not resumed despite Daladier's instruction, sent to General Doumenc on the night of August 21, that France agreed to the passage of Soviet troops through Poland, that is, through the Wilno corridor and, if necessary, also through Galicia and Romania. Delivery of this instruction was delayed by Soviet intelligence for several hours, so it was conveyed by the French general to Voroshilov at 6.30 p.m. the next day. The latter did not find it sufficient because the British delegation had not announced its government's agreement, even though they did not dissent. [Drax was instructed to associate himself with Doumenc on August 24]. Moreover, Voroshilov now made a new demand: that the Polish and Romanian governments themselves give their agreement, and Molotov repeated the same demand to Naggiar.[129] The French government seized on this straw to pursue an agreement with the USSR regardless of the nonaggression pact. In 1946, Daladier defended himself publicly against charges of preventing an Anglo-French-Soviet alliance in 1939. He claimed to have called in Polish Ambassador Łukasiewicz on the morning of August 21 and told him that if he did not inform him that afternoon, after telephoning Warsaw, that the Polish

---

127. For Yakovlev's statement of December 23, 1989 on information received by Stalin on August 19–20 that Britain, France, and Poland did not intend to change their position, and on Polish refusal of the passage of Soviet troops, see *1939 God*, 486, also other sources listed in note 3 above.

128. For Schulenburg's delivery of Hitler's message to Molotov August 21, and the latter's communication of Stalin's agreement to Ribbentrop's arrival on August 23, see *DGFP* D VII, nos. 157, 159; for the Russian texts of the Hitler-Stalin messages, see *GK* 2, nos. 582, 583; Stalin message, *DVP 1939* I, no. 478. Fleischhauer sees August 21 as the date of Stalin's decision to line up with Hitler, *Der Pakt*, 339. The question of Ribbentrop's arrival may have been discussed on the evening of August 20, when Stalin saw 14 visitors, of whom Molotov stayed the longest as usual, from 6 to 10.35 p.m., see: *IA 1995*, 5–6, 48–49.

129. For Daladier to Doumenc, August 21, see DDF, 2nd ser., vol. XVIII, no.182, p.232 and note 5. Voroshilov's conversation with Doumenc, August 22, *SPE* no.342; for Doumenc to Daladier, August 23, 1.32 a.m., *DDF* ibid., no. 268 (the document number is misprinted as 2 instead of 268); Naggiar's report on Molotov to Naggiar, ibid., no. 267. On Drax associating himself with Doumenc, August 24, ibid., no.348.

government agreed to the passage of Soviet troops, he, Daladier, would raise the whole question of the Franco-Polish alliance at a meeting of the Council of Ministers. If, however, the ambassador did not manifest Polish opposition by the afternoon, Daladier would telegraph General Doumenc authorizing him to sign the military convention that was proposed [by the Soviets]. However, Ambassador Łukasiewicz denied Daladier had presented him with this ultimatum. The ambassador wrote that if this had occurred, he would have refused to accept it, or proposed it be sent to Ambassador Noël for delivery in Warsaw, or he would have threatened to resign and made this public, something that would have been very inconvenient for Daladier.[130] As mentioned above, Daladier sent the French agreement to Doumenc anyway.

The Polish government and press received the news of the nonaggression pact calmly. In an instruction of August 23 to Polish diplomatic posts, Beck wrote the pact was proof of the Soviets' double-dealing, indicating they did not want to engage themselves on either side, but would welcome the possibility of a European war. He took comfort from the assumption that like other Soviet nonaggression pacts, this one too must have a clause abrogating the agreement if one of the parties became involved in hostilities with a third party.[131] British Ambassador Kennard reported on August 24 that Polish reaction to the news of the pact was calm; the Polish press was taking the line that Russia was withdrawing from Europe, and nothing had changed.[132] This view, as well as the fact that Britain supported Soviet troop passage only if Germany attacked Poland, made it easier for the Poles to agree to a formula allowing the continuation of the Franco-British-Soviet talks in Moscow. As General Musse wrote in his final report, Ambassador Noël made an urgent démarche to Beck in the late evening of August 23, and the Polish foreign minister accepted a formula that General Doumenc was to use in speaking to the head of the Soviet delegation in Moscow. He could state:

> We have acquired the certainty that, in case of common action against a German aggression, collaboration between Poland and the USSR, in technical conditions to be determined, is not excluded (or is possible).

---

130. For Daladier's claim of what he allegedly said to the Polish ambassador and the latter's rebuttal, see *Diplomat in Paris*, 252–253, Polish text in Juliusz Łukasiewicz, *Dyplomata w Paryżu 1936–1939*, 298–299.

131. For Beck's Instruction, August 23,1939, see *Akty dyplomatyczne*, 75, reprinted in Władysław T. Kowalski, *Polska w polityce międzynarodowej (1939–1945). Zbiór dokumentów, 1939* (Warsaw, 1989), no.163, 466.

132. For Kennard's report of August 24, 1939 on Polish calm, see *British Documents on Foreign Affairs*, part II, series F, vol. 58, *Poland, 1939* (Lanham, MD,1990), doc. 303, 307.

The French and British General Staffs therefore consider that *all* the hypotheses for collaboration should be studied immediately.

The text of the British message to Moscow, as agreed with the Poles, was more specific and closer to Polish thinking. It read:

> We have learned for certain that in the event of common action against German aggression, collaboration under technical conditions to be settled subsequently between Poland and the USSR, is not to be excluded.[133]

However, there was no communication between the Anglo-French military mission and Voroshilov, who did not answer their joint letter to him until August 25 when he met separately with the British and French delegation leaders. When Doumenc reiterated his message to Voroshilov, he was told that the talks between the military delegations could not continue because "political conditions had changed." [The Anglo-Polish Mutual Assistance Treaty was signed in London that afternoon]. When British Admiral Drax asked whether, in view of the change in the international situation, the Soviet government still desired to continue the talks, Voroshilov said he had been unable to reply to the joint letter of the French and British delegations—because he had been on a duck hunt! He then said that, to his regret, the change in the international situation made any further conversations useless.[134]

As is known, the Nazi-Soviet Nonaggression Pact was signed on August 23, while the secret protocol was worked out and signed at the Kremlin on the night of August 23–24. No Russian record of these negotiations has been published, but it is clear the Germans quickly gave up any claims they may have had to East Galicia. Furthermore, according to German sources Stalin demanded the inclusion of the Latvian ports of Libau (Liepaja) and

---

133. For the French version of the formula agreed in the late evening of August 23 between Beck and Noël, see the latter's telegram of August 23, *DDF* 2nd ser. XVIII, no. 275, and Musse report of August 24, ibid., no. 396, p. 480 (trans. A.M.C). Halifax informed Kennard on August 22, that Britain gave general support to France regarding the passage of Soviet troops through Poland, but only if the latter was at war with Germany, *DBFP* 3rd ser. VII, no. 150. For the text of the Polish message, as reported by the British ambassador, see Kennard to Halifax, August 23, 1939, 3. 30 p.m., ibid., no.176. The Polish version, as communicated by Beck to Łukasiewicz, did not mention an eventual agreement between Poland and the USSR; see *Diplomat in Paris*, p. 257.

134. For the meeting between Voroshilov and key members of the Anglo-French Mission, August 25, 1 p.m., see *DDF*, ibid., no. 457 and *DBFP*, ibid., no. 277 (including Voroshilov on duck hunt), and Appendix II, pp. 613–614. Voroshilov also saw the British and French ambassadors, but separately so they could not communicate with each other, see point 7 in report by General T.G. Heywood, *DBFP*, 3rd ser. VI, 607.

Windau (Ventspils) in the Soviet sphere of influence, and Ribbentrop received Hitler's agreement to this by telephone. On August 28, the Pisa River was added, at Molotov's request, to the northern part of the demarcation line in Poland.[135] Indeed, this line, which ran through the middle of Warsaw, was shown as the demarcation line between the Soviet and German armies on the map published in *Pravda* on September 23. This map was published in several Soviet newspapers over the next few days.

In the early hours of September 17, just after Stalin informed the German ambassador that Soviet troops were about to enter Poland, Potemkin read an official note, signed by Molotov, to Polish Ambassador Grzybowski, who was summoned to Potemkin's office at 2 a.m. The note—which the ambassador refused to accept, but was delivered to the Polish embassy during his interview with Potemkin—read as follows:

> The Polish-German war has revealed the internal bankruptcy of the Polish State. In ten days of hostilities, Poland has lost all its industrial regions and cultural centers. Warsaw no longer exists as the capital of Poland. The Polish government has collapsed and shows no signs of life. Therefore, the treaties concluded between the USSR and Poland have ceased to operate. Abandoned to its fate and left without leadership, Poland has become a fertile field for any accidental and unexpected contingency, which may constitute a threat to the USSR. Because of this, the Soviet Government, which had been neutral hitherto, can no longer maintain a neutral attitude toward these facts.
>
> Nor can the Soviet Government remain indifferent when its blood brothers, the Ukrainians and Belorussians living on Polish territory, having been abandoned to their fate, are left without protection.
>
> In view of this state of affairs, the Soviet Government has instructed the high command of the Red Army to order troops across the frontier and to take under their protection the lives and property of the population of Western Ukraine and Western White Russia.
>
> At the same time, the Soviet Government intends to take every step to deliver the Polish people from the disastrous war into which they have been plunged by their unwise leaders, and to give them an opportunity to live a peaceful life.[136]

---

135. On the negotiation of the secret protocol at the Kremlin during the night of August 23–24, see Fleischhauer, *Der Pakt,* 381–399; for German documents, see *DGFP* D VII, nos.205, 206, 210. Herwarth writes that he was sitting at the telephone in the German embassy, passing Soviet requests to Hitler, as transmitted by Ribbentrop. He was surprised that Hitler approved each request immediately, see *Against Two Evils,* 165. For the addition of the Pisa River to the line of August 23, in the agreement signed by Molotov and Schulenburg on August 28, see *GK 2,* no.614, *DVP 1939* I, no. 507.

136. Potemkin note to Grzybowski, September 17, 1939, *PWB* no. 175, *DPSR* I, no.43, Degras, *SDFP* III, 374; Russian text: *DiM* VII, no. 105, *Dokumenty*

Molotov repeated these statements in his radio speech of the same day. To his German partners he explained that these declarations were necessary for both foreign and domestic opinion.[137] Indeed, Soviet opinion was shocked by the pact in August and once the Red Army moved in in September, some citizens were critical of the USSR's apparent collusion with the Germans in the destruction of Poland.[138]

As for the date of Soviet aggression against Poland, the cease-fire signed by the Soviet and Japanese commanders in Nomonhan/Ghalkin Gol on September 16, 1939, does not seem to have been decisive for Stalin's agreement that evening to German pleas for Soviet military action and the order that the Red Army move into eastern Poland the next day. In fact, the Ukrainian and Belorussian fronts had been mobilized on September 7 and only awaited marching orders. These were dated originally September 14, but the date of readiness, end September 16, was inserted later. It was also on this date that the Germans informed Stalin of the allegedly impending fall of Warsaw, and this news, together with reports that the Polish government had crossed the border into Romania, may have been decisive for the Soviet leader, for if the Polish state no longer existed, this could at least technically absolve the USSR of attacking it. However, contrary to the claim regarding the fall of Warsaw, which was based on German disinformation, and proclaimed by Molotov that day on the radio—and repeated by German

---

Vneshnei Politiki, vol. XXII, *1939, Kniga* II (Moscow, 1992) no.597 (henceforth: DVP 1939 II]; for Potemkin record of the conversation, see: ibid., no. 596; for Grzybowski's account, see his "Final Report," *PWB* no.184, *DPSR* I, no.69. The same note was sent to foreign ambassadors in Moscow, see Steinhardt to Secretary of State, September 17, 1939, *FRUS 1939* I, 428–429.

137. In a previous version of this statement, the Soviet government was to say that it was coming to help their Ukrainian and Belorussian brothers threatened by the German Wehrmacht. Molotov explained to the Germans that this was to justify the Soviet intervention in the eyes of the masses, so it would not appear as the aggressor, but Ribbentrop voiced strong objections, see *DGFP* D, VIII (London, Washington, 1954), nos. 46, 70, 78. For Molotov's radio speech of September 17, 1939, see Degras, *SDFP*, III, 374–376.

138. NKVD informants in Leningrad reported shock and confusion among the people at the nonaggression pact, seen as a treaty with "the fascists." When the Red Army entered Poland, there was talk about "secret treaties" and Soviet-German collusion in the destruction of Poland; see Sarah Davies, *Popular Opinion in Stalin's Russia. Terror, propaganda and Dissent, 1934–1914* (Cambridge and New York, 1997), 98–99. See also the memoirs of an erstwhile communist, then a teenager in the USSR, later a professor at Yale University, Wolfgang Leonhard, *Betrayal. The Hitler-Stalin Pact of 1939* (New York, 1989), ch. 2., "The Pact and the People in the Soviet Union," 45–72.

historian Fleischhauer fifty years later[139]—the capital was still defending itself. As for the Polish government, it was still on Polish soil. On September 17, Beck telegraphed the Polish embassies in Paris and London as follows:

> Ambassador Grzybowski has refused to accept M. Molotov's note and has presented a protest against the aggression. I have approved his attitude, instructing him to ask for his passports and to withdraw from Moscow. The Polish Government, which is functioning on Polish territory and is in contact with the Diplomatic Corps, has made a protest against the Soviet insinuation. Our frontier troops have resisted the invasion.

He also instructed the Polish embassies in London and Paris to protest the Soviet invasion.[140]

That same day, however, on learning of the speedy Red Army advance into Poland, which threatened the security of the Polish government itself, the latter decided to cross into neighboring Romania. By this time, having retreated east and southeast ahead of the German armies, they were located, together with the diplomatic corps—which included U.S. Ambassador Anthony J. Drexel Biddle—and high command, on the Polish-Romanian border. Marshal Edward Śmigły-Rydz issued an order to Polish troops not to fight the Red Army unless attacked or threatened with disarmament. President Mościcki issued an address to the nation, condemning the German and Soviet aggression against Poland and explaining the government was going abroad to secure the constitutional continuity of Polish sovereignty.[141] The government and high command crossed into Romania

---

139. For Soviet-German talks on September 16–17, see: *DGFP* D VIII, nos. 78, 80. For Fleischhauer on Stalin sending the Red Army into eastern Poland only after the fall of Warsaw, see *Der Pakt*, 385. For the marching orders to the Belorussian and Ukrainian Fronts, originally dated September 14, then changed to September 16, see Russian Katyn documents: *Katyń. Plenniki nieob'iavlennoi Voiny*, edited by Nataliia S. Lebedeva, Wojciech Materski et al. (Moscow, 1997), doc. nos. 3, 4; Polish text, *Katyń. Dokumenty Zbrodni, 1, Jeńcy nie wypowiedzianej zbrodni* (Warsaw, 1995), doc. no.3 and Supplement 1.

140. For Beck telegram to Polish embassies, September 17, also notes presented by Polish ambassadors in London and Paris protesting the invasion, see *PWB*, nos. 176–178; for Grzybowski telegram to Foreign Ministry and Polish government protest, see *DPSR* I, nos. 44, 45.

141. For Śmigły-Rydz order to Polish troops of September 17, see ibid., doc. no. 6. For a photo copy of President Mościcki's address to the Polish nation, including handwritten corrections, see Dariusz Baliszewski and Andrzej Krzysztof Kunert, eds., *Prawdziwa historia Polaków. Ilustrowane wypisy źródłowe 1939–1945*, vol. I, *1939–1942* (Warsaw, 1999), doc. no.80, 73. For Ambassador Drexel Biddle's report on the war and retreat to Romania, see "The Polish-German Conflict and The Embassy's Activities," *Poland and the Coming of the Second World War. The Diplomatic Papers of A. J. Drexel Biddle Jr. United States Ambassador to Poland,*

on the night of September 17–18, with the intention of proceeding to France to continue the fight there and with a French invitation to do so. However, they were interned in Romania though they were formally still recognized by the Polish diplomatic representatives abroad and by Poland's allies as the Polish government until a new one was established in Paris on September 30.[142] Warsaw defended itself until there was no food or water, and capitulated after a three-week siege on September 27, while General Franciszek Kleeberg's troops, the last Polish force fighting the Germans, laid down its arms at Kock on October 5.[143] There were also some pitched battles between Polish and Soviet troops, and the town of Grodno defended itself for three days.[144]

One day after the surrender of Warsaw, a German-Soviet "Boundary and Friendship Treaty" was signed in Moscow. It established a new frontier between the two countries in Poland, running in the north well to the east of the August 23 line. It gave more Polish territory to Germany (Lublin and the eastern part of Warsaw province) in exchange for German recognition of all of Lithuania—except for the southern part of the country including the Memel [Klaipeda] territory—as belonging to the Soviet sphere of interest, for which Stalin undertook to pay an additional $7 million in gold. Also, the Soviet Union gave the Wilno [Vilnius] region to Lithuania. One of the secret protocols signed on September 28 provided for cooperation against any "Polish agitation which affects the territories of the other party,"[145] that is, against any Polish attempts to restore a Polish state. The new German-Soviet frontier

---

1937–1939, Philip V. Cannistraro, Edward D. Wynot, Jr., Theodore P. Kovalev, eds. (Columbus, OH, 1976), 94–165.

142. On the Polish government's retreat from Warsaw eastward, then south-east to the Polish-Romanian border, and its internment in Romania, see Anna M. Cienciala, "Internowanie rządu R.P. w Rumunii we wrześniu 1939 r." *Niepodległość*, vol. XII [po wznowieniu] (New York and London, 1989), 18–65.

143. See Steven Zaloga & Victor Madej, *The Polish Campaign 1939* (New York, 1985, reprint 1991), 103–152.

144. On the Soviet invasion of eastern Poland, ibid., 152–146. For a comprehensive collection of mostly Russian documents, translated into Polish, on the operations of the Soviet Ukrainian and Belorussian fronts in Poland, September 1939, see Czesław Grzelak, Stanisław Jaczyński, Eugeniusz Kozłowski, eds., *Agresja sowiecka na Polskę w świetle dokumentów. 17 września 1939* (Warsaw, 1994,1995, 1996), vols. 1–3. For a brief Russian account, see Mikhail Meltiukhov, *Sovetsko-Pol'skie Voiny. Voenno-politicheskoe protivostoiianie 1918–1939 gg* (Moscow, 2001), 303–350. The author's interpretation of interwar Polish foreign policy generally follows the old Soviet line.

145. For the English language texts of the German-Soviet Boundary and Friendship Treaty and secret protocols of September 28, 1939 see *DGFP* D VIII (London and Washington, 1954), nos. 157–160, *DPSR* I, nos. 52–55; Russian texts, *DVP* 1939 II, nos. 640–643.

in Poland became known as the Molotov-Ribbentrop Line, similar in the center and south both to the Curzon Line—proposed by British Foreign Secretary Lord Curzon as an armistice line between the Soviet and Polish armies in July 1920—and to the Polish-Soviet frontier established in 1944–45.

It is clear from a study of available Russian and German documents that Polish foreign policy did not play any part in Stalin's decision to align with Hitler. Even at the time, a high Soviet official admitted as much. Deputy Foreign Commissar Solomon S. Lozovskii told a Norwegian diplomat on August 23, that Poland's independent attitude had nothing to do with the conclusion of the German-Soviet pact, because political relations followed naturally from the economic agreement. He also touted the nonaggression pact as a peaceful measure, pointing out that previous Soviet nonaggression agreements always contained a clause that if one of the parties became an aggressor, this did not involve the other.[146] This indicates that he was either ignorant of the details of the pact, which is unlikely, or deliberately misled the Norwegian diplomat. It is true, of course, that the Soviet attitude toward Poland was always one of deep distrust. Her government was portrayed as pro-German and fascist. It was expected to give in to German demands, and even to join the Germans in an attack on the USSR. Still, before Britain granted a guarantee to Poland, Stalin seems to have toyed briefly with the idea of a Popular Front government in Warsaw, presumably to be organized and perhaps led by Polish communists. But he had dissolved the Polish Communist Party in 1938 on charges of infiltration by Polish police, so he allowed the establishment of an "Initiative Group" in Paris in January 1939. These were selected Polish communists whom he apparently viewed as the embryo of a new Polish Communist Party. They published three issues of a bulletin up to and including April 1939, calling for a Polish coalition government to resist Germany. However, after the British guarantee, they called for its overthrow. Stalin shelved them in April, when he apparently decided they were no longer needed.[147] Perhaps he perceived a German attack on Poland as more likely because of Polish acceptance of the British guarantee, and decided at this time to try for an agreement with Hitler to partition Poland.

Whatever the case may be, Soviet policy toward Poland in spring and summer 1939 was characterized by friendly declarations as well as talk of Soviet help and benevolent neutrality. At the same time, however, great distrust is documented in the correspondence between Litvinov, then

---

146. Record of Lozovskii conversation with Norwegian chargé d'affaires, M. Bolstad, August 23, 1939, *DVP 1939* I, no. 486.

147. On the Paris Initiative Group, see Anna M. Cienciala, "The Activities of Polish Communists as a Source for Stalin's Policy Toward Poland in World War II," *International History Review*, vol. VII, no. 1 (1986): 129–145.

Molotov, with the Soviet ambassadors in London and Paris, as well as by Soviet demands regarding the prospective political and military alliance with France and Britain. No official Soviet offer of cooperation was ever made to Poland, nor was there any official proposal for the passage of Soviet troops, though a low-level Soviet sounding was recorded in Wilno in spring 1939.[148] In fact, Lithuania was not included in the Soviet list of states to be guaranteed by the Soviet Union and the Western powers, perhaps because it did not border on the USSR. Also, Litvinov may have assumed—or pretended to assume—that Poland would, in her own interest, come to the defense of Lithuania in case of German aggression. No official Soviet proposal was ever made to the Polish government that Polish officers participate in the Moscow negotiations. Indeed, it is possible that if the Polish government had agreed to the Soviet demand for troop passage, Stalin could have portrayed this at the appropriate time as sanctioning the Soviet occupation and then annexation of eastern Poland. The latter took place officially in early November 1939, when the Supreme Soviet acceded to the "requests" of the Soviets [assemblies] of western Belorussia and western Ukraine [East Galicia]—elected under Soviet rules and in an atmosphere of terror—for union with the Soviet Belorussian and Ukrainian Republics. According to wartime Polish estimates, about one million Polish citizens were deported from these territories into the depths of the USSR, of whom about 50 percent were ethnic Poles and 30 percent were Jews, with Ukrainians and Belorussians making up the rest. (Soviet figures, compiled at the time by the NKVD and released after 1991, put the number of deported Polish citizens at about 325,000, which seems too low) . Furthermore, about four hundred thousand Poles are estimated to have been killed by Soviet authorities in former eastern Poland between September 17, 1939, and June 21, 1941. Finally, according to Soviet sources, of the some two hundred thousand Polish prisoners of war taken in September 1939, 21,857 officers and some civilians were held in special camps as well as prisons in Belorussia and Ukraine. They were murdered by special NKVD troops on orders signed by the Soviet Politburo on March 5, 1940.[149] That is how

---

148. See note 57 above.

149. On Soviet-style elections in eastern Poland, October 1939, and Soviet rule there, see Jan T. Gross, *Revolution from Abroad. The Soviet Conquest of Poland's Western Ukraine and Western Belorussia* (Princeton, N.J., 1988); also Keith Sword, ed., *The Soviet Takeover of the Polish Eastern Provinces, 1939–41* (New York, 1991), and his, *Deportation and Exile. Poles in the Soviet Union, 1939–48* (Basingstoke, England and New York, 1994). The number of deported Polish citizens was estimated by the Polish government-in-exile at about 1,200,000, but NKVD figures released after 1991, put them at about 325,000, which seems too low; see Marek Tuszyński, "Soviet War Crimes against Poland During the Second World War and Its Aftermath. A Review of the Factual Record and Outstanding Questions,"

Stalin brought a "peaceful life" to the Polish population of western Ukraine and Belorussia. At the same time, the "liberation" of the Ukrainians and Belorussians meant terror, arrests, and deportations for "enemies of the Soviet people," with collectivization of the land and nationalization of all means of production imposed on the population.

So when did Stalin decide to align the USSR with Nazi Germany? On the basis of all the documentation available up to now, it is clear that the "Vozhd" was very interested in an agreement with Hitler, if not as far back as 1934—as Krivitsky claims—then certainly in 1935–36, as evidenced by the proposals made by Litvinov to Schulenburg in May 1935, and even more so by Kandelaki to Schacht at the turn of 1936–37. If Stalin had not decided to seek cooperation with Germany earlier, he might have done so after the British guarantee to Poland on March 31, 1939, which he apparently suspected of being directed against the USSR. Or he might have done so with the dismissal of Litvinov on May 3 that year, as surmised by Jonathan Haslam and Lev. I. Ginzburg, and affirmed years later by Andrei Gromyko. If this was so, the primary goal of Soviet diplomacy, at least from this time onward, was an agreement with Germany. In any case, Molotov told Schulenburg on May 20 that a political basis had to be found for the economic agreement between the two countries. After a hiatus in the Molotov-Schulenburg talks—though talks continued in Berlin—the Germans became anxious to make a deal. On August 11, 1939, the Soviet chargé in Berlin, Georgii Astakhov, listed the territorial concessions the Germans were willing to make and Molotov found them of great interest, but said it was now up to the Germans. Perhaps the final decision to start concrete negotiations was made that day, as Yakovlev claimed in December 1989, saying it was due to news of Hitler's impending attack on Poland any time after August 25. However, there is no documentary evidence that Hitler made this decision before he was sure that he could strike a deal with Stalin, and this occurred on August 21. In any case, the Germans were told on August 15 that they could send a negotiator to Moscow. On August 17, Molotov

---

(note 149 continued) *Polish Review*, vol. 44, no. 2 (1999): 183–216. For a brief study of Soviet oppression of Poles and Polish citizens, citing NKVD documents, see Stanisław Ciesielski, Wojciech Materski and Andrzej Paczkowski, eds., *Represje sowieckie wobec Polaków i obywateli polskich* (Warsaw, 2000). For Russian documents on the arrest, imprisonment, and mass murder of Polish prisoners of war in the western USSR in spring 1940, see Nataliia Lebedeva, Wojciech Materski et al., eds. *Katyń. Plenniki neob'iavlennoi voiny*, and, *Katyń. Dokumenty zbrodni. Tom I. Jeńcy niewy-powiedzianej wojny* (see note 140 above); Materski, Lebedeva, et al., eds., *Katyń. Dokumenty Zbrodni; Tom II. Zagłada* (Warsaw, 1998), and Lebedeva, Materski et al., eds., *Katyń. Mart 1940—sentiabr 2000 g. Rasstrel. Sud'by zhivykh. Ekho Katyni. Dokumenty* (Moscow, 2001). The publication of an English language volume by Yale University Press, edited by the author of this article, is expected in 2003.

handed a Soviet aide-mémoire to Schulenburg, proposing a nonaggression pact, and on August 19 he gave the German ambassador the Soviet draft of this pact. Yakovlev stated this was done on that day because Stalin allegedly heard from "documented sources" that the Western powers and Poland would not change their attitude. Fleischhauer writes that Stalin made his decision on August 21, when it was clear the Western powers had not persuaded the Poles to grant the key Soviet demand for passage of troops, also because of the Soviet-Japanese fighting in the Far East. However, Yakovlev said the *decision to* negotiate with the Germans had been made on August 11. If August 21 was the date of the final decision to make a deal with Berlin, Stalin was likely to have made it because he could not afford to refuse Hitler's demand that Ribbentrop arrive in Moscow by August 23.

Summation

While the lack of Russian documents on the decision-making process at this time does not allow fixing the exact date of Stalin's decision, it is clear that Astakhov's talks with German officials in Berlin in the period from mid-April to August 12 paved the way for the Nazi-Soviet agreement. Gorlov's thesis, supported by Roberts, that the absence of any instructions from Molotov to Astakhov during this time proves the latter was acting on his own initiative is clearly untenable. Not only did German officials, including Ribbentrop, treat Astakhov as a bona fide representative of the Soviet government, but it is also clear that he was in close touch with Molotov all the time. Indeed, even Astakhov's published correspondence with Moscow shows that he was not acting on his own. Thus, it is quite possible that Stalin and Molotov decided on an agreement with Germany at least as early as Litvinov's dismissal in early May, if not earlier, and then played a consummate diplomatic game until they were sure that Hitler would grant all their demands. This assumption is supported by Astakhov's Berlin conversations, as well as by the "leaks" provided to the German embassy in London from the "reliable source" who was most likely the Soviet agent in the Foreign Office Communications Department, Francis Herbert King. It is striking that very few such hints and leaks of German-Soviet negotiations were made to the Western powers, and those came from the Germans who informed the French. Also, Molotov's tone in his meetings with the British and French diplomats in Moscow was almost always rough, and even rude, while Western policy was strongly criticized in the Soviet press as insincere at best and exploitive at worst. This was in contrast to the generally polite tone adopted by the Soviet press toward Germany and by Molotov toward Schulenburg.

What is particularly noticeable is the parallelism between the German-Soviet talks and the Franco-British-Soviet negotiations between mid-April and the end of July. This became even more striking in August. Thus,

Astakhov told the Germans on August 12—the day that Franco-British-Soviet negotiations opened in Moscow—that the Soviet government was ready to negotiate and would accept a German negotiator in the Soviet capital. Stalin's readiness to sign a nonaggression pact was expressed by Molotov to Schulenburg on August 17, the day that military negotiations with the French and British were suspended after Stalin learned of a message from Hitler to be delivered by Schulenburg. This was before intensive Anglo-French efforts took place in Warsaw to persuade the Poles to agree to the passage of Soviet troops. Molotov handed the Soviet draft of a nonaggression pact to Schulenburg in the late afternoon of August 19, before the French government, and presumably Doumenc in Moscow, received the news of the Polish refusal that day. It is possible that Stalin judged the time was right to negotiate an agreement with Germany sometime in August 1939, but if so, this was the culmination of a long, preparatory period. At the same time, it is most unlikely that Stalin only made up his mind on August 21, allegedly because he learned that the French and British delegations failed to receive a positive reply from Poland regarding the passage of Soviet troops. In fact, Stalin seems to have expected a negative outcome to these military negotiations. If he did, he may have agreed to them in order to pressure Hitler into an agreement with the USSR—and perhaps, at the same time, receive a Western sanction for entering eastern Poland. As for the Japanese-Soviet fighting in the Far East, it did not amount to a full-scale war. Furthermore, a highly placed Soviet intelligence agent in Tokyo (Richard Sorge) reported in June that Japan was not planning to attack the USSR, so it is unlikely that this fighting played a significant role in Stalin's decision.

Did Stalin fear a German attack on the USSR? Perhaps, but German documents do not indicate that Hitler intended to attack the Soviet Union through Poland in 1939, and Soviet intelligence should have reported this to Stalin. D. C. Watt may be right in his judgment that Stalin expected Hitler to attack France and Britain, not the USSR. Whatever the case may be, one may ask whether Hitler would have attacked Poland if the USSR had an alliance with France and Britain? Setting this question aside, it is clear that the lack of a clause abrogating the German-Soviet nonaggression pact in case one of the two parties engaged in an aggressive war against a third country—a clause present in other nonaggression pacts signed by the USSR before August 1939[150]—was certainly a strong encouragement for Hitler to attack Poland. Bearing all this in mind, can Stalin's policy be

---

150. For example, art. 2 of the Polish-Soviet nonaggression pact of July 25, 1932, stated: "If one of the Contracting Parties commits an act of aggression against a third State, the other Contracting Party shall have the right to be released from the present Treaty without previous denunciation.," *DPSR*, I, no. 6.

described simply as appeasement of Germany, and can he be viewed as a wise statesman for concluding the nonaggression pact with Hitler?[151]

The lack of authoritative Soviet documentation allows the debate on dating Stalin's key policy decision to continue, and the same holds true of the interpretation of Stalin's motives for concluding the pact with Hitler. As far as short-term goals are concerned, one may, for example, ask whether Stalin thought he could sign a military alliance with the Western powers if he obtained their agreement to enter eastern Poland while bound by a nonaggression pact to Nazi Germany? Daladier, for one, was certainly willing to let Soviet troops enter eastern Poland, and presumably stay there, as witness his cable to Doumenc of August 21. The British agreed to this on August 24. This may have encouraged the Soviet leader to speculate that he could have his cake and eat it too, that is, he could have both an alliance with the Western powers and a nonaggression pact with Nazi Germany. This hypothesis seems to be supported by the fact that, between August 23 and 25, both Molotov and the Soviet press proclaimed there was no contradiction between a military alliance with the Western powers and a nonaggression pact with Germany. The Soviet ambassador in Poland also talked as if the situation had not changed. Indeed, as late as September 2, when Poland was already under German attack, he suggested the Poles should ask the USSR for supplies, mentioning Voroshilov's positive statement on this as published in the Soviet press on August 27.[152] Was this simply camouflage aimed to strengthen Polish morale and so make the Poles fight the Germans as long as possible, or was it something else? Did the Soviet talk on August 23–25 that both the pact and the alliance were not inherently

---

151. "Das staatsmannische Interesse Stalins bei Abschluss dieses Paktes bestand in einer Politik der Beschwichtigung, der Pakt selbst war vorrangig, ein Instrument der sowjetischen beschwichtigungspolitik." Fleischhauer, *Der Pakt*, 434.

152. Beck informed the Polish embassy in London on September 2, that the Soviet ambassador had asked why Poland was not negotiating with the Soviet government regarding supplies, since the Voroshilov interview had opened up this possibility, *PWB*, no.171, *DPSR*, I, no.36. Indeed, on August 27, *Izvestiia* had reported Voroshilov's statement that aid in raw materials and war materials was a commercial, not a military question, so no military convention was needed to supply Poland with them, see *PWB*, no 170, also Degras, *SDFP* III, 362, Russian text after *Izvestiia*. *DiM*, VII, no.104. However, on September 8, Molotov informed the Polish ambassador that British and French intervention, of which Voroshilov was unaware when granting the [press] interview, had created an entirely new situation, so the USSR was prepared to supply Poland only with the raw materials provided for in the quotas for the current year, *PWB* no. 172, *DPSR*, I, no. 39; this document and Molotov's statement of September 8 to Grzybowski were not published in *DVP* 1939 II. Of course, France and Britain were not at war with Germany until September 3, while Voroshilov's statement was published on August 27.

contradictory reflect Stalin's policy? It is possible that he may have allowed talk on the compatibility of an alliance with the Western powers and a nonaggression pact with Germany to secure Western agreement to his demand regarding Red Army passage through Poland, or to exert pressure on Hitler to make more concessions to the USSR, or both. Of course, without access to relevant Soviet documents, these questions will remain unanswered.

There are also questions concerning Stalin's long-term aims in concluding the pact with Hitler. As mentioned earlier, some Western, a few Russian, and most Polish historians believe that Stalin deliberately ensured Hitler's attack on Poland, thus risking the outbreak of a European war in which the USSR would gain some territory, stay on the sidelines, and then take advantage of the European powers' exhaustion to expand both Soviet power and communism. This view seemed to find confirmation in a German newspaper report of July 1996 on a documentary "find" by a Russian scholar. This was the text of a speech that Stalin allegedly made to the Politburo on August 19, 1939. As it turned out, the speech had been published as long as ago as 1939, and Stalin denied it at the time. Some historians believe it to be a forgery, while others think it is genuine. Neither opinion can be proved correct without other documents to confirm it, but the date of August 19 was cited by Yakovlev for Stalin's final decision, and the document does reflect Soviet thinking as recorded elsewhere. For these reasons the text is given below:

Peace or war? This question has entered into its critical phase. Its solution depends entirely on the position taken by the Soviet Union. We are absolutely convinced that is we conclude an alliance treaty with France and Great Britain, Germany will see itself obliged to draw back from Poland and to seek a *modus vivendi* with the western powers. In this way, war could be avoided and then, later development of this state of affairs will take on a character dangerous to us.

On the other hand, if we accept the proposal of Germany, that you know, to conclude with her a nonaggression pact, Germany will certainly attack Poland and the intervention of England and France will be inevitable.

In these circumstances, we will have a very good chance to stay out of the conflict, and we will be able to wait our turn with advantage to us. This is precisely what our interest demands.

Thus, our choice is clear: we should accept the German proposal and send the Anglo-French missions back to their countries with a courteous refusal.

It is not difficult to foresee the advantage that we will draw from this way of proceeding. It is evident to us that Poland will be destroyed even before England and France are able to come to her aid. In this case, Germany cedes to us a part of Poland right up to the outskirts of Warsaw—together with Ukrainian Galicia.

Germany leaves us complete freedom of action in the three Baltic states. She does not oppose the return of Bessarabia to Russia. She is ready to cede us Romania, Bulgaria and Hungary as our sphere of influence.

There remains the question of Yugoslavia, the solution of which depends on the position taken by Italy. If Italy remains at Germany's side, she will demand that Yugoslavia be included in her sphere of influence, and it is also through Yugoslavia that she will obtain access to the Adriatic. But if Italy does not march with Germany, the latter will have access to the Adriatic at Italian expense, and in that case Yugoslavia will pass into our sphere of influence.

That is, if Germany is victorious in the war.

However, we should foresee the possibilities which will result from the defeat as well as from the victory of Germany. Let us examine the case of a German defeat. England and France will then have enough power to occupy Berlin and destroy Germany, and we will not be able to give effective help to the latter.

Therefore, our goal is that Germany be able to carry on the war as long as possible, so that England and France are tired and exhausted to such a point that they are no longer able to knock out Germany.

Consequently our position is that while remaining neutral, we help Germany economically, furnishing her with raw materials and food products. But it is obvious that our aid should not exceed a certain limit so as not to compromise our economic situation and not weaken the power of our army.

At the same time, we should, in a general way, conduct an active communist propaganda, especially in the Anglo-French bloc, and especially in France. We should expect that, in this country, our party will be obliged, in time of war, to abandon legal measures and move to clandestine activity. We know that this activity requires a lot of money, but we should consent to these sacrifices without hesitation. If this preparatory work is duly carried out, German security will be assured. The latter can contribute to the sovietisation of France.

Now, let us examine the second hypothesis, that of German victory. Some [people] are of the opinion that this possibility represents the greatest danger to us. There is some truth in this assertion, but it would be erroneous to think that this danger is as near and as great as some imagine.

If Germany wins, she will come out of the war too tired to make war on us for the following decade. Her main concerns will be to keep watch over defeated England and France to prevent them from recovering.

On the other hand, a victorious Germany will have vast colonies at her disposal. Their exploitation and adaptation to German methods will absorb Germany to an equal extent for several decades. It is evident that Germany will be too busy elsewhere to turn against us.

Comrades, concluded Stalin, I have expounded my considerations to you. I repeat that is in your* interest that war breaks out between the Reich and Anglo-French bloc. It is essential for us that this war lasts as long as possible, so that the two sides are exhausted. It is for these reasons that we should accept the pact proposed by Germany and work so that the war, once declared, is prolonged to the maximum. At the same time, we should intensify economic work** in the belligerent countries, so that we are well prepared for the moment when the war ends.

As it turned out, the German newspaper report was based on a document found a few years earlier by the Russian historian Tatiana Bushuyeva, who discovered it among documents seized from the Nazis and then stored

in the former Soviet war booty archive. She published it Russian translation in the Russian journal *Novy Mir* in October 1994. Bushueva believed
that since the text was in French, it was probably written by a French-
speaking Comintern member present at the meeting.[153] There is no confirmation of the text from Russian sources, and many historians believe it is a
forgery.[154] However, on September 7, Georgii M. Dimitrov, then head of
the Comintern, noted Stalin as saying:

We have nothing against their fighting and weakening each other. It
would not be bad if German hands shook up the wealthier capitalist countries (especially England). Hitler, though he does not understand or desire
it, is shaking up and undermining the capitalist system.

On the Soviet Union's role in the war he said: *"We can maneuver, support one side against the other, so that they fight each other all the better."*[155] It would be strange, indeed, if Stalin did not have such thoughts
before the conclusion of the pact with Hitler. Furthermore, there are Czech
and Polish reports on statements made by high Soviet officials in 1940–41

---

153. *"votre" [your interest] should probably be "notre." [our interest]. ** It is
not clear what is meant by "economic work"; perhaps it was to organize worker
unrest so as to impede war production. The English translation by the author of this
article is from the original French text as printed in Eberhard Jäckel, "Über eine
angebliche Rede Stalins vom 19 August 1939," *Vierteljahrshefte für Zeitgeschichte*,
no. 4 (Munich, 1958), 581–582. For the German article of 1996, see Carl Gustav
Strohm, Moscow, "Stalins Strategie für Krieg und Frieden. Geheime Dokumente
beweisen: Sowjetischer Diktator hat Hitlers Angriff auf Polen einkalkuliert," *Die
Welt*, July 16, 1996; Russian translation from French by T. Bushueva in section
"Knizhnoe Obozrenie," *Novy Mir,* 10 (1994): 232–233..

154. According to Eberhard Jäckel, the text of the alleged Stalin speech, first
summarized in a report by the French news agency *Havas*, was provided by an
unnamed source to Henry Ruffin, the *Havas* correspondent in Geneva. Jäckel noted
that the "speech" was published in Geneva in the *Revue du Droit International*
no.3 for July-September 1939, and that Stalin's denial appeared in *Pravda*, 30 November 1939. The denial was also published in the German press, while the text
was reprinted in the Geneva journal in 1941 and in the Vichy France *Revue
Universelle* in 1944. Jäckel concludes that Stalin's motives, as portrayed in the alleged speech, were "historically incorrect," and that it was a piece of "prophetic
fiction" written by a specialist on Bolshevism, see: Jäckel, "Über eine angebliche
rede Stalins," 589.

155. Emphasis added, A M..C. See F. I. Firsov, in *Komintern: opyt, traditsii,
uroki,* Moscow, 1989, 21; cit. in Nataliia S. Lebedeva, M.M. Narinskii, eds.,
Komintern i Vtoraia Mirovaia Voina, chast 1 do 22 iuniia 1941g., Moscow, 1994,
10–11. Ivo Banac, ed., *The Diary of Georgii Dimitrov, 1933–1949,* New Haven &
London, 2003, pp. 115–116.

about Soviet plans for the Red Army to march into an exhausted Europe, which would then become communist.[156]

It is, of course, possible to explain Stalin's decision to align the USSR with Germany because he expected the latter to invade Poland without any significant military reaction by France and Britain, and because he needed time to rearm. On this hypothesis, it would be obviously in the Soviet interest to prevent the Germans from taking all of Poland and perhaps Lithuania, Latvia, and Estonia as well, while making an ally of Finland. However, it seems rather restrictive to view Stalin's policy only in terms of traditional "realpolitik," based on the need to assure Soviet security while totally ignoring the role of communist ideology. Instead, it seems more appropriate to see Stalin's policy in 1939 as a combination of "realpolitik" *and* the old goal of world revolution—in this case, the establishment of Soviet-dominated communist governments in Europe after an exhausting war.

In conclusion, it seems most likely Stalin decided sometime in spring 1939 to align with Hitler. He must have calculated that he could risk having the German army and air force much nearer to Moscow through a partition of Poland, because he expected Hitler to become bogged down in a long war with France and Britain. Therefore, he conducted negotiations with the Western powers in order to pressure Hitler into an agreement with the USSR. Such a policy would form part of the long-term Soviet goal of gaining lasting security for the USSR, which was always identified with the spread of communism across the world, but first of all in Europe. Like Lenin in 1917–19, Stalin seems to have expected such a state of affairs only in the wake of an exhausting war. Again, like Lenin, he seems to have viewed Germany as the key European country in an expanded communist

---

156. Two Czech reports written in 1940–41 mention statements by Soviet officials about plans to communize Europe, and one even forecast an autonomous Czech republic as part of the USSR; see reports to President Edvard Beneš of November 6, 1940 and August 10, 1941, Jan Němeček et al., eds., _eskoslovensko-sovětské vztahy v diplomatických jednáních 1939–1945. Dokumenty, díl 1 (březen 1939—červen 1943)_ (Prague, 1998), nos. 98, 163. Statements by high NKVD officials on the Red Army marching to the English Channel and a postwar communist Europe were recorded by a Polish cavalry captain, a surviving prisoner of war, interviewed for military service by the head of the NKVD, Lavrenty P. Beria and his deputy, Feodor A. Merkulov in fall 1940, see Narcyz Lopianowski, *Rozmowy z NKWD, 1940–1941* (Warsaw, 1990), 32, 85 ff. Lopianowski joined a group of Polish officers willing to cooperate with the Soviet government, led by General Zygmunt Berling, but did so in order to report on the group to his own commanding general, see ibid., 93.

bloc, which included Poland as the land bridge between Germany and the USSR. Finally, all the available documentation indicates that Poland did not play any role in Stalin's decision to align with Hitler in 1939, except as a convenient scapegoat for breaking off the negotiations for a Soviet alliance with France and Britain. Stalin's view of Poland is probably best reflected in a statement noted by Dimitrov during the latter's meeting with the "Vozhd" on September 7, 1939. Stalin characterized it as "fascist state" which oppressed Ukrainians and Belorussians, and said:

> The destruction of this state in present circumstances would mean one bourgeois, fascist, state less! Would it be a bad thing if, as a result of the defeat of Poland, we expanded the socialist system to new territories and populations?[157]

It is more than likely that these were also Stalin's thoughts about Poland for a long time before he concluded his fateful agreement with Hitler in August 1939.

---

157. See Lebedeva and Narinskii, *Komintern*, cit. note 155 above; trans. A.M.C.

Chapter 7

Poland, the GDR, and the "Ulbricht Doctrine"[1]

Douglas Selvage

Most of the existing scholarship on the cold war in Europe during the 1960s posits the existence of an "Ulbricht Doctrine": an East German dictate, forced upon the other Warsaw Pact states, not to establish diplomatic relations with Bonn until it first recognized the GDR. Most accounts date the "Ulbricht Doctrine" back to the meeting in February 1967 of the Warsaw Pact foreign ministers in Warsaw.[2] The term itself originated in the Federal Republic of Germany (FRG), where analysts began to suggest in early 1967 that at the very moment when Bonn was ready to drop (or at least revise) the Hallstein Doctrine to permit diplomatic relations with Eastern Europe, the GDR had stepped in with its own doctrine—an "Ulbricht Doctrine"—to prevent their establishment. Such theorizing is in keeping with most West German scholarship on the GDR, which tends to focus on

1. This article is based upon a paper presented to the National Convention of the American Association for the Advancement of Slavic Studies (AAASS) in Boston, Massachusetts, on November 15, 1996. Research for this article was supported in part by a grant from the International Research and Exchanges Board (IREX), with funds provided by the National Endowment for the Humanities, the United States Information Agency, and the U.S. Department of State, which administers the Russian, Eurasian, and East European Research Program (Title VIII). I would also like to thank the Bradley Foundation, the German Academic Exchange Service (DAAD), and International Security Studies at Yale for their support of this project.
2. See, for example, Timothy Garton Ash, *In Europe's Name: Germany and the Divided Continent* (New York, 1993), 55–6; Peter Bender, *Die "Neue Ostpolitik" und ihre Folgen: Vom Mauerbau bis zur Vereinigung,* 3rd rev. ed. (Munich, 1995), 143–4; William E. Griffith, *The Ostpolitik of the Federal Republic of Germany* (Cambridge, MA, 1978), 151; Michael J. Sodaro, *Moscow, Germany and the West: From Khrushchev to Gorbachev* (Ithaca, NY, 1990), 100; Jochen Stadt, *Die geheime Westpolitik der SED 1960–1970: Von der gesamtdeutschen Orientierung zur sozialistischen Nation* (Berlin, 1993), 230.

comparisons and interactions between the two German states and to ig-
nore linkages among the GDR and the other socialist states, with the possible exception of the Soviet Union.[3]

The situation within the Warsaw Pact, however, was more complicated
than that suggested by the "Ulbricht Doctrine" thesis. In fact, Poland's
communist leader, Władysław Gomułka, stood behind the successful convocation of the Warsaw Pact foreign ministers' meeting in February 1967.
The secret agreement that came out of the conference reflected as much
Polish, as East German, thinking. It listed a number of preconditions that
Bonn would have to meet before the other socialist states would be allowed to establish diplomatic relations with the FRG, including not only
recognition of the GDR, but also recognition of Poland's western border,
the Oder-Neisse Line. Within the Soviet bloc, this list of demands came to
be known as the "Warsaw Package," and not the "Ulbricht Doctrine."[4]

The "Warsaw Package" had its origins in the threat of isolation that
arose for both Warsaw and East Berlin as a result of Bonn's adoption of a
more active *Ostpolitik* in 1966. At a time when the FRG still refused to
recognize either the GDR or Poland's western border, the Oder-Neisse Line,
the other Warsaw Pact states were on the verge of normalizing relations
with Bonn. Both the "Southern Tier" of the pact (Hungary, Romania, and
Bulgaria) and, increasingly, Czechoslovakia saw in closer political relations
with Bonn an opportunity to increase trade and obtain much-needed capital to purchase investment goods from the West. These differences of opinion found expression in the Warsaw Pact's Bucharest Declaration of July
1966: a compromise, brokered by the Soviet Union, between the hard-line,
anti-West German stance of Poland and the GDR, and Romania's wish,
vaguely backed by Hungary, to improve economic and political ties with
Bonn. One section of the declaration had recognized the existence of
antirevanchist, "peace-loving" elements in West Germany and had called
for an improvement in cultural and economic relations among all European states—including, of course, the FRG. In accordance with Polish and
East German thinking, yet another section of the declaration had condemned
"revanchism" and "militarism" in West Germany. This section demanded
that Bonn recognize, not only the GDR and the Oder-Neisse Line, but also
acknowledge the invalidity of the Munich Agreement, *ex tunc*; renounce
its claim to West Berlin; and forswear access to nuclear weapons in any
form. The declaration did not make these demands a precondition for dip-

---

3. Beate Ihme-Tuchel, *Das "nördliche Dreieck": Die Beziehungen zwischen der
DDR, der Tschechoslowakei und Polen in den Jahren 1954 bis 1962* (Köln, 1994),
16.

4. Jan Ptasiński, Ambassador of the People's Republic of Poland (PRL) in Moscow, "Radzieckie opinie o polityce zagranicznej PRL w sprawie niemieckiej," 4
January 1970. Archiwum Akt Nowych (AAN), KC PZPR, p. 123, t. 75, pp. 9–21.

lomatic relations with Bonn, however. At the time, the FRG was still cling-
ing to the Hallstein Doctrine, which forbade diplomatic relations with any
country that recognized the GDR. Diplomatic relations were thus a moot
point for the GDR's Warsaw Pact allies.[5]

This began to change, however, in the fall of 1966. Bonn began to re-
consider its eastern policy, including the Hallstein Doctrine. Warsaw and
East Berlin awakened to a threat of isolation following the visit of the
FRG's economics minister, Kurt Schmücker, to Bucharest in September 1966.
During his visit, the Romanian communists expressed a willingness to establish diplomatic relations without any preconditions; they would allow
Bonn to retain its "legal standpoint" on the German question.[6] This legal
standpoint impinged, however, upon the vital interests of both Poland (recognition of the Oder-Neisse Line) and the GDR (recognition of its existence). The question arose: If Bonn revised the Hallstein Doctrine to allow
for diplomatic relations with Eastern Europe, should the Warsaw Pact place
its own preconditions upon diplomatic relations with Bonn? Clearly, Romania did not think so.

Within a month, both Ulbricht and Gomułka were in Moscow to com-
plain about Romania and to discuss methods for blunting Bonn's political
offensive to the east. Ulbricht, who visited Moscow one week after
Schmücker's visit to Bucharest in September, proposed a unilateral East
German response, backed by Moscow, to Bonn's offensive. The GDR, he
suggested, should submit an aide-mémoire to the other socialist states warning about Bonn's new tactics and conclude friendship treaties with its so-
cialist-bloc neighbors, Poland and Czechoslovakia (ČSSR).[7] In contrast,
when Gomułka visited Moscow in October, the Polish leader called for a
multilateral response by the entire Warsaw Pact. He explained to Brezhnev:
"We cannot rule out that [Bonn] might abandon the Hallstein Doctrine in

---

5. See the speeches of the Warsaw Pact foreign ministers from the preparatory
conference held from June 6–17 in Moscow: "Im Auftrage des Genossen Kohrt
anbei Reden und Bemerkungen auf der Beratung der Außenminister der Staaten des
Warschauer Vertrages," 11 June 1966, in Stiftung Archiv der Parteien und
Massenorganisationen der DDR im Bundesarchiv (SAPMO BA), J IV 2/202–258.
On the Soviet Union's role, see Hegen, Staatssekretär und Erster Stellvertreter des
MfAA, to Ulbricht, Stoph, Honecker, and Axen, 15 June 1966, in ibid. On Hun-
gary: Herbert Krolikowski, Stellv. des Ministers für Auswärtige Angelegenheiten to
Ulbricht, Stoph, Honecker, and Axen, 16 June 1966, in ibid. For the Bucharest
Declaration of July 5, 1966, see *Dokumente zur Deutschlandpolitik* (Bonn, 1970),
Vol. IV/12: 1061–71. Henceforth, *DzDP*.

6. "Interview des Bundesministers Schmücker für die Deutsche Welle in Bukarest,"
6 September 1966. *DzDP*, IV/12: 1293–97.

7. "AUFZEICHNUNG ÜBER DAS GESPRÄCH ZWISCHEN GENOSSEN
WALTER ULBRICHT UND L.I. BRESHNEW IM ZK DER KPdSU IN MOSKAU
AM 10. SEPTEMBER 1966 (Zweiter Teil)," n.d. SAPMO BA, J IV 2/201–735.

relation to the socialist states. The question arises: Will we conduct a common policy, or will every country act independently? . . . It seems to me that a common policy is needed here." Implying that it should serve as a model for the entire alliance, Gomułka repeated Warsaw's three conditions for diplomatic relations with Bonn: its recognition of the existing borders, including the Oder-Neisse Line; *de facto* recognition of the GDR, and renunciation of access to nuclear weapons in any form. When Brezhnev brought up Ulbricht's idea for friendship treaties, Gomułka expressed his support, but questioned its timeliness. He proposed a *series* of friendship treaties among Warsaw, Prague, and East Berlin in order to build a "central core" for the Warsaw Pact.[8] In other words, the treaties should provide more than just bilateral support for the GDR.

During his talks with Ulbricht and Gomułka, Brezhnev never took a stance on diplomatic relations between the socialist states and Bonn. This most likely reflected differences of opinion within the Soviet leadership.[9] At the time, Moscow was more concerned about its relations with China. Since the launching of the Cultural Revolution in August 1966, the Chinese Communist Party (CCP) had escalated its propaganda attacks against Moscow. Mobs were blocking the streets outside the Soviet embassy in Beijing. Moscow's preoccupation with China, as opposed to the FRG, was reflected in Brezhnev's remarks to Ulbricht. He admonished the East German leader to exercise a "maximum of comraderie and patience" in dealing with the other socialist states, especially Romania. If the GDR sent a letter to the Romanians, it should be written in a "comradely tone." The Warsaw Pact meeting in June, he said, had "had its effect" upon the Romanians. At the meeting, despite their balancing act between Moscow and Beijing, the Romanians had approved a joint declaration by the Warsaw Pact on Vietnam—a sore point in Sino-Soviet relations.[10]

Moscow's failure to take a stance on diplomatic relations led the other socialist states to explore a rapprochement with Bonn; Warsaw and East Berlin grew increasingly isolated. By December 1966, Bulgaria, Hungary, and Czechoslovakia had joined Romania in considering diplomatic relations.[11] During that month, at a conference of foreign relations institutes in Warsaw, an argument broke out among the delegations from the various

---

8. "Wizyta polskiej delegacji partyjno-rządowej w ZSRR, 10–15 października 1966 r.," AAN KC PZPR, p. 114, t. 131.

9. Sodaro, *Moscow, Germany, and the West*, 88–90.

10. "AUFZEICHNUNG ÜBER DAS GESPRÄCH ZWISCHEN GENOSSEN WALTER ULBRICHT UND L.I. BRESHNEW . . . "; *China and the Soviet Union, 1949–84*, Keesing's International Studies, compiled by Peter Jones and Sian Kevill (London, 1985), 73.

11. Both Budapest and Prague had expressed their willingness to establish diplomatic relations with Bonn through secret contacts with the West German SPD. See

Warsaw Pact states over how to apply the Bucharest Declaration to the new situation. The Poles and East Germans argued that until Bonn recognized the status quo in Europe, there could be no talk of diplomatic relations. The Czechoslovak delegation, which favored an improvement in economic and cultural relations with Bonn, disagreed. Its chairman declared: "[T]he demand for a normalization of relations between West Germany and the GDR could be viewed as a Hallstein-Doctrine-in-reverse, and would be unacceptable to the FRG." Although the other delegations were more reticent on the issue of diplomatic relations, they were more optimistic than the Poles or East Germans about the upcoming formation of a grand coalition in Bonn. The leader of the Soviet delegation, for one, believed that the participation of the West German Social Democrats (SPD) in the coalition government would have a moderating effect upon Bonn's foreign policy. The Poles and East Germans disagreed. If the new government in Bonn employed more flexible methods, the Polish delegation declared, these would only be "salami tactics" aimed at "undermining the unity of the socialist states, isolating the GDR, and better preparing the ground for [Bonn's] aggressive aims."[12]

Indeed, the new West German chancellor, Kurt Georg Kiesinger, had little to offer either the Polish or East German communists in his inaugural address on December 13, 1966. In the speech, he declared his government's willingness to improve relations with Eastern Europe, up to and including diplomatic relations. At the same time, however, he renewed Bonn's legal stances on sole representation, West Berlin, and the Polish-German border.[13] On December 15, Ulbricht publicly dismissed Kiesinger's program as a mere continuation of Bonn's "revisionist" policies. In effect, he publicly warned the other socialist states not to normalize relations with Bonn until

---

Hans-Jürgen Wischnewski to Willy Brandt, Fritz Erler, Herbert Wehner, Helmut Schmidt, and Egon Bahr, "Aktennotiz," 4 November 1966. Archiv der sozialen Demokratie der Friedrich-Ebert-Stiftung (AdSD), Bestand SPD-Bundestagsfraktion, 5. WP, Büro Herbert Wehner, Bd. 1930; Erhard Eppler, "Aktennotiz für den Bundesaussenminister über ein Gespräch mit dem Leiter der Ungarischen Nachrichtenagentur MTI Pecsi Ferenc in Anwesenheit des Bonner Korrespondenten Denes Polgar," 9 December 1966, in ibid., Bd. 1922.

12. "Bericht über die wissenschaftliche Konferenz zu Fragen der eur'n Sicherheit vom 7.–10.12.1966 in Warschau," 12 December 1966. SAPMO BA, NL 182/1301, pp. 179–87; cf., "Informacja o międzynarodowej konferencji naukowej na temat 'Bezpieczeństwo europejskie i współczesne koncepcje Zachodu' /Warszawa, 8–10 grudnia 1966r./", [n.d.], AAN, KC PZPR, p. 125, t.87.

13. See the excerpts from Kiesinger's speech in *DzDP* V/1: 56–62. Although Kiesinger expressed his understanding for Poland's desire "to live in a state with secure borders," he also reiterated Bonn's stance on the Polish-German border: " . . . [T]he borders of a reunified Germany can only be fixed in a freely-reached agreement with an all-German government."

it had done so with the GDR. For Prague's benefit, Ulbricht expounded at some length upon Kiesinger's failure to declare the Munich Agreement invalid *ex tunc*.[14]

Warsaw, for its part, avoided making public demands upon its allies. In keeping with Moscow's wait-and-see attitude, it initially held off on criticizing the Kiesinger government.[15] In order to avoid isolation alongside the GDR, it continued to stall on a friendship treaty with East Berlin.[16] At the same time, Gomułka pressured the Soviets to call a meeting of the Warsaw Pact foreign ministers. On December 28, he told Yuri Andropov and Boris Ponomarev of the Soviet Central Committee: "We should work out a common line for dealing with the Kiesinger government. No one should act according to his own whims. The Warsaw Pact does, after all, obligate us to something." Andropov reassured Gomułka that Moscow was considering such a meeting.[17] Thus reassured, Warsaw renewed its attacks against Bonn. On January 11, 1967, the Polish foreign minister, Adam Rapacki, finally received his East German counterpart, Otto Winzer, in Warsaw to discuss a draft friendship treaty. During the talks, Rapacki made it clear that a Polish-East German treaty depended upon Prague's willingness to conclude similar agreements with both Warsaw and East Berlin.[18] This stipulation was of great importance. At the time of the Polish-East German talks, a delegation from the West German Foreign Office was in Prague to discuss diplomatic relations.

---

14. "Rede des Staatratsvorsitzenden Ulbricht auf der 14. Tagung des ZK der SED," 15 December 1966. *DzDP* V/1: 114–24.

15. On Moscow's attitude, see J. F. Brown, "Eastern Europe and the Kiesinger Offensive," *Radio Free Europe Research*, 4 February 1967, in Radio Free Europe, *Background Reports: Foreign Relations Series—East-West Relations* (Radio Free Europe, 1982), fiche 24.

16. Ulbricht had proposed a Polish-East German friendship treaty to Gomułka in a letter dated October 11, 1966. Over a month later, Gomułka expressed his acceptance of the offer in a November 19 letter to Ulbricht. He noted with approval East Berlin's plans to sign a similar treaty with Prague. By the beginning of December, however, the East Germans had concluded that Poland was stalling on the matter. Letter, Ulbricht to Gomułka, 11 October 1966; Letter Gomułka to Ulbricht, 19 November 1966; Letter Winzer to Ulbricht, Stoph, Honecker and Axen, 5 December 1966, and attachment, "Abschrift: Telegramm Nr. 133/66 v. 2.12.1966 vom Genossen Mewis, Warschau"; Mewis, Warsaw, "Vermerk über ein Gespräch mit Genossen Kliczko [sic]," 5 December 1966, SAPMO BA, J IV 2/202–371.

17. "Protokó_ ze spotkania I sekretarza KC PZPR Władysława Gomułki z sekretarzami KC KPZR—Jurijem Andropowem i Borisem Ponomariewem /28 grudnia 1966r./," n.d. AAN, KC PZPR, sygn. 2641, 644–58.

18. "Protokoll der Ausführungen des Genossen Rapacki am 11.1.1967," n.d. SAPMO BA, J IV 2/202–371; Kohrt, Staatssekretär und Erster Stellvertreter des Ministers für Auswärtige Angelegenheiten, to Ulbricht, Stoph, Honecker and Axen, 12 January 1967, ibid.

It was January 13, 1967, before Moscow finally took a stance on the Kiesinger government. It only contributed, however, to the existing confusion within the Soviet bloc. In a speech at Gorky, Brezhnev combined harsh words for the FRG and declarations of support for the GDR with veiled encouragement for a change in policy in Bonn. "We shall support everything sensible and useful for peace in Europe," he declared, "including appropriate steps by the FRG, should such steps be taken." Although he declared "unconditional recognition" of the GDR a "basic precondition" for a "true normalization" in Europe, he did not make it a precondition for diplomatic relations with Bonn. He failed even to mention the issue of Poland's western border.[19]

In the week following Brezhnev's speech, it became obvious that Moscow intended to sneak an initiative past Poland and the GDR permitting the other socialist states to establish diplomatic relations with Bonn. During talks with Ulbricht and the East German leadership on January 17, Soviet Deputy Foreign Minister Vladimir Semenov discussed a memo that Moscow was planning to send to the other socialist states. Although the memo, like Brezhnev's speech, harshly criticized Bonn, it also intimated for the first time that Moscow would permit individual socialist states to establish diplomatic relations. The Soviets were working from the assumption, Semenov explained, that this would lead to a "further breakdown in the Hallstein Doctrine." To assure that this would be the case, Moscow would ask the other socialist states to adopt the same stance that it had in establishing relations with Bonn in 1955—namely, to declare the existence of two German states, stress the final character of the borders in Europe, and underline that the "FRG's jurisdiction applied exclusively to its own territory."[20]

Ulbricht expressed strong misgivings about the Soviet memo. He doubted that the other socialist states, especially Romania, would follow Moscow's wishes. More importantly, the Bucharest Declaration, he argued, not the "Moscow 1955 model," marked the proper point of departure for the socialist states. "No formulations may be used or tolerated," he declared, "like it happened with Adenauer in 1955, when he wrote about reunification and the Paris Treaties." He joined Gomułka in calling for a foreign ministers' meeting. By the end of the talks, however, he made the mistake of suggesting that the Soviets could discuss their memorandum with the other socialist states.[21]

---

19. See the excerpts from Brezhnev's speech in *DzDP*, V/1: 305–7.
20. "Vermerk über die Unterredung zwischen Genossen Walter Ulbricht und Genossen W.S. Semjonow, Stellvertreter des Ministers für Auswärtige Angelegenheiten der UdSSR (17.1.67)," n.d. SAPMO BA, J IV 2/201–1094.
21. Ibid.

Brezhnev exploited Ulbricht's concession the following day, January 18, during secret talks with Gomułka and the Polish leadership in eastern Poland. Moscow, he informed Gomułka, was planning to send a letter to the "fraternal parties" about the Kiesinger government and its policies. Gomułka asked if the Soviets thus considered a foreign ministers' meeting unnecessary. "One does not preclude the other," Brezhnev replied. It would be difficult, however, for Moscow to tell the other socialist states not to establish diplomatic relations with Bonn when Moscow had already done so. The best the Soviets could do, he said, was to ask that they adopt the same stance that Moscow had in 1955. At this point, Brezhnev declared: "We consulted with Comrade Ulbricht about the letter . . . He fully agrees with the stance contained in it, 100%. He told this to Semenov . . . Soon, our ambassadors will be going to work. We did not want to begin this action, however, before we discussed the matter with you." It later came out during the meeting that the Soviets had in fact already distributed the memorandum to their ambassadors in the other East European states.[22]

After the Soviets read their memorandum, Gomułka launched into a bitter tirade against disunity within the Warsaw Pact and Moscow's failure to counter it. The situation, he said, was beginning to remind him of what Khrushchev had accused Beria of doing in 1953—i.e., selling out the GDR. He dismissed the "Moscow 1955 model" and repeated Warsaw's three conditions for diplomatic relations with Bonn—including de facto, not de jure, recognition of the GDR. He was particularly unnerved that Moscow had put in writing that it was not opposed to diplomatic relations with Bonn. When Brezhnev protested that there was nothing else that Moscow could do, Gomułka accused the Soviets of secretly favoring the movement within the alliance towards diplomatic relations with Bonn.[23] If the Soviets could not block the establishment of diplomatic relations themselves—and indeed wanted to block it, Gomułka implied—then a Warsaw Pact meeting was all the more necessary.[24] At one point, he snapped: "If Romania establishes diplomatic relations with Bonn without any preconditions, I would tell them: Go to hell."[25]

If Gomułka was playing the role of tutor, by the end of the meeting, Brezhnev was acting like his chastened pupil. Brezhnev blamed the other socialist states for the movement towards normalization with Bonn; Andrei

22. "Protokók ze spotkania przywódców Polskiej Zjednoczonej Partii Robotniczej i Komunistycznej Partii Związku Radzieckiego /18 stycznia 1967 roku—Łańsk/," n.d. AAN, KC PZPR, sygn. 2642, p. 11.

23. "We received news from Cologne," Gomułka said, "about a statement by Tsarapkin . . . that the USSR has approved the establishment of diplomatic relations by other countries." Ibid.

24. Ibid.

25. Ibid.

Gromyko and his other advisors were responsible for the offending passage in the Soviet letter. He promised to phone Moscow the same day and have the Politburo vote on a foreign ministers' meeting. After the vote, Gromyko would immediately contact the other Warsaw Pact first secretaries to inform them about the meeting, which would be held in a matter of days, preferably in East Berlin. The Soviet leader's promise seemed to placate Gomułka, at least for the time being.[26]

It was January 24, 1967, almost a week later, before Moscow announced the foreign ministers' meeting, to be held from February 6–8 in East Berlin. By that time, the East Germans had already sprung into action. On January 18, a day after Semenov's departure, Ulbricht had received an analysis of the "Moscow 1955 model" from the International Division of the SED Central Committee. The documents exchanged between Bonn and Moscow in 1955, it reported, had all contained wording suggesting that problems relating to Germany as a whole could be resolved without the GDR's participation. "If today, in 1967, the establishment of diplomatic relations between a socialist state and the West German Federal Republic ensued in such a form and with similar formulations," the analysis concluded, "then it would be . . . a serious setback that we could not bear."[27] On January 24, the day of Moscow's announcement, the SED Politburo ordered the GDR foreign ministry to distribute its own memorandum on relations with Bonn to the socialist states. The final memorandum, dated January 25, asked the GDR's allies not to enter into negotiations with Bonn until the Warsaw Pact had established a common stance on diplomatic relations. If the GDR's allies felt that they had to establish diplomatic relations, it asked that they take three steps: first, inform the states of the "anti-Hitler coalition" that their act should contribute to a normalization of relations between both German states; second, publicly reaffirm their support for the demands addressed to Bonn in the Bucharest Declaration; and third, notify neutral and nonsocialist countries that they recognized the existence of two German states.[28]

---

26. Ibid.

27. Gerhard Kegel, ZK SED, to Ulbricht, "'Moskauer Modell 1955' bei evt. Aufnahme diplomatischer Beziehungen zwischen der UdSSR und Westdeutschland," 18 January 1967. SAPMO BA, J IV 2/202–79. The memo's title suggests where the GDR's greatest fears lay—with the USSR.

28. On the day of the Soviet memorandum, the SED Politburo ordered the GDR foreign ministry to revise a memorandum that it had prepared for distribution to the other socialist states as an aide-mémoire. "Protokoll Nr. 3/67 der Sitzung des Politbüros des Zentralkomitees am 24. Januar 1967," SAPMO BA, J IV 2/2–1.095, pp. 1–7; and attachment, "Erwägungen des Ministeriums für Auswärtige Angelegenheiten der DDR zur Frage der diplomatischer Beziehungen sozialistischer Staaten mit der westdeutschen Bundesrepublik," 24 January 1967, in ibid., pp. 77–80. For the final version of the aide-mémoire, see the "Denkschrift" dated 25 January

Both the GDR's unilateral action and Moscow's continued foot-dragging on a foreign ministers' meeting clearly upset Warsaw. The Poles made their displeasure known. At a press conference in Paris on January 27, 1967, Rapacki listed only two factors as having an influence upon Polish-West German relations: Bonn's stance on nuclear weapons and its attitude towards the existing borders in Europe, including the Oder-Neisse Line. He made only passing reference to the GDR.[29] Having issued their warning, the Poles returned to their original three conditions within a matter of days.[30]

It was Romania, in the end, which forced Moscow to take a clear stance on relations with Bonn. On January 31, 1967, Bucharest established diplomatic relations. Ignoring both the "Moscow 1955 model" and the GDR's memorandum, the Romanians allowed the West Germans to repeat their claims to sole representation and to the borders of 1937. On February 3, *Neues Deutschland* charged the Romanians with violating the Bucharest Declaration.[31] On February 4, Bucharest responded by accusing the GDR of "interven[ing] in the internal affairs of another socialist state."[32] After the exchange, Romania refused to attend the Warsaw Pact foreign ministers' meeting unless it was postponed and held somewhere other than East Berlin. To preserve a facade of unity, Brezhnev rescheduled the gathering for February 8–10 in Warsaw.[33] Privately, the Soviets expressed their dis-

---

(note 28 continued) 1967, in SAPMO BA, J IV 2/202–79. Winzer's subsequent speech in Warsaw confirmed that the aide-mémoire had been distributed to the GDR's allies. See "Rede des Ministers für Auswärtige Angelegenheiten der DDR, Genossen Otto Winzer," p. 15, in "Stenographische Niederschrift der Konferenz der Außenminister der Warschauer Vertragsstaaten in Warschau," 8–10 February 1967. SAPMO BA, J IV 2/202–260.

29. According to the Polish Press Agency (*Polska Agencja Prasowa, PAP*) as cited in *DzDP* V/1: 398–400.

30. On January 29, *Życie Warszawy* declared that Bonn's recognition of the Oder-Neisse Line by itself, while of value in 1955, would be worthless in 1967 without Bonn's recognition of the GDR. See A. Ross Johnson, "Survey of Poland's Relations with West Germany, 1956–1967," 26 February 1968, in Radio Free Europe, *Background Reports: Foreign Relations Series, East-West Relations* (Radio Free Europe, 1982), fiche #29, 22. Also see the comments of Edward Ochab, the head of Poland's State Council, on January 31, 1967, in *DzDP* V/1: 436–38.

31. "Europäische Sicherheit erfordert Verzicht auf Revanchepolitik," *ND* (3 February 1967), as cited in *DzDP* V/1: 470–72.

32. As cited in ibid., 475–9.

33. When Brezhnev informed Ulbricht of Romania's demands, the Soviet leader suggested that the meeting be moved to Budapest. Ulbricht replied that Budapest would be "inappropriate." He recommended that the meeting be held either in Moscow or in Warsaw. Brezhnev decided on Warsaw. "Telefonat des Genossen Breshnew mit Genossen Ulbricht am 4. Februar 1967, 10 Uhr," n.d. SAPMO BA, J IV 2/2–1097, pp. 5–6.

pleasure with the SED's decision to attack Romania publicly in the pages of *Neues Deutschland*.[34]

If the desire for unity led the Soviets, on the one hand, to adopt a conciliatory stance towards Bucharest, it also compelled them, on the other, to reimpose bloc discipline upon the remaining socialist states. On February 6, 1967, Brezhnev and Andropov paid a "friendship visit" to Prague. Brezhnev informed the Czechoslovak leadership that Moscow expected all the socialist states to follow a common line on relations with Bonn. Since the conflict with Beijing and support for Vietnam demanded Moscow's full attention, Brezhnev asked that Czechoslovakia support Moscow's stance at the upcoming foreign ministers' meeting. The Czechoslovaks reluctantly consented.[35]

The East Germans and Poles made their own preparations for the meeting in Warsaw. On February 4, the GDR Ministry of Foreign Affairs finished a proposal for an "informal, oral agreement" by the Warsaw Pact foreign ministers. According to the proposal, if the GDR's allies established relations with Bonn, they would promise to reject Bonn's claims to sole representation or any territorial changes; reaffirm that the FRG's rule applied only to its own territory; and declare that West Berlin was an independent political entity.[36] Bucharest had failed to take any of these steps. On February 7, the Politburo ordered the GDR foreign ministry to distribute an aide-mémoire to the Warsaw Pact first secretaries, repeating the GDR's stance from January 25. Apparently, the original memorandum, addressed to the foreign ministries, had not been enough.[37]

Warsaw tried to use the meeting's change in venue to play the role of honest broker.[38] Although Warsaw opposed Romania's decision to establish

---

34. Hegen, Staatssekretär und Erster Stellvertreter des Ministers für Auswärtige Angelegenheiten, to Ulbricht, Honecker and Axen, 10 February 1967. SAPMO BA, NL 182/1232.

35. Hegen to Ulbricht, Honecker and Axen, 10 February 1967. By the beginning of February, the increasingly violent demonstrations outside the Soviet embassy in Beijing had compelled Moscow to evacuate the families of embassy staff. *China and the Soviet Union, 1949–84*, 77–9.

36. MfAA, "Entwurf: Vorschlag für eine formlose mündliche Übereinkunft der Außenminister der Staaten des Warschauer Vertrages," 4 February 1967. SAPMO BA, J IV 2/201–1129.

37. "Protokoll Nr. 6/67 der Sitzung des Politbüros des Zentralkomitees am 7.2.1967," SAPMO BA, J IV 2/2–1098, p. 2; "Stellungnahme des Politbüros des Zentralkomitees der SED zur Frage der Aufnahme diplomatischer Beziehungen zwischen sozialistischen Ländern und der westdeutschen Bundesrepublik (Beschluß des Politbüros des ZK der SED vom 7. Februar 1967)," 7 February 1967, SAPMO BA, J IV 2/202–79.

38. See A. Korab, "Unbehagen über Bonns Ostpolitik," *Tagesspiegel* (8 February 1967), as reprinted in *DzDP* V/1: 486–8.

diplomatic relations, it refrained from lodging any official complaints in Bucharest. It wanted to assure Romania's attendance at the Warsaw meeting. Rapacki invited Gromyko, East German Foreign Minister Otto Winzer, and Czechoslovak Foreign Minister Václav David to Warsaw a day early, February 7, to discuss strategy for the upcoming meeting.[39] At a dinner hosted by the Polish premier, the four ministers tried to work out a common stance. Despite their apparent failure, Rapacki, Gromyko, and Winzer would continue to caucus throughout the foreign ministers' meeting, sometimes joined by Foreign Minister David. Earlier in the day, Gromyko had clearly stated Moscow's stance during talks with Winzer: For the time being, it would be "inappropriate" for any of the remaining socialist states to establish diplomatic relations with Bonn. He also "proposed" that the GDR withdraw its latest aide-mémoire. Since Gromyko was adopting a harder line than the GDR had expected, Winzer backed the Soviets' stance.[40]

Speeches filled the first day of the foreign ministers' meeting, February 8. In a display of national sovereignty, Bucharest sent only its deputy foreign minister. He began the meeting by opposing the publication of a press release.[41] In the first speech of the day, Rapacki accused Bonn of trying to isolate the GDR and underlined the importance of the proposed triangle of friendship treaties.[42] David struggled in his speech to minimize the importance of Prague's recent contacts with Bonn. In the future, he said, Prague would remind Bonn that it had to meet certain preconditions for diplomatic relations; he recited the demands contained in the Bucharest Declaration.[43] David's speech closely paralleled Gromyko's, presented the following day.[44]

Winzer's speech aroused a great deal of interest. He openly criticized the "Moscow 1955 model"—which he attributed to West Germany!—and indirectly accused the Soviets of violating the GDR's sovereignty. The 1955 model, he argued, ignored the fact that Moscow had recognized the GDR's

---

39. Oskar Fischer, Stellvertreter des Ministers für Auswärtige Angelegenheiten, "Vermerk über eine Unterredung zwischen Genossen Oskar Fischer und dem Botschafter der VR Polen, Genossen F. Baranowski, am 4.2.1967," 5 February 1967. SAPMO BA, J IV 2/202–261.

40. Stellv. Abteilungsleiter, Abt. Internationale Verbindungen [KC SED], "Vermerk," 7 February 1967. SAPMO BA, J IV 2/201–1129.

41. P. Markowski, MfAA, to Ulbricht, 8 February 1967. SAPMO BA, J IV 2/202–261.

42. See the German translation of Rapacki's speech in "Stenografische Niederschrift der Konferenz der Außenminister der Warschauer Vertragsstaaten in Warschau," 8–10 February 1967. SAPMO BA, J IV 2/202–260.

43. See David's speech, esp. pp. 13–16, in ibid.

44. In his speech, Gromyko reaffirmed Moscow's support for the catalog of demands addressed to Bonn in the Bucharest Declaration. "Rede des Ministers für Auswärtige Angelegenheiten der UdSSR am 9. Februar 1967," p. 3, in ibid.

sovereignty in 1955 and had reaffirmed it in its 1964 friendship treaty with East Berlin. Echoing Gromyko's private remarks, he declared: "The GDR is of the opinion that the establishment of diplomatic relations . . . [with] the West German Federal Republic is not appropriate at present."[45] Although the foreign ministers of both Hungary and Bulgaria—according to the East German record—gave rather weak speeches, Romania's isolation within the Warsaw Pact seemed complete.[46]

On the evening of February 8, the troika of Rapacki, Gromyko, and Winzer finished work on an agreement. It listed the conditions that Bonn would have to meet before the remaining socialist states would establish diplomatic relations: "recognition of the existing borders, including the Oder-Neisse border and the border between the Federal Republic and the GDR"; recognition of the invalidity of the Munich Agreement, *ex tunc*; "recognition of the fact that two German states exist; resignation from the presumption to sole representation, the attempt to gain access to nuclear weapons in any form, and the illegal claim to West Berlin."[47] The troika met privately with individual colleagues to gather signatures.

The highlight of the three-day meeting was Gomułka's speech to the foreign ministers on February 9. He implicitly criticized Romania for establishing relations with Bonn and then declared point-blank: "[A]ll this eagerness to establish diplomatic relations with Bonn disturbs us." The Western press, he said, was reporting that the socialist states were "standing in line to establish diplomatic relations." Although Gomułka spent most of his speech emphasizing the importance of the GDR's recognition (de facto) for the security of the entire socialist bloc, he embedded this demand in Warsaw's longstanding package of three conditions. Lest Gomułka's speech be misunderstood, Gromyko declared in the name of the Soviet Central Committee that it also represented Moscow's position. Winzer made a similar proclamation; the East German delegation, he added, was "deeply moved" by Gomułka's kind words for the GDR. The Romanian delegation, for its part, remained unimpressed.[48]

By February 10, 1967, Gromyko, Rapacki, and Winzer gained the approval of all the delegations—except the Romanians, whom they did not

---

45. "Rede des Ministers für Auswärtige Angelegenheiten der DDR, Genossen Otto Winzer," pp. 5, 17, 20–21, in ibid.

46. Markowski to Ulbricht, 8 February 1967. SAPMO BA, J IV 2/202–261.

47. "PROTOKOLLNIEDERSCHRIFT EINER VEREINBARUNG," attached to ibid. The Polish-language version can be found in AAN, KC PZPR, sygn. 2949, pp. 28–9.

48. Stanisław Trepczyński, "Protokół ze spotkania I sekretarza KC PZPR Władysława Gomułki z uczestnikami narady Ministrów Spraw Zagranicznych państw-członków Układu Warszawskiego /Warszawa, 9 lutego 1967 r./," AAN, KC PZPR, p. 129, t. 103.

ask—for their draft agreement. Gromyko did not even bother to speak with the Hungarian foreign minister, Janos Peter. The Soviet ambassador to Budapest met with the head of the International Division of the Hungarian Central Committee. Acting on orders from Gromyko, he demanded that the Hungarian leadership simply telephone Peter and order him to sign the agreement, sight unseen. Hungarian First Secretary Janos Kádár reluctantly complied with Gromyko's request.[49] The last holdout was David. He signed the agreement on February 10 after gaining a few cosmetic changes. Gromyko and Rapacki convinced Winzer to accept the changes for the sake of unanimity.[50] The final agreement remained a secret, even to the Romanians at the conference; this explains in part the subsequent speculation about an "Ulbricht Doctrine." The final communiqué from the conference, approved by the Romanian delegation, merely stated that a "friendly exchange of opinions over international questions had taken place."[51]

In the end, Moscow, Warsaw, and East Berlin could declare the foreign ministers' meeting a success. For the time being, they had halted Bonn's diplomatic offensive to the east and preserved unity within the Warsaw Pact. For Warsaw and East Berlin, the threat of isolation had passed—at least temporarily. The GDR had gained acceptance for its demands that none of the remaining socialist states establish diplomatic relations with Bonn until it recognized the GDR and renounced its claim to West Berlin. Warsaw had gained acceptance for its three preconditions: Bonn's de facto recognition of the GDR, renunciation of access to nuclear weapons, and recognition of the existing borders in Europe. The agreement specified the Oder-Neisse Line as one of the borders to be recognized. The Soviets, for their part, had restored unity within the bloc without ostracizing the Romanians. They succeeded in preventing a further breach in bloc discipline at a time when Sino-Soviet tensions were at a peak.

An examination of the origins, course, and results of the Warsaw meeting demonstrate that its outcome was not an "Ulbricht Doctrine". It was Gomułka who successfully pushed the Soviets to call the meeting; he gained acceptance of Warsaw's three conditions, plus a few more. He prevented the Soviet Union and the GDR from deciding on their own what preconditions—if any—to place upon diplomatic relations with Bonn. By pressur-

---

49. See Kádár's account of the matter in "Protokół z nieoficjalnej wizyty tow.W. Gomułki i tow. J. Cyrankiewicza na Węgrzech/Budapeszt 8–9 marca 1967 r./," n.d. AAN, KC PZPR, sygn. 2600, pp. 245–47.

50. Minister Winzer, Warsaw, to Ulbricht, Honecker, Alfred Neumann, and Staatssekretär Hegen, "Blitz-Telegramm," 10 February 1967. SAPMO BA, J IV 2/201–1129, m.n.p.; cf. "PROTOKOLLNIEDERSCHRIFT EINER VEREINBARGUNG."

ing the Soviets, he had derailed Moscow's letter and contributed indirectly to the withdrawal of the GDR's aide-mémoire. The meeting's outcome was neither an Ulbricht nor a "Gomułka Doctrine," but a compromise.[52] It remained to be seen how the individual socialist states would put this compromise into practice.

51. "Kommuniqué über die Tagung der Außenminister der Teilnehmerstaaten des Warschauer Vertrages in Warschau," 10 February 1967. *DzDP*, V. Reihe, Bd. 1, 517–18.

52. Cf. Korab, "Unbehagen über Bonns Ostpolitik," *DzDP* V/1: 486–8.

Writings of Piotr S. Wandycz

Books

Czechoslovak Polish Confederation and the Great Powers 1940–1943 (Bloomington, IN, 1956 [reprinted 1980]), 152 pp.

France and Her Eastern Allies 1919–1925: French-Czechoslovak-Polish Relations from the Paris Peace Conference to Locarno (Minneapolis, MN, 1962 [reprinted 1974]), 454 pp.
Awarded George Louis Beer Prize of the American Historical Association, 1962.

Zjednoczona Europa: teoria i praktyka (in collaboration with Ludwik Frendl) (London, 1965), 305 pp.

Soviet-Polish Relations 1917–1921 (Cambridge, MA, 1969), 403 pp.

The Lands of Partitioned Poland 1795–1918 (Seattle, WA, 1974, [reprinted, 1984]), 432 pp.

The United States and Poland (Cambridge, MA, 1980), 465 pp.

August Zaleski, minister spraw zagranicznych RP 1926–1932 w świetle wspomnień i dokumentów (Paris, 1980), 138 pp.

Polska a zagranica (Paris, 1986), 290 pp.

Stracone szanse: stosunki polsko-amerykańskie 1939–1987 (Warsaw, 1987), 163 pp.

The Twilight of French Eastern Alliances 1926–1936: French-Czechoslovak-Polish Relations from Locarno to the Remilitarization of the Rhineland (Princeton, NJ, 1988), 537 pp.
Awarded George Louis Beer Prize of the American Historical Association, and Wayne Vucinich Prize of the American Association for the Advancement of Slavic Studies, 1989.

Z Dziejów dyplomacji (London, 1988 [reprinted, 1989]), 154 pp..

Polish Diplomacy 1914–1945: Aims and Achievements (London, 1988), 139 pp.

The Price of Freedom: A History of East Central Europe from the Middle Ages to the Present (London, New York, 1992); [2nd revised edition, 2001], 330 pp.
A History Book Club selection.

Die Freiheit und ihr Preis: IVM-Vorlegungen zur modernen Geschichte Zentraleuropas (Vienna, 1993), 127 pp.

Pod zaborami, 1795–1918: Ziemie Rzeczypospolitej w latach 1795–1918 (Warsaw, 1994), 551 pp.
The Polish version of *The Lands of Partitioned Poland 1795–1918*.

Cena wolności: Historia Europy środkowo-Wschodniej od sredniowiecza do współczesności (Kraków, 1995), 488 pp.

The Polish version of *The Price of Freedom.*
Laisves kaina Vidurio Rytu: istorija nuo viduramz'iu iki dabarties (Vilnius, 1997), 348 pp.
The Lithuanian version of *The Price of Freedom.*
Str'ednâ Evropa v de'jinach od str'edove'ku do souc'asnosti: Cena svobody (Prague, 1998), pp. 301.
The Czech version of *The Price of Freedom.*
Tsenata na svobodata. Istoriia na Iztochna Tsentralna Evropa ot srednovekovieto do dnes (Sofia, 1999), pp. 396.
The Bulgarian version of *The Price of Freedom.*
Prezzo dela Liberta: Storia dell'Europa centro-orientale dal medioevo a oggi (Bologna, 2001), pp. 454.
Italian version of *The Price of Freedom.*
Z Piłsudskim i Sikorskim: August Zaleski Minister Spraw Zagranicznych 1926–32, i 1939–41 (Warsaw, 1999), pp. 264.
Historia Europy Srodkowo-wschodniej. Coauthor. 2 vols. (Lublin, 2000), I, 416–531, II, 139–186, 203–236.
Pax Europaea 1915–1914 (Wrocław, 2002). Forthcoming.

Articles

"A Historical Example of a Regional Federation: The Polish-Lithuanian Union," *Cahiers de Bruges*, II (1951): 33–38.
"The Polish Precursors of Federalism," *Journal of Central European Affairs*, XII (1952–53): 346–355.
"Beneš-Sikorski Agreement," *Central European Federalist*, I (1953): 3–9.
"The Theory of International Relations," *Review of Politics*, XVII (1955): 189–205.
"Wilson, Czechoslovaks and Poles in Paris, 1919," *Central European Federalist*, IV (1956): 177–184.
"The Soviet System of Alliances in East Central Europe," *Journal of Central European Affairs*, XVI (1956–57): 177–184.
"Regionalism and European Integration," *World Affairs Quarterly*, XXVIII (1957): 229–259.
"The Treatment of East Central Europe in History Textbooks," *American Slavic and East European Review*, XVI (1957): 513–523.
"Czechoslovak-Polish Rapprochement of 1921," *Central European Federalist*, VI (1958): 6–10.
"American Policy toward East Central Europe: The Polish Case 1956–58," *Indiana Academy of Social Science Proceedings*, III (1958): 17–23.
"U źródeł Paktu Skirmunt-Beneš," *Kultura*, 11/133 (1958): 119–126.
"Problematyka historii najnowszej," *Teki Historyczne*, IX (1958): 88–95.
"Sojusz polsko-francuski z 1921," *Kultura*, 11/145 (1959): 108–122.

"General Weygand and the Battle of Warsaw of 1920," *Journal of Central European Affairs*, XIX (1959–60): 357–365.

"Regionalism and World Federalism," *Current History* (August, 1960): 87–91.

"Czechoslovakia and Poland, 1918–1939: Bibliographical Indications," *Central European Federalist*, X (1962): 26–29.

"Henrys i Niessel, dwaj pierwsi szefowie francuskiej misji wojskowej w Polsce," *Bellona*, I/II (1962): 3–19.

"Studium stosunków polsko-sowieckich," *Kultura*, 6/176 (1962): 78–87.

"Trzy dokumenty: przyczynek do zagadnienia wojny prewencyjnej," *Zeszyty Historyczne*, Vol. 3 (1963): 7–14 .

"French Diplomats in Poland 1919–1926," *Journal of Central European Affairs*, XXIII (1963–64): 440–450.

"Germany, Poland, and the USSR before Hitler's Advent to Power," *Polish Review*, IX (1964): 94–101.

"Nieznane listy Petlury do Piłsudskiego," *Zeszyty Historyczne*, Vol. 8 (1965): 181–186.

"Secret Soviet-Polish Talks in 1919," *Slavic Review*, XXIV (1965): 425–449.

"The Poles in the Habsburg Monarchy," *Austrian History Yearbook*, III, pt. 2 (1967): 262–286.

"Z zagadnień wspołpracy polsko-ukraińskiej w latach 1919–1920," *Zeszyty Historyczne*, 12 (1967): 2–24.

"Attempts at Czechoslovak-Polish Cooperation: Achievements and Failures," in Miloslav Rechcigl, Jr., ed., *Czechoslovakia Past and Present* (The Hague, 1968), 673–681

"Legion czechosłowacki w Polsce w r.1939," *Kultura*, 10/253 (1968): 75–86.

"Poland: History," in Paul L. Horecky, ed., *East Central Europe: A Guide to Basic Publications* (Chicago, 1969), 647–662.

"Odezwa Rządu Tymczasowego z marca 1917 r. a interwencja angielska" *Zeszyty Historyczne*, 15 (1969): 230–235.

"The Treaty of Riga: Its Significance for Inter-War Polish Foreign Policy," *Polish Review*, XIV (1969): 31–36.

"Dwie próby stworzenia związków regionalnych w Europie wschodniej," *Tematy*, 31–32 (1969): 391–409.

"Recent Traditions of the Quest for Unity: Attempted Polish-Czechoslovak and Yugoslav-Bulgarian Confederations 1940–1948," in Jerzy Łukaszewski, ed., *The People's Democracies After Prague* (Bruges, 1970), 35–93.

Polish Federalism 1919–20 and its Historical Antecedents," *East European Quarterly*, IV (March, 1970): 25–39.

"Jeszcze o misji Jerzego Potockiego w 1933 roku," *Zeszyty Historyczne*, 18 (1970): 81–83.

"Fascism in Poland 1918–1939," in Peter F. Sugar, ed., *Native Fascism in the Successor States 1918–1945* (Santa Barbara, 1971), 92–97.

"Sprawa Józefa Becka jako attache; wojskowego w Paryżu," *Zeszyty Historyczne*, 22 (1972): 34–40.

"Poland in International Politics," *Canadian Slavonic Papers*, XIV, 3 (1972): 401–420.

"*Foreign Policy of Edvard Beneš 1918–1938*," Victor Mamatey and Radomâr Luža, eds., *A History of the Czechoslovak Republic 1918–1948* (Princeton, NJ, 1973), 216–238.

"Pierwsza Republika a Druga Rzeczpospolita" *Zeszyty Historyczne*, 28 (1974): 3–20.

"Wypowiedzi Marszałka Piłsudskiego na konferencji byłych premierów 7 marca 1934 roku" Niepodległość; , IX (1974): 345–350.

"A Study of Polish History," in Stanislaus A. Blejwas, ed., *East Central European Studies: A Handbook for Graduate Students* (New York, 1974), 9–10.

"Polish Foreign Policy: Some Observations," *Polish Review*, XX (Feb. 1975): 58–63.

"O dwóch historykach," *Zeszyty Historyczne*, 32 (1975): 61–65.

"MSZ widziane oczyma amerykańskiego dyplomaty," *Zeszyty Historyczne*, 32 (1975): 153–157.

"Partitions of Poland and the Diplomacy of the Partitioning Powers," in Victor Erlich et al., eds., *For Wiktor Weintraub: Essays in Polish Literature, Language and History, Presented on the Occasion of his 65th Birthday* (The Hague, Paris, 1975), 559–570.

"MSZ w okresie międzywojennym: ankieta ," *Zeszyty Historyczne*, 35 (1976): 3–6.

"Stany Zjednoczone a Europa środkowo-wschodnia w okresie między-wojennym 1921—1939," *Zeszyty Historyczne*, 37 (1976): 3–38.

"MSZ w okresie międzywojennym: odpowiedzi na ankietę," *Zeszyty Historyczne*, 38 (1976): 120–155.

"Czy Hołówko rozmawiał z Leninem i Trockim w 1918 r." *Zeszyty Historyczne*, 41(1977): 225–119.

"Próba nawiązania przez Marszałka Piłsudskiego kontaktu z Hitlerem jesienia 1930r.," *Niepodległość*, XI (1977): 127–138.

"The United States and Poland: An Attempt at Historical Synthesis," in Frank Mocha, ed., *Poles in America: Bicentennial Essays* (Stevens Point, WI, 1978), 387–396.

"Die Aussenpolitik von Edvard Beneš 1918–1938," in Victor Mamatey and Radomâr Luža, eds., *Geschichte der Tschechoslowakischen Republik 1918–1948* (Vienna, 1980), 232–256.

"The American Revolution and the Partitions of Poland," Jaroslav Pelenski ed., *The American and European Revolutions 1776–1840s: Sociopolitical and Ideological Ramifications* (Iowa City, IA, 1980), 95–110.

"Orientacja rosyjska w polskiej walce niepodległośociowej," *Zeszyty Historyczne*, 51 (1980): 57–65.

"Colonel Beck and the French: Roots of Animosity," *The International History Review*, III (1981): 115–127.

"The Little Entente: Sixty Years Later," *Slavonic and East European Review*, 59 (1981): 548–564.

"La Pologne face à la politique locarnienne de Briand," *Revue d'Histoire Diplomatique*, no. 2–3–4 (1981): 237–263.

"Similarities and Dissimilarities in the Political Development of Poland 1945–1948," Nikolaus Lobkowicz and Friedrich Prinz, eds., *Schicksalsjahre der Tschechoslowakei 1945–1948* (Munich & Vienna, 1981), 155–164.

"The Poles in the Habsburg Monarchy," Andrei S. Markovits and Frank E. Sysyn, eds., *Nationbuilding and the Politics of Nationalism: Essays on Austrian Galicia* (Cambridge, MA, 1982), 68–93.

"The Polish National Idea in the 19th Century," *Kosmas*, I (Summer 1982): 19–25.

"Listy Piłsudskiego do Masaryka i Focha," and "Rozmowa Marszałka Piłsudskiego z Marszałkiem Franchet d'Esperey 17 listopada 1927 roku," *Niepodległość*, XV (1982): 108–112 and 130–136.

"Ocena traktatów sojuszniczych polsko-francuskich: dokument," *Niepodległość*, XVI (1983): 61–74.

"La Crisi delle ideologie nei rapporti internationali," *Il Nuovo Aeropago*, 26 (1983): 65–75.

"Louis Barthou o swej wizycie w Polsce w kwietniu 1934 r.: dokument," *Niepodległość*, XVII (1984): 107–121.

"L'Alliance franco-tchécoslovaque de 1924: exchange de lettres Poincaré–Beneš," *Revue d'Histoire Diplomatique*, nos. 3–4 (1984): 328–333.

"Poland and Russia: The Perennial Question," *International History Review*, VII (February, 1985): 2–18.

"Poland in World History: Inspiration or Trouble Maker?" *Cross Currents: A Yearbook of Central European Culture*, (1986): 195–208.

"Poland between East and West," in Gordon Martel, ed., *The Origins of the Second World War Reconsidered: The A.J.P. Taylor Debate After Twenty-Five Years* (Boston, 1986), 187–209.

"O Juliuszu Mieroszewskim," *Zeszyty Historyczne*, 76 (1986): 223–226.

"Wizyta Aleksandra Skrzyńskiego w Stanach Zjednoczonych w 1925 r.," *Roczniki Humanistyczne*, 34, II (1986): 501–506.

"Harriman a Polska," *Zeszyty Historyczne*, 79 (1987): 88–115.

"Czechoslovak-Polish Relations: A Polish View," *Kosmas*, VI (Summer, 1987): 25–35.

Preface to Z. Musialik, *General Weygand and the Battle of Warsaw* (London, 1987), 9–12.

"La Politique étrangère d'Edvard Beneš," in Victor Mamatey and Radomâr

Luža, eds., *La République tchécoslovaque 1918–1948* (Paris, 1987), 201–223.

"Historyczne dylematy polskiej polityki zagranicznej," in Józef Jasnowski, ed., *Nowoczesna Historia Polski (Prace Kongresu Kultury Polskiej,* III, London, 1987), 11–29.

"Telegram Ambasadora Steinhardta," *Zeszyty Historyczne,* 84 (1988): 204–207.

"East Central Europe 1918: War and Peace, Czechoslovakia and Poland," in Peter Pastor, ed., *Revolutions and Interventions in Hungary and its Neighboring States, 1918–1919* (Boulder, CO, 1988), 397–408.

"Narodowa Demokracja a polityka zagraniczna II Rzeczypospolitej," *Więź,* XXXII, nos.7–8 (July-August 1989): 152–168.

"Polish Foreign Policy: An Overview," in Timothy Wiles, ed., *Poland between the Wars 1918–1939* (Bloomington, 1989), 65–73.

"Poland on the Map of Europe in 1918," *The Polish Review,* XXIV, 4 (1990): 19–25.

Also published separately in *70th Anniversary of Independent Poland* (Chicago, 1988), 4–7.

"Polska międzywojenna," in Jerzy Kłoczowski, ed., *Uniwersalizm i swoistość kultury polskiej* (2 vols., Lublin, 1990): II, 261–291.

"Historyk a tradycja: refleksje," *Fermentum massae mundi: Jackowi Wozniakowskiemu w siedemdziesiątą rocznicę urodzin* (Warsaw, 1990), 248–253.

"Wspomnienie o Henryku Wereszyckim," *Zeszyty Historyczne,* 92 (1990): 90–98.

"Poland's Place in Europe in the Concepts of Piłsudski and Dmowski," *East Europe Politics and Society,* IV, 3 (Fall, 1990): 451–468.

"I Progetti di una confederazione polacco-cecoslovacca durante la seconda guerra mondiale," *Il Nuovo Areopago,* IX, 335 (1990): 97–114.

"Próby stworzenia konfederacji polsko-czechosłowackiej podczas II wojny światowej," *Znaki Czasu,* 20 (Oct.-Dec. 1990):130–149.

"In memoriam," *Zeszyty Historyczne,* 91 (1990): 205–206.

"August Zaleski and His Times," *East European Quarterly,* XIV, 1 (January, 1991): 409–423.

"August Zaleski o polskiej polityce zagranicznej w 1941 r.: dokument," *Zeszyty Historyczne,* 98 (1991): 95–106.

"Historiographies of the Countries of Eastern Europe: Poland," *The American Historical Review,* 97 (October, 1992): 1011–1025.

"Tentatives et projets d'union regionale en Europe Centrale, XVIIIe , XIXe et XXe siècles," in Gerard Beaupretre, ed., *L'Europe Centrale, realité , mythe, enjeu XVIIIe-XXe siècles,* Cahiers de Varsovie (Warsaw, 1992) , 433–443.

"List Jana Masaryka do Stalina," *Zeszyty Historyczne,* 100 (1992): 83–87.

"Między Wschodem a Zachodem: Polska-Czecho-Słowacja-Węgry," *Obóz,* 24 (Fall 1992): 1–17.

"East European History and its Meaning: The Halecki-Bidlo-Handelsman Debate," in Pal Jonas et al., eds., *Kiraly Bela emlekkonyv* (Budapest, 1992), 308–321.

"Dmowski's Policy at the Paris Peace Conference: Success or Failure?" in Paul Latawski, ed., *The Reconstruction of Poland, 1914–23* (London, 1992), 117–132.

"Henri Rollet," *Zeszyty Historyczne*, 99 (1992): 188.

"Beneš o pakcie Ribbentrop-Mołotow," *Przegląd Wschodni*, II, 4(8) (1992–93): 891–893.

"Some Myths in Polish History," in Ferenc Glatz, ed., *Europa vonzasaban: emlekkonyv Kosary Domokos* (Budapest, 1993), 19–21.

"Liberal Internationalism: The Quest for a Polish Variant," *Polish Western Affairs*, XXXIV, 2 (1993): 13–39.

"Instytut Józefa Piłsudskiego na tle życia naukowego i kulturalnego emigracji," *Niepodległość*, XXVI (1993): 73–82.

"Wspomnienie o Wacławie Jędrzejewiczu," *Kultura*, 1556–2557 (1994): 160–171.

"Trzy próby poprawy stosunków polsko-czechosłowackich 1921–1926–1933," *Z dziejów polityki i dyplomacji polskiej: Studia poświęcone pamięci Edwarda hr. Raczyńskiego* (Warsaw, 1994): 223–235.

"O stosunkach polsko-czechoslowackich: garść refleksji," *Zeszyty Historyczne*, 108 (1994): 112–120.

"Historycy i historia na emigracji," in *Nauka polska wobec totalitaryzmów. W 55 rocznicę wybuchu II wojny światowej. Materiały Sympozjum 15–17 IX 1994*, Warsaw. 78–8.

"Rola powstań w dziejach nowożytnych Polski," *Kwartalnik Historyczny*, CI (1994): 4, 73–86.

"O polskich percepcjach Rzeczypospolitej Obojga Narodów," Instytut Europy Środkowo-Wschodniej: *The Foundations of Historical and Cultural Traditions in East Central Europe* (Rome, 1994), 35–43.

"Adam Rapacki and the Search for European Security," in Gordon Craig and Francis Loewenheim, eds, *The Diplomats 1939–1979* (Princeton, NJ, 1994), 289–315,

"Western Images and Stereotypes of Central and Eastern Europe," in André Gerits and Nanci Adler, eds., *Vampires Unstaked: National Images, Stereotypes and Myths in East Central Europe* (Amsterdam, 1995), 5–23.

"The French *barrière de l'est* or *Cordon sanitaire?*," in John S. Micgiel, ed., *Wilsonian East Central Europe: Current Perspectives* (New York, 1995), 113–122.

"Erazm Piltz a koncepcje polityki środkowoeuropejskiej," *Międzymorze: Polska i kraje Europy środkowo-wschodniej XIX-XX wiek. Studia ofiarowane Piotrowi Łossowskiemu w siedemdziesiątą rocznicę urodzin* (Warsaw, 1995), 215–225.

"Benešuv rozhovor se Sikorským 3. unora 1941," *Acta Universitatis Carolinae—Philosphica et Historica 3, Studia Historica* XLII (1995): 345–353.

"Challenges and Opportunities; The Foreign Policy of Post-Communist Poland," Stanislaus A. Blejwas, ed., *Perspectives in Polish History: Occasional Papers in Polish and Polish American Studies,* no.1 (New Britain, CT, 1996), 29–43.

"The Spirit of 1920 in America's NATO Debate: This Time, Will America Do the Right Thing?" *Transactions,* vol. IV, no. 5 (October, 1997): 52–58.

"The United States and Poland: Historical Reflections," *The Summit Times,* vol. V, nos. 16–17, 1997, 1, 16–19.

"Teaching Polish History," *NewsNet,* v. 37, no.5, (Nov. 1997): 7.

"Beneš a Polska i Polacy," Michał Pułaski et al., eds., *Z Dziejów Europy środkowo-wschodniej w XX w. Studia ofiarowane Henrykowi Batowskiemu w 90. rocznicę urodzin* (Krakow, 1997), 143–145.

"Two Revolutions 1788–1792, 1980–1990," in Samuel Fiszman, ed., *Constitution and Reform in Eighteenth-Century Poland* (Bloomington, IN, 1997), 531–554.

"The Polish Road to 1989: The Role of American Foreign Policy: Introduction," *Polish Review,* 1997, nr. 4, 187–188.

"Polska," in Jerzy Kłoczowski and Paweł Kras, eds., *Historiografia Krajów Europy Środkowo-Wschodniej* (Lublin, 1997), 21–45

"The Polish Question," in Manfred F. Boemke, Gerald D. Feldman, Elisabeth Glaser, eds., *The Treaty of Versailles: A Reassessment After 75 Years,* (Washington D.C. and Cambridge, 1998), 313–335.

"Przystanki do niepodległości: Bilans strat i dokonań," in Wojciech Wrzesiński, ed., *Do Niepodległości 1918, 1944, 1989: Wizje-drogi-spelnienia* (Warsaw, 1998), 311–326.

"O Mieroszewskim i Mieroszewskich," in *Jerzy Giedroyć—Juliusz Mieroszewski Listy 1949–1956* (Warsaw, 1999): I, 34–47.

"Miejsce Polski w stosunkach międzynarodowych," *Więź,* no. 103 (July, 2000): 102–132.

"Zapoznany Instytut," *Zeszyty Historyczne,* 133, (2000): 58–68.

"Aleksander Skrzyński w oczach współczesnych: Sylwetka dyplomaty," in Marek Andrzejewski, ed. *Gdańsk-Gdynia-Europa-Stany Zjednoczone w XIX i XX w* (Gdansk, 2000), 252–264.

"Czechoslovakia in the Proceedings of the Polish Government in Exile 1939–1941," *Evropa mezi Ne'meckem a Ruskem. Sbornâk Pracâ k sedmdesatim Jaroslava Valenty* (Prague, 2000), 409–420.

"1000 Jahre gemeinsames Erbe: Mitteleuropa zwischen dem Jahr 1000 und 2000," Alfried Wieczorek and Hans–Martin Hinz, eds., *Europas Mitte um 1000* (Stuttgart, 2000) vol. 2, 918–928.

"Polnische Geschichtsschreibung im Exil," in Hannes Siegrist, ed., *Komsum und Region im 20. Jahrhundert* (Leipzig, 2001), 128–137.

"The Place of the French Alliance in Poland's Foreign Policy," *Batir une nouvelle sécurité; La cooperation militaire entre la France et les états d'Europe centrale et orientale de 1919 à 1929* (Vincennes, 2001), 183–207.

"The Totalitarian Challenge to East Central Europe," Jerzy Kłoczowski, Wojciech Lenarczyk, Sławomir Łukasiewicz, eds., *Churches in the Century of the Totalitarian Systems* (2 vols., Lublin, 2001), vol. II, 9–19.

"Historyk emigracyjny—refleksje," *Rocznik Polskiej Akademii Umiejętności,* 2000, 218–221.

"Piłsudski et Weygand à la bataille de Varsovie (with Tomasz Schramm): *Revue d'histoire diplomatique,* Vol. 3 (2001): 203–212.

"Mity i kopleksy Europy środkowo-wschodniej," *Przegląd Polityczny,* 51 (2001): 44–47.

"Między starymi a nowymi laty" in E. Orman and Antoni Cetnarowicz, eds., *Henryk Wereszycki (1898–1990)* (Kraków, 2001), 263–272.

"The Myths and Complexes of East Central Europe" *The Polish Foreign Affairs Digest,* 1 (2001): 133–138.

"Cztery listy Juliusza Mieroszewskiego," *Zeszyty Historyczne,* 139 (2002): 189–199.

"La Pologne dans ses relations internationales" *Organon,* nos. 28–30 (1999–2001): 49–77.

"*Zeszyty Historyczne,*" in Krzysztof Pomian, ed., *Jerzy Giedroyć: Redaktor, Polityk, Człowiek* (Lublin, 2001), 276–287.

Encyclopedia Entries

"Czartoryski" in *Encyclopedia Americana 1974.*
"Czartoryski, Adam Jerzy" in *Encyclopedia Americana 1974.*
"Długosz, Jan" in *Encyclopedia Americana 1974.*
"Poland: History" in *Encyclopedia Britannica,* 15th ed. 1998, Vol. 25, 940–956.
"Little Entente" in Richard Frucht, ed., *Encyclopedia of Eastern Europe* (New York, 2000), 458.

Semi-Popular Articles, Notes, Interviews

"Poles and the English Left," *Labour Review,* vol. VII, 3, 21 Feb. 1947, 7–8.
In *Trybuna:*
"Dwie koncepcje," 29 (June, 1949).
"Poszukiwanie koncepcji," 40 (September, 1952).
"Egzamin życia," 49 (December, 1953).
"Zasady współpracy, 50 (March, 1954).

"Polska myśl federalna," 1/57 (l969), 31–35.
"Jałta w pamiętnikach zachodnich uczestników," 4/60 (1970), 12–17.
"W dwuchsetną rocznicę I-go Rozbioru," 11/67 (1972), 7–11.
"Stany Zjednoczone a Polska," 12/79 (1976), 6–11.
"Roosevelt wobec Polski," 30/86 (1978), 22–25.
"Wyprawa kijowska," 36/92 (1980), 20–24.
"Zachód wobec II-ej Rzeczypospolitej," 43/99 (1983), 12–15.
"Realizm a idealizm w dziejach Polski," 50/106–51/107 (1985), 38–42.
"Dyplomacja polska 1914–1945," 57/113 (1988), 21–31.
"O federacji polsko-czechosłowackiej," 63/119 (1990), 33–37.
"Polska, Czecho-Słowacja, Węgry," 69/125 (1991), 19–22.
"Evropske: dojmy," Nov. Dec. 1955.
In *Tygodnik Powszechny*:
"Kompromis,"19 December 1982.
"Realizm, idealizm a historia," 31 July 1983.
"Magistra vitae," 9 September 1984.
"Laboratorium historii: Polska, Czechosłowacja, Węgry," 22 September 1985.
"Appeasement, bezpieczeństwo, niepodległość," 21 September 1986.
"O historycznej tożsamości Europy środkowo-wschodniej," 7 June 1987.
"Jak powstają i giną wielkie mocarstwa," 21 August 1988.
"Emigracja i kraj," 2 June 1989.
"O Niemczech trochę inaczej," 26 November 1989.
"Widziane z za Atlantyku: Rzeczypospolitej egzamin z samodzielności,"
    11 July 1990.
"Śmierć prezydenta,"4 November 1990.
"Państwo Masaryka" O modelu ustrojowym międzywojennej Czech-
    osłowacji," 7 June 1991.
"O trójkątach, pentagonach i heksagonach," 6 October 1991.
"Królestwo Kongresowe i PRL," 19 July 1992.
"Cień Jałty czy tradycyjna orientacja" 2 January 1994.
"O dyplomatach," 31 July 1994.
"Prymat polityki wewnętrznej," 28 April 1996.
"List z Kijowa," 22 June 1997.
"Znaki dobre i złe" Apokryf, Nr. 11, June 1997.
"Zdrada jest tu . . . ," 17 August 1997.
"Przeszłość, terazniejszość; i przystość: Europy środko-wowschodniej,"
    26 October 1997.
"Powtórka z historii: tolerancja Polska nota," 16 August 1998.
"Pożegnania," 6 September 1998.
"1918—państwo odzyskane," *Apokryf,* nr. 13, November 1998.
"Myśli o dyplomacji polskiej" 14 March 1999.
"List z Ameryki," 4 July 1999.
"Krakowski Zjazd Polskiego Instytutu Naukowego: Powrót do korzeni,"
    18 June 2000.

"Jakim go znałem," 24 September 2000.
"Czy historia ma krzepić; czy *odbrązawiać,* 22 April 2001 (reprinted in *Przegląd Polityczny,* 51, 2001).
"Wypisy z Dmowskiego," 26 May 2002
"Wspomnienie o moim Ojcu," *Kultura,* 1328–2329 (1975): 139–149.
"Emigranci o Sobie: Piotr Wandycz," *Arka,* 15, 1986.
"Historia, poezja, literatura. Wokół pojęcia polskości, Ankieta," *Znak,* II, Vol. XL, no. 394, March, 1998, 94–95.
"Więcej źródeł," *Res Publica,* 1. 1, 1988.
"Czy emigracja jest jeszcze potrzebna,?" *Kultura,* 10/505 (1989): 3–15.
"Czy Jałta może się zostać? Rozmowa," *W Drodze,* 10/194 (1989): 8–13.
"Ankieta: Pytanie dla Historyków," *Arka,* 29 (1990): 40–42.
"Nowe spojrzenie z amerykańskiej perspektywy, " *Perspektywy,* 6. 3. 1990.
"Nie rzucać się na szyję: rozmowa," *Nowy Dziennik,* 18. 5. 1990.
"Post-Communist Eastern Europe: A Survey of Opinion." *EEPS,* IV, 2 (Spring 1990): 154, 184, 187, 193, 204–205.
"Czy Polacy sa małym narodem?: rozmowa," *Arka,* 34/4 (1991): 91–98.
"Historyk jest przewodnikiem," *Nowy Dziennik,* 9. 1. 1992.
"Zakurzony szyld," *Plus-Minus* (dodatek do *Rzeczypospolitej*), 16–17. 4. 1994
"Żyjemy w czasach saskich: rozmowa," *Dziennik Bałtycki,* 23. 9. 1994
"Długi marsz: o próbach integracji Europy Środkowo-wschodniej," *Plus Minus* (dodatek do *Rzeczypospolitej*), 5–6, 11, 1994.
"Mosty nad przeszłością: rozmowa," *Przegląd Polityczny,* 26 (zima, 1994): 54–58.
"Społeczeństwo polskie w oczach historyka," *Nowy Dziennik,* 14, 4, 1995.
"Węgierskie migawki," *Kultura,* 9/576 (1995): 63–68.
"Dwugłos o NATO," *Arcana,* 3 (9), 1996, 45–49.
"Siły zbrojne Trzeciej Rzeczypospolitej: Myśli i rozważania," ed. Janusz Zadzik, (Warsaw, 1996), 394–395.
"Wstęp," *Spór o PRL.* Krakow, 1996, 7–16.
"Rozmowa braci po latach," *Plus-Minus,* 18–29. 6. 1997.
"Ośrodek studiów w Lipsku, *Kultura,* 1/604–2/605 (1998): 153–154.
"Rowmund Piłsudski," *Kultura,* 9/612, 1998, 155–158.
"Rozmowa," *Poczta Polska,* 5 July 1998, 16–17.
"O potrzebie historii," *Arcana* 33 (5), 1998, 8–10.
"Current Issues in Polish Foreign Policy," East European Studies, Woodrow Wilson International Center for Scholars, *Newsletter,* 1998, 6–7.
"Pożegnanie Aleksandra Gieysztora," *Zeszyty Historyczne,* nr. 128 (1999): 137–142.
"Wywoływanie europejskiego ducha" *Unia Polska,* nr. 17 (2), 30 Sept. 1999, 17.
"Gdyby nie Davies . . . ," *Gazeta Wyborcza,* Sept. 21, 1999.
"Historia prawda naznaczona: rozmowa," *Nowy Dziennik,* 28 June 2000.

"Wojna polsko-bolszewicka 1919–1920—alternatywy i konsekwencje (ankieta)," *Arcana* 35 (5/2000): 30–34.

"Rzecz o historii i jej interpretowaniu: rozmawia Jolanta Szepieniec," *Przegląd Polski*, 25 maja, 2001.

"Ankieta: Polska Jesień; 2001," *Arcana*, 404 (2001): 25–29.

"Niezastąpiony," *Nowy Dziennik*, 6–7 October, 2001.

"Jörg Hoensch (1935–2001)," *Zeszyty Historyczne*, 137, (2001), 173–174.

"Dyskusja historyków—Polska wielu narodów," *Plus Minus*, 10–11 November, 2001

Book Reviews and Review Articles

L. G. Dabinus, *Die Landliche Bevölkerung Pomerellens*, in *Journal of Central European Affairs*, XV (1955): 191–192.

N. Gąsiorowska, *W Stulecie Wiosny Ludów*, in *American History*, 63 (1957): 125–127.

Hans Roos, *Polen und Europai*, in *Journal of Modern History*, XXIX (1957): 404

Titus Komarnicki, *Rebirth of the Polish Republic*, in *Polish Review*, II, 4 (1957): 95–98.

John W. Wheeler-Bennett, *Brest-Litovsk—The Forgotten Peace*, in *The Historian*, XX (1957): 100–101.

"Drętwa mowa," in *Kultura*, 5/115 (1957): 64–69.

"Cui bono," in *Polish Review*, II (1957): 114–117.

Stefan Kiniewicz, *Ruch chłopski w Galicji* and J. Deresiewicz, ed., *Materiały do dziejów chłopa wielkopolskiego w XVIII w.*, in *American Historical Review*, 63, (1958): 416–417.

George Liska, *International Equilibrium*, in *World Affairs Quarterly*, XXIX (1958): 301–302.

K. M. Pospieszalski, *Hitlerowskie prawo okupacyjne w Polsce*, and R. L. Koehl, *German Resettlement and Occupation Policy*, in *Journal of Modern History*, XX (1958): 381–383.

Elisabeth Wiskemann, *Germany's Eastern Neighbours*, in *The Historian*, XX (1958): 362–363.

R. Yakemtchouk, *La Ligne Curzon et la IIe guerre mondiale*, in *Journal of Modern History*, XXXI (1959): 389–390.

M. K. Dziewanowski, *The Communist Party of Poland*, in *Slavic and East European Journal*, 17, 3 (1959): 409–411.

"Portrait of America: Letter of Henry Sienkiewicz," in *Indiana Magazine of History*, LV (1959): 309–310.

"Hitler i Stalin," in *Kultura*, 3/137 (1959): 136–141.

Alexandre Bregman, *Najlepszy sojusznik Hitlera* and Yakemtchouk, *La Ligne Curzon*, in *Central European Federalist*, VII (1959): 33–35.

"Konferencja w Spa," in *Kultura*, 6/140 (1959): 136–138.

Michael Howard, *Disengagement in Europe*, in *Central European Federalist*, VII (1959): 51–55.

Historia Polski II, pts I and II, in *American Slavic and East European Review*, 19 (1960): 126–128.

Arno Mayer, *Political Origins of the New Diplomacy*, in *The Historian*, XXII (1960): 314–315.

W. Markert, *Osteuropa—Handbuch Polen*, in *Journal of Central European Affairs*, XX (1960–61): 225–228.

Frank Gibney, *The Frozen Revolution* and S. L. Sheiderman, *The Warsaw Heresy*, in *Slavic and East European Journal*, 4 (18) (1960): 186–187.

Roman Kopecký, *Ceskoslovensky odboj*, in *Kultura*, 4/150 (1960): 96–104.

Tadeusz Jędruszczak, *Górny Śląsk*, in *Kultura*, 9/155 (1960): 139–144.

Hugh Seton-Watson, *Neither War nor Peace*, in *The Historian*, XXIII (1961): 378–379.

Historia Polski II cz. III, in *American Slavic and East European Review*, 20 (1961): 231–232.

Wacław Jędrzejewicz, *Poland in the British Parliament, Vol. II*, in *American Slavic and East European Review*, XX (1961): 329–330.

Immanuel Geiss, *Der polnische Grenzstreifen*, in *Journal of Central European Affairs*, XXI (1961): 231–232.

Historia Polski II cz. IV, in *American Slavic and East European Review*, 20 (1961): 530.

H. H. Kaplan, *The First Partition of Poland*, in *Slavic and East European Journal*, 7 (1963): 89.

J. K. Zawodny, *Death in the Forest*, in *Slavic and East European Journal*, 7 (1963): 233.

E. Birke, *Frankreich und Ostmitteleuropa*, in *Journal of Central European Affairs*, XXIII (1963): 91–92.

Roman Dębicki, *Foreign Policy of Poland*, in *Polish Review*, VIII (1963): 113–115.

Richard Staar, *Poland 1944–1962*, in *Slavic and East European Journal*, 7 (1963): 445.

Jerzy Krasuski, *Stosunki polsko-niemieckie* and Henryk Batowski, *Kryzys dyplomatyczny*, in *Central European Federalist*, XI (1963): 39–41.

Bohdan Budurowycz, *Polish-Soviet Relations 1932–39*, in *Journal of Central European Affairs*, XXIII (1963–64): 383–384.

I. I. Kostiushko, *Krestanskaia reforma 1864g v Tsartsvo Polskom*, in *American Historical Review*, 69 (1964): 842–843.

R. F. Leslie, *Reform and Insurrection in Russian Poland 1856–65*, in *Journal of Modern History*, XXXVI (1964): 213–214.

"O polskiej polityce zagranicznej Dwudziestolecia," in *Kultura*, 1/195–2/196 (1964): 199–208.

Wacław Jędrzejewicz, ed., *Poland in the British Parliament, III,* in *Journal of Modern History,* XXXVI (1964): 12l.

"*Teki Historyczne,* in *Zeszyty Historyczne,* 6 (1964): 225–227.

Jerzy Kozeński, *Czechosłowacja w polskiej polityce zagranicznej 1932–38,* in *American Historical Review,* 70 (1965): 780–781.

"Karta z przeszłości," in *Zeszyty Historyczne,* 7 (1965): 197–201.

"O Lidze Narodowej," in *Zeszyty Historyczne,* 8 (1965): 221–227.

"Druga wojna widziana z Ankary," in *Zeszyty Historyczne,* 9 (l966): 216–217.

"Dwa wydawnictwa," in *Kultura,* 4/234 (1967): 125–127.

H. E. Volkmann, ed., *Die Krise des Parlamentarismus in Ostmitteleuropa zwischen den beiden Weltkriegen,* in *Slavic Review,* XXVII (1968): 142 *Kryzys polskiego parlamentaryzmu w II Rzeczypospolitej,* in *Zeszyty Historyczne,* 14 (1968): 216–221.

Wiesław Balcerak, *Polityka zagraniczna Polski w dobie Locarna* in *Slavic Review,* 27 (1968): 562.

A. E. Senn, *The Great Powers, Lithuania and the Vilna Question 1920–28* in *Slavic Review,* 28 (1969): 334.

Stosunki polsko-sowieckie podczas drugiej wojny światowej, in *Zeszyty Historyczne,* 16 (1969): 208–211.

Documents diplomatiques français, 1932–34, vol. IV, in *American Historical Review* 74 (1969): 1642–1643.

"Na marginesie książki *Roman Dmowski,*" in *Kultura,* 7/274–8/275 (1970): 221–225.

M. K. Dziewanowski, *Joseph Piłsudski: A European Federalist* in *Russian Review,* 29 (July, 1970): 344.

"Nowa historia Polski po angielsku," and "Nowy tom *Diariusza Szembeka,*" in *Zeszyty Historyczne,* 17 (1970): 198–218.

P. N. Olshansky, *Rizhsky mir* in *Slavic Review,* 30 (1971): 153.

"Pseudohistoria," in *Zeszyty Historyczne,* 19 (1971): 218–228.

Stefan Kieniewicz, "*Historia Polski, 1795–1918,*" in *Slavic Review,* 31 (1972): 211–212.

Edward Chmielewski, *The Polish Question in the Russian Duma* in *Jahrbücher fur Geschichte Osteuropas,* 20 (1972): 156.

Jon Jacobson, *Locarno Diplomacy,* in *Slavic Review,* XXXI (1972): 915–917.

"Polska a Francja w okresie międzywojennym," *Zeszyty Historyczne,* 22 (1972): 211–218.

Letter re Wiktor Sukiennickis "Memoriał Paderewskiego" and Zbigniew Siemaszko, *White Eagle* by Norman Davies in *Zeszyty Historyczne,* 27 (1974): 215–220.

Gaines Post, Jr., *The Civil-Military Fabric of Weimar Foreign Policy,* in *Social Science Quarterly,* LV (1974): 543–544.

Jörg Hoensch, *Sozialverfassung und politische Reform,* in *Slavic Review,* 33 (1974): 792–793.

Josef Korbel, *Detente in Europe,* in *American Historical Review,* 79 (1974): 1148–1149.

Norman Davies, *White Eagle, Red Star,* in *American Historical Review,* 79 (1974): 1593–1594.

"Ostatni tom Diariusza Szembeka," in *Zeszyty Historyczne* 29 (1974): 211–217.

Antony Polonsky, *Politics in Independent Poland 1921–1939,* in *East Central Europe,* (1975): 183–184.

Emanuel Halicz, *Partisan Warfare in 19th Century Poland,* in *American Historical Review,* 81 (1976): 900.

Edward Wynot, *Polish Politics in Transition,* in *The Historian,* XXXVIII (1976): 747.

P. F. Cannistraro et al., *Poland and the Coming of the Second World War,* in *American Historical Review* 82 (1977): 398.

"*Historia Polski dla mlodzieży,*" in *Zeszyty Historyczne,* 42 (1977): 234–235.

Anthony T. Komjathy, *The Crises of France's East Central European Diplomacy,* in *American Historical Review,* 82 (1977): 985.

M. K. Dziewanowski, *Poland in the 20th Century,* in *Polish Review,* XXII, 3 (1977): 111–112.

Antony Polonsky, *Great Powers and the Polish Question, 1941–1945,* in *East Central Europe ,* 4 (1977): 218–219.

"Kronika życia Józefa Piłsudskiego," and "Stany Zjednoczone a Polska: nowe publikacje," in *Zeszyty Historyczne,* 46 (1978): 232–242.

"Książki Andrzeja Garlickiego o Józefie Piłsudskim," in *Zeszyty Historyczne,* 48 (1979): 221–223.

Norman Davies, *Poland, Past and Present: A Select Bibliography,* in *Slavic Review,* 38 (1979): 702–703.

Walter A. McDougall, *France's Rhineland Diplomacy,* in *International History Review,* 1 (1979): 575–577.

Kai Lundgreen-Nielsen, *The Polish Problem at the Paris Peace Conference,* in *American Historical Review ,* 85 (1980): 94.

Wacław Jędrzejewicz, *Kronika życia Józefa Piłsudskiego,*" in *Canadian Slavonic Papers,* 22 (1980): 434.

"U źródeł drugiej wojny światowej," in *Zeszyty Historyczne,* 53 (1980): 213–215.

"Nowe ksiązki," in *Zeszyty Historyczne,* 54 (1980): 181–183.

Gy. Juhasz, *Hungarian Foreign Policy, 1919–45,* in *International History Review,* II (1980): 668–671.

"Bić się czy nie bić?" in *Kultura,* 7/394–8/395 (1980): 35–38.

Eliza Campus, *The Little Entente and the Balkan Alliance,* in *Slavonic and East European Review,* 59 (1981): 128.

"Nowe ksiązki i dawniejsze," in *Zeszyty Historyczne,* 58 (1981): 185–188.

R. F. Leslie, ed., *The History of Poland since 1863*, in *Slavonic and East European Review*, 59 (1981): 452–453.

Kai Lundgreen-Nielsen, *The Polish Problem at the Paris Peace Conference*, in *Niepodległość*, XIV (1981): 251–254.

G. Wagner, *Deutschland und der polnisch-sowjetische Krieg*, in *Jahrbücher für Geschichte Osteuropas*, 29 (1981): 132–133.

M. M. Drozdowski, *Ignacy Jan Paderewski*, in *Polish Review*, XXVI , 1 (1981): 127–128.

Daniel E. Kaiser, *Economic Diplomacy and the Origins of the Second World War*, in *East Central Europe*, 8 (1982): 134–135.

Lisanne Radice, *Prelude to Appeasement*, in *Russian Review*, Vol. 41, No. 3 (1982): 360–361.

"Historia Dwudziestolecia," in *Zeszyty Historyczne*, 60 (1982): 207–210.

"*Igrzysko Boże* Normana Daviesa," in *Zeszyty Historyczne*, 61 (1982): 3–25.

"Zyciorys Józefa Piłsudskiego," in *Zeszyty Historyczne*, 61 (1982): 211–213.

Norman Davies, *God's Playground*, in *American Historical Review*, 88 (1983): 436–437.

"Nowe wydawnictwa z historii Polski," in *Zeszyty Historyczne*, 65 (1983): 221–223.

"Polityka zagraniczna Francji podczas II wojny światowej," and "Polonica na amerykańskim rynku wydawniczym," in *Zeszyty Historyczne*, 66 (1983): 196–206.

Gordon A. Craig and Alexander George, *Force and Statecraft*, in *International History Review*, VI (1984): 481–483.

Patricia Gajda, *Postscript to Victory*, in *Slavonic and East European Review*, 62 (1984): 136–137.

"Polonia Resituta czyli Noël redivivus" (with Anna M. Cienciala), in *Zeszyty Historyczne*, 72 (1985): 147–159.

Leon Noël, *La Tchécoslovaquie d'avant Munich*, in *East Central Europe* (1985): 223–224.

"Dwugłos o książce J. Karskiego," in *Zeszyty Historyczne*, 74 (1985): 158–167

"Świadomość narodowa w Polsce," in *Kultura*, 4/451 (1985): 130–134.

K. Hovi, *Alliance de revers*, in *Slavic Review*, 44 (1985): 558.

Jan Karski, *The Great Powers and Poland*, in *International History Review*, VIII (1986): 453–455.

K. Doss, *Zwischen Weimar und Warschau*, in *International History Review*, VIII (1986): 638–639.

"Nowe książki," in *Zeszyty Historyczne*, 75 (1986): 216–218.

"Nowe książki," in *Zeszyty Historyczne*, 77 (1986): 156–159.

Taras Hunczak, *Ukraine and Poland in Documents*, in *Harvard Ukrainian Studies*, X, 1–2 (1986): 260–263.

Józef Garliński, *Poland in the Second World War*, in *East Central Europe*, 13 (1986): 238–239.

Tadeusz Żenczykowski, *Samotny bój Warszawy*, in *International History Review*, IX (1987): 168–170.

"Nowe książki," in *Zeszyty Historyczne*, 81 (1987): 180–185.

"Nowe książki," in *Zeszyty Historyczne*, 82 (1987): 221–225.

"Nie bójmy się prawdy" *Puls*, 35 (Autumn 1987): 97–103.

"A Guide to Polish History for Americans in Poland," in *Polish American Studies*, XLIV (Spring, 1987): 75–79.

Adam Zamoyski, *The Polish Way*, in *New York Times*, July 17, 1988.

"Nowa historia Polski," in *Niepodległość*, XXI (1988): 238–245

"Nowe książki," and "ZSRR a Polacy," in *Zeszyty Historyczne*, 86 (1988): 199–201 and 223–227.

S. A. Garrett, *From Potsdam to Poland*, in *Political Science Quarterly*, 1031 (Spring 1988): 190–191.

Anita Prażmowska, *Britain, Poland and the Eastern Front*, in *Russian Review*, 47 (1988): 343–344.

Jerzy Wiatr, *The Soldier and the Nation*, in *Polish Review*, XXXIV, 2 (1989): 175–178.

"O polityce zagranicznej Polski międzywojennej," in *Niepodległość*, XXII (1989): 249–251.

Jerzy Borejsza, *Antysławizm Adolfa Hitlera*, in *International History Review*, XI (1989): 376–377.

George Lerski, *Poland's Secret Envoy*, in *East Central Europe*, 16 (1989): 223–224.

"Nowe książki," in *Zeszyty Historyczne*, 88 (1989): 216–219.

G. T. Berend, *Crisis Zone*, in *East Central Europe*, 16 (1989): 196–197.

"Nowe książki," in *Zeszyty Historyczne*, 92 (1990): 226–229.

Czesław Bloch, *Władysław Sikorski, Ignacy Paderewski*, in *Niepodległość*, XXIII (1990): 211–217.

Keith Sword, Norman Davies, and Jan Ciechanowski, *The Formation of the Polish Community in Great Britain*, in *Slavonic and East European Review*, 68 (1990): 579–580.

"Nowe książki," in *Zeszyty Historyczne*, 98 (1991): 200–205.

August G. Kanka, *Poland: An Annotated Bibliography of Books in English* (with Lee Blackwood), in *Slavic Review*, 50 (1991): 1068.

Thomas C. Fiddick, *Retreat from Poland*, in *Russian Review*, 51 (January 1992): 130–131.

"O polskiej dyplomacji," in *Zeszyty Historyczne*, 100 (1992): 198–201.

"Nowe książki," in *Zeszyty Historyczne*, 102 (1992): 180–184

N. Jordan, *Popular Front and Central Europe*, in *American Historical Review*, 98 (1993): 885–886.

"O dyplomacji II Rzeczypospolitej," in *Zeszyty Historyczne*, 103 (1993): 182–184.

"Nowe książki," in *Zeszyty Historyczne,* 106 (1993): 159–170.

"Nowa wersja Kronika życia Piłsudskiego," in *Zeszyty Historyczne,* 111 (1995): 182–186.

"Trzy Europy," in *Przegląd Polityczny,* 30 (wiosna, 1996): 103–105.

Stanley Kirschbaum, *A History of Slovakia,* in *Polish Review,* XLI, 1 (1996): 112–116.

"Nowe książki," in *Zeszyty Historyczne,* 116 (1996): 151–158.

"Konfederacja polsko-czechosłowacka: dokumenty," in *Zeszyty Historyczne,* 116 (1996): 186–190.

Michael Palij, *The Ukrainian-Polish Defensive Alliance 1919–21,* in *Polish Review,* XLI, 2 (1996): 233–241.

"Zapomniana książka," in *Kultura,* 12/591 (1996): 149–151.

Włodzimierz Suleja, *Józef Piłsudski,* in *Niepodległość,* XLVIII (1996): 256–262.

"Szkoda," in *Kultura,* 11/602 (1997): 131–136.

"Nowe książki," in *Zeszyty Historyczne,* 122 (1997): 194–197.

"Lux et Veritas," in *Kultura,* 3/606 (1998): 145–147.

"Nowe książki," in *Zeszyty Historyczne,* 125 (1998): 155–161.

"Krytyka i pochwala" in *Zeszyty Historyczne,* 126 (1998):171–175.

"Zagłada Drugiej Rzeczypospolitej, 1945–1947," and "Na bezdrożach," in *Zeszyty Historyczne,* 129 (1999): 159–171 and 172–184.

"Polonica w czeskich publikacjach," in *Teki Historyczne,* XXII (1999): 303–310.

"With Fire and Sword—The Film: Views of a Trilogy Enthusiast," in *Polish Review,* no. 3 (2000): 318–320.

Oleg Ken, *Collective Security of Isolation: Soviet Foreign Policy and Poland* (St. Petersburg, 1995), in *Polish Review,* no. 1 (2001): 108–11.

"Nowe Dzieje Polski," in *Zeszyty Historyczne,* 137 (2001): 206–219.

"Znakomita książka," in *Zeszyty Historyczne,* 139 (2002): 217–114.

"The Pitfalls of East European History: An Overview," in *Polish Review,* no. 1 (2002): 104–106.

Contributors

M. B. B. BISKUPSKI holds the S. A. Blejwas Endowed Chair in Polish history at Central Connecticut State University. He previously taught at Yale University, the University of Rochester, and was Fulbright Research Professor at the Instytut Historyczny of the University of Warsaw. He is the author of *The History of Poland* (2000); *Polish Democratic Thought* (1991); *Poland and Europe: Historical Dimensions* (1993), and several other works as well as the forthcoming volumes, *The United States and Poland, 1914–1918* and *The Rise of Modern Polish Democracy.* Biskupski is a director of the Polish Institute of Arts and Sciences, and past president of the Polish American Historical Association. He was awarded the Officer's Cross of the Order of Merit by the government of Poland in 2001 and inscribed in the "Honour Roll of Polish Science" by the Polish Ministry of Education in 2001. He earned his doctorate under Piotr S. Wandycz at Yale in 1981.

WILLIAM L. BLACKWOOD taught at Yale and the Jagiellonian University in Kraków as a Fulbright Professor. His essays on international relations have appeared in a number of journals. He is currently studying law at New York University. Blackwood completed his doctorate under Wandycz at Yale in 1996.

ANNA M. CIENCIALA is Professor of History, Emerita, at Kansas University. She is the author of *Poland and the Western Powers, 1938–1939* (1968), *From Versailles to Locarno: Keys to Polish Foreign Policy, 1919–1925* (1984). She edited James W. Headlam-Morley's *A Memoir of the Paris Peace Conference* (1972) and Józef Beck's *Polska polityka zagraniczna, 1926–1939.* She completed her doctorate under Wandycz at Indiana University in 1962.

BRUCE GARVER is Professor of History at the University of Nebraska at Omaha, where he chairs the department. He is the author of *The Young Czech Party, 1874–1901* (1978), as well as many shorter studies on Czech and Slovak history. He is the editor of the journal *Kosmas: Czechoslovak and Central European Journal.* He completed his doctorate under Wandycz at Yale in 1979.

NEAL PEASE is Associate Professor of History at the University of Wisconsin-Milwaukee. He is the author of the volume *Poland, the United States and the Stabilization of Europe, 1919–1933* (1986), as well as a number of essays, particularly regarding the role of the Roman Catholic Church in Polish public life. He earned his doctorate under Wandycz at Yale in 1982.

ANTONY POLONSKY, D.Phil., Oxford, is Albert Abramson Professor of Holocaust Studies at Brandeis University and the U.S. Holocaust Memorial Museum. He previously taught at the London School of Economics and Political Science. He chairs the editorial board of the journal *Polin*. Among his many books are *Politics in Independent Poland* (1972); *The Little Dictators* (1975); and *The Great Powers and the Polish Question* (1976). He is the coauthor of *A History of Modern Poland* (1980) and *The Beginnings of Communist Rule in Poland* (1981).

DOUGLAS SELVAGE is at the Office of the Historian of the U.S. Department of State. He is the author of a number of studies regarding the GDR and Poland in the cold war era. He completed his doctorate at Yale under Wandycz in 1999.

STEVEN BÉLA VÁRDY is McAnulty Distinguished Professor of European History at Duquesne University. He is the author of seventeen books and almost five hundred shorter works. He is a member of the Hungarian Writers' Federation, a board member of the World Federation of Hungarian Historians, and a member of International P.E.N. Among his many awards are the Gold Medal of the Árpád Academy, the Berzsenyi Prize, and the Knight's Cross of Hungary. He received his doctorate at Indiana University under Wandycz in 1967.

INDEX